The Developing Labor Law

Fourth Edition
2001 Cumulative Supplement

(covering 1999–2000)

BNA Books Authored by the
ABA Section of Labor & Employment Law

Covenants Not to Compete: A State-by-State Survey

The Developing Labor Law

Discipline and Discharge in Arbitration

Elkouri & Elkouri: How Arbitration Works

Employee Benefits Law

Employee Duty of Loyalty: A State-by-State Survey

Employment Discrimination Law

Equal Employment Law Update

The Fair Labor Standards Act

How to Take a Case Before the NLRB

International Labor and Employment Laws

Labor Arbitration: A Practical Guide for Advocates

Labor Arbitration: Cases and Materials for Advocates

Labor Arbitrator Development: A Handbook

Occupational Safety and Health Law

The Railway Labor Act

Trade Secrets: A State-by-State Survey

For details on these titles visit BNA Books' home page on the Internet at **http://www.bnabooks.com** or call **800-960-1220** to request a catalog. All BNA books are available on a 30-day free-examination basis.

The Developing Labor Law

The Board, the Courts, and the National Labor Relations Act

Fourth Edition
2001 Cumulative Supplement
(covering 1999–2000)

Editors-in-Chief

Richard S. Cleary
Greenebaum Doll & McDonald PLLC
Louisville, KY

Howard Z. Rosen
Posner & Rosen, LLP
Los Angeles, CA

Barry J. Kearney
National Labor Relations Board
Washington, DC

Committee on the Development of the Law
Under the National Labor Relations Act

Section of Labor & Employment Law
American Bar Association

The Bureau of National Affairs, Inc., Washington, DC

The materials contained herein represent the opinions of the authors and editors and should not be construed to be those of either the American Bar Association or the Section of Labor and Employment Law. Nothing contained herein is to be considered as the rendering of legal advice for specific cases, and readers are responsible for obtaining such advice from their own legal counsel. These materials and any forms and agreements herein are intended for educational and informational purposes only.

**Library of Congress Cataloging-in-Publication Data
(Revised for vol. suppl.)**

The developing labor law : the board, the courts, and the National Labor Relations Act / editor in chief, Patrick Hardin ... [et al.].–4th ed.
    p. cm.
  Includes index.
  ISBN 1-57018-151-9 (set) –ISBN 1-57018-149-7 (v. 1) –ISBN 1-57018-150-0 (v. 2)
    1. Labor laws and legislation–United States. 2. United States. National Labor Relations Act. 3. United States. National Labor Relations Board. I. Hardin, Patrick.

KF3369 .D48 2002
344.7301–dc21

2001052867

Published by BNA Books, 1231 25th St., NW, Washington, DC 20037
http://www.bnabooks.com

International Standard Book Number 1-57018-279-5
Printed in Canada

KEVIN HARREN
New York State United
  Teachers
Albany, NY

CHRISTOPHER T. HEXTER
Schuchat, Cook & Werner
St. Louis, MO

JOHN S. IRVING
Kirkland & Ellis
Washington, DC

RICHARD P. JAMES
Allotta & Farley Co., L.P.A.
Toledo, OH

DAVID E. KHOREY
Varnum, Riddering, Schmidt
  & Howlett LLP
Grand Rapids, MI

MARY L. KNOBLAUCH
Fruth & Anthony
Minneapolis, MN

TODD A. LYON
Davies, Roberts & Reid
  L.L.P.
Seattle, WA

ARMIN J. MOELLER, JR.
Phelps Dunbar LLP
Jackson, MS

MICHAEL J. MUELLER
Akin, Gump, Strauss, Hauer
  & Feld, L.L.P.
Washington, DC

WENDY L. NUTT
Schiff Hardin & Waite
Chicago, IL

ANGELA PACE
United Steelworkers of
  America
Pittsburgh, PA

PATTY L. PARSONS
Dickerson, MD

WARREN PYLE
Pyle, Rome & Lichten, P.C.
Boston, MA

JOHN RAUDABAUGH
Matkov, Salzman, Madoff
  & Gunn
Chicago, IL

FRED M. REICHMAN
Lewis, Rice & Fingersh, L.C.
St. Louis, MO

RICHARD M. RESNICK
Sherman, Dunn, Cohen,
  Liefer & Yellig, P.C.
Washington, DC

FRANK C. SABATINO
Schnader Harrison Segal
  & Lewis LLP
Philadelphia, PA

JUDITH BATSON SADLER
Bruckner & Sykes, LLP
Houston, TX

W.V. (BERNIE) SIEBERT
Sherman & Howard L.L.C.
Denver, CO

ARTHUR F. SILBERGELD
Proskauer Rose LLP
Los Angeles, CA

LEONARD SINGER
Interestate Brands Corp.
Overland Park, KS

ARTHUR B. SMITH, JR.
Murphy, Smith & Polk
Chicago, IL

ARLUS STEPHENS
United Steelworkers of
   America
Pittsburgh, PA

ROBERT M. STONE
Musick, Peeler & Garrett LLP
Los Angeles, CA

JESSE H. STRAUSS
Reitman Parsonnet P.C.
Newark, NJ

JONATHAN WALTERS
Markowitz & Richman
Philadelphia, PA

IRA WEINSTOCK
Harrisburg, PA

ALLAN H. WEITZMAN
Proskauer Rose LLP
Boca Raton, FL

RICHARD A. WILLIAMS
Williams and Iversen, P.A.
Roseville, MN

CONTRIBUTING EDITORS

GEORGE D. ADAMS
Greenebaum Doll
   & McDonald PLLC
Louisville, KY

DAVID ADELSTEIN
Geffner & Bush
Burbank, CA

HARVEY M. ADELSTEIN
Neal, Gerber & Eisenberg
Chicago, IL

JOSEPH J. ALLOTTA
Allotta & Farley Co., L.P.A.
Toledo, OH

DAN ALTCHECK
Proskauer Rose LLP
New York, NY

BROOKS R. AMIOT
Miles & Stockbridge, P.C.
Baltimore, MD

MARIA ANASTAS
Jackson Lewis Schnitzler
   & Krupman
Chicago, IL

ANGELA ANDERSON
National Labor Relations
   Board
Washington, DC

SCOTT B. ANGLEHART
Coughlin & Gerhart
Binghamton, NY

ROBIN B. APPLEBAUM
Clifton Budd & DeMaria
   LLP
New York, NY

GAVIN S. APPLEBY
Kimberly-Clark Corp.
Roswell, GA

ROMAN ARCE
Marshall & Melhorn
Toledo, OH

ELLIOT STEPHEN AZOFF
Baker & Hostetler LLP
Cleveland, OH

JAMES G. BAKER
Spencer, Fane, Britt & Browne
   LLP
Overland Park, KS

LINDA BARGE-MILES
American Federation of State,
   County and Municipal
   Employees
Tallahassee, FL

NED H. BASSEN
Hughes Hubbard & Reed,
   LLP
New York, NY

TIMOTHY R. BAUMAN
Blitman & King LLP
Rochester, NY

SEAN BECKER
Ropes & Gray
Boston, MA

WILLIAM L. BECKER
Laner, Muchin, Dombrow,
   Becker, Levin and
   Tominberg, Ltd.
Chicago, IL

LISA L. BEHM
Quarles & Brady, LLP
Milwaukee, WI

GREGORY D. BELLEW
Kansas City, MO

THOMAS J. BENDER, JR.
Littler Mendelson PC
Philadelphia, PA

WILLIAM BERGER
Stettner, Miller and Cohn,
   PC
Denver, CO

STEVEN M. BERNSTEIN
Fisher & Phillips LLP
Atlanta, GA

PAUL J. BERRA III
Lewis, Rice & Fingersh
St. Louis, MO

HOLGER BESCH
Jones, Day, Reavis & Pogue
Los Angeles, CA

WILLIAM BEVAN III
Reed, Smith, Shaw & McClay
   LLP
Pittsburgh, PA

CHERYL BLACKWELL
Holleb & Coff
Chicago, IL

JORDAN L. BLOOM
Littler Mendelson PC
San Francisco, CA

MELISA L. BODNAR
Haynesworth Baldwin Johnson
   & Greaves LLC
Macon, GA

KEITH R. BOLEK
O'Donoghue & O'Donoghue
Washington, DC

PAUL BOSANAC
National Labor Relations
   Board
Milwaukee, WI

JENNIFER CABRANES BRACERAS
Ropes & Gray
Boston, MA

NATHAN P. BRENNA
Fruth & Anthony
Minneapolis, MN

MARK E. BRENNAN
Webster, Mrak & Blumberg
Seattle, WA

LOUIS P. BRITT III
McKnight Hudson Lewis
   & Henderson
Memphis, TN

RICHARD S. BROOK
Law Office of Richard S.
   Brook
Mineola, NY

LOVIC A. BROOKS
Ellzey & Brooks, LLC
Columbia, SC

RICKLIN BROWN
Bowles, Rice, McDavid, Graff
   & Love PLLC
Charleston, WV

NORMAN R. BUCHSBAUM
Law Offices of Norman R.
   Buchsbaum
Baltimore, MD

PETER BULMER
Jackson Lewis Schnitzler
   & Krupman
Chicago, IL

KAREN CAIN
Jones, Day, Reavis & Pogue
Cleveland, OH

ROBERT K. CARROL
Littler Mendelson PC
San Francisco, CA

DONALD C. CARROLL
Law Offices of Carroll
   & Scully, Inc.
San Francisco, CA

JAMES L. CARROLL
Carr Flora Carroll & Driscoll,
   P.C.
El Paso, TX

AGNIS CHAKRAVORTY
Woods, Rogers & Hazlegrove,
   P.L.C.
Roanoke, VA

NEELAM CHANDNA
Reich, Adell, Crost & Cvitan
Los Angeles, CA

STEVEN M. CHANLEY
Sinsheimer, Schiebelhut
   & Baggett
San Luis Obispo, CA

JAMES S. CHESLOCK
Cheslock, Deely & Rapp
San Antonio, TX

FRANCISCO CHEVERE
McConnell Valdés
San Juan, PR

ROBERT J. CHOVENEC
Warner, Norcross & Judd
Grand Rapids, MI

ANDREA S. CHRISTENSEN
Kay, Scholer, Fierman, Hays
   & Handler, LLP
New York, NY

LEONARD E. COHEN
Piper & Marbury, L.L.P.
Baltimore, MD

STUART I. COHEN
Husch & Eppenberger, LLC
St. Louis, MO

BETH LINCOW COLE
Buchanan Ingersoll, P.C.
Princeton, NJ

ADAM COLLIER
Bullard Korshoj Smith
   Jenstedt
Portland, OR

J. MICHAEL COLLOTON
Moss & Barnett
Minneapolis, MN

ROSEMARY M. COLLYER
Crowell & Moring LLP
Washington, DC

MAIREAD CONNOR
Chamberlain D'Amanda
Oppenheimer
   & Greenfield
Syracuse, NY

RICHARD L. CONNORS
Stinson, Mag & Fizzell
Kansas City, MO

PETER REED CORBIN
Corbin & Duvall
Jacksonville, FL

MARTIN COSTELLO
Hughes & Costello
St. Paul, MN

STACY L. COWAN
Morgan, Brown & Joy, LLP
Boston, MA

WILLIAM B. COWEN
Cowen & Associates
Arlington, VA

MATTHEW COYLE
Lockheed Martin Corp.
Olney, MD

GRANT CRANDALL
United Mine Workers
Washington, DC

JOHN CURLEY
AT&T
Morristown, NJ

JOSEPH F. DANNER
SAAD's Healthcare
Mobile, AL

ELLEN J. DANNIN
California School of Law
San Diego, CA

DOUGLAS A. DARCH
Seyfarth, Shaw, Fairweather
   & Geraldson
Chicago, IL

FRANCIS X. DEE
Carpenter, Bennett
   & Morrissey
Newark, NJ

KRISTINA DETWILER
Rinehart, Robblee & Hannah
Seattle, WA

JAMES R. DICKENS
Miller, Nash, Werner, Hager
   & Carlsen LLP
Seattle, WA

NICHOLAS DiGIOVANNI, JR.
Morgan, Brown & Joy, LLP
Boston, MA

MICHAEL J. DiMATTIA
Ross & Hardies
New York, NY

NATALE V. DiNATALE
Durant, Nichols, Houston,
   Hodges & Cortese-Costa, P.C.
Bridgeport, CT

JOHN R. DOLL
Logothetis, Pence & Doll
Dayton, OH

JOHN M. DONOGHUE
Donoghue, Thomas,
  Auslander & Drohan
Hopewell Junction, NY

JEFFREY S. DUBIN
Huntington, NY

ADRIANE J. DUDLEY
Dudley, Clark & Chan
St. Thomas, VI

E. TERRY DURANT
Durant, Nichols, Houston,
  Hodges & Cortese-Costa,
  P.C.
Bridgeport, CT

BRIAN EASLEY
Jones, Day, Reavis & Pogue
Chicago, IL

DAVID B. ELLIS
Foley, Hoag & Eliot, LLP
Boston, MA

WILLIAM J. EMANUEL
Jones, Day, Reavis & Pogue
Los Angeles, CA

SHELDON ENGELHARD
Boca Raton, FL

HOLLACE J. ENOCH
National Labor Relations
  Board
Washington, DC

BLAIR B. EVANS
McKnight Hudson Lewis
  & Henderson
Memphis, TN

STEVEN I. FARBMAN
Reed Smith Shaw & McClay
  LLP
Pittsburgh, PA

ERIC M. FINK
Willig, Williams
  & Davidson
Philadelphia, PA

JONATHAN S. FORMAN
Duvin, Cahn & Hutton
Cleveland, Ohio

DIANA R. FRANCIS
Harrison, Dowell, Fisher,
  & Harris, L.C.
Chesterfield, MO

LOURDES GARCIA
Wohlner, Kaplon, Phillips,
  Young & Cutler
Encino, CA

THOMAS GIOTTO
Klett Lieber Rooney
  & Schorling
Pittsburgh, PA

DENNIS GLADWELL
Gibson, Dunn & Crutcher
  LLP
Irvine, CA

DAVID M. GLANSTEIN
O'Donnell, Schwartz,
    Glanstein & Rosen
New York, NY

JOEL C. GLANSTEIN
O'Donnell, Schwartz,
    Glanstein & Rosen
New York, NY

CYNTHIA L. GLEASON
Fisher & Phillips LLP
Atlanta, GA

N. VICTOR GOODMAN
Benesch, Friedlander, Coplan
    & Aronoff LLP
Columbus, OH

DEBORAH E. GODWIN
Agee, Allen, Godwin, Morris
    & Laurenzi
Memphis, TN

MERRITT GREEN
Cowen & Associates
Arlington, VA

BRIAN S. GREIG
Fulbright & Jaworski L.L.P.
Austin, TX

JULIE GUTMAN
National Labor Relations
    Board
Los Angeles, CA

W. MELVIN HAAS III
Constangy Brooks & Smith
Macon, GA

LEWIS R. HAGOOD
Arnett, Draper & Hagood
Knoxville, TN

ALLYSON C. HALL
National Labor Relations
    Board
Washington, DC

SPENCER HAMER
Musick, Peeler
    & Garrett LLP
Los Angeles, CA

J. RICHARD HAMMETT
Brown McCarroll & Oaks
    Hartline
Houston, TX

DAVID R. HANSEN
Hansen & Connolly, P.C.
Denver, CO

PATRICIA L. HARDAWAY
Gay & Hardaway
New York, NY

JENNIFER A. HARDGROVE
Neal, Gerber & Eisenberg
Chicago, IL

RICHARD HARDICK
National Labor Relations
    Board
Washington DC

MICHAEL T. HARREN
Chamberlain, D'Amada,
    Oppenheimer
    & Greenfield
Rochester, NY

WILLIAM HAUS
Kelly & Haus
Madison, WI

SAMUEL HELDMAN
Gardner, Middlebrooks,
    Fleming, Gibbons & Kittrell,
    P.C.
Mobile, AL

JOSHUA M. HENDERSON
Seyfarth, Shaw, Fairweather
    & Geraldson
Chicago, IL

TOM HENDERSON
Lewis Fisher Henderson
    & Claxton
Memphis, TN

BARRY HERSH
Jenkens & Gilchrist
Dallas, TX

ROBERT L. HOBBINS
Dorsey & Whitney LLP
Minneapolis, MN

C. JOHN HOLMQUIST, JR.
Charfoos Reiter Peterson
    Holmquist &
    Pilchak, P.C.
Farmington Hills, MI

NORMAN HOLTZ
Holtz Gilman Grunebaum
Boston, MA

MELVIN R. HUTSON
Melvin Hutson, P.A.
Greenville, SC

PAUL D. INMAN
Klein, Zelman, Rothermel
    & Dichter, L.L.P.
New York, NY

CYNTHIA L. JACKSON
Baker & McKenzie
Palo Alto, CA

KEITH R. JEWELL
Beverly Enterprises
Fort Smith, AR

RICHARD L. E. JOCELYN
Hinkley Allen & Snyder
Providence, RI

FLORENCE M. JOHNSON
Perkins, Johnson, and Settle
Memphis, TN

JEFFREY T. JOHNSON
Holland & Hart LLP
Denver, CO

SHELLEY BABER JONES
Benesch, Friedlander, Coplan
    & Aronoff LLP
Columbus, OH

LAURA P. JURAN
Atshuler, Berzon, Nussbaum,
    Rubin & Demain
San Francisco, CA

MARK L. JUSTER
Laner, Muchin, Dombrow,
    Becker, Levin and
    Tominberg, Ltd.
Chicago, IL

RAYMOND L. KALMANS
Neel, Hooper & Kalmans, P.C.
Houston, TX

MEL R. KANG
Schwerin, Campbell & Barnard
Seattle, WA

JOEL I. KEILER
Reston, VA

DR. JAMES A. KEIM
Husch & Eppenberger, LLC
St. Louis, MO

ELIZABETH KELLY
Law Offices of John
   McKendree
Denver, CO

SIOBHAN KELLY
National Labor Relations
   Board
Washington DC

THOMAS J. KENNEDY
Gallagher & Kennedy P.A.
Phoenix, AZ

WESLEY KENNEDY
Allison, Slutsky & Kennedy,
   P.C.
Chicago, IL

JAY W. KIESEWETTER
Kiesewetter Wise Kaplan
   Schwimmer & Prather,
   P.C.
Memphis, TN

PAUL J. KINGSTON
Kingston & Hodnett
Boston, MA

MICHAEL K. KIRK
Wyatt, Tarrant & Combs
Louisville, KY

CAROLYN KLARQUIST
United Mine Workers
Washington, DC

RONALD J. KLEPETAR
Rexon, Freedman, Klepetar
   & Hambleton
Los Angeles, CA

RICHARD M. KOBDISH
Fulbright & Jaworski L.L.P.
Dallas, TX

FRANK L. KOLLMAN
Kollman & Sheehan, PA
Baltimore, MD

JOHN J. KRIMM, JR.
Schottenstein, Zox and
   Dunn
Columbus, OH

BRIAN KURTZ
Matkov, Salzman, Madoff
   & Gunn
Chicago, IL

RICK KUYKENDALL
Gardner, Middlebrooks,
   Fleming, Gibbons & Kittrell,
   P.C.
Mobile, AL

DAVID W. LARRISON
Ferrara, Fiorenza, Larrison,
    Barrett & Reitz P.C.
East Syracuse, NY

ROBERT LAVITT
Schwerin, Campbell & Barnard
Seattle, WA

ELIZABETH LEO
Rosenn, Jenkins & Greenwald,
    L.L.P.
Wilkes-Barre, PA

ALAN S. LEVINS
Littler Mendelson PC
San Francisco, CA

ARIANNA LEVINSON
Holguin & Garfield, APLC
Los Angeles, CA

JAY J. LEVIT
Levit, Mann & Halligan, PC
Richmond, VA

TARA LEVY
Jersey City, NJ

BRIAN LEWIS
Littler Mendelson PC
San Francisco, CA

BRIAN E. LEWIS
Hinckley, Allen & Snyder LLP
Boston, MA

MICHAEL LIGHTNER
National Labor Relations Board
Newark, NJ

D. MICHAEL LINIHAN
McMahon, Berger, Hanna,
    Linihan, Code & McCarthy
St. Louis, MO

RICHARD J. LOFTUS, JR.
Littler Mendelson PC
San Jose, CA

ROBERT C. LONG
Seyfarth, Shaw, Fairweather
    & Geraldson
Chicago, IL

TINA L. LORLEBERG
Faegre & Benson LLP
Minneapolis, MN

THOMAS M. LUCAS
McGuireWoods LLP
Norfolk, Virginia

ELIZABETH WELCH LYKINS
Miller, Johnson, Snell
    & Cummiskey
Grand Rapids, MI

STEPHEN W. LYMAN
Hall Render Killian Heath
    & Lyman
Indianapolis, IN

PAUL V. LYONS
Foley Hoag & Eliot LLP
Boston, MA

JOSEPH MACK III
Thorp Reed & Armstrong
Pittsburgh, PA

J. Warren Mangan
O'Connor & Mangan, P.C.
Long Island City, NY

Thomas J. Marcoline
Holtz Gilman Grunebaum
Boston, MA

Stefan Jan Marculewicz
Miles & Stockbridge
Baltimore, MD

Robert D. Mariani
Law Offices of Robert D.
   Mariani
Scranton, PA

John Markle, Jr.
Drinker Biddle & Reath, LLP
Berwyn, PA

Barry W. Marr
Marr Jones & Pepper
Honolulu, HI

Elicia L. Marsh-Watts
National Labor Relations
   Board
Washington DC

Gary S. Marshall
McGuireWoods LLP
Richmond, VA

Martin P. Marta
D'Ancona & Pflaum LLC
Chicago, IL

Francis A. Mastro
Apruzzese, McDermott,
   Mastro & Murphy
Liberty Corner, NJ

Mark S. Mathison
Gray, Plant, Mooty, Mooty
   & Bennett, P.A.
Minneapolis, MN

Stephen B. Maule
McMahon, Berger, Hanna,
   Linihan, Code & McCarthy
St. Louis, MO

James N. McCauley
Law Office of James N.
   McCauley
Ithaca, NY

John W. McKendree
Law Offices of John McKendree
Denver, CO

Charles W. McManigal
Laird, Heiny, McManigal,
   Winga, Duffy & Stambaugh,
   P.L.C.
Mason City, IA

Gregg R. Melinson
Drinker Biddle & Reath LLP
Philadephia, PA

Arthur P. Menard
Menard, Murphy & Walsh LLP
Boston, MA

TERESE MERRILL
United Steelworkers of
  America
Pittsburgh, PA

JUSTINE MEYERS
Sheppard, Mullin, Richter
  & Hampton LLP
San Francisco, CA

STACEY A. MEYERS
Schuchat, Cook & Werner
St. Louis, MO

JOLYNNE MILLER
National Labor Relations
  Board
Washington, DC

STEPHANIE A. MINER
Blitman & King LLP
Syracuse, NY

MICHAEL J. MOBERG
Briggs and Morgan
St. Paul, MN

SCOTT MOORE
Baird Holm
Omaha, NE

ROBERT W. MORGAN
Berry Moorman, PC
Detroit, MI

SAMUEL MORRIS
Allen, Godwin, Morris,
  Laurenzi & Bloomfield P.C.
Memphis, TN

JEFFREY E. MYERS
Blank, Rome, Comisky
  & McCauley LLP
Philadelphia, PA

CLIFFORD H. NELSON, JR.
Wimberly Lawson Steckel
  Nelson & Schneider, P.C.
Atlanta, GA

FRANK A. NEMIA
Coughlin & Gerhart
Binghamton, NY

RAYMOND D. NEUSCH
Frost Brown Todd, LLC
Cincinnati, OH

STUART NEWMAN
Jackson Lewis Schnitzler
  & Krupman
Atlanta, GA

JOHN W. NOBLE, JR.
Holleb & Coff
Chicago, IL

DONALD T. O'CONNOR
Buchanan Ingersoll, P.C.
Pittsburgh, PA

THOMAS L. P. O'DONNELL
Ropes & Gray
Boston, MA

ERNEST B. ORSATTI
Jubelirer, Pass & Intieri
Pittsburgh, PA

MATTHEW ORTIZ
Catron, Catron & Sawtell
Santa Fe, NM

PAUL M. OSTROFF
Lane, Powell, Spears
  & Lubersky, LLP
Portland, OR

SUELLEN OSWALD
Duvin, Cahn & Hutton
Cleveland, OH

LOYD E. OWEN, JR.
Lathrop & Gage, L. C.
Kansas City, MO

TYLER M. PAETKAU
McCutchen, Doyle, Brown
  & Enersen, LLP
East Palo Alto, CA

JEFFREY W. PAGANO
King, Pagano & Harrison
New York, NY

ALBERT W. PALEWICZ
National Labor Relations
  Board
Baltimore, MD

PATRICIA E. PALMERI
Law Office of Richard S. Brook
Mineola, NY

PETER M. PANKEN
Parker Chapin Flattan
  & Klimpl, LLP
New York, NY

RICHARD R. PARKER
Ogletree, Deakins, Nash,
  Smoak & Stewart
Nashville, TN

ROBERT E. PAUL
Zwerdling, Paul, Leibig, Kahn,
  Thompson & Driesen, P.C.
Washington DC

JESSICA S. PECORARO
Rider, Bennett, Egan
  & Arundel, LLP
Minneapolis, MN

CHRISTOPHER PEDERSON
Atshuler, Berzon, Nussbaum,
  Rubin & Demain
San Francisco, CA

JOHN W. PELINO
Pelino & Lentz, P.C.
Philadelphia, PA

LETICIA PEÑA
National Labor Relations
  Board
Denver, CO

JOHN W. ROBINSON IV
Fowler, White, Gillen,
   Boggs, Villereal &
   Banker, P.A.
Tampa, FL

WILLIAM J. ROGERS
Collier, Shannon, Rill & Scott,
   PLLC
Washington, DC

JACQUELINE R. ROLFS
Faegre & Benson LLP
Minneapolis, MN

JEFFREY K. ROSS
Seyfarth, Shaw, Fairweather
   & Geraldson
Chicago, IL

NELSON G. ROSS
Ropes & Gray
Boston, MA

RICHARD ROUCO
Whatley Drake
Birmingham, AL

ANTONIO RUIZ
VanBourg, Weinberg, Roger
   & Rosenfeld
Oakland, CA

CHRISTOPHER J. RUSEK
Klett, Lieber, Rooney
   & Schorling
Philadelphia, PA

TIMOTHY F. RYAN
Morrison & Foerster, LLP
Los Angeles, CA

RICHARD C. RYBICKI
Littler Mendelson PC
Santa Rosa, CA

STANLEY SAUNIER, JR.
Lexington, KY

ANN SCARPINO
National Labor Relations
   Board
Washington DC

CRAIG A. SCHLOSS
San Diego, CA

LORRAINE SCHMALL
Northern Illinois University
   School of Law
DeKalb, IL

MARK W. SCHNEIDER
Rider, Bennett, Egan &
   Arundel
Minneapolis, MN

TODD W. SCHNELL
Dorsey & Whitney, LLP
Minneapolis, MN

WILLIAM F. SCHOEBERLEIN
Otten Johnson Robinson
   & Neft
Denver, CO

MARK M. SCHORR
Erickson & Sederstrom
Lincoln, NE

STEPHEN J. SCHULTZ
Merrill, Schultz & Wolds, Ltd.
San Diego, CA

CARL A. SCHWARZ, JR.
Schwarz & DeMarco LLP
Garden City, NY

J. TRENT SCOFIELD
Ogletree, Deakins, Nash,
   Smoak & Stewart, P.C.
Birmingham, AL

THEODORE R. SCOTT
Luce, Forward, Hamilton
   & Scripps LLP
San Diego, CA

ANNE SENTER
Rinehart, Robblee
   & Hannah
Seattle, WA

STEPHANIE R. SETTERINGTON
Varnum, Riddering, Schmidt
   & Howlett LLP
Grand Rapids, MI

SCOTT T. SILVERMAN
Zinober & McCrea, P.A.
Tampa, FL

HOWARD S. SIMONOFF
Cherry Hill, NJ

WILLIAM E. SIZEMORE
Thompson, Sizemore
   & Gonzalez
Tampa, FL

HENRY W. SLEDZ, JR.
Schiff, Hardin & Waite
Chicago, IL

THOMAS DWIGHT SLOAN
Balch & Bingham, L.L.P.
Birmingham, AL

KENNETH A. SPRANG
Springfield, PA

TRACEY E. SPRUCE
Foley, Hoag & Eliot, LLP
Boston, MA

STEPHEN J. STANFORD
Fuller & Henry P.P.L.
Toledo, OH

M. JEFFERSON STARLING III
Johnston Barton Proctor
   & Powell LLP
Birmingham, AL

ROBERT S. STEINBERG
Menard, Murphy & Walsh LLP
Boston, MA

TODD M. STENERSON
Akin, Gump, Strauss, Hauer
   & Feld, L.L.P.
Washington, DC

James H. Stock, Jr.
Weintraub Stock, Bennett
& Grisham, P.C.
Memphis, TN

James M. Stone
McDonald, Hopkins, Burk
& Haber
Cleveland, Ohio

Laurence E. Stuart
Baker & McKenzie
Houston, TX

Peter C. Swanson
Cornfield and Feldman
Chicago, IL

Eric A. Taussig
Philip Morris, Inc.
New York, NY

Sally M. Tedrow
O'Donoghue & O'Donoghue
Washington, DC

Gabriel A. Terrasa
Albertini, Singleton, Gendler
& Darby, L.L.P.
Baltimore, MD

David M. Thomas
Phelps Dunbar, L.L.P.
Jackson, MS

George J. Tichy II
Littler Mendelson PC
San Francisco, CA

William C. Tidwell III
Hand Arendall, LLC
Mobile, AL

Robert P. Tinnin, Jr.
Hinkle Cox
Albuquerque, NM

Robert W. Tollen
Bronson Bronson
& McKinnon L.L.P.
San Francisco, CA

Joseph J. Torres
Winston & Strawn
Chicago, IL

Regis J. Trenda
Borg Warner Inc.
Chicago, IL

Abril B. Turner
Gibson, Dunn & Crutcher
LLP
Irvine, CA

James S. Urban
Jones, Day, Reavis & Pogue
Pittsburgh, PA

Jason J. Valtos
Davies, Roberts & Reid L.L.P.
Seattle, WA

Sybil Villanueva
Holguin & Garfield
Los Angeles, CA

FREDERICK W. VOGT
Mackall, Crounse & Moore,
   PLC
Minneapolis, MN

JEFFERY S. VOGT
James & Hoffman, P.C.
Washington DC

THOMAS M. VOGT
Falhaber, Larson, Fenlon
   & Vogt
Minneapolis, MN

HENRY JARED WALLACE, JR.
New Kensington, PA

MARK A. WASSERMAN
Mitchell, Silberberg & Knupp
   LLP
Los Angeles, CA

STUART S. WAXMAN
Donoghue, Thomas,
   Auslander & Drohan
Hopewell Junction, NY

RICHARD E. WAYLAND
King & Ballow
Nashville, TN

J. ROY WEATHERSBY
Littler Mendelson PC
Atlanta, GA

NORMAN I. WHITE
McNees, Wallace & Nurick
Harrisburg, PA

PATRICIA P. WHITE
Littler Mendelson PC
San Jose, CA

MARILYN L. WIDMAN
Allotta & Farley Co., L.P.A.
Toledo, OH

ROBERT A. WIESEN
Clifton Budd & DeMaria
New York, NY

MICHELLE A. WILCK
Hughes Hubbard & Reed, LLP
New York, NY

JAMES R. WILLARD
Spencer Fane Britt & Browne
   LLP
Overland Park, KS

STANLEY D. WILLIAMS
National Labor Relations
   Board
Overland Park, KS

STUART A. WILLIAMS
Eckert, Seamans, Cherin
   & Mellott
Pittsburgh, PA

ANNE M. WILSON
Faegre & Benson LLP
Minneapolis, MN

BRENT L. WILSON
Elarbee, Thompson
   & Trapnell, LLP
Atlanta, GA

JEFFREY D. WINCHESTER
Jones, Day, Reavis & Pogue
Columbus, OH

DAVID W. WOLF
Philadelphia, PA

BRIAN N. WOOLEY
Lathrop Cage, LC
Kansas City, MO

DAVID J. WOOLF
Drinker Biddle & Reath LLP
Philadephia, PA

AMANDA STULMAN WRIGHT
Jackson Lewis Schnitzler
   & Krupman
Atlanta, GA

PORTIA WU
Bredhoff & Kaiser
Washington, DC

JACQUELINE YOUNG
National Labor Relations Board
Washington, DC

ANDREW E. ZELMAN
Klein, Zelman, Rothermel
   & Dichter, LLP
New York, NY

JOHN ZENOR
Bullard Korshoj Smith
   Jenstedt
Portland, OR

LAWRENCE T. ZIMMERMAN
Sanders, Schnabel,
   Brandenburg &
   Zimmerman, P.C.
Washington, DC

JOHN ZIMRING
Holleb & Coff
Chicago, IL

EDGAR A. ZINGMAN
Wyatt, Tarrant & Combs
Louisville, KY

BENNET D. ZUROFSKY
Reitman Parsonnet P.C.
Newark, NJ

FOREWORD

Since 1945 the ABA Section of Labor and Employment Law has had among its stated purposes (1) to study and report on continuing developments in the field of labor and employment law, (2) to assist the professional growth and development of practitioners in the field of labor and employment law, and (3) to promote justice, human welfare, industrial peace, and the recognition of the supremacy of law in labor-management relations and the employment relationship.

Through the publication of books such as *The Developing Labor Law*, and through annual and committee meeting programs designed to provide a forum for the exchange of ideas, the Section has pursued these stated goals. Gradually, the Section has built a library of comprehensive legal works intended for the use of the Section membership as well as the bar generally.

The Section of Labor and Employment Law is pleased to provide this Supplement to its classic treatise on the National Labor Relations Act as part of its library of books published by BNA Books, a Division of The Bureau of National Affairs, Inc. The combined efforts of many individual authors from the Committee on the Development of the Law under the National Labor Relations Act of the Section are reflected in this Supplement.

The Sections wishes to express its appreciation to the committee, and in particular to the editors-in-chief, Richard S. Cleary, Howard Z. Rosen, and Barry J. Kearney, and the associate editors. This group has tried to accomplish two primary objectives: (1) to be equally balanced and nonpartisan in their viewpoints, and (2) to ensure the book is of significant value to the practitioner, student, and sophisticated nonlawyer.

The views expressed herein do not necessarily represent the views of the American Bar Association, or its Section of Labor and Employment Law, or any other organization, but are simply the collective, but not necessarily the individual views of the authors.

Information on the affiliation of government employees who contributed to this work is for informational purposes and does not constitute any official endorsement of the information provided herein.

SORRELL LOGOTHETIS
Chair

JANA HOWARD CAREY
Chair-Elect

Section of Labor
and Employment Law
American Bar Association

October 2001

PREFACE

This second cumulative Supplement to the fourth edition follows the organization of the fourth edition exactly. It updates the main volume through 2000. This Supplement does not contain headings where there have been no significant developments under that heading since publication of the fourth edition.

The efforts of all the members of the Committee toward publication of this Supplement are deeply appreciated. This is truly a working and producing Committee. In addition, we wish to express our appreciation for the support and assistance of the staff of BNA Books who have spent many hours editing and proofing the manuscript and otherwise working with us on this Supplement. Special thanks are also given to the Section of Labor and Employment Law and its governing Council for their valuable support and encouragement in this endeavor.

We believe that the final product is ample justification for the efforts of all involved.

RICHARD S. CLEARY
HOWARD S. ROSEN
BARRY J. KEARNEY

TABLE OF CONTENTS

PART III

THE REPRESENTATION PROCESS AND
UNION RECOGNITION

PART V

ARBITRATION AND THE ACT

PART VIII

ADMINISTRATION OF THE ACT

PART I

HISTORY OF THE NATIONAL LABOR RELATIONS ACT

HISTORICAL DEVELOPMENTS

There have been no changes or developments in the law since publication of the Fourth Edition.

PART II

PROTECTED EMPLOYEE ACTIVITY

CHAPTER 6

INTERFERENCE WITH PROTECTED RIGHTS

I. OVERVIEW

B. Section 7—Rights of Employees

2. *To Refrain From Such Activities*

The Section 7 right guaranteeing employees the right to refrain from engaging in concerted activities was violated by the Virgin Islands Wrongful Discharge Act.[1] The Act specified nine lawful grounds for dismissal of employees in the Virgin Islands, and allowed those grounds for dismissal to be modified only through a collective bargaining agreement. The court held that the law impermissibly forced employees to join unions, and forced employers to enter into labor contracts, if they wanted to modify the statutorily established grounds for dismissal.

3. *Other Concerted Activities*

Section 7 protects concerted employee activity unrelated to union organization.[2] While the scope of Section 7 remains very broad, employee activity still must be "concerted" in order to be protected.[3]

Courts, in agreement with the Board, continue to hold that it is not necessary that an employee's co-workers appoint him or her to represent their interests for the employee's actions taken on their behalf to be concerted.[4] Employees who espouse the cause of other

---

[1]24 V.I.C. §76. *See* Claytor v. Chenay Bay Beach Resort, 79 F. Supp. 2d 577, 163 LRRM 2378 (D.V.I. 1999); Bell v. Chase Manhattan Bank, 40 F. Supp. 2d 307, 163 LRRM 2370 (D.V.I. 1999).

[2]Mojave Elec. Coop. Inc., 327 NLRB 13, 163 LRRM 1288 (1998) (employee and co-workers petitioned for injunctive relief against harassment by two officials of employer's subcontractor).

[3]Mobil Exploration & Producing U.S. v. NLRB, 200 F.3d 230, 163 LRRM 2387 (5th Cir. 1999) (employee's statements to co-workers in lunchroom that employer was trying to fire him and had security investigator after him for "trying to right a wrong" and about his opposition to union president was concerted activity); Office Depot, 330 NLRB No. 99, 163 LRRM 1169 (2000) (employee telling individual who was picking up order for newspaper whose employers were on strike "Oh, you work for the scab newspaper," was protected concerted activity, where employee's use of term "scab" was expression of support for striking newspaper employees and amounted to making common cause with protected concerted activity of employees of another employer); *Mojave, supra* note 2. *Cf.* Yale Univ. Graduate Employees & Students Org., 330 NLRB No. 28, 162 LRRM 1393 (1999) (grade strike by teaching fellows was a partial strike and, therefore, unprotected).

[4]NLRB v. Main St. Terrace Care Ctr., 218 F.3d 531, 164 LRRM 2833 (6th Cir. 2000).

employees are engaged in concerted activity.[5] Partial strikes, however, remain unprotected.[6]

The Board and the courts continue to hold that an individual employee's action to enforce the terms of a collective bargaining agreement, even though pursued singly, constitutes concerted activity under Section 7.[7]

While activity by a single employee for the individual's own personal benefit is not concerted activity, the fact that self-interest is a factor in an employee's decision to engage in the activity at issue does not deprive otherwise concerted activity of protection under the Act.[8] Likewise, although an individual employee's assertion of a statutory right enjoyed by other employees is not always concerted activity, employees who collectively seek to improve their working conditions through resort to administrative or judicial forums have been found to be engaged in concerted activity.[9]

Once concerted activity is found, however, the Board and courts continue to broadly interpret the protective umbrella of Section 7,[10]

---

[5]Caval Tool Div., Chromalloy Gas Turbine Corp., 331 NLRB No. 101 (2000).

[6] Yale Univ., *supra* note 3.

[7]New Orleans Cold Storage & Warehouse Co. v. NLRB, 201 F.3d 592, 163 LRRM 2330 (5th Cir. 2000) (employer violated Act by taking adverse employment action against employee because of number of grievances filed by employee under collective bargaining agreement); United States Postal Serv., 332 NLRB No. 28 (2000) (employees engaged in protected concerted activity when they refused to work overtime after employer failed to provide 1-hour notice required by collective bargaining agreement).

[8]St. Luke's Episcopal-Presbyterian Hosp., Inc., 331 NLRB No. 87 (2000).

[9]*See* Mojave Elec. Coop., Inc. v. NLRB, 206 F.3d 1183, 163 LRRM 2917 (D.C. Cir. 2000) (co-workers jointly filing, with the support of other employees, judicial petition seeking an injunction against harassment from contractors hired by employer engaged in concerted activity); Tri-County Transp., Inc., 331 NLRB No. 152 (2000) (employer violated §8(a)(1) by terminating employees who acted collectively in filing for unemployment benefits); 127 Restaurant Corp., 331 NLRB No. 32 (2000) (employees joining to file civil action against their employer regarding payment of wages engaged in concerted activity).

[10]*E.g.*, Frazier Indus. Co. v. NLRB, 213 F.3d 750, 164 LRRM 2516 (D.C. Cir. 2000) (union supporter who persistently discussed union with co-workers was engaged in protected activity, despite employer's contention that employee was impermissibly harassing co-workers during work time); Mojave Elec. Coop., Inc, 327 NLRB 13, 163 LRRM 1288 (1998) (employee and his co-worker, pursuant to common concern for workplace safety, petitioned for injunctive relief against harassment by two officials of employer's subcontractor, and employee's actions not found disloyal so as to lose protection); Epilepsy Found. of Northeast Ohio, 331 NLRB No. 92, 164 LRRM 1233 (2000) (written memos in which employee, along with co-worker, had attempted to dismiss their supervisor and raised issues related to employees' terms and conditions of employment, were protected); Office Depot, 330 NLRB No. 99, 163 LRRM 1169 (2000).

though concerted activity that is in breach of contract or is found an impermissible strike continues to be found unprotected.[11]

Section 7 protections can extend to situations in which employees seek to improve terms and conditions of employment through channels outside the immediate employee-supervisor relationship, such as situations in which an employee raises complaints regarding working conditions in the media,[12] in group meetings called by the employer,[13] or by distributing literature to the public.[14]

In *Petrochem Insulation*[15] the Board held that petitioning state governmental agencies with objections to environmental standards of employer contracts is protected area-standards activity within the meaning of the mutual aid or protection provision of Section 7 of the Act. According to the Board, working conditions may include the safety and health of all employees who may eventually be employed at a particular worksite.

---

[11]*See* District 17 v. Island Creek Coal Co., 179 F.3d 133, 161 LRRM 2463 (4th Cir. 1999) (employees fired for picketing over grievable disputes in violation of labor contract were not engaged in protected activity).

[12]*See* Allstate Ins. Co., 332 NLRB No. 66, 165 LRRM 1293 (2000) (employer unlawfully disciplined employee for magazine interview critical of employer where several employees participated and interview was done in part to alert other employees of the complained-of conditions); St. Luke's Episcopal-Presbyterian Hosp., Inc., 331 NLRB No. 87 (2000) (employer unlawfully terminated employee for airing complaints in regard to working conditions in television interview where, prior to interview, employee and her co-workers were engaged in ongoing labor dispute with employer over these conditions).

[13]*See* CKS Tool & Eng'g, Inc., 332 NLRB No. 162 (2000) (employee who protested employer's position regarding employee productivity at meeting called by employer was protesting on behalf of co-workers with whom he had previously discussed issue and appealing to his co-workers to support protest, and therefore his actions constituted concerted activity); Caval Tool Div., Chromalloy Gas Turbine Corp., 331 NLRB No. 101 (2000) (employee who questioned and commented on employer's proposed change in company's break policy at employer-called meeting was espousing cause of her co-workers and was therefore engaged in concerted activity); 127 Restaurant Corp., 331 NLRB No. 32 (2000) (employee expressing employee concerns about working conditions at meeting called by employer engaged in concerted activity); Bethlehem Temple Learning Ctr., Inc., 330 NLRB No. 166, 167 LRRM 1006 (2000) (employees raising concerns about signing noncompetition agreements at employer-called meeting engaged in concerted activity); *cf.* Mobil Exploration & Producing U.S., Inc. v. NLRB, 200 F.3d 230, 163 LRRM 2387 (5th Cir. 1999) (affirming Board's conclusion that employee's statements to group of employees during work break qualified as concerted activity).

[14]*See* Arlington Elec. Inc., 332 NLRB No. 72, 166 LRRM 1049 (2000) (employee who discussed formation of employee association with co-workers was seeking to initiate, induce, or prepare for group activities by distributing flyers critical of employer's insurance coverage and was therefore engaged in protected concerted activity).

[15]330 NLRB No. 10, 163 LRRM 1276 (1999), *enforced*, 240 F.3d 26, 166 LRRM 2433 (D.C. Cir. 2001).

The Board continues to hold that employee conduct on behalf of the employees of another employer who are engaged in protected concerted activity is itself concerted activity under Section 7.[16] Similarly, in some, but not all, circumstances employee protests regarding nonemployees such as supervisors can constitute concerted activity.[17]

C. Employer Interference With Section 7 Rights: Section 8(a)(1)

3. *Motive Not an Essential Element of Section 8(a)(1) Violations*

The Board continues adhering to its position that motive is not an essential element of a Section 8(a)(1) violation.[18] The Board continues applying the principles set forth in *NLRB v. Burnup & Sims.*[19] When an employer discharges an employee for misconduct arising out of a protected activity, the employer has the burden of showing that it held an honest belief that the employee engaged in serious misconduct. Once the employer establishes that it had such an honest belief, the burden shifts to the General Counsel to affirmatively show that the misconduct did not in fact occur.[20] The courts tend to follow this rule as well.[21]

---

[16]*See* Office Depot, 330 NLRB No. 99, 163 LRRM 1169 (2000) (employee's use of term "scab" to person crossing picket line of employees of another employer was expression of support for striking employees and amounted to making common cause with protected concerted activity of those employees).

[17]*See* Southern Pride Catfish, 331 NLRB No. 81 (2000) (employee walkout over discharge of supervisor fired because employees she supervised were wearing union t-shirts was concerted activity); Senior Citizens Coordinating Council of Riverbay Cmty. Inc., 330 NLRB No. 154, 166 LRRM 1074 (2000) (employee actions in seeking to replace executive director constituted protected concerted activity). For complete treatment of this subject, see Section III.A.3. [Other Concerted Activity; Protected Concerted Activity: In General; Employee Activity for "Other Mutual Aid or Protection], *infra*.

[18]*See* Eckert Fire Protection, Inc., 332 NLRB No. 18 (2000); Multi-Ad Servs., Inc., 331 NLRB No. 160, 165 LRRM 1157 (2000); SOS Staffing Servs., Inc., 331 NLRB No. 97, 165 LRRM 1011 (2000); Medic One, Inc., 331 NLRB No. 56 (2000); Yoshi's Japanese Restaurant, Inc., 330 NLRB No. 174 (2000); Westwood Health Care Ctr., 330 NLRB No. 141, 163 LRRM 1225 (2000).

[19]379 U.S. 21 (1964).

[20]Pepsi-Cola Co., 330 NLRB No. 69, 164 LRRM 1013 (2000) (case remanded to judge for explicit determination of whether employer affirmatively established that it had honest belief that employee made statements calling for work stoppage and whether General Counsel carried its burden of showing that employee did not engage in misconduct).

[21]*See* Webco Indus., Inc., 217 F.3d 1306, 164 LRRM 2845 (10th Cir. 2000), *relying on* NLRB v. Burnup & Sims, Inc., 379 U.S. 21, 22–23, 57 LRRM 2385 (1964).

The courts continue to look to state law to determine whether an employer has a property interest sufficient to exclude non-employees from its premises.[22] The D.C. Circuit declined to defer to the Board's interpretation of property rights under state law, and held that in the case at bar the nonowner, nonlessee employer did not have the right under Virginia trespass law to exclude union organizers from the sidewalks in front of its stores.[23] In *R&R Plaster & Drywall Co.*[24] a divided panel of the Board held that factual questions precluded the dismissal of a complaint alleging that a subcontractor unlawfully threatened to arrest union organizers for entering onto property that the subcontractor did not control. The Board distinguished a Pennsylvania state court decision holding that an independent contractor, not the landowner, had possession and control of a work area for tort liability purposes.

D. Union Restraint and Coercion—Section 8(b)(1)(A)

2. *Nature of the Violation*

The Board continues to hold that it is not a violation of Section 8(b)(1)(A) for a union to enforce its own valid rules against its members.[25] The Board, however, continues to find various attempts by unions to discipline members in violation of Section 8(b)(1)(A).[26] The Board held that imposition of a window-period limitation on the filing of *Beck* objections on employees who have recently resigned their union membership violates Section 8(b)(1)(A) because it con-

---

[22]Communication Workers Local 400 v. NLRB, 222 F.3d 1030 (D.C. Cir. 2000) (quoting Indio Grocery Outlet, 323 NLRB 1138, 1141 (1997), *enforced,* 187 F.3d 1080 (9th Cir. 1999), for the proposition that "there is a threshold burden on the [employer] to establish that it had, at the time it expelled the Union representatives, an interest which entitled it to exclude individuals from the property.").

[23]*Id.*

[24]330 NLRB No. 22, 163 LRRM 1105 (1999).

[25]Teamsters Local 710, 333 NLRB No. 159 (2001); Service Employees Local 254, 332 NLRB No. 103 (2000); Office & Professional Employees Local 251, 331 NLRB No. 193 (2000).

[26]NLRB v. Teamsters Local 439, 175 F.3d 1173, 161 LRRM 2571 (9th Cir. 1999) (Act prohibits union from disciplining member for reporting co-worker misconduct, when member is required to do so by his employer); Auto Workers v. NLRB, 168 F.3d 509, 160 LRRM 2955 (D.C. Cir. 1999) (union rule that discriminates between members and nonmembers in processing of grievances violates Act); Operating Eng'rs Local 3, 331 NLRB No. 60 (2000); Electrical Workers (IBEW) Local 3, 331 NLRB No. 150 (2000) (rule requiring following IBEW Constitution in hiring hall violates Act).

stitutes an arbitrary restriction on the right to resign from union membership.[27] The Board overruled its decision in *Pepsi-Cola Bottling Co.*,[28] and held that union photographing or videotaping of employees engaged in protected activities during an election campaign, without more, does not necessarily interfere with employees' Section 7 rights.[29]

The Board does not require evidence of unlawful intent to support a finding of a violation of Section 8(b)(1)(A). Under appropriate circumstances, an implied threat may constitute a violation. *National Ass'n of Letter Carriers Local 3825*[30] involved a charge that the union violated Section 8(b)(1)(A) by implicitly threatening in a union newsletter to refuse to represent employees who make complaints against union officers and who cooperate in employer investigations of union officers. The Board concluded that the newsletter, which criticized union–member informants as ungrateful, and which contained a statement that "what goes around comes around" did not constitute an implied threat of retaliation in violation of Section 8(b)(1)(A).

E.   "Freedom of Speech"—Section 8(c) in General

1.   *Threat or Prophecy?*

The Board and courts continue to consider the effect of statements made during a union election campaign from the employee's perspective, taking into account "the economic dependence of the employees on their employers, and the necessary tendency of the former, because of that relationship, to pick up intended implications of the latter that might be more readily dismissed by a more disinterested ear."[31] Statements beyond mere expression of opinion

---

[27]Transportation Workers, 329 NLRB No. 56 (1999).

[28]289 NLRB No. 736 (1988).

[29] Randell Warehouse of Arizona, 328 NLRB 1034, 161 LRRM 1265 (1999).

[30]333 NLRB No. 41, 166 LRRM 1217 (2001).

[31]NLRB v. St. Francis Healthcare Ctr., 212 F.3d 945, 164 LRRM 2324 (6th Cir. 2000) (employer's chief executive officer unlawfully threatened closure of healthcare facility when he predicted that no entity would affiliate with facility if employees elected union, where only likely affiliate had expressed concerns about possible unionization of facility. Viewed from perspective of employees, CEO's exaggeration of the objective evidence was material); Multicraft Int'l, 328 NLRB 85, 161 LRRM 1080 (1999) (employer that provides assembly services to company that manufactures dashboards for Mercedes automobile violated §8(b)(1) when its general manager told employee that company had contract with Mercedes that

continue to be found to be outside Section 8(c) protection,[32] although employers remain entitled to freely express the opinion that the company does not need a union.[33]

An employer violated Section 8(a)(1) when, following the announcement of a union election victory, one manager told his employees "you're going to regret this all year." Viewing this statement in the context of other unlawful statements, and based on the totality of the relevant circumstances, the Board determined that the statement violated the Act.[34]

Similarly, the Board found that an employer's inquiry to an employee about a union-organizing meeting constituted interrogation and created an impression of surveillance in violation of Section 8(a)(1).[35] The employer asked the employee "how it went with the organizers today." Under all the circumstances, the inquiry, coupled with other statements made by the owner, violated Section 8(a)(1).

---

would not let a union happen, and if a union got formed, company would lose its contract with Mercedes, employees would leave, and employees would lose their jobs); ITT Automotive v. NLRB, 188 F.3d 375, 161 LRRM 3132 (6th Cir. 1999) (statements did not merit §8(c) protection because they reasonably tended to coerce employees. Supervisors' economic predictions that after unionization plant might close if they became unprofitable or that strikes might occur as result of employer's refusal to give in to union demands were not supported by objective facts that "did not refer to matters over which [employees] exercised no control"); Wallace Int'l de Puerto Rico, 328 NLRB 29 (1999) (employer unlawfully threatened employees, by showing video suggesting that plant closure would result if they voted for union).

[32]E.g., Sheridan Manor Nursing Home v. NLRB, 225 F.3d 248, 165 LRRM 2133 (2d Cir. 2000) (Board reasonably found employer violated §8(a)(1) when, one week before scheduled vote on ratification of tentative labor contract, it distributed to employees memo that criticized exclusion of nonunion members from ratification process; despite contention that memo was employer speech protected by §8(c). The court reasoned that the memo, which used phrases such as "you should object now and refuse being on membership board if you have not already" constituted conduct beyond mere expression of opinion and beyond §8(c) protection. However, the court also questioned whether protection of §8(c) is limited only to speech that is unrelated to unfair labor practice charge).

[33]Pacific Custom Materials, 327 NLRB 75 (1998) (employer lawfully maintained handbook stating that there was no need for union at company, that all its employees were treated fairly, and that "an employee who would want to become a member of union in the future should expect nothing more than an employee who is not a union member").

[34]Ebenezer Rail Car Servs., 333 NLRB No. 18 (2001).

[35]Fred'k Wallace & Son, Inc., 331 NLRB No. 113 (2000).

II. Organizational and Preelection Activity

A. In General: Relation of Unfair Labor Practices to "Laboratory Conditions" Required for Elections

The Board addressed an employer grant of wage increases during an organizational effort in *Overnite Transportation Co.*[36] At the height of the union's organizing effort, in what the Board referred to as a "carrot and stick campaign," Overnite granted its unrepresented workers an unprecedented wage increase just months after granting their normal annual pay raises. Simultaneously, it announced in the company newsletter that "unfortunately" employees at the four facilities that had elected union representation "will not get these pay increases," but will "have to wait for negotiations." This, coupled with a variety of other violations, led the Board to find the issuance of a bargaining order appropriate. The Fourth Circuit denied review and granted the cross-petition for enforcement.[37]

B. Unlawful Employer Conduct

1. *Employer's Restrictions on Union and Employee Activity on Employer's Property*

a. Basic Presumptions

The Board continues to hold that employer no-distribution rules are only presumptively valid if employees have the right to distribute union literature on company property in nonworking areas when neither they nor the employee recipients are expected to be actively working.[38] The Board also requires that valid no-distribution rules allow distribution of union literature in mixed-use areas, as long as both the person doing the distributing and the person receiving the literature are not on working time.[39]

---

[36]329 NLRB No. 91 (1999).
[37]240 F.3d 325 (4th Cir. 2001). A petition for rehearing was pending at the time of publication of this supplement.
[38]Eby-Brown Co., L.P., 328 NLRB No. 75 (1999).
[39]Saia Motor Freight, 333 NLRB No. 117 (2001).

b. Rights of Employees Over Nonemployees

The Board and courts continue tugging at each other over the rights of employees versus nonemployee organizers in reaching other employees at different business entities. When a union does not have a reasonably effective means of communicating with employees away from the employees' job sites, Section 7 compels the employer to allow nonemployee union organizers access to its property for organizational purposes.[40]

In *Sandusky Mall Co. v. NLRB*[41] the Sixth Circuit refused to enforce the Board's findings that union organizers were engaged in protected activity. Union organizers attempted to handbill mall patrons because one mall tenant had hired a nonunion contractor, and threatened to handbill another tenant for the same reason and purpose. The owner of the mall permitted distribution by a charitable organization, but prohibited union handbilling. The court distinguished between nonorganizational solicitation by "charitable, civic and even commercial organizations to enter a mall for solicitations, displays, and presentations,"[42] and handbilling by nonemployee union organizers, based on the manner in which the mall wished to present itself to the public. The court reaffirmed its earlier decision in *Cleveland Real Estate Partners*[43] that "alleged 'discriminatory' conduct in allowing solicitation and handbilling required that the 'discrimination be among comparable groups or activities' and that the activities themselves under *consideration* must be '*comparable*,'" which was not the case here.

In *6 West Ltd. Corp. v. NLRB*[44] the court held that employee solicitation of other employees at a Chicago restaurant was not protected activity, although in the past the restaurant had permitted employee selling of Christmas cookies, hand-made Christmas ornaments, hand-painted water bottles, theater tickets, and raffle tickets.[45] The court extended the distinction drawn by the Sixth Circuit in *Sandusky Mall Co.*[46] and *Cleveland Real Estate Partners*[47] to include

---

[40]North Alaska Drilling, Inc. v. NLRB, 190 F.3d 1008, 162 LRRM 2197 (9th Cir. 1999).

[41]242 F.3d 682, 166 LRRM 2641 (6th Cir. 2001).

[42]*Id.* at 690.

[43]95 F.3d 457, 153 LRRM 2338 (6th Cir. 1996).

[44]237 F.3d 767, 166 LRRM 2221 (7th Cir. 2001).

[45]*Id.*

[46]Sandusky Mall Co. v. NLRB, 242 F.3d 682, 166 LRRM 2641 (6th Cir. 2001).

[47]95 F.3d 457, 153 LRRM 2338 (6th Cir. 1996).

employees engaging in "an activity as innocent as the sale of girl scout cookies or the sale of hand-blown Christmas ornaments during the yuletide season," as opposed to efforts by some employees to organize others.[48]

In *NLRB v. Calkins*[49] the Ninth Circuit enforced a Board order prohibiting a stand-alone grocery store from threatening non-employee union organizers with arrest for trespassing on its parking lot and walkway. A California statute prohibited owners of shopping malls and general access supermarkets from excluding speech activity on their private adjacent sidewalks and parking lots. The court rejected the employer's assertion that the California law was pre-empted by the need for uniform application of Section 7 access rights across the country. Because the California statute enhanced Section 7 protection and did not conflict with or frustrate the federal scheme, the court held that the Board's ruling, which granted more union accommodation than federal law requires, was rational and consistent with the Act.[50]

c. No-Solicitation and No-Distribution Rules Generally

The Board and the courts continue distinguishing between employee solicitation and distribution of literature. Solicitation by employees can be prohibited only during working time,[51] although employers cannot prohibit employees from discussing unionization during working times if other work time discussions are not prohibited.[52] Employers may lawfully prohibit distribution of literature by employees in work areas at any time.[53] Employers may not prohibit distribution in nonwork areas, or in mixed areas, during nonworking time.[54]

The Board continues treating employee efforts to obtain signatures on authorization cards as solicitation rather than distribution of literature.[55]

---

[48] *6 West, supra* note 44 at 780, 166 LRRM at 2229–2230.

[49] 187 F.3d 1080, 161 LRRM 3121 (9th Cir. 1999).

[50] *Id.* at 1095, 161 LRRM at 3131–3132.

[51] Valmont Indus. v. NLRB, 244 F.3d 454, 166 LRRM 2782 (5th Cir. 2001).

[52] Frazier Indus. Co., 328 NLRB No. 89, 163 LRRM 1024 (1999).

[53] United Parcel Serv., 327 NLRB 317, 160 LRRM 1148 (1998), *aff'd*, 228 F.3d 772, 165 LRRM 2358 (6th Cir. 2000); RCN Corp., 333 NLRB No. 45 (2001).

[54] *Id.*

[55] Mid-Mountain Foods, Inc., 332 NLRB No. 19, n.2 (2000).

(1) Presumptions of Validity

Recent decisions confirm that a presumptively valid rule prohibiting solicitation may still be unlawful if it is promulgated or enforced in a discriminatory manner.[56] An invalid rule violates the Act even if the rule is not enforced.[57]

(2) Facial Validity of Rule

Employers may not draw no-solicitation rules so broadly as to en-compass nonworking time; such a rule is presumptively unlawful.[58]

In *Flamingo Hilton-Laughlin*[59] the Board held that the employer's no-solicitation policy was overbroad to the extent that it covered off-duty employees in public areas of the employer's property. The Board refused, however, to find that it was overbroad to the extent that it covered gaming areas, because the retail department store "selling area" exception covers gaming areas.

In *Cooper Health Systems*[60] the Board held that a hospital's prohibition against solicitation in all work areas was presumptively invalid because it applied to nonworking time in working areas other than immediate patient care areas. Further, the hospital failed to show that solicitation in working areas that are not immediate patient care areas would either disrupt care or disturb patients, a showing that is required to justify the exception for health care institutions.

The Board and the courts continue holding that describing the period in which solicitation and distribution is prohibited as "working hours" is ambiguous, and, thus, overly broad and facially invalid.[61]

(3) Unlawful Promulgation or Enforcement

The Board continues holding that evidence of a discriminatory purpose in the adoption or application of a presumptively valid rule

---

[56]Webco Indus. v. NLRB, 217 F.3d 1306, 164 LRRM 2845 (10th Cir. 2000); Wexler Meat Co., 331 NLRB No. 26 (2000).

[57]Beverly Health & Rehab. Servs., 332 NLRB No. 26 (2000).

[58]*Wexler Meat Co., supra* note 56; Waste Management of Palm Beach, 329 NLRB No. 20, 167 LRRM 1059 (1999) (rule prohibiting solicitation and distribution of literature during nonwork time in nonwork areas is facially invalid); Eby-Brown Co. L.P., 328 NLRB 496 (1999).

[59]330 NLRB No. 34 (1999).

[60]327 NLRB 1159 (1999).

[61]St. George Warehouse, Inc., 331 NLRB No. 55 (2000).

will rebut the presumption of validity.[62] In *Pioneer Hotel v. NLRB*[63] the employer's hotel policy, prohibiting employees from access to the hotel dining room 30 minutes before their shift, was valid on its face. However, the policy could not be enforced selectively to block efforts to circulate petitions. Similarly, when evidence demonstrated that a hospital employer had previously allowed commercial and other nonunion solicitation and distribution in immediate patient care areas, it could not lawfully enforce its no-solicitation/no-distribution policy against union organizing activity by its employees in such areas.[64]

The Board and certain courts continue to disagree regarding the rights of employees and nonemployees with respect to the enforcement of solicitation and distribution rules.[65] The Board takes the position that a violation of the Act occurs when an employer denies union representatives access while regularly allowing nonunion organizations to solicit and distribute literature on its property.[66] The Sixth Circuit disagrees, and held in *Sandusky Mall Co. v. NLRB*[67] that a mall owner's nonsolicitation policy could be applied differently to nonemployee union handbillers than it was applied to private, civic, and religious organizations' solicitations, because Section 7 of the Act does not protect nonemployees.

d. Implementation of Rules: Timing as an Element of Legality

The Board continues considering the timing of implementation of a no-solicitation or no-distribution rule an important factor in determining the rule's validity.[68]

---

[62]Clinton Elecs., Inc., 332 NLRB No. 47 (2000); Waste Mgmt. of Palm Beach, 329 NLRB No. 20 (1999).

[63]182 F.3d 939, 161 LRRM 2785 (D.C. Cir. 1999).

[64]Cooper Health Sys., 327 NLRB 1159 (1999).

[65]See discussion at Section II.B.1.h. [Organizational and Preelection Activity; Unlawful Employer Conduct; Employer's Restriction on Union and Employee Activity on Employer's Property; Prohibiting Protected Activity on Private Property Open to the Public]; *see also* 6 West Ltd. Corp. v. NLRB, 237 F.3d 767, 166 LRRM 2221 (4th Cir. 2001); Guardian Indus. Corp. v. NLRB, 49 F.3d 317, 148 LRRM 2665 (7th Cir. 1995); Riesbeck Food Mkts. v. NLRB, 91 F.3d 132, 153 LRRM 2320 (4th Cir. 1996) (unpublished decision).

[66]Cleveland Real Estate Partners v. NLRB, 316 NLRB 158, 149 LRRM 137 (1995), *enf. denied*, 95 F.3d 457, 153 LRRM 2338 (6th Cir. 1996).

[67]242 F.3d 682, 166 LRRM 2641 (6th Cir. 2001), *rev'g* 329 NLRB No. 62, 162 LRRM 1191 (1999). *See* factual summary of *Sandusky*, notes 41–43, *supra.*

[68]Waste Mgmt. of Palm Beach, 329 NLRB No. 20 (1999); (solicitation and distribution policy implemented in response to union organizing campaign violated Act); *In re* Teledyne Advanced Materials, 332 NLRB No. 53, 166 LRRM 1033 (2000).

e. Union Buttons and Insignia

The Board continues adhering to its position that an employer may lawfully promulgate and enforce a rule prohibiting the wearing of union buttons and insignia only if "special circumstances" exist.[69] An employer's attempt to prohibit wearing union insignia will be difficult to justify if it is not based on an announced, generally applicable rule.[70] A rule banning decals or union stickers from company hardhats has been upheld where there were special circumstances and where employees were permitted to wear union insignia on their own clothing.[71] An "overly broad" rule prohibiting the wearing of union insignia, however, was invalidated in its entirety where it was promulgated for unlawful retaliatory reasons, even though the employer asserted a "special circumstances" defense.[72] The Board considers the size of union insignia as a significant factor in determining whether an employer may prohibit displaying the insignia.[73]

An employer's offering of antiunion buttons to employees,[74] or making negative remarks about employees wearing union buttons,[75] also may be unlawful under Section 7 of the Act.

g. No-Access Rules

In defining the right of off-duty employees to enter or remain on plant premises for purposes of engaging in union activities, the Board continues applying the principle of *Tri-County Med. Center.*[76]

---

[69]Pioneer Hotel, Inc. v. NLRB, 182 F.3d 939, 161 LRRM 2785 (D.C. Cir. 1999); *In re* Eckert Fire Protection, Inc., 332 NLRB No. 18 (2000); NLRB v. St. Francis Healthcare Centre, 212 F.3d 945, 957–960, 164 LRRM 2324 (6th Cir. 2000). *See also* Flamingo Hilton-Laughlin, 330 NLRB No. 34 (1999) (customer exposure to union insignia alone is not special circumstance allowing employer to prohibit display of union insignia by employees).

[70]NLRB v. Autodie Int'l, Inc., 169 F.3d 378 (6th Cir. 1999).

[71]Eastern Omni Constructors, Inc. v. NLRB, 170 F.3d 418, 160 LRRM 2669 (4th Cir. 1999); Timken Co., 331 NLRB No. 86 (2000). *But see* Eby-Brown Co. L.P., 328 NLRB 496 (1999) (employer may not normally prohibit union insignia on company-issued property if its placement does no damage to that property).

[72]E & L Transp. Co. LLC, 331 NLRB No. 83 (2000).

[73]Produce Warehouse of Coram, Inc., 329 NLRB No. 80 (1999).

[74]ITT Automotive v. NLRB, 188 F.3d 375, 161 LRRM 3132 (6th Cir. 1999).

[75]Decca Ltd. Partnership, 327 NLRB 980, 164 LRRM 1040 (1999); Manor Care of Decatur, 327 NLRB No. 173 (1999) (negative comment on performance evaluation about employee's wearing of union button).

[76]222 NLRB 1089, 91 LRRM 1323 (1976). *See also* Timken Co., 331 NLRB No. 86 (2000) (application of *Tri-County* test to employee handbillers); Flamingo Hilton-Laughlin, 330 NLRB No. 34 (1999) (holding that employer's policy violated §8(a)(1) because it barred employees from patronizing the employer's property

Where the employer does not have an actual rule banning employees' off-duty access to the employer's property, the Board does not apply the principles of *Tri-County*.[77]

h. Prohibiting Protected Activity on Private Property Open to the Public

A difference of opinion exists between the Board and certain courts regarding the disparate application of solicitation and distribution policies to union representatives on employers' private property. In *Lechmere, Inc. v. NLRB*[78] the Supreme Court provided guidance in this general area by holding that "[s]o long as nonemployee union organizers have reasonable access to employees outside an employer's property,"[79] an employer may prohibit all access by such individuals to its premises. Questions continue arising, however, on the access issue when an employer permits nonemployee access for such activities as Girl Scout cookie sales, but denies nonemployee union representatives access.

The Board continues holding that *Lechmere* will not shield an employer that discriminates by allowing solicitation or distribution by other persons and groups while denying like access to a union.[80] However, in *6 West Ltd. Corp. v. NLRB*,[81] the Seventh Circuit ruled that prohibiting employee solicitation for union support, while allowing employee solicitation for Girl Scout cookies, Christmas ornaments, and raffle tickets did not constitute discriminatory application of the employer's no-solicitation policy. The court held that the latter activities were not "similar" to union solicitations and, therefore, allowing them while banning the union solicitations did not violate Section 8(a)(1). The court also found that the union solicitations were disruptive in the workplace because some employees complained to management. The court found, on the other hand, that

---

during the eight hours before their shift but failed to establish a business reason for the rule); R&R Plaster & Drywall Co., 330 NLRB No. 22, 163 LRRM 1105 (1999) (employer's failure to provide evidence of its property interest precludes it from proving its right to exclude union representation from its site).

[77]Santa Fe Hotel, Inc., 331 NLRB No. 88 (2000) (Board affirmed ALJ determination that employer violated §8(a)(1) by enforcing its no-distribution policy so as to prohibit off-duty employees from distributing union-related literature in nonworking area).

[78]Lechmere, Inc. v. NLRB, 502 U.S. 527, 139 LRRM 2225 (1992).

[79]*Id.* at 538.

[80]See discussion in Main Edition; *see also* Albertson's, Inc., 332 NLRB No. 104 (2000).

[81]237 F.3d 767, 166 LRRM 2221 (7th Cir. 2001).

an "activity as innocent as the sale of girl scout cookies" was "beneficial to all employees."[82] Other courts have reached similar conclusions in refusing to enforce Board orders in this area.[83]

The Board's supplemental decision in *Farm Fresh, Inc.*,[84] a case on remand from the D.C. Circuit, provides certain additional guidance in this area. The Board accepted the D.C. Circuit's finding that the employer did not rely solely on its no-solicitation rule when it ejected union organizers from the snack bar. In fact, the employer had no such policy, and evicted the union organizers because of prior trespass warrants issued against them. The Board ruled that the record contained no evidence of discrimination against union solicitation and reaffirmed that the employer did not violate Section 8(a)(1). This decision reflects the Board's principle that where an employer has met the nondiscrimination requirements, the *Lechmere* analysis applies, and the employer's right to exclude is derived from the relevant state property law. In applying Virginia law, however, the Board found that the employer lacked a sufficient exclusionary interest to eject union organizers from the sidewalk outside its store.[85]

i. Prohibiting Distribution of Political Materials

Handbilling is protected under *Eastex, Inc. v. NLRB*,[86] where employees, in nonworking areas on nonworking time, distribute "political" material regarding laws that have a significant and direct bearing on a basic concern of employees as employees.

---

[82] *Id.* at 780.

[83] *See, e.g.*, Sandusky Mall Co. v. NLRB, 242 F.3d 682, 166 LRRM 2461 (6th Cir. 2001); Guardian Industrial Corp. v. NLRB, 49 F.3d 317, 148 LRRM 2665 (7th Cir. 1995).

[84] 326 NLRB 997, 159 LRRM 1201 (1998), *petition for review granted*, 222 F.3d 1030 (D.C. Cir. 2000), *on remand to*, 332 NLRB No. 156 (2000).

[85] *Id. See also* NLRB v. Calkins, 187 F.3d 1080, 161 LRRM 3121 (9th Cir. 1999), *cert. denied*, 529 U.S. 1098, 164 LRRM 2256 (2000) (holding that, as a threshold matter, the employer must show a property right entitling it to exclude individuals engaged in §7 conduct; without such a showing, any exclusion or threat of exclusion from the property is a violation of §8(a)(1)).

[86] 437 U.S. 556, 98 LRRM 2717 (1978); Kenworth Truck Co., Inc., 327 NLRB 497, 166 LRRM 1215 (1999) (employee engaged in protected activity when he distributed, during nonwork time and outside the work site, political material advocating repeal of a new law that reduced benefits available to workers under Ohio's worker's compensation system).

j. Effect of Contractual Waiver of Right to Solicit or Distribute

The Board and the courts continue applying *NLRB v. Magnavox Co.*[87] in a variety of situations, including holding that a collective bargaining agreement, absent specific waiver language, cannot be read to restrict employee rights to distribute campaign material in support of the bargaining agent.[88]

In *Hotel & Restaurant Employees Local 5 v. Honolulu Country Club*[89] *Magnavox* was discussed, but distinguished on the facts. In that case, the court ruled that "working hours" included the paid meal breaks given to employees. Therefore, a provision in the parties' collective bargaining agreement that prohibited solicitation "during working hours" was only a partial waiver of the employees' Section 7 rights. *Magnavox,* said the court, focused on the unions' power to consent to the total elimination of either distribution or solicitation. Relying on *NLRB v. United Tech Corp.,*[90] the court upheld this partial limitation on solicitation by the union.

2. *Specific Conduct That Violates Section 8(a)(1)*

a. Threats to Withdraw, and Withdrawals of, Benefits

The Board will closely examine the discontinuation of existing benefits in the context of union activity among employees. In *Climatrol, Inc.,*[91] an employer's termination of vacation benefits and holiday pay violated Section 8(a)(1) when the benefit termination followed one of the most successful years in the employer's history and was announced on the heels of recent union activities by the employees. In *Overnite Transp. Co.,*[92] an employer violated Section 8(a)(1) by implying that employees who voted for the union would forfeit future pay increases when it announced a pay increase that excluded all employees working at a certain location where the Teamsters had recently been certified. In *Eby-Brown Co. L.P.,*[93] an em-

---

[87]415 U.S. 322, 85 LRRM 2475, *reh'g denied,* 416 U.S. 952 (1974).
[88]Summa Health Sys., Inc., 330 NLRB No. 197 (2000); Mead Corp., 331 NLRB No. 66 (2000).
[89]100 F. Supp. 2d 1254, 164 LRRM 3021 (D. Haw. 1999).
[90]706 F.2d 1254, 113 LRRM 2326 (2d Cir. 1983).
[91]329 NLRB No. 83 (1999).
[92]329 NLRB No. 91, 166 LRRM 1101 (1999), *enforced,* 240 F.3d 325. 166 LRRM 2577 (2001).
[93]328 NLRB No. 496 (1999).

ployer violated Section 8(a)(1) when an executive told employees that the only reason they had no retirement plan was because the company had spent so much money fighting employee grievances.

The withdrawal of, or threat to withdraw, benefits need not entail a significant change. Any threatened or actual change may be found unlawful, even where the change is slight.[94] The Board continues to examine the context of the employer's statements in determining whether the overall effect of the message conveys an unlawful threat.[95]

(1) Permissible Predictions and Prohibited Threats

Over 30 years after *NLRB v. Gissel Packing Co.*,[96] the Board and the courts continue struggling with the distinction between permissible predictions and unlawful threats of reprisal.[97] To avoid violating Section 8(a)(1), an employer must provide an objective factual basis, outside its own control, for predictions of adverse consequences of unionization.[98] In *President Riverboat Casinos of Missouri, Inc.*[99] a manager responded to an employee's question about whether wages would go down by stating that this was a "possibility." Because the manager made no reference to the collective bargaining process, any economic necessities, or other objective facts when making this statement, the Board held that it was coercive and implied reprisal if the union was voted in.

One result of the difficulty that the Board and the courts have experienced in evaluating the objective basis offered by employers to support their predictions is that considerable scrutiny is often given

---

[94]NLRB v. General Fabrications Corp., 222 F.3d 218, 231, 164 LRRM 2974, 2982–2983 (6th Cir. 2000) (employer statements that threaten employee working conditions, "however slightly," necessarily affect employee sentiment regarding the union), citing United Artists Theatre Circuit, Inc., 277 NLRB 115, 121, 121 LRRM 1283 (1985).

[95]Venture Indus., Inc., 330 NLRB No. 159, 164 LRRM 1173 (2000) (employer statement that "UAW" means "You Ain't Working" held, in context, to be an unlawful threat that employees would lose jobs, and CEO's statement that as far as he was concerned, the plant would never be a union shop, held, in context, to be a threat that "voting for union representation was futile").

[96]395 U.S. 575, 71 LRRM 2841, *reh'g denied*, 396 U.S. 869 (1969).

[97]Webco Indus., Inc. v. NLRB, 217 F.3d 1306, 1316, 164 LRRM 2845 (10th Cir. 2000).

[98]Office Depot, 330 NLRB No. 99, 163 LRRM 1169 (2000) (the employer's statement "was not supported by any objective facts"); NLRB v. General Fabrications Corp., 222 F.3d 218, 230, 164 LRRM 2974, 2975 (6th Cir. 2000) (the employer's statement violated §8(a)(1) because it was "not a factual prediction about the likely future").

[99]329 NLRB No. 10, 162 LRRM 1081 (1999).

to every word used in the communication in question. For example, in *NLRB v. St. Francis Healthcare Center*,[100] the Sixth Circuit held that the employer's prediction that "no company" would affiliate with it if the union won the election was unlawful because it "exaggerated" the facts. Focusing on the employer's precise language, the Sixth Circuit found that while the objective evidence may have supported the prediction that certain companies would not affiliate with the employer, it "hardly support[ed] the prediction that no company would."[101]

(2) Futility of Organizing

In a case on remand from the D.C. Circuit, the Board held that certain language in an employer handbill, that stated the extremely divergent positions prior to bargaining, was lawful and served an objective basis for additional statements indicating the potential for "long bitter negotiations" and "a long and ugly strike."[102] The Board majority found that this language was indistinguishable from language found unlawful in prior Board decisions because the employer "was not telling its employees that union representation would be futile. Rather, the Respondent's explanation was consistent with how the Act operates in practice. If parties are sharply divided . . . , negotiations, can indeed, become protracted and bitter."[103]

(3) Inevitability of Strikes or Violence

The Board continues closely scrutinizing statements depicting strikes as a possible consequence of unionization. Thus, where statements depict the possibility of a strike after hard bargaining, the Board will not find a violation of Section 8(a)(1).[104] When, on the other hand, two days after threatening to close the doors if the union got in, the employer stated that the union would call a strike and the employees would be replaced by new workers earning less money, the Board found such conduct to be a violation of Section 8(a)(1).[105]

---

[100]212 F.3d 945, 164 LRRM 2324 (6th Cir. 2000).

[101]*Id.* at 955.

[102]General Elec. Co., 332 NLRB No. 91, 2000 WL 1663427, *2, 165 LRRM 1335, 1337 (2000). *See also* Overnite Transp. Co., 329 NLRB No. 91, 166 LRRM 1101 (1999) (employer repeated statement at another of its facilities, where despite 13 years of bargaining and a strike, the union had not been able to negotiate a collective bargaining agreement).

[103]*General Elec., supra* note 102, 2000 WL 1663427, *3,

[104]*Id.*

[105]Rankin & Rankin, Inc., 330 NLRB No. 148, 165 LRRM 1221, 1222 (2000).

(4) Assessing Recurrent Phrases and Themes

(b) "Bargaining Will Start From Scratch. " "Bargaining will start from scratch" statements continue to be the subject of litigation, with the context in which such statements are made, the timing of the statement, and the opportunity for the union to respond being the key factors in determining whether the Act was violated.[106] For example, an employer violated Section 8(a)(1) when one of its representatives told its employees, "if [a union] was voted in, then that means [the employees] would have to start from scratch," referring to the negotiations between the employer and the union.[107] Another employer violated Section 8(a)(1) when it warned employees that the company would bargain "very hard" and, as a consequence, employees may not "end up with as good a wage benefit package as [they] have now!"[108]

Conversely, an employer in the Sixth Circuit was found not to have engaged in unlawful conduct when it stated bargaining would start "from scratch" or "from zero" if the employees voted for union representation.[109] The Sixth Circuit held that while such statements in isolation may be objectionable conduct, in this case the statements were made to a small number of employees, the union had ample time to respond, and the employer also distributed literature during the pre-election period stating that "employees could expect to remain at their current levels of pay and benefits during negotiations but could ultimately lose or gain benefits as a result of the bargaining process."[110]

(c) Statements Regarding Plant Closings. The Board and courts continued grappling with cases involving statements concerning plant closings. In some instances, the cases involved substantial interplay between Sections 8(c) and 8(a)(1) and are analyzed as if there was some objective basis for the prediction of a plant closure.[111] In other instances, the statements were naked assertions not coupled with

---

[106]Automation & Measurement Div. Bendix Corp. v. NLRB, 400 F.2d 141, 146, 69 LRRM 2157 (6th Cir. 1968).

[107]Overnite Transp. Co., 329 NLRB No. 91 (1999).

[108]ITT Automotive v. NLRB, 188 F.3d 375, 385, 161 LRRM 3132 (6th Cir. 1999).

[109]NLRB v. St. Francis Healthcare Ctr., 212 F.3d 945, 164 LRRM 2324 (6th Cir. 2000).

[110]*Id.* at 957.

[111]*St. Francis Healthcare, supra* note 109 at 954–55; *ITT Automotive, supra* note 108.

factors outside the employer's control.[112] Indeed, unlike interrogation, which is coercive only if a reasonable person would perceive it as such, a threat of plant closure is a per se violation of Section 8(a)(1).[113]

In *Springs Indus., Inc.*[114] the Board established a "rebuttable presumption" test regarding dissemination of threats of plant closure, for purposes of evaluating the effect of such threats on a representation election. The Board overruled *Kokomo Tube Co.*,[115] in which a supervisor's threat of plant closure was found to be insufficient to set aside an election absent evidence of dissemination to other employees.[116] The Board held that it will, in such future cases, require the employer to demonstrate, through record evidence, "either that the employees threatened did not tell other employees about the threat, or that those employees whom they told did not in turn tell any other employees about the threat."[117]

b. Promises and Grants of Benefits

The Board continues applying its presumption that benefits conferred during an organizing campaign are meant to influence employees to relinquish their support for the union. For example, in *Waste Mgmt. of Palm Beach*,[118] the employer accelerated its announcement of an increase in its matching contribution to the company's 401(k) plan, announcing the increase at a "benefits dinner" three days before the union election. The record indicated that the company previously had not planned to announce the increase at that time. On the other hand, the Board found no violation where, in

---

[112]*See* NLRB v. General Fabrications Corp., 222 F.3d 218, 230, 164 LRRM 2974 (6th Cir. 2000); V&S Pro Galv., Inc. v. NLRB, 168 F.3d 270, 278, 160 LRRM 2518 (6th Cir. 1999) (a CEO's response to unionization attempt that the company would lock its doors and the employees could kiss the investment goodbye); Bonham Heating & Air Conditioning, Inc., 328 NLRB 432, 161 LRRM 1113 (1999); ITT Automotive v. NLRB, 188 F.3d 375, 386, 161 LRRM 3132 (6th Cir. 1999) (employer violated §8(a)(1) when it expressly suggested that plants might close if employees voted in the union without an objectively articuable basis for its belief).

[113]Avondale Indus., Inc., 329 NLRB No. 93 (1999).

[114]332 NLRB No. 10, 2000 WL 1344548, 165 LRRM 1161 (2000).

[115]280 NLRB 357, 122 LRRM 1254 (1986).

[116]The Board cited *General Stencils, Inc.*, 195 NLRB 1109, 1110, 79 LRRM 1608, *enforcement denied*, 472 F.2d 170, 82 LRRM 2081 (2d Cir. 1972), and *Coach & Equip. Sales Corp.*, 228 NLRB 440, 94 LRRM 1391 (1977). *But see* Caron Int'l, 246 NLRB 1120, 103 LRRM 1066 (1979) (threats to discharge union proponents are not presumed to be disseminated).

[117]*Springs Indus., supra* note 114, 2000 WL 1344548, *3.

[118]329 NLRB No. 20 (1999).

order to maintain a competitive wage package, an employer granted wage adjustments to its employees before an election.[119] In that case, the employer had conducted a local wage survey and planned to grant wage adjustments before learning of union activity.

(1) Employer Inducements

In *V&S ProGalv, Inc. v. NLRB*[120] the Sixth Circuit affirmed the Board's finding that the employer's proposal of a plan to match union dues in a savings fund violated Section 8(a)(1) by promising employees an additional benefit if they rejected the union. Similarly, the Eighth Circuit affirmed the Board's finding of a violation where the employer tried to dissuade an employee from joining the union and later tried to encourage the employee to withdraw his membership after he had joined.[121] The president of the company offered the employee $2.00 per hour above the union pay scale if he would refrain from joining. The president later told the employee that he "would like to do away with the union" and offered him a company-sponsored health plan and offered to reimburse his union initiation fee if he would withdraw his membership.

In *Atlantic Limousine, Inc.*[122] the Board reversed its position in *Sony Corp. of America*[123] and adopted a ban of all raffles if "(1) eligibility to participate in the raffle or win prizes is in any way tied to voting in the election or being at the election site on election day or (2) the raffle is conducted at any time during a period beginning 24 hours before the scheduled opening of the polls and ending with the closing of the polls."[124] The Board explained that the opportunity to win a prize in a raffle that is tied to the voting could be viewed as "something extra" which could make employees feel obligated to vote against the union.

(2) Soliciting or Remedying Employee Grievances

The Board continues to hold that an employer who solicits grievances or complaints from employees during a period of organizing activity may be considered to have made an implied promise that

---

[119]Insight Communications Co., 330 NLRB No. 64 (2000).

[120]168 F.3d 270, 277–78, 160 LRRM 2518 (6th Cir. 1999).

[121]McKenzie Eng'g Co. v. NLRB, 182 F.3d 622, 628, 161 LRRM 2641 (8th Cir. 1999).

[122]331 NLRB No. 134, 2000 WL 1178160, 165 LRRM 1001 (2000).

[123]313 NLRB 420, 145 LRRM 1242 (1993).

[124]*Atlantic Limousine, supra* note 122, 2000 WL 1178160, *8. *See also* Comcast Cablevision-Taylor v. NLRB, 232 F.3d 490, 497, 165 LRRM 2803 (6th Cir. 2000).

grievances elicited will be favorably resolved. Such an implied promise, if made for the purpose of influencing employee choice, is unlawful.[125] However, an employer that has a past practice of soliciting and resolving employee grievances may continue that practice during organizing activity.[126] Moreover, without a promise to take action on a grievance, an employer's solicitation is permissible under the Act. Courts have also found that a supervisor's request for information about "problems leading to the Union campaign and employee dissatisfaction with management" do not constitute grievance solicitation under the Act.[127]

(3) Withholding Benefits During an Election Campaign

It remains the general rule that an employer's legal obligation during a campaign is to proceed with the conferral of benefits that would otherwise have been granted. In *NLRB v. Aluminum Casting & Eng'g Co.*[128] the Seventh Circuit affirmed the Board's finding of a violation when the employer failed to give an annual across-the-board wage increase during an organizing campaign.

In *Noah's Bay Area Bagels, LLC*[129] the Board found a violation where the employer restored a particular health benefits plan at the request of its managers for all of its store units except the one in the midst of an organizing campaign. The employer notified the employees that "no change can be made for you at this time" because it wanted to "avoid any risk of improper influence on any upcoming election" through "buying votes." The Board opined that the employer should have either: (1) provided assurances that withholding the more desirable health plan from the unionizing store was only temporary, and that the plan would be restored retroactively to them following the election, regardless of the outcome; or (2) provided the new plan to the employees and proven that there was a persuasive business reason demonstrating that the timing of the grant of benefits was governed by factors other than the union campaign.[130]

---

[125]Overnite Transp. Co., 329 NLRB No. 91, 166 LRRM 1101 (1999), *review denied*, 240 F.3d 325, 166 LRRM 2577 (4th Cir. 2001); Traction Wholesale Ctr. Co., 328 NLRB 1058, 164 LRRM 1266 (1999); National Health Care L.P., 327 NLRB No. 195, 161 LRRM 1152 (1999), *aff'd in part, vacated in part*, 234 F.3d 1269, 166 LRRM 2768 (6th Cir. 2000).

[126]6 West Ltd. Corp., 330 NLRB No. 77, 163 LRRM 1113 (2000), *enforcement denied*, 237 F.3d 767, 166 LRRM 2221 (7th Cir. 2001).

[127]Health Mgmt., Inc., 326 NLRB 801, 160 LRRM 1059 (1998), *enforced in part*, 210 F.3d 371, 164 LRRM 2128 (6th Cir. 2000).

[128]230 F.3d 286, 290–92, 165 LRRM 2513 (7th Cir. 2000).

[129]331 NLRB No. 17, 2000 WL 678727, 166 LRRM 1175 (2000).

[130]*Id.*, 2000 WL 678727, *6.

c. Interrogation and Polling

(1) Systematic Polling

In *Sea Breeze Health Care Center, Inc.*[131] the Board held that the employer's distribution of a "Union Truth Quiz," consisting of 17 questions with an antiunion bias, was tantamount to polling employees about their union sentiments. The prize for completing the quiz by the day before the election was $1,427.60, which, according to the employer, represented the amount of money the union would receive in monthly dues payments. Under the circumstances, the employer's conduct was coercive and violated Section 8(a)(1).

Improper polling was also found where a company leadman found an envelope in his truck bearing the words "National Labor Relations Board."[132] The envelope contained a piece of paper that read, "I no longer want [the union] to represent me," with spaces for employees to sign. The leadman showed the company president the petition and the president denied placing the envelope in his truck, but told the leadman to see if he could get some signatures on it and later told the leadman to circulate another petition after the first one was lost. The Board concluded this amounted to "instigating and soliciting the employee drafting and circulation of a petition seeking the decertification of the Union"[133] in violation of Section 8(a)(1).

(2) Individual or Isolated Questioning

The Board continues evaluating whether an interrogation is coercive in light of all the surrounding circumstances. For example, requiring job applicants to disclose their union membership or affiliation violated Section 8(a)(1).[134] In *Fixtures Mfg. Corp.*[135] the Board found that the employer violated Section 8(a)(1) when an employer's supervisor called the employee to a meeting with the company's vice president after the employee had signed a union authorization card and had distributed union literature during his break periods. The

---

[131]331 NLRB No. 149 (2000).

[132]V&S ProGalv, Inc. v. NLRB, 168 F.3d 270, 276–77, 160 LRRM 2518 (6th Cir. 1999).

[133]*Id.* at 275.

[134]Richland Mellow Elec. Contractor Corp., 327 NLRB 1112 at 1112, 116 LRRM 1018 (1999).

[135]332 NLRB No. 55 (2000); Naomi Knitting Plant, 328 NLRB 1279 (1999) (employee questioning in supervisor's office by employer's labor consultant and manager regarding status of union campaign was coercive interrogation and violated §8(a)(1)).

vice president accused the employee of distributing literature on company time and asked him why he was interested in the union.

Although inquiries conducted in a joking atmosphere are not generally considered coercive, the Board found a violation where a company's CEO addressed an employee by saying in a sarcastic fashion, "Oh, by the way, did you have fun talking with the NLRB yesterday?"[136]

(3) Preparation of Defense for Trial of Unfair Labor Practice Case

The Board recently applied the *Johnnie's Poultry Co.*[137] principles to employer interrogation of employees in preparation for arbitration hearings. In *Grandview Health Care Center,* an employer unilaterally implemented a new policy under which an employee would face discipline for, among other things, "[r]efusing to cooperate in the investigation of any . . . alleged violation of company rules, laws, or government regulations."[138] Finding that employees would reasonably conclude that the word "investigation" includes all phases of the prearbitration process, the Board concluded that the employer's ability to coerce cooperation under the policy constituted a *Johnnie's Poultry* violation of the Act.

d. Surveillance and Photographing

The Board continues finding employer or supervisor conduct unlawful where it is intended to impede or discourage employee organization, such as creating an impression among employees that the employer is engaged in surveillance of their protected activities[139] and unjustified photographing or videotaping of protected activity.[140]

---

[136]*V&S ProGalv, Inc., supra* note 132, at 280.

[137]146 NLRB 770, 55 LRRM 1403 (1964).

[138]332 NLRB No. 26 (2000).

[139]*See* Beverly Cal. Corp. v. NLRB, 227 F.3d 817, 842, 165 LRRM 2257 (7th Cir. 2000) (violation where employee who had visited a co-worker's home the previous night to discuss the union was met by administrator, who said, "Good morning, Mrs. Black, I understand you had a busy night last night," and asked her to meet with him later); Newlonbro, LLC (Connecticut's Own) Milford, 332 NLRB No. 146 (2000) (violation where manager told employee, "I understand you went to the Union meeting," which reasonably led employee to believe that his activities were under surveillance); Seton Co., 332 NLRB No. 89 (2000) (employer created an impression of surveillance among employees when supervisor told employee to be careful because the employer was watching the union hall and noting the comings and goings of employees).

[140]*See* Timken Co., 331 NLRB No. 86 (2000) (employer's photographing and videotaping of handbilling activity not justified by desire to protect itself from

e. Employer's Responsibility for Third-Party Conduct

The Board continues applying the doctrine of apparent authority to determine whether rank-and-file employees are agents of the employer for purposes of the Act.[141]

g. Discipline and Discharge of Supervisors

Individuals meeting the Section 2(11) definition of "supervisor" under the Act do not enjoy statutory protection and remain subject to discipline for engaging in union activity or other concerted activity.[142]

3. Other Unlawful Employer Interference

b. Requests for Employee Statements to the NLRB

An employer violated the Act by asking employees whether they had provided statements or affidavits to the Board, even though the employees had signed a voluntary release form.[143]

c. Employer Conduct Relating to Authorization Cards

An employer's request that an employee sign a decertification petition, or conditioning a promotion on signing such a petition, violates Section 8(a)(1).[144] An employer is guilty of unlawful assistance, in violation of the Act, if it provides the language for a decertification petition and requests that a signed petition be sent to company headquarters.[145] On the other hand, an employer does not

---

false accusations of assault and battery; surveillance was continuous and unlimited rather than limited to encounters between management and handbillers); Decca Ltd. Partnership, 327 NLRB No. 173, 164 LRRM 1040 (1999) (employer violated §8(a)(1) by photographing employees handbilling outside employer's facility because employer could not show a necessity for taking photographs of employees while they were engaged in protected concerted activity); Manor Care of Decatur, 327 NLRB No. 173, 164 LRRM 1040 (1999) (employer failed to establish necessity for taking photographs of employee-protected activity); Climatrol, Inc., 329 NLRB No. 83 (1999) (employer violated §8(a)(1) when its agent took pictures of an employee while employee sat in a company truck and talked with a union organizer during employee's lunch break).

[141]PCC Structurals, Inc., 330 NLRB No. 131, 164 LRRM 1350 (2000); Tim Foley Plumbing Serv., Inc., 332 NLRB No. 158, 166 LRRM 1061 (2000).

[142]Westwood Health Care Ctr., 330 NLRB No. 141, 163 LRRM 1225 (2000).

[143]Wire Prod. Mfg. Corp., 326 NLRB 625, 163 LRRM 1261 (1998), *enforced sub nom.* NLRB v. R.T. Blankenship & Assoc., 210 F.3d 375, 163 LRRM 2896 (7th Cir. 2000).

[144]Fritz Cos., 330 NLRB No. 183 (2000).

[145]Bridgestone/Firestone, Inc., 332 NLRB No. 56 (2000).

violate the Act by merely telling employees that revocation forms are available in the break room.[146]

III. Other Concerted Activity

A. Protected Concerted Activity: In General

2. Individual Versus Concerted Activity: Employee Claim of Right Under Employment, Safety, and Other Laws

The Board and courts continue applying the basic *Meyers Indus.*[147] rule that the activities of a single employee are "concerted," within the meaning of the Act, when undertaken with or on the authority of other employees and not solely by and on behalf of the individual.[148] Decisions in this area continue following the rule that once the activity is found to be concerted, a *prima facie* case for a violation of Section 8(a)(1) is established if: (1) the employer knew of the concerted nature of the employee's activity; (2) the concerted activity was protected by the Act; and (3) the adverse employment action at issue was motivated by the employee's protected activity.[149]

---

[146]Mid-Mountain Foods, Inc., 332 NLRB No. 19 (2000).

[147]268 NLRB 493, 115 LRRM 1025 (1984), *rev'd sub nom.* Prill v. NLRB, 755 F.2d 941, 118 LRRM 2649 (D.C. Cir. 1985), *decision on remand sub nom.* Meyers Indus., 281 NLRB 882, 123 LRRM 1137 (1986), *aff'd,* 835 F.2d 1481, 127 LRRM 2415 (D.C. Cir. 1987).

[148]*See, e.g.,* CKS Tool & Eng'g, Inc., 332 NLRB No. 162 (2000) (employee's activities were undertaken "with or on the authority of other employees" where he participated in joint employee, pre-meeting discussions during which a consensus was reached); Allstate Ins. Co., 332 NLRB No. 66, 165 LRRM 1293 (2000) (employee engaged in protected concerted activity when speaking with a reporter of a major publication about terms and conditions of employment where employee was expressing her personal concerns as well as those of similarly situated employees); Labor Ready, Inc., 331 NLRB No. 187 (2000) (two employees engaged in protected concerted activity when they refused to return to work with the purpose of pressuring their employer to reverse its decision to discharge a third employee); Halle Enters., Inc., 330 NLRB No. 163 (2000) (participation in protected concerted activity was found where 11 employees jointly complained about working conditions, including wage increases, uniforms, safety equipment, and tools); Mobil Exploration & Producing U.S., Inc. v. NLRB, 200 F.3d 230, 241–242, 163 LRRM 2387 (5th Cir. 1999) (employee that informed co-workers of his sentiment that employer was "trying to dig something up" on him was engaged in protected concerted activity where the statement was made in an attempt to enlist the support of others in opposition to the current union leadership and not merely a personal complaint).

[149]Tradesmen Int'l, Inc., 332 NLRB No. 107, 165 LRRM 1347 (2000) (employee's appearance and testimony at administrative hearing on behalf of the

3. Employee Activity for "Other Mutual Aid or Protection"

In *Beta Steel Corp. v. NLRB*[150] the circuit court reviewed the Board's decision on the issue of whether an employee's submission of safety suggestions and complaints to management constituted concerted protected activity. An employee was suspended after he submitted a safety suggestion to management on behalf of another employee. Because the employee had filed the complaint on behalf of fellow employees, the Seventh Circuit upheld the Board's finding that the employee was engaged in protected activity.[151]

In *NLRB v. Main St. Terrace Care Center*[152] an employee's statement to the effect that, if the employees had a union they would be treated better, was overheard by a member of management. Three days later the employee was fired. Relying on the Fifth Circuit's decision in *Scooba Manufacturing Co. v. NLRB*,[153] the employer argued that the employee's statement arose out of a personal dispute and was, therefore, not protected concerted activity. In *Scooba*, the employee got into an argument with her supervisor and angrily proclaimed: "It would be nice if it [sic] was a union here. A whole lot of things going on wouldn't be going on."[154] Because the employee's statement involved merely a personal dispute, rather than action on behalf of her fellow employees, the *Scooba* court held it did not constitute protected concerted activity. In contrast, the employee in *Main Street* made the remark "during a conversation with a fellow employee regarding unionization,"[155] under circumstances where no personal dispute was involved, and the same employee "had engaged in other protected activity . . . in the past."[156] These factors led the Sixth Circuit to conclude that the employee's remark constituted protected concerted activity.

---

union constituted protected concerted activity where employer knew of the concerted nature of the activity and there was a nexus between the activity and legitimate employee concerns about employment-related matters).

[150]Nos. 98-3658 and 98-4063, 2000 U.S. App. LEXIS 4112 (7th Cir. 2000) (unpublished disposition).

[151]*See also* Cormier v. Simplex Techs., Inc., No. 98-500-JD, 1999 U.S. Dist. LEXIS 21516 at *13 (D.N.H. 1999) (finding that mutual aid and protection clause was satisfied because, as a member of the safety committee, plaintiff was "clearly acting on behalf of other employees").

[152]218 F.3d 531, 536, 164 LRRM 2833, 2835 (6th Cir. 2000).

[153]694 F.2d 82, 112 LRRM 2113 (5th Cir. 1982).

[154]*Id.* at 82.

[155]*Main St. Terrace, supra* note 152, at 540.

[156]*Id.* at 531.

The Board continued expanding the Supreme Court's decision in *Eastex, Inc. v. NLRB*[157] with its ruling in *Tradesmen International, Inc.*[158] There, the company was in the business of supplying skilled workers to primarily nonunion facilities, and the charging party contacted the company to inquire about obtaining work. He subsequently applied for a position, and disclosed that he was employed as a full-time union organizer. He was told that, while he was qualified, there was no work available. After learning that the company had not complied with a city ordinance requiring a bond to be posted by subcontractors who performed work for the city, the charging party contacted the city's chief building inspector and informed him of this. In his role as a union representative, the charging party later appeared before the city's Board of Building Standards at a hearing to determine whether the company met the ordinance's definition of a "subcontractor." The charging party argued that it did not meet the definition, and was thus required to comply. The charging party was subsequently told by the company's vice-president that he would never be put to work because he had tried to hurt the company.

The Board found that the charging party's appearance at the hearing was protected concerted activity because it "ensur[ed] that the [company], a nonunion contractor, did not have an unfair competitive advantage by virtue of its noncompliance with the surety bond ordinance."[159] In the Board's view, this "nexus between [the charging party's] activit[ies] and employees' legitimate concern over their continued employment"[160] was sufficient to find in accord with the dictates of *Eastex*, that the concerted activities were protected by the Act.

4. Limits on Protection of Concerted Activity [New Topic]

In *District 17, Mine Workers v. Island Creek Coal Co.*[161] the Fourth Circuit affirmed an arbitrator's decision upholding the discharge of two union members who engaged in a workplace protest over unpaid wages, vacation time, and sick leave. The court found that the employees' activities did not constitute protected concerted activity

---

[157]437 U.S. 556, 565, 98 LRRM 2717 (1978) (noting §7 encompasses attempts to improve terms or conditions of employment "through channels outside the immediate employee-employer relationship").

[158]332 NLRB No. 107, 2000 WL 1679479, 165 LRRM 1347 (2000).

[159]*Id.*, WL 1679479, *4.

[160]*Id.*

[161]179 F.3d 133, 161 LRRM 2463 (4th Cir. 1999).

because, under the controlling collective bargaining agreement, such matters were subject to a grievance procedure and picketing over grievable matters was a dischargeable offense. The court also rejected the union's argument that the arbitrator's award did not draw its essence from the contract, noting that the "gravamen of the Union's complaint [was] not with [the arbitrator's] failure to properly construe the contract, but with his findings of fact."[162]

In *Eastern Omni Constructors, Inc. v. NLRB* the court considered a supervisor's statement that "if [the foreman] saw the Union guy giving out Union literature on the job [or on company time] [the foreman] was going to send [the union member] up the hill."[163] At the time of the event, the company had a rule prohibiting distribution of literature during working time. While it was disputed whether the supervisor used the phrase "on the job" or "on company time," the Fourth Circuit held that this was irrelevant because the "statement, placed in context, did not coerce, deter, or interfere with the exercise of protected activity."[164] This conclusion was based on the validity of the company's no-distribution rule, the fact that the statement was made under circumstances free from any unfair labor practice charge, and the lack of evidence to support the notion that the supervisor's words amounted to an unlawful threat.

A separate issue presented in *Eastern Omni* was whether the company could properly prohibit the wearing of union decals on hardhats.[165] The company used decals to designate employees' particular area of skill or expertise, such as first-aid training or the ability to work with high-voltage equipment. Noting that valid safety concerns justified the ban, the court accepted the company's proffered reason that "non-company authorized decals on hardhats could create, and delay reaction to, dangerous situations in its industrial facility."[166] The court also recognized that because employees were still allowed to wear union decals on their clothing, it "simply strain[ed] credulity to conclude" that the employees' right to effectively communicate "with each other regarding unionization was somehow stymied by" the company's hardhat ban. Accordingly, it refused to en-

---

[162]*Id.* at 138.
[163]170 F.3d 418, 423–24, 160 LRRM 2669, 2673 (4th Cir. 1999).
[164]*Id.* at 424.
[165]*Id.*
[166]*Id.* at 425.

force that portion of the Board's order that found the ban violated Section 8(a)(1).[167]

The Eighth Circuit held, in *Carleton College v. NLRB*,[168] that whether the employee, an adjunct professor and organizer for a committee of adjunct professors, was involved in concerted activity was irrelevant because his misconduct was unprotected. The employee was asked to meet with the dean of the college to discuss professional expectations. During the meeting, the employee was sarcastic, used vulgarities, referred to the music department as a "laughingstock" and a "pig," expressed loyalty only toward the students and other adjunct faculty, and avoided the dean's request for a commitment to abide by the school's professional expectations. Because of the employee's actions, the dean decided not to offer him a contract. The ALJ found that the employee's involvement with the committee was a protected activity, that the college had animus toward the committee, that it acted upon that animus by refusing to extend a contract to the employee, and that the reasons cited by the college for dismissing the employee were pretextual. The Board adopted these findings, and ordered that the professor be reinstated.

On appeal, the Eighth Circuit held that "misconduct that is 'flagrant or render[s] the employee unfit for employment' is unprotected," and factors to be considered in this regard include "the nature of the misconduct, the nature of the workplace, and the effect of the misconduct on the employer's authority."[169] The court then found that the Board did not consider the college's interest in fostering and maintaining mutual respect among the faculty, which it described as not only a legitimate concern, but a necessary one. The employee's actions evidenced his disrespect for the music department and his unwillingness to commit to behaving in a professional manner. Accordingly, the court denied enforcement of the Board's order.

In *CKS Tool & Engineering*[170] the Board again held that an employee's use of loud, profane language at an employee meeting did not remove the protections of the Act. In response to the plant

---

[167] *Cf.* Aldworth Co., Inc., 200 NLRB LEXIS 241 at *262 (2000) (finding no safety concerns justified company's hardhat insignia ban).

[168] 230 F.3d 1075, 1080–81, 165 LRRM 2670, 21674–75 (8th Cir. 2000).

[169] *Id.* at 1081, 165 LRRM at 2675, quoting Earle Indus., Inc. v. NLRB, 75 F.3d 400, 406–07, 151 LRRM 2300 (8th Cir. 1996).

[170] No. 7-CA-40332, 332 NLRB No. 162, 2000 WL 1920357 (2000).

manager's statements regarding the high scrap rate and the need for increased teamwork to ensure quality production rates, the employee asked several questions and made several comments to the manager regarding his fellow workers. The employee's language was interspersed with obscenities and he was subsequently asked to leave the meeting. Adhering to the rule enunciated in *Meyers Indus.*[171] that "the guarantees of Section 7 . . . extend to concerted activity which in its inception involves only a speaker and a listener," the Board determined the employee's speech was uttered on behalf of his co-workers and also constituted an appeal to them to support his protest of the manager's expressed goals. Thus, the Board held it constituted concerted activity. Because argumentative, vulgar language was commonly tolerated by management at these meetings, the Board rejected the company's contention that the employee's manner and conduct took his speech outside the protections of the Act.

a. Employer Property and Business Interests [New Topic]

In *Tracer Protection Services, Inc.*[172] the Board found that a guard who overheard an informal management discussion and then reported on it to a union member was engaged in protected concerted activity. Because the company discharged the guard, but failed to take action against other employees who violated written company policies, the Board determined that the discharge violated Section 8(a)(1).

Similarly, in *Mobil Exploration & Producing U.S., Inc. v. NLRB*,[173] an employee union member expressed dissatisfaction with the union's president during a work break conversation that was overheard by his supervisor. He was subsequently terminated for interfering with an internal investigation and for insubordination. In light of the principle that Section 7 "encompasses the right of employees to oppose the policies and actions of their incumbent union leadership and to seek to persuade other employees to take steps to align the union with"[174] those opposing views, the Fifth Circuit affirmed the Board's finding that the employee's conduct constituted protected concerted activity.

In *NLRB v. Main St. Terrace Care Center*[175] the Sixth Circuit upheld the Board's finding that the promulgation of a rule prohibiting

---

[171]268 NLRB 493, 494 (1984).
[172]328 NLRB No. 94, 162 LRRM 1079 (1999).
[173]200 F.3d 230, 163 LRRM 2387 (5th Cir. 1999).
[174]*Id.*, at 240.
[175]218 F.3d 531, 538, 164 LRRM 2833, 2836 (6th Cir. 2000).

the discussion of wages constituted an unfair labor practice. The court noted that the test for determining whether the rights granted by Section 7 are violated is "whether the employer's conduct tends to be coercive or tends to interfere with the employees' exercise of their rights."[176] The court pointed out that two managers had told the employees not to discuss their wages, and that one of these managers testified at the hearing that the owner of the facility did not want employees to discuss their wages with each other. It reasoned, therefore, that a "rule prohibiting employees from communicating with one another regarding wages, a key objective of organizational activity, undoubtedly tends to interfere with the employees' right to engage in protected concerted activity."[177]

B. Protected Concerted Activity: Specific Conduct

1. Work Stoppages

In *District 17, Mine Workers v. Island Creek Coal Co.*[178] the Fourth Circuit upheld an arbitrator's determination that picketing aimed at causing a work stoppage, over matters that the collective bargaining agreement explicitly provided would be subject to arbitration, is not a protected concerted activity. The union contended on appeal that the picketing was intended merely to publicize its dispute with management. The court rejected this notion, instead accepting the arbitrator's findings that the workers gathered along strategic points on the only access road to the company, that this action caused the other workers to refuse to work, and that the protesters "knew that their actions would cause a work stoppage."[179] While the workers were also protesting non-grievable medical benefits, the court accepted the arbitrator's determination that the protest was "over predominantly grievable matters."[180]

In *Bethany Medical Center*[181] employees of a cardiac catheterization laboratory walked off the job, giving notice of their walkout only 15 minutes before the first scheduled procedure of the day. Because the employees were not part of a labor organization, the Board affirmed the ALJ's decision that the strike notice requirement

---

[176]*Id.* at 537.
[177]*Id.*
[178]179 F.3d 133, 140, 161 LRRM 2463, 2468 (4th Cir. 1999).
[179]*Id.* at 140.
[180]*Id.*
[181]328 NLRB No. 161, 1999 WL 596222, 162 LRRM 1403 (1999).

of Section 8(g) was inapplicable to the case.[182] The company contended that the strike was "indefensible" conduct, in that it endangered the lives of patients at the laboratory, and, therefore, removed the workers' actions from the protection of the Act. The Board held the correct test for whether the workers' action was indefensible was "whether [the workers] failed to prevent such imminent damage as foreseeably would result from their sudden cessation of work."[183] The Board noted the routine nature of all the procedures scheduled that day, the lack of emergency patients, the fact that approximately 20 other hospitals in the vicinity were capable of performing the procedure, and that the cardiologists who worked there were often tardy, requiring that procedures be rescheduled. Thus, the Board held that the workers' actions "did not foreseeably create such a risk of harm to patients"[184] as to justify depriving the employees of the protections of the Act.

In *Senior Citizens Coordinating Council of Riverbay Community, Inc.*[185] workers at a social service organization threatened, by letter, to not report for work unless the acting director was expeditiously replaced with a more qualified, full-time director. One of these workers was forced to sign a letter retracting her statements about the organization, and the others were terminated. Conceding the concerted nature of the employees' letter, the Board concluded that writing the letter was also protected activity because it asserted that a lack of proper supervision directly affected the employees' terms and working conditions. This conclusion, however, was based not on the contents of the letter itself, but on testimony and other evidence elicited at the hearing.

4. Weingarten: *Employee Request or Demand for Union Representation During Investigation*

b. Rights of Unrepresented Employees

On July 10, 2000, in *Epilepsy Foundation of Northeast Ohio*,[186] the Board reversed 12 years of precedent, ruling that *Weingarten*[187] rights

---

[182]*See also* Hospital Del Maestro, Nos. 24-CA-8001, 8003, 2000 NLRB LEXIS 60 at *29 (2000).

[183]*Id.*, 1999 WL 596222, *2.

[184]*Id.*

[185]330 NLRB No. 154, 166 LRRM 1074 (2000).

[186]331 NLRB No. 92, 2000 WL 967066, 164 LRRM 1233 (2000) (Given the recency of this decision, no court of appeals has yet to review the Board's decision. The Board's decision was met with sharp criticism from dissenting Board members, Peter Hurtgen and J. Robert Brame, III).

[187]NLRB v. J. Weingarten, Inc., 420 U.S. 251, 88 LRRM 2689 (1975).

should extend to nonunion employees in nonunion workplaces. Accordingly, nonunion employees now have the right to have a co-worker present at any investigatory interview that the employee reasonably believes might result in disciplinary action.

In *Epilepsy Foundation*[188] two employees prepared a memo that was critical of their supervisor. The employer's Executive Director asked one of the employees to meet with her and the supervisor who had been criticized. The employee was intimidated by the prospect of meeting with the Executive Director and the supervisor, because at a previous meeting with them he had received a reprimand. The employee asked to meet with the Executive Director alone, or to have the other author of the memo present to support his position. The Executive Director refused both requests. The employee then declined to meet with the Executive Director and the supervisor, and was fired the next day for insubordination because he refused to participate in the meeting.

The ALJ followed existing Board precedent, set forth in *E.I. Du Pont de Nemours & Co.*,[189] and held that the employee's discharge did not violate Section 8(a)(1) of the Act because employees in nonunion workplaces do not have the right to have a co-worker present at a disciplinary meeting.

While the Board recognized that the ALJ properly adhered to *DuPont*, it overruled that decision, finding it inconsistent with the U.S. Supreme Court's decision in *Weingarten*, and the purposes of the Act. In so doing, the Board noted that *Weingarten* was based on Section 7 of the Act, which protects the rights of employees to act in concert generally, whether unionized or not. The Board found that having a co-worker present at a disciplinary meeting "greatly enhances employees' opportunities to act in concert to address their concerns that an employer does not initiate or continue a practice of imposing punishment unjustly."[190] Because the discharged employee, under the Board's reasoning, was attempting to act in concert with another employee, the Board found that his termination for attempting to have a co-worker present at the meeting was an unlawful act in violation of the Act.

As a practical matter, *Weingarten*, and, thus, *Epilepsy Foundation*, does not require employers to inform employees of their right to request and have present a co-worker at any investigatory interview that the employee reasonably believes might result in disciplinary

---

[188] *Supra* note 186.
[189] 289 NLRB 627, 128 LRRM 1233 (1988).
[190] *Epilepsy, supra* note 186, 2000 WL 967066, at *4.

action. Moreover, it is likely that employees who are aware of their right under *Epilepsy Foundation* will not be permitted to request the attendance of a co-worker who is not present at the workplace at the time of the requested meeting. Significantly, the Board claimed that its decision would not force an employer to deal with a mini-union or an employee representative because the employer is "free to forego the investigatory interview and pursue other means of resolving the matter."[191] Accordingly, employers retain the option of terminating employees without first requesting their attendance at an investigatory interview meeting. Employers also retain the option of requiring an employee to submit a written explanation of his or her conduct, in lieu of an investigatory interview.

5. Safety-Related Protests

The Board held, in *TNS, Inc.*,[192] that a walkout at a plant that manufactured ammunition from depleted uranium, motivated in part by concerns over exposure to radiation and toxic heavy metal, was protected by Section 502. Likewise, employees' circulation of a petition raising safety concerns is protected concerted activity under the Act.[193]

6. Protests Relating to Employment Discrimination

An employee who engaged in a discussion with a co-worker, urging her to bring a race discrimination claim against their employer for its refusal to hire the co-worker's daughter, was engaged in protected concerted activity.[194]

C. Unprotected Concerted Activities

1. Sit-Down Strikes

The Board held, in *Yale University*,[195] that the withholding of grades, or a "grade strike," by teaching fellows in an effort to force recognition of their union was a partial strike and thus unprotected activity. Their conduct was analogized to a sit-down strike.

---

[191]*Id.* at *5.
[192]329 NLRB No. 61, 166 LRRM 1018 (1999).
[193]Avondale Indus., 329 NLRB No. 93, 165 LRRM 1228 (1999).
[194]Dearborn Big Boy No. 3, 328 NLRB No. 92 (1999).
[195]330 NLRB No. 28, 162 LRRM 1393 (1999).

3. Other Unprotected Activity

In *Bethany Medical Center*[196] hospital catheterization laboratory employees who walked out to protest working conditions did not lose their protection under the Act for an "indefensible" action. The test of whether a work stoppage loses its protection, and becomes an indefensible action, is whether the employees failed to prevent imminent damage that was foreseeable as a result of their work stoppage. Whether actual injury occurs is irrelevant.

a. Breach of Confidentiality

A security guard was engaged in protected concerted activity when he disclosed to the union a plan, by the supervisors at the company to which he had been assigned to work, to discipline certain union officials.[197] The guard had overheard the conversation in which the supervisors discussed their plan. The security company violated the Act when it discharged the guard at the request of the company to which he was assigned.

In *Beverly California v. NLRB*[198] the Seventh Circuit overruled the Board's determination that the employer violated Section 8(a)(3) by discharging a known union organizer for copying co-workers' names and telephone numbers and removing them from the premises. The Board concluded that the personnel information was not confidential, and, therefore, disagreed with the ALJ's finding that the employee had engaged in unprotected activity in violation of the employer's rules. The court found that the information was confidential, thus the employee had not obtained the information in an open and unobjectionable manner and, based on the totality of circumstances surrounding other employees' behavior, the employer had proper grounds for discharging him.

An employer's rule against speaking about medical restrictions justified by the Americans with Disabilities Act was overly broad because it impacted on working conditions of other employees and was the subject of a possible grievance.[199]

---

[196]328 NLRB No. 161, 162 LRRM 1403 (1999).

[197]Tracers Protection Servs., Inc., 328 NLRB No. 94, 162 LRRM 1075 (1995).

[198]227 F.3d 817, 165 LRRM 2257 (7th Cir. 2000), *enforcing in part, vacating in part, and remanding* 326 NLRB No. 29, 159 LRRM 1049 (1998) and 326 NLRB No. 30, 159 LRRM 1033 (1998).

[199]Lockheed Martin Astronautics, 330 NLRB No. 66, 163 LRRM 1051 (2000).

b. False Allegations or Affidavits Concerning the Employer

The Tenth Circuit enforced the Board's decision in *Mojave Electric Cooperative, Inc. v. NLRB*,[200] finding that the employer unlawfully terminated an employee for filing a petition seeking a civil injunction, with the support of co-workers, to prohibit the employer and a subcontractor's supervisor from contacting him and a co-worker at work and at home. The employee did not act out of malice or bad faith, even though the business relationship between the employer and subcontractor might have been disrupted.

c. Disparagement of the Employer or its Business Activities

The Board, in *American Golf Corp.*,[201] determined that distribution of a handbill at a city council meeting addressing the impact of capital investment on quality of services was unprotected.

However, the Board determined that it was unlawful for an employer to refuse to hire a known union organizer as a result of his testimony at a city board meeting.[202] While the organizer testified that the employer was not in compliance with the city's bonding ordinance, his testimony did not cause harm to the employer, as contemplated by *NLRB v. Electrical Workers (IBEW) Local 1229.*[203]

A magazine reporter's interview of an employee regarding employment conditions was protected concerted activity.[204]

IV. UNION RESTRAINT AND COERCION

A. Section 8(b)(1)(A): Restraint and Coercion of Employees

Unions may violate Section 8(b)(1)(A) with respect to their treatment of nonmembers; nonmembers cannot be discriminated against in the processing of contract grievances.[205]

Enforcing the union-security clause of the contract, to collect dues and fees from nonmember employees who object to paying

---

[200]206 F.3d 1183, 163 LRRM 2917 (D.C. Cir. 2000), *enforcing* 327 NLRB 13, 163 LRRM 1228 (1998).

[201]330 NLRB No. 172, 164 LRRM 1049 (2000).

[202]Tradesmen Int'l, 332 NLRB No. 107, 165 LRRM 1347 (2000).

[203]346 U.S. 464, 33 LRRM 2183 (1953).

[204]Allstate Ins. Co., 332 NLRB No. 66, 165 LRRM 1293 (2000).

[205]Auto Workers v. NLRB, 168 F.3d 509, 160 LRRM 2955 (D.C. Cir. 1999), *enforcing* 323 NLRB 530, 160 LRRM 1158 (1998).

dues in excess of the amounts spent on representation, violates Section 8(b)(1)(A).[206] However, allocating expenditures for organizing is chargeable to objecting nonmember employees, and expending dues and fees collected from them for such activities did not violate Section 8(b)(1)(A).[207]

The union did not violate Section 8(b)(1)(A) when it required employees, who had "withdrawn dishonorably" from the union, to pay a fee equivalent to the dues for the period of nonmembership if they should seek to rejoin the union, while allowing employees who had "honorably withdrawn" to rejoin without having to pay such a fee.[208] According to the union's policy, a resignation is dishonorable when the employee remains in a bargaining unit position, while an honorable withdrawal refers to an employee who took a position outside of the unit. The Board, applying *Scofield v. NLRB*,[209] found the union's policy was not coercive or discriminatory and constituted a legitimate exercise of the union's right to prescribe rules of membership.

2. Fines and Discipline of Union Members

A union violated Sections 8(b)(1)(A) and 8(b)(2) by (1) refusing to provide employees who had recently resigned, and made *Beck* objections asking for, a unit-by-unit allocation of representational and nonrepresentational expenditures, and charging them extra for unit expenditures; (2) charging nonmember objectors for certain nonrepresentational expenditures; and (3) refusing to accept the resignation and process the objections of an employee, failing to give the employee pertinent financial information, and failing to give him a refund for the nonrepresentational portion of his dues.[210]

In *Operating Engineers Local 3*[211] the union was found to have violated Section 8(b)(1)(A) when it disciplined four members for continuing to work for a nonunion employer after being directed to cease working. Without deciding whether the union had properly

---

[206]Painters District Councils No. 8, 16, and 33 and Local 4, 327 NLRB No. 180, 162 LRRM 1173 (1999).

[207]United Food & Commercial Workers, 329 NLRB No. 69, 162 LRRM 1177 (1999).

[208]Auto Workers Local 1853 (Saturn Corp.), 333 NLRB No. 43 (2001).

[209]394 U.S. 423 (1969).

[210]Transport Workers, 329 NLRB No. 56 (1999).

[211]331 NLRB No. 60, 164 LRRM 1217 (2000).

adopted a rule prohibiting such employment, the Board held that it had been disparately enforced. The union's defense, that it had taken this action in response to having lost an election and for the lawful purpose of obtaining recognition, was rejected.

A union's punishment of a member for complying with his employer's instructions to report co-workers' misconduct also violated Section 8(b)(1)(A).[212]

b. Impact of Discipline on Employee Relationship

In *Office & Professional Employees Local 251 (Sandia National Laboratories)*[213] the Board overruled *Carpenters Local 22 (Graziano Construction Co.)*[214] and its progeny and determined that section 8(b)(1)(A) does not proscribe wholly intraunion conduct and discipline. The Board determined that a purely intraunion dispute between rival union officers, resulting in impeachment petitions, did not affect the relationship of the participants with their employer or impair the policy of the Act.

The Board, in *Service Employees Local 254 (Brandeis University)*,[215] consistent with its *Sandia* decision, determined that there was no Section 8(b)(1)(A) violation where a union removed a member from his position as a shop steward and as the union representative on the labor-management committee. The removal did not impact upon the member's relationship with his employer, impair his access to the Board's processes, pertain to unacceptable methods of coercion (such as violence), or otherwise impair policies imbedded in the Act.

Notably, subsequent to its decision in *Sandia*, the Board expressly affirmed the continuing validity of those cases in which a union was found to have violated Section 8(b)(1)(A) by conduct that interferes with an employee's employment relationship. The Board ruled that a union violates Section 8(b)(1)(A) whenever it causes an employer to discriminate against a union member for reasons other than the member's failure to tender dues.[216] The Board found that unions

---

[212]NLRB v. Teamsters Local 439, 175 F.3d 1173, 161 LRRM 2571 (9th Cir. 1999), *enforcing* 324 NLRB 1096, 157 LRRM 1190 (1997).

[213]331 NLRB No. 193, 165 LRRM 1089 (2000).

[214]195 NLRB 1, 79 LRRM 1194 (1972).

[215]332 NLRB No. 103, 165 LRRM 1321 (2000).

[216]Laborers Local 1184 (Nicholson Radio West Dam Joint Venture), 332 NLRB No. 104 (2000), citing Wenner Ford Tractor Rentals, 315 NLRB 964, 148 LRRM 1075 (1994) (union violated Act by causing employer to remove member from his position as master mechanic because he had opposed union's officers in election).

violated Section 8(b)(1)(A) where they (1) demanded that an employer discharge an employee–member who had unsuccessfully challenged a union incumbent for his office;[217] (2) asked an employer to deny an employee–member's earned seniority, so that the union president's son-in-law would have top seniority;[218] or (3) threatened to run an employee–member off the job unless he transferred his membership from a sister union to the local.[219]

Likewise, a union violated Section 8(b)(1)(A) when it threatened to have employees discharged if they did not pay a market recovery program dues owing from their employment on Davis-Bacon jobs.[220] The Board found payments to support such programs are not "periodic dues" for purposes of the Act, because requiring such payment is "inimical to public policy."

e. Discipline for Intraunion Activity

The Board, in *Office & Professional Employees Local 251 (Sandia National Laboratories)*,[221] expressly overruled a number of cases,[222] holding that Section 8(b)(1)(A) does not proscribe wholly intraunion conduct. The Board ruled that "Section 8(b)(1)(A)'s proper scope, in union discipline cases, is to proscribe union conduct against union members that impacts on the employment relationship, impairs access to the Board's processes, pertains to unacceptable methods of union coercion (such as physical violence in organizational or strike contexts), or otherwise impairs policies imbedded in the Act."[223] In *Sandia*, the Board ruled that the union did not violate Section 8(b)(1)(A) when it imposed internal union discipline against its members for opposing the policies of the union's president. In reaching its conclusion, the Board ruled:

---

[217]USF Red Star, 330 NLRB No. 15, 162 LRRM 1409 (1999), *enforced*, 230 F.3d 102, 165 LRRM 2665 (4th Cir. 2000).

[218]327 NLRB 1033, 164 LRRM 1339 (1999).

[219]United Refining Co., 327 NLRB No. 143 (2000).

[220]Electrical Workers (IBEW) Local 48 (Kingston Contractors Inc.), 332 NLRB No. 161, 166 LRRM 1090 (2000).

[221]331 NLRB No. 193, 2000 WL 1279158, 165 LRRM 1089 (2000).

[222]*See, e.g.*, Carpenters Local 22 (Graziano Constr. Co.), 195 NLRB 1, 79 LRRM 1194 (1972); Teamsters Local 579 (Janesville Auto Transp.), 310 NLRB 975 (1993), *enforcement denied*, 145 LRRM 2200 (7th Cir. 1994); Laborers Local 324 (AGC of Cal.), 318 NLRB 589 (1995), *enforcement denied in relevant part*, 123 F.3d 1176 (9th Cir. 1997); Laborers Local 652 (Southern Cal. Contractors Ass'n), 319 NLRB 694, 151 LRRM 1088 (1995).

[223]*Sandia, supra* note 221, 2000 WL 1279158, at *4.

What is of critical significance in our judgment is that the only sanctions visited on the Charging Parties by the victorious intraunion faction were internal union sanctions, such as removal from union office and suspension or expulsion from union membership. The relationship between the Charging Parties and their Employer, Sandia, was wholly unaffected by the discipline. Nor are any policies specific to the National Labor Relations Act implicated by the union discipline at issue.[224]

Consistent with the Board's modified application of Section 8(b)(1)(A), the Board cited, with approval, the Seventh Circuit's decision in *Operating Engineers Local 139 (Associated Gen. Contractors of America, Wisconsin Chapter).*[225] There, the court refused to enforce the Board's finding that a union violated Section 8(b)(1)(A) by bringing charges against and fining a member who circulated a newsletter critical of the local's leadership.

---

[224]*Id.* at *3.

[225]273 NLRB 992, 118 LRRM 1396 (1984), *enforcement denied,* 796 F.2d 985, 123 LRRM 2021 (7th Cir. 1986).

CHAPTER 7

DISCRIMINATION IN EMPLOYMENT

II. Employer Discrimination

A. Persons Within the Protection of Section 8(a)(3)

The Board continues to hold that a company violates Sections 8(a)(3) and (1) of the Act by failing and refusing to hire a union organizer because of his or her protected activity.[1]

Undocumented aliens whose discharges from employment have been determined to be unlawfully discriminatory are entitled to reinstatement with backpay provided that, within a reasonable time period, they complete the documentation necessary to enable the employer to meet its obligations under the Immigration Reform and Control Act.[2]

B. Purpose of the Discrimination

Courts continue to hold that discrimination generally designed to encourage or discourage union activities or support is unlawful.[3]

1. Conduct Requiring Proof of Union Animus: The Wright Line Rule

The Board has held that, because the motive of the employer is at issue, it is appropriate to use the *Wright Line* analytical framework when considering Section 8(a)(3) allegations arising from alleged

---

[1]Tradesmen Int'l Inc., 332 NLRB No. 107, 165 LRRM 1347 (2000). *See also* Main Edition, Chapter 7, "Discrimination in Employment," at Section II.C.7. [Employer Discrimination; Specific Conduct; Discrimination Against Union Organizers and "Salts"].

[2]8 U.S.C. §132a et seq. *See* County Window Cleaning Co., 328 NLRB No. 26, 163 LRRM 1221 (1999); Hoffman Plastic Compound Inc. v. NLRB, 2001 U.S. App. LEXIS 571, 166 LRRM 2257 (D.C. Cir. 2001).

[3]Wright Elec. Co. v. NLRB, 200 F.3d 1162, 163 LRRM 2353 (8th Cir. 2000) (nonunion electric contractor was motivated by antiunion animus, violating §8(a)(3) of Act by refusing to hire union electrician); Hospital Shared Servs., 330 NLRB No. 40, 166 LRRM 1051 (1999) (employer that provides security services to hospital violated Act when it refused to rehire security officer, where reason was for earlier activity on behalf of union and union activity in general); Ross Stores Inc. v. NLRB, 235 F.3d 669, 166 LRRM 2207 (D.C. Cir. 2000) (employer violated §8(a)(3) when it discharged prounion employee, allegedly for violating employer's written time-off policies, where employer knew that employee was participating in

8(b)(1)(A) and (2) conduct by a union.[4] The Board has also determined that *Wright Line* applies when deciding whether employer discipline of a worker allegedly to protect another disabled employee from an alleged "hostile" work environment within the scope of the Americans with Disabilities Act (ADA) and that the ADA does not bar the Board from finding that disciplinary action violates the Act.[5]

The Board continues its practice of not applying the framework set forth in *Wright Line* in striker misconduct cases,[6] but instead applies the analysis developed in *Clear Pine Mouldings*[7] and *Rubin Bros.*[8] In addition, the *Wright Line* framework is not applied in situations that do not involve a dual motive for employer action.[9]

Under *Wright Line*, once the general counsel's burden has been met, it is the respondent's burden to show that in the absence of the union activity it *might* have taken the action it did and also to show that it *would* have done so.[10]

In *Starcon v. NLRB*[11] the Seventh Circuit agreed with the Sixth Circuit's ruling in *NLRB v. Fluor Daniel, Inc.*,[12] concerning the appli-

---

ongoing union organization campaign); Beverly Cal. v. NLRB, 227 F.3d 817, 165 LRRM 2257 (7th Cir. 2000) (employer violated §8(a)(3) when its assistant director required active union supporter to obtain formal certification before she returned to work after she experienced one bout of nausea early in her pregnancy, whereas other employees were able to work during their pregnancies); Frazier Indus. Co. v. NLRB, 213 F.3d 750, 164 LRRM 2516 (D.C. Cir. 2000) (employer's discharge of union supporter who persistently discussed union with co-workers violated §8(a)(3)); NLRB v. Hospital San Pablo Inc., 207 F.3d 67, 163 LRRM 2999 (1st Cir. 2000) (hospital violated §8(a)(3) when it discharged known union activist during union-organizing campaign, allegedly for insubordination in leaving work early, but substantial evidence established that employee was discharged because of hospital's antiunion animus).

[4]Nationsway Transp. Serv., 327 NLRB 1033, 164 LRRM 1339 (1999).
[5]PCC Structurals Inc., 330 NLRB No. 131, 164 LRRM 1350 (2000).
[6]Siemens Energy & Automation, Inc., 328 NLRB No. 164, 162 LRRM 1083 (1999).
[7]268 NLRB 1044, 1046, 115 LRRM 1113 (1984), *enforced,* 765 F.2d 148, 120 LRRM 2631 (9th Cir. 1985), *cert. denied,* 474 U.S. 1105, 121 LRRM 2368 (1986); General Tel. Co., 251 NLRB 737, 105 LRRM 1288 (1980); Axelson, Inc., 285 NLRB 862, 129 LRRM 1344 (1987).
[8]99 NLRB 610, 30 LRRM 1109 (1952).
[9]*See* Nor-Cal Beverage Co., 330 NLRB No. 91, 163 LRRM 1268 (2000); USF Red Star, Inc. v. NLRB, 230 F.3d 102, 108 n.3, 165 LRRM 2665, 2669 n.3 (4th Cir. 2000).
[10]*See* Becker Group, Inc., 329 NLRB No. 9 (1999); Avondale Indus., Inc., 329 NLRB No. 93 (1999); Coyne Int'l Enters. Corp., 326 NLRB 1187, 163 LRRM 1080 (1998).
[11]176 F.3d 948, 161 LRRM 2233 (7th Cir. 1999).
[12]161 F.3d 953, 159 LRRM 2794 (6th Cir. 1998).

cation of *Wright Line* in cases involving an employer's refusal to hire "salts." Both circuits held that the employer must be allowed at the hearing to show on the merits that it would not have hired the discriminatees even in the absence of their union activity or affiliation. This was contrary to the Board's position that deferred consideration of the employer's defense until the compliance stage of proceedings. The Seventh Circuit disagreed, however, with the Sixth Circuit's holding in *Fluor Daniel* that as part of meeting its burden of proof on the merits in a refusal-to-hire violation, the general counsel must match qualified applicants with job openings. Instead, the court in *Starcon* determined that to meet its *Wright Line* burden on the merits, the general counsel need only show that one applicant was discriminated against to establish a refusal-to-hire violation warranting a cease-and-desist order.

In *FES, a Division of Thermo Power*[13] the Board revised its approach to applying *Wright Line* in refusal-to-hire and in refusal-to-consider cases. The Board accepted the Seventh Circuit's *Starcon* application of *Wright Line* to refusal-to-hire cases, emphasizing that the general counsel in the case on the merits must show that the employer was hiring or had concrete plans to hire, that the applicants had the training or experience relevant to the openings, and that antiunion animus contributed to the employer's refusal to hire. Once these showings have been made, then the employer in the case on the merits would be permitted to show that it would not have hired the applicants in the absence of their union activity.

In refusal-to-consider cases, the Board ruled in *FES* that the general counsel's *Wright Line* burden on the merits was to show that the employer excluded applicants from the hiring process and that antiunion animus contributed to the decision not to consider, and that this burden could be met even when no hiring is occurring. The Board held that once this burden is met by the general counsel, the burden shifts to the employer to show that it would not have considered the applicants even in the absence of union activity. The appropriate remedy for a refusal-to-consider violation, the Board ruled, is a cease-and-desist order; an order to consider the discriminatees for future openings in accord with nondiscriminatory criteria; and an order to notify the discriminatees, the charging party, and the regional director of future openings for which the discriminatees applied or for substantially equivalent positions.

---

[13]331 NLRB No. 20, 164 LRRM 1065 (2000).

Finally, in *FES*, the Board also provided direction on the appropriate use of compliance proceedings in connection with job openings arising after the unfair labor practice trial has begun in both refusal-to-hire cases and refusal-to-consider cases.

C. Specific Conduct

1. Discharge or Discipline for Union Activity

c. Employer's Knowledge of Employee's Union Activity

In the Board's view, a prima facie case may be established without proving that an employer had specific knowledge of an employee's union sympathies or activities where it is reasonable to infer from other circumstances that the employer suspected or had information permitting the probable identification of union supporters. Such circumstances include knowledge of general union activity, antiunion hostility, the timing of the employer's adverse employment action, the assertion of pretextual reasons for the action, and the existence of a close relationship between the employee and a known union supporter.[14]

d. Inferential Proof of Employer's Animus

With respect to the evidence of animus necessary to support an inference that the motivation of a discharge was unlawful, the Eighth Circuit has cautioned that, "While hostility to [a] union is a proper and highly significant factor for the Board to consider when assessing whether the employer's motivate was discriminatory . . . general hostility toward the union does not itself supply the element of unlawful motive."[15] A discharge resulting from the enforcement of a rule that is unlawful under the Act will itself be unlawful.[16] The Seventh Circuit rejected the Board's imputation of antiunion animus to an employer based on a supervisor's knowledge of union activity on the ground that the supervisor who recommended the discharges of two employee union supporters for gross misconduct, apparent theft, and insubordination was prounion.[17]

---

[14]Regional Home Care, Inc., 329 NLRB No. 6, 166 LRRM 1112 (1999); Martech MDI, 331 NLRB No. 57 (2000).

[15]GSX Corp. v. NLRB, 918 F.2d 1351, 1356, 135 LRRM 3001 (8th Cir. 1990), cited in Carleton College v. NLRB, 230 F.3d 1075, 165 LRRM 2670 (8th Cir. 2000).

[16]Frazier Indus. Co., 328 NLRB No. 89, 163 LRRM 1024 (1999), *enforced*, 213 F.3d 750, 164 LRRM 2516 (D.C. Cir. 2000).

[17]Vulcan Basement Waterproofing of Ill., Inc. v. NLRB, 219 F.3d 677, 164 LRRM 2961 (7th Cir. 2000).

2. Lockouts

The D.C. Circuit has reiterated that the motive or purpose underlying an employer's lockout of its employees continues to be the critical factor in determining whether the lockout constitutes a Section 8(a)(3) violation. In *Electrical Workers (IBEW) Local 702 v. NLRB*[18] the court denied the union's petition for review of a Board order finding that the employer, Central Illinois Public Service Co., did not violate the Act by locking out its employees in response to "inside-game" tactics used by the two unions in lieu of a strike during contract negotiations. The court concluded that the Board's decision[19] to reverse the ALJ on the Section 8(a)(3) charge was in accord with the law and was supported by substantial evidence.

The court first determined that the lockout was not "inherently destructive of employee rights," under *American Ship Building Co. v. NLRB*,[20] and therefore did not fall into the category of cases in which the Board may truncate its inquiry into employer motivation. The court found that the Board correctly applied the Supreme Court's decision in *NLRB v. Great Dane Trailers*[21] in concluding that the inquiry is "whether the Respondent possessed a legitimate and substantial business justification for the lockout"[22]—in other words, a legitimate defense against the union's inside-game tactics. The court agreed with the Board's determination that the employer had "substantial and legitimate business objectives"[23] for locking out the employees and that their good-faith attempts to reach a contract settlement as well as a long history of a stable bargaining relationship mitigated against a finding of improper motivation. The court also found that letters from the employer to the union on the day the lockout was initiated supported the Board's finding that the motivation for the lockout was to facilitate a successful conclusion to contract negotiations.

---

[18]215 F.3d 11, 164 LRRM 2193 (D.C. Cir.), *cert. denied*, 121 S. Ct. 654, 165 LRRM 3056 (2000).

[19]Central Ill. Publ. Serv. Co., 326 NLRB 928, 159 LRRM 1217 (1998), *review denied sub nom.* Electrical Workers (IBEW) Local 702 v. NLRB, 215 F.3d 11 (D.C. Cir. 2000), *cert. denied*, 148 L.Ed.2d 558 (2001).

[20]380 U.S. 300, 58 LRRM 2672 (1965).

[21]388 U.S. 26, 65 LRRM 2465 (1967).

[22]*Central Ill., supra* note 19, at 931, 159 LRRM at 1220.

[23]*Electrical Workers, supra* note 18, at 18, 164 LRRM at 2197.

3. Plant Closings

b. Partial Closings

A partial closing or a transfer of work may violate Section 8(a)(3). The Board continues to determine the legality of partial closings by focusing on the motive underlying the employer's decision. In *Bonham Heating & Air Conditioning, Inc.*[24] the Board held that an employer engaged in plumbing, heating, and air conditioning work violated Section 8(a)(3) when it ceased its plumbing business, slowed down bidding, and laid off employees after a majority of them had signed a petition requesting union representation. Similarly, in *Electrical South, Inc.*[25] the employer's closing of its engineering department shortly after the employees voted in favor of union representation was found to be discriminatorily motivated, where the employer's economic justifications were unsupported by substantial evidence. However, in *Coyne International Enterprises Corp.*,[26] the Board held that the employer lawfully closed its terminal, even though union animus was a factor in its decision, where the employer proved that it would have closed the terminal in any event because of a continuing and escalating loss of sales.

c. Transfer of Work: The "Runaway Shop"

In *Reno Hilton Resorts v. NLRB*[27] the court upheld the Board's determination that a hotel unlawfully contracted out its security service and laid off security workers after a union election victory, notwithstanding the evidence of cost savings presented by the employer. In *O'Dovero v. NLRB*[28] the D.C. Circuit enforced the Board's determination that the diversion of work from a unionized entity to the nonunion entity of a family-owned integrated enterprise violated Section 8(a)(3) because it had been shown that the diversion occurred

---

[24]328 NLRB No. 61, 161 LRRM 1113 (1999).

[25]327 NLRB No. 270, 160 LRRM 1202 (1998).

[26]326 NLRB 1187, 163 LRRM 1080 (1998).

[27]196 F.3d 1275, 162 LRRM 2961 (D.C. Cir. 1999), *enforcing* 326 NLRB 375, 162 LRRM 1405 (1998). *See also* Westchester Lace Inc., 326 NLRB 1227, 163 LRRM 1181 (1998) (employer unlawfully subcontracted all of its bargaining-unit work in response to employee grievance filings where there was no showing subcontracting would have occurred in absence of grievance activity); GT Terminal Packaging Co., 326 NLRB 114, 160 LRRM 1169 (1998) (employer unlawfully transferred potato-packing operations).

[28]193 F.3d 532, 162 LRRM 2618 (D.C. Cir. 1999).

in response to union efforts to organize the nonunion entity's employees and because the employer failed to show that the diversion would have taken place in the absence of union activity.

5. Replacement and Reinstatement of Economic Strikers

a. Development of the Law

The Board ruled that employees who quit work in circumstances governed by Section 502 of the Act, which protects refusals to work in the face of "abnormally dangerous" working conditions, are not economic strikers for purposes of the rules pertaining to permanent replacement of economic strikers and are, therefore, entitled to immediate reinstatement to employment on making an unconditional offer to return to work.[29]

In *Detroit Newspaper Agency*[30] the Board declined to overrule *Service Electric Co.*,[31] and adhered to the established doctrine that an employer is not obligated to bargain with a union concerning the terms and conditions of employment for replacements hired during a strike. The Board continues, however, to follow its rule that once the strike has ended any replacements who remain employed assume the same status as other unit employees. Such employees are no longer strike replacements, the terms under which they work will be governed by the newly bargained contract,[32] and the union is presumptively entitled to their names and addresses.

b. Nature of the Duty to Reinstate

The Board continues to grant preferential reinstatement rights to economic strikers.[33] The Board held that an offer to return to work under the terms of an expired contract, after an employer had lawfully implemented its final offer for a new contract, was not an "unconditional" offer.[34]

The Board continues to impose the duty on a striking employee to advise the employer, personally or through the union, that he or she is ready to return to work. In the absence of an offer to return, the employer could not have known of a striker's desire to return and the employer, therefore, has no duty to reinstate the striker.[35]

---

[29]TNS, Inc., 329 NLRB No. 61, 166 LRRM 1018 (1999).
[30]327 NLRB 871, 161 LRRM 1033 (1999).
[31]281 NLRB 633, 124 LRRM 1318 (1986).
[32]Grinnell Fire Protection, 332 NLRB No. 120, 165 LRRM 1345 (2000).
[33]Forsyth Elec. Co., Inc., 332 NLRB No. 68 (2000).
[34]Taylor Lumber & Treating, Inc., 326 NLRB 1298, 161 LRRM 1031 (1999).
[35]Sacramento Theatrical Lighting, 333 NLRB No. 47 (2001).

The Board continues to hold that unreinstated economic strikers are entitled to preferential reinstatement to job vacancies created by the departure of strike replacements.[36]

c. Defenses and Limitations

The Board continues to follow its rule that, to show replacements were hired permanently, the employer is required to show that it had a "mutual understanding" with the replacements that they were permanent.[37] Based on the limited allegations of the complaint, the Board held that an employer did not violate the Act by not displacing crossovers during a 3-day period following a 1-day strike, where the employer was operating under a 4-day contract for the supply of temporary workers.[38]

The Board's "substantially equivalent position" definition, as set out in *Rose Printing*,[39] was applied to require the employer to reinstate a striker to a newly created position of "polisher" because it was substantially equivalent to the apprentice painter job.[40]

7. *Discrimination Against Union Organizers and "Salts"*

The Board continues to apply strict standards in evaluating employer defenses attempting to demonstrate that refusal to consider or hire union organizers and "salts" would have occurred even absent knowledge of union-organizing activity, and, in most cases, has rejected the defenses.[41] In those cases in which no violations were

---

[36]Pirelli Cable Corp., 331 NLRB No. 158 (2000).

[37]Dino & Sons Realty, 330 NLRB No. 106 (2000).

[38]AMI/HTI Tarzana-Encino, 332 NLRB No. 90 (2000).

[39]302 NLRB 1076, 138 LRRM 1188 (1991).

[40]Towne Ford, 327 NLRB 193, *enforced sub nom.* Machinists Peninsula Lodge No. 1414 v. NLRB, 238 F.3d 429 (9th Cir. 2000) (unpublished).

[41]*E.g.*, H.B. Zachry Co., 332 NLRB No. 110, 165 LRRM 1351 (2000) (employer claim that phone calls to salt applicants to offer employment went unanswered deemed a sham because evidence revealed that caller hung up as soon as call was answered); Merit Elec. Co., 328 NLRB No. 29, 163 LRRM 1196 (1999) (employer failed to show hiring would not have occurred in absence of knowledge that applicants were "salts"); Lin R. Rogers Elec. Contractors, Inc., 328 NLRB No. 163, 161 LRRM 1297 (1999) (employer failed to prove that it exclusively followed policy of hiring only employees who have worked at its other job sites); North Bay Plumbing, Inc., 327 NLRB 899, 161 LRRM 1139 (1999) (employer failed to prove that it followed policy of not hiring individuals who had formerly been in competing business, and applicant no longer operated competing business in any event); Custom Top Soil, Inc., 327 NLRB 121, 161 LRRM 1142 (1999) (reasons for not hiring found to be pretextual); *see also* Kentucky General, Inc. v. NLRB, 178 F.3d 1294, 161 LRRM 2435 (6th Cir. 1999) (enforcing Board order finding failure of employer to prove that it followed policy of hiring only those applicants whose skills were already known to employer).

found, the employers were successful in either establishing lack of knowledge of union activity or showing an application of valid non-discriminatory hiring criteria.[42]

The Board's rule that a backpay award for a paid union organizer wrongfully denied employment by a nonunion contractor need not be offset by earnings received from the union during the backpay period has been accepted by the Second Circuit.[43]

III. UNION INDUCEMENT OF EMPLOYER TO DISCRIMINATE

A. Union Inducements as Unfair Labor Practices Prohibited by Section 8(b)(2)

The Board continues to find that a union violates Section 8(b)(2) by attempting to cause or causing an employer to discharge a member for criticizing the union. Types of protected intraunion activity include filing internal charges against incumbent union officers and running for office against incumbents.[44] Recent cases also continue to hold that a union violates Section 8(b)(2) by attempting to cause or causing an employer to discriminate against those who choose not to support the union, either by being nonmembers or crossing picket lines.[45]

The cases also continue to hold that discrimination under Section 8(b)(2) can involve refusals to hire or rehire,[46] to offer over-

---

[42]*E.g.*, TNT Techs., Ltd., 330 NLRB No. 23, 163 LRRM 1009 (1999) (no showing that refusals to hire were result of union activity); Little Rock Elec. Contractors, Inc., 327 NLRB 932, 164 LRRM 1100 (1999) (employer established that it validly applied its rule against considering or hiring applicants who held simultaneous employment with another entity); J.O. Mory Inc., 326 NLRB 604, 161 LRRM 1109 (1999) (employer lawfully applied its policy of not hiring those who currently earn more than employer's entry-level wage).

[43]NLRB v. Ferguson Elec. Co., 242 F.3d 426, 166 LRRM 2513 (2d Cir. 2001), *enforcing* 330 NLRB No. 75, 163 LRRM 1081 (2001).

[44]Painters Local 466 (Skidmore College), 332 NLRB No. 41, 165 LRRM 1195 (2000); USF Red Star, Inc., 330 NLRB No. 15, 162 LRRM 1409, *enforced*, 230 F.3d 102, 165 LRRM 2665 (4th Cir. 2000); Nationsway Transp. Serv., 327 NLRB 1033, 164 LRRM 1339 (1999).

[45]Letter Carriers Branch 3126 (U.S. Postal Serv.), 330 NLRB No. 85, 163 LRRM 1190 (2000); Newspaper & Mail Deliverers (City & Suburban Delivery), 332 NLRB No. 77 (2000).

[46]*Newspaper & Mail Deliverers*, *supra* note 45; *Painters Local 466*, *supra* note 44.

time opportunities,[47] or to honor an employee's seniority.[48] In *Laborers Local 1184 (Nicholson Rodio)*[49] union representatives complained to an employer that a member was a troublemaker, told the employer that it was not obligated to hire the individual despite the union's referral, and reminded the employer that it was not obligated to hire all referrals. The Board found that the union had unlawfully induced the employer not to hire the member.

B. Violations Relating to Seniority Provisions

The Board continues to hold that a union violates Section 8(b)(2) when it agrees with an employer to base seniority on whether employees have exercised or refrained from exercising their Section 7 rights. In *Newspaper & Mail Deliverers' Union (City & Suburban Delivery System)*[50] a union unlawfully caused the employer to refuse to recognize the seniority of certain casual employees in making permanent hiring decisions, because those employees had worked during an earlier strike. The union's actions violated Section 8(b)(2) even though the individuals had no contractual seniority rights and the contract did not provide for seniority to be used as a basis for hiring; the employer's expressed desire was to use seniority as the basis for hire.

The Board addressed a putative superseniority issue in *Nationsway Transport Service*,[51] in which an employee was denied a top seniority position because the union and employer had entered into an agreement to award the first seniority spot to an employee who would act as the union's "spokesperson" or "shop steward." The Board reasoned that the union violated Section 8(b)(2) because the union and the employer's particular agreement did not trump the parties' past practice of placing employees on a seniority list in the order that they arrived at a new trucking terminal. In reaching its ruling, the Board did not discuss its *Dairylea Cooperative*[52] line of cases or its *Gulton* rule[53] relating to superseniority issues.

---

[47] *Letter Carriers Branch 3126, supra* note 45.

[48] *Nationsway Transp., supra* note 44.

[49] 332 NLRB No. 124 (2000).

[50] 332 NLRB No. 77 (2000).

[51] 327 NLRB 1033, 164 LRRM 1339 (1999).

[52] Dairylea Coop., Inc., 219 NLRB 656, 89 LRRM 1737 (1975), *enforced sub nom.* NLRB v. Teamsters Local 338, 531 F.2d 1162, 91 LRRM 2929 (2d Cir. 1976).

[53] Gulton Electro-Voice, 266 NLRB 406, 112 LRRM 1361 (1983), *enforced sub nom.* Electrical Workers (IUE) Local 900 v. NLRB, 727 F.2d 1184, 115 LRRM 2760 (D.C. Cir. 1984).

C. Violations Relating to Union-Security Provisions

1. Introduction and Overview

Under Section 8(b)(2), a union may lawfully cause the discharge of an employee under a union-security clause for the employee's failure "to tender the periodic dues and the initiation fees uniformly required as a condition of acquiring or retaining membership."[54] There are, however, limitations on a union's ability to enforce a union-security clause.

For example, in *Flying Dutchman Park, Inc.*,[55] the Board found that a union violated Section 8(b)(2) when it enforced a union-security clause that contained a requirement that the employee obtain a "referral" from the union before commencing employment. The Board found that the union and the employer, which was not engaged in the construction industry, negotiated a collective bargaining agreement that lacked a hiring-hall provision but contained a union-security clause that required employees to obtain a "referral" from the union. The Board found that the union-security clause was unlawful on its face. However, the inclusion of this clause did not justify the employer's refusal to sign the agreement and did not render the entire contract unenforceable.

The Board also held that a union violated Section 8(b)(2) of the Act by accepting recognition as exclusive representative of a bargaining unit of employees in which it did not represent an uncoerced majority.[56] The Board found the union violated the Act by telling employees that it would seek their termination if they did not pay dues and fees and by arbitrating the employer's failure to terminate employees for failing to pay those dues and fees.

In *Incisa, U.S.A., Inc.*[57] the Board held that a union's acceptance of voluntary recognition under Section 9(a) while a valid election petition was pending did not implicate Section 8(b)(2) but did violate Section 8(b)(1)(A). The contract was originally a Section 8(f) prehire agreement in which the union-security clause was permissible without majority status.

A union did not violate Sections (b)(1)(A) and 8(b)(2) by negotiating the return of bargaining-unit work that was being performed

---

[54]29 U.S.C. §158(a)(3).
[55]329 NLRB No. 46, 162 LRRM 1283 (1999).
[56]Keystone Shipping Co., 327 NLRB 892, 160 LRRM 1225 (1999).
[57]327 NLRB 563, 167 LRRM 1228 (1999).

by previously unrepresented employees and by applying the collective bargaining agreement to those employees.[58] In that case, the general counsel did not allege that the employer and the union were attempting to expand the bargaining unit to include employees who were historically excluded from the unit. Rather, the union and the employer negotiated the transfer of 26 employees who were performing bargaining-unit work into the unit.

2. Discriminatory Enforcement Prohibited

A union violates Section 8(b)(1)(A) by collecting full membership dues from a *Beck* objector, but the union does not thereby violate Section 8(b)(2) as long as the union does not attempt to cause the employer to discharge or discriminate against the objector.[59] Also, a union does not violate Section 8(b)(2) by attempting to collect an amount equal to the *Beck* objector's share of the representational expenses.[60]

3. Dues and Fees That May Be Exacted

In *Electrical Workers Local 48 (Kingston Constructors, Inc.)*[61] the Board clarified the precedent relating to the phrase "periodic dues and initiation fees uniformly required as a condition of acquiring or retaining membership."[62] In particular, the Board addressed whether market-recovery dues constituted periodic dues or assessments. Market-recovery dues are part of job targeting programs, in which unions subsidize part of the employees' wages to allow union contractors to bid competitively on construction projects. In addressing this issue, the Board found that its decision in *Teamsters Local 959 (RCA Service*

---

[58]Lockheed Martin Tactical Aircraft Sys., 331 NLRB No. 190, 165 LRRM 1145 (2000).

[59]Transport Workers (Johnson Controls World Servs., Inc.), 329 NLRB No. 56 (1999); Steelworkers (George E. Failing Co.), 329 NLRB No. 18, 162 LRRM 1097 (1999); Polymark Corp., 329 NLRB No. 7, 162 LRRM 1033 (1999). *See also* Lamson & Sessions Co., 328 NLRB No. 154, 161 LRRM 1019 (1999) (noting ALJ found union did not violate §8(b)(2) because there was no evidence union took affirmative action to enforce allegedly unlawful union-security clause).

[60]*Polymark, supra* note 59; Kroger, Inc., 327 NLRB 1237 (1999). *But see* Teamsters Local 75 (Schreiber Foods), 329 NLRB No. 12, 162 LRRM 1057 (1999) (modifying ALJ's decision to find violation of only §8(b)(1)(A) but not 8(b)(2) for the union's attempt to enforce union-security clause without informing objectors of their *Beck* rights).

[61]332 NLRB No. 161, 2000 WL 1920355, 166 LRRM 1090 (2000).

[62]*Id.*, 2000 WL 1920355, at *4.

Co.),[63] which held that the term "periodic dues" referred only to those payments that are for the purpose of supporting the union's role as a collective bargaining agent, was implicitly overruled by its later decision in *Detroit Mailers Local 40*.[64] In the latter case, the Board held that "periodic dues" included any payments under a union-security clause "so long as they are periodic and uniformly required and not devoted to a purpose which would make their mandatory extraction otherwise inimical to public policy."[65]

Applying *Detroit Mailers* to market-recovery dues, the Board found that unions could collect market-recovery dues from employees on non–Davis-Bacon projects. However, the Board also found that the union could not enforce a union-security clause to recover market-recovery dues from employees on Davis-Bacon projects. Relying on the Davis-Bacon Act and Wage Appeals Board decisions, the Board found that the extraction of market-recovery dues pursuant to a union-security clause was inimical to public policy under the Davis-Bacon Act, which limits the instances in which employees' wages can be returned to contractors and prohibits the deduction of employees' wages that benefit employers.

The Board also found that under Section 8(b)(2), as well as Section 8(a)(3), a union may require employees to pay initiation fees pursuant to the union-security clause in their collective bargaining agreement.[66] Unions may also notify employees that they are required to pay initiation fees under the union-security clause.[67]

4. Union Must Supply Information to Employees

A union violates Section 8(b)(2) by seeking the discharge of an objector under a union-security clause without providing notice of the right to remain a nonmember and giving the objector a reasonable time to comply with the union-security obligations.[68]

---

[63]167 NLRB 1042, 66 LRRM 1203 (1967).

[64]192 NLRB 951, 78 LRRM 1053 (1971).

[65]*Id.*, at 952.

[66]Paperworkers (Sun Chem. Corp. of Mich.), 327 NLRB 1011, 161 LRRM 1028 (1999).

[67]*Id.* The Board noted that any such notice must be consistent with the requirements of *California Saw & Knife Works*, 320 NLRB 224 (1995), 151 LRRM 1121 (1999), *enforced sub nom. Machinists v. NLRB*, 133 F.3d 1012, 157 LRRM 2287 (7th Cir. 1998), *cert. denied*, 525 U.S. 813, 160 LRRM 2064 (1998).

[68]Yellow Freight Sys. of Ind., 327 NLRB 996 (1999); Incisa USA, Inc., 327 NLRB 563 (1999).

In *International Union, Automobile, Aeronautics and Agricultural Implement Workers (Various Employers)*[69] the Board dismissed a *Beck* complaint alleging that the international union violated Section 8(b)(2) by seeking the discharge of a nonmember after he failed to comply with the union's demand for payment of dues. There was no allegation that the employee ever exercised his right under *Beck* to object to the payment of dues for nonrepresentational activities. The international union had distributed a *Beck* notice to the nonmember; however, the international union had provided a report on the breakdown of its expenditures only to known *Beck* objectors. On these facts, the Board found the international union satisfied its duty to provide the *Beck* notice. The Board also found that the nonmember failed to comply with the union's request for the payment of dues and that the union's subsequent attempts to have the nonmember discharged were lawful. On appeal, however, the D.C. Circuit found that its previous decision in *Penrod v. NLRB*[70] was controlling. In *Penrod*, the court held that potential objectors were entitled to be informed of the amounts that their fees would be reduced if they became *Beck* objectors. Because the international union had not provided information about the breakdown to the nonmember, the D.C. Circuit remanded the case to the Board to determine the remedy.[71]

5. Obligations of Employers

With respect to an employer's obligation to remit dues to the union, the Board found in *Polymark Corp.*[72] that an employer does not violate Section 8(a)(3) by collecting an amount equal to the full union dues after the objector perfects his or her *Beck* objection but before the union informs the employer of the reduced dues owed for chargeable expenses. The Board found the circumstances in *Polymark Corp.* were governed by its decision in *Auto Workers Local 1752 (Schweitzer Aircraft Corp.).*[73] In the latter case, the Board held

---

[69]328 NLRB No. 175, 164 LRRM 1177 (1999), *enforced in part, remanded in part sub nom.* Thomas v. NLRB, 213 F.3d 651, 164 LRRM 2577 (D.C. Cir. 2000). This case also involved the validity of the "local presumption" for determining "chargeable and nonchargeable expenses." The Board held that it was permissible for an international union to apply the same ratio of its expenses to the fees and dues expended by its local union.

[70]203 F.3d 41, 163 LRRM 2513 (D.C. Cir. 2000).

[71]*Thomas, supra* note 69.

[72]329 NLRB No. 7, 162 LRRM 1033 (1999).

[73]320 NLRB 528, 115 LRRM 1286 (1995), *enforced sub nom.* Williams v. NLRB, 105 F.3d 787, 153 LRRM 2986 (2d Cir. 1996).

that an employee's "resignation of membership . . . under a lawful security clause does not privilege the employee to make an untimely revocation of his checkoff authorization, and therefore a union's efforts aimed at continued enforcement of that checkoff after the employee's resignation do not violate the Act."[74] An employee's resignation does not completely void his or her dues obligation. Likewise, an employee's resignation does not revoke his or her checkoff authorization. Employees are required to continue to pay dues until they perfect their *Beck* objection. After that time, the union may lawfully seek to enforce the checkoff provision for an amount equal to the employee's share of representational expenses.[75]

D. Violations Relating to Hiring and Referral Halls

The Board continues to hold that a union violates Sections 8(b)(1)(A) and 8(b)(2) of the Act by refusing to refer a person from an exclusive hiring hall because he or she is not a union member.[76]

The Board in *Theatrical Stage Employees Local 720*[77] dismissed charges against a union that refused to permit an individual who earlier had been expelled from use of its exclusive hiring hall because of a history of alleged misconduct toward employers, other employees, and clients. The union's actions were found to be within an acceptable wide range of reasonableness and not arbitrary, even though it did not act pursuant to an explicit written policy. The union had demonstrated that its conduct was necessary to protect the representative role that it performed in administering the hiring hall.

The Board in *Laborers Local 294 (Associated General Contractors of California)*[78] reversed an ALJ and deferred to an arbitrator's resolution of claims that a union had dispatched individuals out of order to a job site, allegedly in violation of Sections 8(b)(1)(A) and 8(b)(2). The grievant–employees were represented by independent counsel in the arbitration proceeding, and the Board found that the arbitration proceeding met the *Spielberg* fairness criteria.

---

[74]*Id.*, at 531.
[75]*Polymark Corp., supra* note 72.
[76]*In re* Electrical Workers Local 3 (White Plains), 331 NLRB No. 150 (2000).
[77]332 NLRB No. 3, 165 LRRM 1163 (2000).
[78]331 NLRB No. 28, 164 LRRM 1169 (2000).

In *Jacoby v. NLRB*[79] the D.C. Circuit reversed and remanded the Board's decision in *Steamfitters Local 342 (Contra Costa Electric)*,[80] in which the Board held that mere negligence in failing to follow hiring hall procedures does not violate Sections 8(b)(1)(A) and 8(b)(2) of the Act independent of the duty of fair representation. The Board found that contrary precedents were inconsistent with Supreme Court decisions in *Steelworkers v. Rawson*[81] and *Air Line Pilots Ass'n v. O'Neill*.[82] The Court of Appeals held that the Board misinterpreted this Supreme Court precedent. The Court held that the union had a "heightened duty of fair dealing in the context of a hiring hall," and remanded the case for the Board to readdress the legal issues related to the union's duty of fair representation. The Court recognized that the Section 8(b)(2) issues were different, as a result of that section's focus on discrimination, and remanded those allegations to the Board to address the issue of whether breaches of the duty of fair representation in this context are themselves violations of Section 8(b)(2).

IV. DISCRIMINATION BECAUSE OF INVOLVEMENT WITH NLRB PROCEDURES: SECTION 8(a)(4)

In *NLRB v. Lampi, LLC*[83] the Eleventh Circuit concluded that the Board's decision that the employer had violated Section 8(a)(4) by firing an employee because of her testimony adverse to the employer in an unfair labor practice case was not supported by sufficient evidence linking the termination to protected activity. In doing so, the court rejected the reliance that the Board had placed on a statement made by the employer's president to a television reporter, saying that he did not like unions.

[**Editor's Note:** The D.C. Circuit has endorsed the Board's application of the *Bill Johnson Restaurants*[84] framework for determining whether lawsuits brought against unions are retaliatory and unlaw-

---

[79]233 F.3d 611, 165 LRRM 2993 (D.C. Cir. 2000).

[80]329 NLRB No. 65, 162 LRRM 1156 (1999). The Board reaffirmed its decision in *Steamfitters Local 342* in subsequent cases, before the Court of Appeals' decision in *Jacoby*. *See* Plumbers Local 375 (H.C. Price Constr. Co.), 330 NLRB No. 55, 163 LRRM 1041 (1999).

[81]495 U.S. 362, 134 LRRM 2153 (1990).

[82]59 U.S.L.W. 4175, 136 LRRM 2721 (1991).

[83]240 F.3d 931, 166 LRRM 2321 (11th Cir. 2001).

[84]461 U.S. 731, 113 LRRM 2647 (1983).

ful under Section 8(a)(1) when it enforced the Board's determination that suits filed under RICO and the Sherman Act for unions' pursuit of environmental objections to a nonunion contractor's zoning and construction permits had an impermissible retaliatory motive. Also enforced was the Board's order that the employer reimburse the unions for their legal costs incurred in defending the action.[85]]

---

[85]Petrochem Insulation, Inc. v. NLRB, 240 F.3d 26, 166 LRRM 2433 (D.C. Cir. 2001), *enforcing* 330 NLRB No. 10, 163 LRRM 1276 (1999), and adopting Board's reasoning in *BE&K Constr. Co.*, 329 NLRB No. 68, 162 LRRM 1217 (1999); *see also* Beverly Health & Rehabilitation Servs., Inc., 331 NLRB No. 121, 164 LRRM 1345 (2000).

Chapter 8

EMPLOYER DOMINATION OF AND ASSISTANCE TO LABOR ORGANIZATIONS

I. Introduction: Section 8(a)(2)

Section 8(a)(2) of the Act prohibits employer domination of, interference with the formation or administration of, or contribution of financial or other support to any labor organization.[1] Recent decisions have generally followed the cases in the Main Edition.

---

[1]The additional language of §8(a)(2) reads as follows: "Provided, That subject to the rules and regulations made and published by the Board pursuant to Section 6, an employer shall not be prohibited from permitting employees to confer with him during working hours without loss of time or pay."

An employer violates Section 8(a)(2) by recognizing a union that does not represent a majority of the employees, even if the action is taken in good faith. In determining whether a violation of Section 8(a)(2) has occurred, the Board engages in a two-pronged inquiry. First, the Board determines whether the employee group at issue is a labor organization, as defined by Section 2(5) of the Act. If the group is considered a labor organization under the Act, the Board next considers whether the employer has dominated, interfered with the formation or administration of, or supported the labor organization, compared with merely cooperating with the organization.[2]

The Board continues to draw a line between prohibited employer *support* and permitted employer *cooperation*, a line that at times may be difficult to perceive, particularly when good-faith intention is not material to a violation.[3] For example, in *NLRB v. Autodie International*,[4] a prospective purchaser of a business violated Section 8(a)(2) when it recognized a shop committee and later a successor organization, because the petition signed by a majority of the seller's employees did not necessarily represent a majority of those who would be employed by the purchaser and because the petition merely indicated that the signers preferred an in-house committee over the UAW. Likewise, in *Deferiet Paper Co.*,[5] the Board found that the employer violated Section 8(a)(2) when, despite dismissal of its unit-clarification petition seeking accretion of employees represented by one labor organization, it recognized another labor organization as the exclusive bargaining representative of those employees.

II. LABOR ORGANIZATION DEFINED

Section 2(5) of the Act defines a labor organization as

any organization of any kind, or any agency or employee representation committee or plan, in which employees participate and which

---

[2]Polaroid Corp., 329 NLRB No. 47, 162 LRRM 1129, 1129–30 (1999), citing Electromation, Inc., 309 NLRB 990, 996, 142 LRRM 1001 (1992), *enforced*, 35 F.3d 1148, 147 LRRM 2257 (7th Cir. 1994).

[3]Addicts Rehabilitation Ctr. Fund, Inc., 330 NLRB No. 113 (2000) (it is not necessary to establish union animus or other unlawful motive to find §8(a)(2) violation).

[4]169 F.3d 378, 160 LRRM 2681 (6th Cir. 1999), *enforcing* 321 NLRB 688, 153 LRRM 1242 (1996).

[5]330 NLRB No. 89, 166 LRRM 1040 (2000), *enforcement denied on other grounds*, 235 F.3d 581, 166 LRRM 2107 (D.C. Cir. 2000).

exists for the purpose, in whole or in part, of dealing with employers concerning grievances, labor disputes, wages, rates of pay, hours of employment, or conditions of work.

Based on this statutory definition, the Board has ruled that an organization can only be considered a labor organization if "(1) employees participate; and (2) the organization exists, at least in part, for the purpose of 'dealing with' employers; and (3) these dealings concern conditions of work or concern other statutory subjects, such as grievances, labor disputes, wages, rates of pay, or hours of employment."[6] The definition of a labor organization is broad, and includes "very loose, informal, unstructured, and irregular meeting groups."[7] The cases generally focus on two statutory prerequisites: employee participation and having the purpose of dealing with employers.

A. Requirement of Participation by "Employees"

Groups composed of individuals excluded from the definition of employees under Section 2(3), such as public employees, are not labor organizations within the meaning of Section 2(5).[8]

B. Requirement of "Dealing With" Employers

Both the Board and the courts continue to interpret the "dealing with" language broadly.[9] The Board has ruled that "dealing with" involves a bilateral mechanism that entails "a pattern or practice in which a group of employees, over time, make proposals to management, and management responds to those proposals by acceptance or rejection by word or deed."[10] The Board has ruled repeatedly that employee committees that interact and "deal with" management

---

[6]*Polaroid, supra* note 2.

[7]*Id. See also Addicts Rehabilitation Ctr., supra* note 3 (2000) (ALJ noted that "there may also be a requirement that the employees in the committee act in representational capacity").

[8]Pacific N. Maritime Ass'n v. Local 63, Longshoremen (ILWU), 198 F.3d 1078, 162 LRRM 3037 (9th Cir. 1999).

[9]V&S Progalv v. NLRB, 168 F.3d 270, 160 LRRM 2518 (6th Cir. 1999), *enforcing* 323 NLRB 801, 157 LRRM 1255 (1997).

[10]*Polaroid, supra* note 6, citing E.I. du Pont de Nemours & Co., 311 NLRB 893, 894, 143 LRRM 1268 (1993).

constitute labor organizations.[11] In *Polaroid Corp.*[12] the Board ruled that the employer-created Employee-Owners Influence Council (EOIC) was a labor organization because it functioned as a bilateral mechanism in which employees, acting in a representational capacity, made group proposals relating to concerns such as conditions of work and employee benefits. The Board placed emphasis on the fact that the EOIC process went beyond mere group proposals and entailed the employer's response to such proposals.[13]

Similarly, in *V&S Progalv v. NLRB*,[14] the Sixth Circuit enforced the Board's determination that the employer's "in-house committee" was "dealing with" the employer. The committee was formed at the behest of the company president and raised employment issues and proposals that it presented to the company. Subsequently, the company president met with the committee to discuss the proposals. The Sixth Circuit noted that "all that is required to satisfy the definition of 'dealing with' is that management respond to the proposal, either by acceptance *or rejection.*"[15]

In *EFCO Corp.*[16] the Board held that the employer's employee benefits and policy review committees were labor organizations. Both committees operated in representational capacities on behalf of the employees, formulating and presenting proposals to management,

---

[11]*E.g.*, Summa Health Sys., Inc., 330 NLRB No. 197, 2000 WL 57344, *13, *15 (2000) (employer's "process enhancement teams" were labor organizations, dealing with the employer, because they were "created, formed, funded, directed, and constituted" by the employer, they were designed to represent the employees, and there was an "interactional exchange of proposals, a discussion, and a reaching of consensus between managerial team participants."); Beverly Cal. v. NLRB, 227 F.3d 817, 165 LRRM 2257 (7th Cir. 2000), *enforcing in part* 326 NLRB No. 29, 159 LRRM 1049; 326 NLRB No. 30, 159 LRRM 1033 (1998) (management-created employee council was labor organization because evidence revealed that (1) unit employees were going to participate in council; (2) at least part of purpose of council was to deal with employer; and (3) dealings with employer would have concerned grievances, labor disputes, wages, rates of pay, hours of employment, or conditions of work); Addicts Rehabilitation Ctr. Fund, Inc., 330 NLRB No. 113 (2000) (employer violated Act by creating and supporting "pro-action committee" that dealt with employer with regard to employee grievances); Naomi Knitting Plant, 328 NLRB No. 180 (1999) (a design team was a labor organization under Act, because committee went far beyond "brainstorming" and addressed issues of drug testing and job-bidding procedure).

[12]*Id.*

[13]*Id.*

[14]V&S Progalv v. NLRB, 168 F.3d 270, 160 LRRM 2518 (6th Cir. 1999), *enforcing* 323 NLRB 801, 157 LRRM 1255 (1997).

[15] *Id.* Emphasis in original.

[16]327 NLRB No. 71, 160 LRRM 1049 (1998).

which it would either accept or reject.[17] Similarly, the employer's safety committee was held to be a labor organization because it involved employees who made proposals to management about safety policies and programs, including proposals about employee compensation.[18]

Although the Board had broadly defined the "dealing with" provision, it has set forth a number of safe havens for employee involvement that do not violate Section 8(a)(2). In *Polaroid Corp.*[19] the Board ruled that employee proposals made to the employer and implemented without the give-and-take of negotiations do not violate the Act. For example, suggestion boxes and "brainstorming" groups do not violate the Act where the purpose is merely to develop ideas that management may or may not adopt.[20] The Board has also reaffirmed the principle that there must be a pattern or practice in which a group of employees makes proposals, over time, to management, and management responds to such proposals.[21]

III. EMPLOYER DOMINATION

Prohibited domination of a labor organization exists when the organization is controlled or directed by the employer, rather than by the employees. The Board and the courts continue to apply the *Electromation, Inc.*[22] standards for determining when a labor organization is "dominated." Recent cases confirm that the Board and courts are in agreement that domination exists where the employer plays a significant role in the creation of the committee and the selection of members for the committee. For example, in *Beverly California Corp. v. NLRB*,[23] the Seventh Circuit enforced the Board ruling that the employer dominated an employee council because it was the "creature of the facility's management."[24] In *V&S Progalv, Inc. v. NLRB*[25]

---

[17]*Id.*

[18]*Id.*

[19]329 NLRB No. 47, 162 LRRM 1129, 1130 (1999).

[20]*Id.*; EFCO Corp., 327 NLRB No. 71, 160 LRRM 1049 (1998) (employee suggestion screening committee was not labor organization because it "performed clerical or ministerial function that facilitated employer's consideration of suggestions made by the employees").

[21]*Id.*

[22]309 NLRB 990 (1992), *enforced*, 35 F.3d 1148 (7th Cir. 1994).

[23]227 F.3d 817, 165 LRRM 2257 (7th Cir. 2000), *enforcing in part* 326 NLRB No. 29, 159 LRRM 1049; 326 NLRB No. 30, 159 LRRM 1033 (1998).

[24]*Id.*, 227 F.3d at 836.

[25]168 F.3d 270, 160 LRRM 2518, 2528 (6th Cir. 1999), *enforcing* 323 NLRB 801, 157 LRRM 1255 (1997).

the Sixth Circuit ruled that substantial evidence supported the Board's determination of employer domination of an employee committee when there was testimony that the employees had been told how many employees should be on the committee, how they should be chosen, and how the committee should function.

The Board continues to hold that a labor organization is unlawfully dominated where an employer exerts control over the organization, such as control of the organization's agenda and involvement in the operation of the organization.[26] In *Summa Health System*[27] the Board ruled that the employer dominated its "process enhancement teams" when it created the teams, funded them, played a role in selecting the employee participants, and controlled the teams' operations and agendas. In *Addicts Rehabilitation Center Fund*[28] the Board found that an employer dominated an employee committee charged with conveying employee grievances to management because the employer "dominated the process of forming the committee."[29] The Board also noted that the employer determined the committee's structure and agenda and provided its space and material needs.[30]

IV. EMPLOYER INTERFERENCE

A. Unlawful Recognition or Other Assistance

Unlawful assistance, which occurs when a union is deemed capable of functioning as a union once the unlawful interference or assistance is eliminated, is misconduct that is less severe than domination. Unlawful assistance is found most commonly where a labor organization is recognized at a time when it does not have majority status.[31] In *Keystone Shipping Co.*[32] the Board held that the employer violated Sections 8(a)(2) and (1) by recognizing a union as repre-

---

[26]*E.g.*, Addicts Rehabilitation Ctr. Fund, Inc., 330 NLRB No. 113 (2000) (employer violated Act by creating and supporting "pro-action committee"); Naomi Knitting Plant, 328 NLRB No. 180 (1999) (employer violated Act by creating and organizing design team).

[27]330 NLRB No. 197 (2000).

[28]330 NLRB No. 113, 2000 WL 248214 (2000).

[29]*Id.*, 2000 WL 248214, at *19.

[30]*Id.*

[31]Planned Bldg. Servs., Inc., 330 NLRB No. 116 (2000); Gulf Caribe Maritime, Inc., 330 NLRB No. 120 (2000); Incisa USA, Inc., 327 NLRB 563 (1999); Ryder Integrated Logistics, Inc., 329 NLRB No. 89 (1999).

[32]327 NLRB 892, 160 LRRM 1225 (1999).

sentative of employees on two ships as part of a fleetwide bargaining unit when it assumed control of the vessels, where there had been a separate bargaining unit for the two vessels with another union and there was no showing of majority support for the change. In *Deferiet Paper Co.*[33] the employer violated Section 8(a)(2) when, despite dismissal of its unit-clarification petition seeking accretion of employees represented by one labor organization it recognized another labor organization that did not represent a majority of employees in the bargaining unit. In *Wayne County Legal Services*[34] the employer violated Section 8(a)(2) when it continued to recognize an incumbent and deducted union dues after the union failed to accumulate enough votes in an election to be on the ballot in a runoff election.

However, the Board ruled that there was no unlawful accretion to a bargaining unit when a job audit showed that nonunit employees were performing unit work, and the company and the union negotiated a procedure for returning work to the bargaining unit, under which nonunit employees performing the work would be offered transfers into the unit.[35] The Board reasoned that the work performed by the nonunit employees belonged to the unit; therefore, the employer merely returned work that rightfully belonged to the unit.

Unlawful assistance has been found in a variety of other circumstances. An employer violates Section 8(a)(2) when it grants one labor organization access to its facility to campaign and denies such access to another union.[36] Although the Board has traditionally held that a supervisor's participation in the solicitation of authorization cards constitutes a violation of the Act,[37] in *Millsboro Nursing & Rehabilitation Center, Inc.*,[38] the Board determined that the solicitation of authorization cards by supervisors in and of itself is not objectionable where "nothing in the words, deeds, or atmosphere of a supervisor's request for authorization cards contains the seeds of potential reprisal, punishment, or intimidation."[39] Likewise, an em-

---

[33]330 NLRB No. 89, 166 LRRM 1040 (2000), *enforcement denied on other grounds*, 235 F.3d 581, 166 LRRM 2107 (D.C. Cir. 2000).

[34]333 NLRB No. 15, 166 LRRM 1169 (2001).

[35]Lockheed Martin Tactical Aircraft Systems, 331 NLRB No. 190, 165 LRRM 1145 (2000).

[36]Regal Recycling, Inc., 329 NLRB No. 38, 163 LRRM 1245 (1999).

[37]Planned Bldg. Servs., Inc., 330 NLRB No. 116 (2000), and chapters cited therein.

[38]327 NLRB 879, 160 LRRM 1209 (1999).

[39]*Id.* at 880.

ployer violates the Act by deducting dues payable to a union that does not represent a majority of the employees in the applicable unit.[40] In *Lockheed Martin Tactical Aircraft Systems*[41] the employer violated Section 8(a)(2) by threatening employees with discharge if they did not agree to sign a union checkoff authorization card or join the union.

B. Employer Preference Among Contending Unions

Actions of an employer[42] that aid one labor organization over another constitute unlawful "assistance" in violation of Section 8(a)(2).[43] Similarly, in *Ryder-Integrated Logistics, Inc.*[44] the Board held that the employer violated Section 8(a)(2) when it threatened employees with plant closure if they supported a particular union seeking recognition over its rival union.

V. THE REQUIREMENT OF EMPLOYER NEUTRALITY

Section 8(a)(2) prohibits an employer from contributing "support" to a labor organization, but in the absence of unlawful interference, it does not prohibit expressions of preference for one union over another.

B. When a Union Is Incumbent

In *JASCO Industries, Inc.*[45] the Board held that an employer violates Section 8(a)(5) of the Act when, after a rival union files a petition, the employer refuses to bargain with the incumbent union because of the petition and the expiration of the certification year. The Board reasoned that the certification year had been extended by the employer's initial refusal to bargain and that even if the certification year had expired, previous Board decisions require the employer to continue to bargain in good faith, notwithstanding the filing of a petition by a rival union.[46]

---

[40]Wayne County Legal Servs., 333 NLRB No. 15, 166 LRRM 1169 (2001); Ryder Integrated Logistics, Inc., 329 NLRB No. 89 (1999).

[41]331 NLRB No. 190, 165 LRRM 1145 (2000).

[42]Regal Recycling, Inc., 329 NLRB No. 38, 163 LRRM 1245 (1999).

[43]An employer violates §8(a(2) by granting access to its facilities to a labor organization for campaigning and discussion of issues, when it denied such access to a union that was attempting to organize the work force.

[44]329 NLRB No. 89 (1999).

[45]329 NLRB No. 27, 162 LRRM 1255 (1999).

[46]*Id.*, citing Dorn Plastic Mach. Co., 300 NLRB 278, 135 LRRM 1160 (1990), *enforced*, 939 F.2d 402, 1380 NLRB 2102 (6th Cir. 1991); Dominguez Valley Hosp.,

C. When No Union Is Incumbent

The Board continues to hold that an employer violates Sections 8(a)(1) and 8(a)(2) of the Act by recognizing a union after a rival union files a valid representation petition.[47] Following its *Bruckner Nursing Home* decision,[48] the Board held that an employer unlawfully recognized a union based on a majority of authorization cards after a rival union filed a petition, even though the rival union subsequently withdrew its petition as a result of an AFL-CIO umpire's ruling that awarded the union the exclusive right to organize the employees.[49] Finally, the Board continues to hold that during the period after the lawful recognition of a union but before the parties finalize an initial agreement, the "recognition serves as a bar for a reasonable period of time to allow the parties to bargain free from challenge to the union's majority status."[50]

VI. SUPPORT VERSUS COOPERATION

The Board continues to hold that an employer provides unlawful assistance to a union where it improperly deducts union dues on behalf of a union that does not represent a majority of the employees in the applicable bargaining unit.[51]

VII. THE UNION AS PARTY TO THE EMPLOYER'S DOMINATION, ASSISTANCE, OR SUPPORT

Employer conduct that violates Section 8(a)(2) often involves a derivative violation of Section 8(b)(1)(A) by the union, as the union is deemed to have restrained or coerced the employees by accepting the employer's unlawful support or assistance. The Board continues to rule that a union that accepts recognition without majority sup-

---

287 NLRB 149, 151, 127 LRRM 1065 (1987), *enforced sub nom.* NLRB v. National Med. Hosp. of Compton, 907 F.2d 905, 134 LRRM 2787 (9th Cir. 1990).

[47]Incisa USA, Inc., 327 NLRB 563, 167 LRRM 1228 (1999).

[48]262 NLRB 955, 110 LRRM 1374 (1982).

[49]McLaren Health Care Corp., 333 NLRB No. 31 (2001).

[50]Livent Realty, 328 NLRB No. 1, 161 LRRM 1038 (1999) (reasonable time had not passed; therefore, recognition of union barred petition by rival union); MGM Grand Hotel, Inc., 329 NLRB No. 50, 162 LRRM 1202 (1999) (Board barred decertification petition filed before parties had reached tentative agreement).

[51]Wayne County Legal Servs., 333 NLRB No. 15, 166 LRRM 1169 (2001) (employer violated Act by continuing to deduct dues from union that had failed to garner enough votes in election to be on ballot in runoff election).

port or executes a collective bargaining agreement when it represents a minority of employees violates Section 8(b)(1)(A).[52] A union also violates Section 8(b)(1)(A) when it accepts recognition from an employer at a new facility in the absence of a lawful accretion.[53] A union is also guilty of a Section 8(b)(1)(A) violation when it threatens to have employees fired if they refuse to sign a union membership application and a dues checkoff authorization card or when it actually causes an employer to terminate an employee because of his or her refusal to join the union.[54]

VIII. REMEDIES

Where the Board determines that an employer's violations are limited to unlawful interference and support but do not rise to the level of domination, the Board orders the employer to cease and desist from such conduct.[55] If the employer unlawfully recognizes a minority union that is not dominated, the Board generally will issue a cease-and-desist order that prohibits the employer from recognizing the union and from giving any effect to any contract between the parties until the union is properly certified.[56] In *President Container, Inc.*[57] the Board set aside an election. On the eve of the election the employer's owner announced at a bargaining session with the incumbent union, in front of 25 employees, that he would not deal or

---

[52]McLaren Health Care Corp., 333 NLRB No. 31 (2001); Gulf Caribe Maritime, Inc., 330 NLRB No. 120 (2000) (union violated §8(b)(1)(A) when it accepted recognition based on tainted authorization cards); Incisa USA, Inc., 327 NLRB 563, 167 LRRM 1228 (1999) (union violated §8(b)(1)(A) by seeking and accepting recognition at time when valid recognition petition was pending before Board).

[53]Keystone Shipping Co., 327 NLRB 892, 160 LRRM 1225 (1999).

[54]Lockheed Martin Tactical Aircraft Sys., 331 NLRB No. 190, 165 LRRM 1145 (2000); Keystone Shipping Co., 327 NLRB 892, 160 LRRM 1225 (1999) (union violated §8(b)(1)(A) by telling employees that it would ask employer to discharge them if they did not pay dues and fees; by requesting that employer discharge employees; and by receiving aid, assistance, and support from employer in form of dues deducted from wages of employees); Incisa USA, Inc., supra note 52 (union violated Act by causing employer to terminate employee because of his refusal to join union).

[55]*Wayne County Legal Servs., supra* note 51.

[56]*Id.*; *McLaren Health, supra* note 52; Deferiet Paper Co., 330 NLRB No. 89, 166 LRRM 1040 (2000), *enforcement denied on other grounds*, 235 F.3d 581, 166 LRRM 2107 (D.C. Cir. 2000); Planned Bldg. Servs., Inc., 330 NLRB No. 116 (2000); *Gulf Caribe, supra* note 52; *Keystone, supra* note 53; *Incisa USA, supra* note 52; Ryder Integrated Logistics, Inc., 329 NLRB No. 89 (1999).

[57]328 NLRB No. 181, 162 LRRM 1254 (1999).

negotiate further with the incumbent union. The Board found this conduct discredited the union in the eyes of the employees and affected their ability to freely choose in the election. However, it remains the Board's policy to order disestablishment where company unions or employee committees are dominated by an employer.[58]

When the Board prohibits an employer from giving effect to any contract with an unlawfully assisted union, the employer is not required to cease giving effect to the wages, benefits, and conditions provided under the agreement.[59] In *Keystone Shipping Co.*[60] the Board stated that "nothing in the remedial order shall require [the employer] to withdraw or eliminate any wage increases or other benefits, terms or conditions of employment which may have been established pursuant to any such [collective bargaining] agreement." When union dues or initiation fees have been collected pursuant to unlawful recognition of a union, the employer and union will be ordered to reimburse all unit employees for fees and moneys deducted from their pay, with interest.[61]

The Board continues to impose *Gissel* bargaining orders to remedy serious violations of Section 8(a)(2), but where the violations are not serious enough to warrant imposition of a bargaining order, the Board will direct the employer to cease and desist from unlawful assistance and order a new election. For example, in *Regal Recycling*,[62] the employer violated Section 8(a)(2) by denying access to its employees and facility to one labor organization but providing such access to another. The Board refused to impose a *Gissel* bargaining order because of the lengthy delay in processing the case at the Board. Rather, the Board ordered that (1) a second election be held in the event that the rival organization did not prevail in the first election, and (2) the employer, on request, provide to the rival organization the names and addresses of all current unit employees.

---

[58]Summa Health Sys., 330 NLRB No. 197 (2000); Addicts Rehabilitation Ctr. Fund, Inc., 330 NLRB No. 113 (2000); Naomi Knitting Plant, 328 NLRB No. 180 (1999); Polaroid Corp., 329 NLRB No. 47, 162 LRRM 1129, 1130 (1999). *See also* EFCO Corp., 327 NLRB No. 71, 160 LRRM 1049 (1999).

[59]Gulf Caribe Maritime, Inc., 330 NLRB No. 120 (2000); Keystone Shipping Co., 327 NLRB 892, 160 LRRM 1225 (1999).

[60]*Id.*

[61]*Id.*; Planned Bldg. Servs., Inc., 330 NLRB No. 116 (2000); Ryder Integrated Logistics, Inc., 329 NLRB No. 89 (1999).

[62]329 NLRB No. 38, 163 LRRM 1245 (1999).

Part III

THE REPRESENTATION PROCESS AND UNION RECOGNITION

CHAPTER 9

RESTRICTIONS ON PREELECTION ACTIVITY: "LABORATORY CONDITIONS"

I. Introduction

A. The Board's Authority Under Section 9

1. Relation to Unfair Labor Practices

In a consolidated unfair labor practice and representation case, the Board noted that the "traditional practice is to presume dissemination of at least the most serious threats, such as threats of plant closure, absent evidence to the contrary." Thus the

> presumption that a threat of plant closure by an employer to one or more employees will be widely disseminated among the employees is a rebuttable presumption. The employer may rebut the presumption by establishing through record evidence either that the employees threatened did not tell other employees about the threat, or that those employees whom they told did not in turn tell any other employees.[1]

A threat to terminate an employee for defacing the employer antiunion literature was found to warrant setting aside the election where the Board found that the threat was effectively disseminated among employees.[2]

B. Timing of "Laboratory Period"

The Board continues to hold that unfair labor practices or objectionable conduct occurring before the date of the petition cannot form the basis for setting aside an election, but that such conduct may be considered when it adds meaning and dimension to related postpetition conduct.[3]

In one case, the Board did not find the required relationship that would warrant considering pre-petition conduct in its analysis of conduct that might have affected election results.[4]

---

[1]Springs Indus., 332 NLRB No. 10 (2000).
[2]Waste Mgmt., Inc., 330 NLRB No. 96 (2000).
[3]VJNH, Inc., dba Vestal Nursing Ctr., 328 NLRB No. 16 n.34 (1999).
[4]National League of Professional Baseball Clubs, 330 NLRB No. 112 (2000).

Likewise the Board continues to hold that activity occurring after an election cannot form the basis for objectionable conduct to set aside an election.[5]

II. Grounds for Setting Aside Elections

A. Employer and/or Union Conduct

1. *Misrepresentations*

b. *Hollywood Ceramics* Overruled: Voters Allowed to Assess Misrepresentations

(2) *Return to* Shopping Kart: Hollywood Ceramics *Again Abandoned*

The Board continues to apply the *Midland National* rule,[6] holding that employees should be left the task of evaluating campaign propraganda by themselves and that the Board will not set aside elections based on campaign misrepresentations absent evidence of the use of forged documents.[7] The courts also continue to apply *Midland National*, refusing to set aside an election based on misrepresentations not involving forgery.[8] The Sixth Circuit, however, continues to apply a modified form of the *Midland National* rule, holding that an employee's free and fair choice will be affected where the misrepresentation is so persuasive and the deception so artful that employees will be unable to separate truth from untruth, even where no forgery can be proved.[9]

---

[5]Naomi Knitting Plant, 328 NLRB No. 180 (1999).

[6]Midland Nat'l Life Ins. Co., 263 NLRB 127, 110 LRRM 1489 (1982).

[7]*Professional Baseball Clubs, supra* note 4 (overruling objections to election based on misrepresentations that were addressed and debated during election and did not involve use of forged documents).

[8]NLRB v. Queensboro Steel Corp., 2000 U.S. App. LEXIS 21590 (4th Cir. 2000).

[9]NLRB v. St. Francis Health Care Ctr., 212 F.3d 945, 964, 164 LRRM 2324 (6th Cir. 2000) (applying five-factor test, including (1) timing of misrepresentation; (2) whether employer had opportunity to respond; (3) nature and extent of misrepresentation; (4) whether source of misrepresentation was identified; and (5) whether there is evidence that employees were affected by misrepresentation); NLRB v. Gormac Custom Mfg., 190 F.3d 742, 162 LRRM 2156 (6th Cir. 1999) (Board erred in refusing to have evidentiary hearing on whether the union unlawfully misrepresented extent of support among employees by distributing handbill 2 to 3 hours before election that listed names and purported signatures of 31 of 45 eligible voters allegedly supporting union, where at least three of the employees whose signatures appeared on handbill did not support union); Maremont Corp. v. NLRB,

3. *Misuse of the Board's Election Process*

c. **Electioneering at the Polls**

In *S.F.D.H. Associates*[10] the union's observer spoke to five or six (of approximately 100) voters in the polling area during the election. Each conversation was brief, lasting a few seconds to a minute, and the content of the conversations was innocuous. The Board determined that these "brief remarks to a few voters could not have affected the results of the election and are not sufficient grounds for setting it aside."[11]

In a subsequent decision, the Board determined that a union observer's outbursts against the employer in close proximity to the doorway to the hallway where approximately 20 employees were waiting to vote did not reasonably tend to interfere with those employees' free choice. Accordingly, the Board refused to set aside the results of the election.[12]

In another decision, the Board determined that a union observer's actions did constitute improper electioneering and therefore set aside the election results.[13] The union's observer told four separate employees, as they approached the observer table, to vote for the union. The persons standing in line repeated this message to other employees waiting to vote. The union observer also gave the "thumbs up" signal to other employees as they approached the table.

The Board has expanded its previously stated prohibition against an employer using a supervisor as its election observer.[14] The Board

---

177 F.3d 573, 161 LRRM 2338 (6th Cir. 1999) (upholding Board's conclusion that union's "vote yes" handbill containing signatures of 446 of 664 eligible voters did not constitute grounds for setting aside representation hearing); NLRB v. Dave Transp. Servs. Inc., 176 F.3d 484 (9th Cir. 1999) (reiterating the Ninth and a majority of Circuit's adoption of the *Midland National* standard, and recognizing that the Sixth and First Circuits have established exceptions to that standard even absent forgery of Board documents).

[10]330 NLRB No. 98, 163 LRRM 1173 (2000).

[11]*Id.*

[12]Midway Hosp. Medical Ctr., Inc., 330 NLRB No. 199, 164 LRRM 1090 (2000); ITT Automotive v. NLRB, 188 F.3d 375, 161 LRRM 3132 (6th Cir. 1999) (employer coerced employees by positioning supervisors in aisle through which employees had to pass to vote).

[13]Brinks Inc., 331 NLRB No. 10, 164 LRRM 1140 (2000).

[14]Family Serv. Agency, San Francisco, 331 NLRB No. 103, 164 LRRM 1305 (2000).

created a new general rule prohibiting any party, employer, or union, from using a supervisor as its election observer.[15]

d. Other Conduct In and Around the Polls

The Board continues to hold that keeping a list of employees who have voted (aside from the official eligibility list used to check off voters as they receive their ballots) is objectionable conduct that interferes with an election.[16] The Board upheld an employer's objection to an election where the union observer kept a list of those whom he thought were voting "yes" and "no" during the election. Some employee voters saw the observer keeping the list of names. The Board found that because the employee voters witnessed the union observer keeping a list, the voters reasonably could have concluded that the observer was keeping track of how people voted.[17]

The Board continues to hold that observers may not keep lists of those who have voted. In *Elizabethtown Gas Co.*[18] the Fourth Circuit found no merit to employer objection that its observer kept a piece of paper on his lap during the voting.[19] The Board agent instructed the observers not to keep any lists of those who had voted. At the instruction of the employer's lawyer, the employer's observer kept a duplicate list of the names of all of the voters and checked off the names of those who had actually voted. The employer's observer kept the list on his lap after the Board agent noticed that he was holding a piece of paper and instructed him to place any paper or list other than the official voter eligibility list on his lap. There was no evidence that any voters saw the list kept by the employer's observer. The employer lost the election but contended that the election should overturned because its observer was allowed to keep a list of voters on his lap. The court enforced the Board's decision to certify the election. The court agreed that the employer should not be permitted to overturn an election based on its own misconduct. In addition, because there was no evidence that any voter noticed

---

[15]*Id.* The Board found that the union's use of a statutory supervisor as its observer in the election constituted objectionable conduct and ordered a new election be conducted.

[16]Cross Pointe Paper Corp., 330 NLRB No. 101 (2000).

[17]*Id.*

[18]212 F.3d 257, 164 LRRM 2257 (4th Cir. 2000).

[19]*Id.*

the employer's observer's recording of their vote, there was no basis to conclude that maintaining the list affected any voter.[20]

4. Appeals to Racial Prejudice

In two recent cases, the federal courts enforced Board decisions, finding that appeals to racial prejudice during the preelection period do not constitute grounds for setting aside a representation election.[21] These cases were decided on the specific factual situations involved and have not changed the underlying principles set forth by the Board in *Sewell Manufacturing Co.*,[22] which govern such comments.

5. The 24-Hour Rule Barring Speeches to Massed Employees

The Board's *Peerless Plywood*[23] rule prohibits election speeches to mass assemblies of employees in the 24-hour period before an election. Although both employees and unions are restricted by the 24-hour rule, the vast majority of *Peerless* cases involve allegations of employer-sponsored captive-audience speeches. For example, in *Montgomery Ward*, the Board held that a question-and-answer session, organized by the employer less than 24 hours before an election, unlawfully interfered with the election.[24] The rule does not limit the

---

[20]*Id.* at 266–67, 164 LRRM at 263–64.

[21]Family Serv. Agency of San Francisco v. NLRB, 163 F.3d 1369, 160 LRRM 2288 (D.C. Cir. 1999) (union did not use appeals to racial prejudice to interfere with vote, even assuming union was responsible for turmoil between African American and Latina employees over alleged existence of rule prohibiting employees from speaking Spanish at work—union statements were reasonably accurate description of facts and were not calculated to spark racial prejudice); NLRB v. Flambeau Airmold Corp., 178 F.3d 705, 161 LRRM 2385 (4th Cir. 1999) (representation election union won by two votes was not rendered invalid by racially inflammatory rumor, spread day before the election, that white managers had used racial slurs because neither employer nor union was responsible for starting rumor—and rumor did not so inflame and taint atmosphere as to make reasoned choice impossible).

[22]138 NLRB 66, 50 LRRM 1532 (1962).

[23]Peerless Plywood Co., 107 NLRB 427, 33 LRRM 1151 (1953). *But see* Nebraska Consol. Mill, 165 NLRB 639, 65 LRRM 1361 (1969) (assemblies at which attendance is purely voluntary and on employees' own time do not violate *Peerless* restriction).

[24]Montgomery Ward & Co., 124 NLRB 343, 44 LRRM 1375 (1959); *but see* Adel Jewelry Corp., 326 NLRB 53, 159 LRRM 1295 (1998) (employer's handing out campaign leaflets and answering unsolicited questions posed by employees did not violate *Peerless* doctrine).

distribution of campaign materials[25] or restrict every conversation between a supervisor and a small group of employees.[26] Rather, it is designed to ensure sober and thoughtful choice and to avoid "mass psychology" that would give an unfair advantage to the party that uses the captive audience to obtain "the last most telling word."[27] The Board has applied *Peerless* to the use of sound trucks to communicate with employees during shift changes or to broadcast union songs,[28] and has found a breach of the rule where the union used a sound truck to communicate with employees while they were at work.[29]

a. Mail Ballots

In mail-ballot elections, the time restriction on massed assemblies begins with the date of the mailing of the ballots by the regional director. To avoid unwitting violation of the *Peerless* doctrine, the Board requires that the parties be given notice of the date ballots will be mailed.[30]

b. Paychecks

The Board applied the 24-hour rule to prohibit any changes in the normal paycheck process during this period.[31] The Board held that the *Peerless* rule prohibits employers from altering the paycheck or the timing, the method, or location of paycheck distribution within 24 hours before an election. The Board views a paycheck as "a singular document" that cannot be equated to an ordinary piece of campaign literature, and is therefore exempt from the *Peerless* rule.

---

[25]General Elec. Co., 161 NLRB 618, 63 LRRM 1289 (1966).

[26]Electro Wire Prods., 242 NLRB 960, 101 LRRM 1271 (1979); Associated Milk Producers, 237 NLRB 879, 99 LRRM 1212 (1978); Business Aviation, 202 NLRB 1025, 82 LRRM 1710 (1973) (solicitation by union business agent at employer premises).

[27]*Peerless Plywood, supra* note 23; 162 LRRM 1399; *see also* Great Atl. & Pac. Tea Co., 111 NLRB 623 (1955) (employer's speeches to 80 out of 6,300 eligible voters violated *Peerless* doctrine).

[28]Bro-Tech Corp., 330 NLRB No. 7 (1999) (union songs); Crown Paper Bd. Co., 158 NLRB 440, 62 LRRM 1041 (1966) (appeals to vote during shift changes).

[29]United States Gypsum Co., 115 NLRB 734, 37 LRRM 1374 (1956) (7 hours of speeches).

[30]Red Cross Blood Servs., 322 NLRB 401 (1996) (notice contained election stipulation); Oregon Wash. Tel. Co., 123 NLRB 339, 43 LRRM 1430 (1959).

[31]Kalin Constr. Co., 321 NLRB 649, 152 LRRM 1226 (1996).

B. Employer Conduct

3. Voter Eligibility List

The Board continues to apply its *Excelsior* rule requiring that the employer provide a list of the full names and addresses of the unit employees. Failure to comply with the rule is grounds for setting aside the election and the Board will do so where the union is "prevented from making full use of the *Excelsior* list because of its delayed receipt," even though the delay was not caused by the employer.[32] Where the list is incomplete or inaccurate, the Board will determine whether the employer has substantially complied with *Excelsior* by examining (1) the number of names omitted in relation to the overall electorate, (2) whether the number of names omitted involves a determinative number of voters, and (3) the employer's reasons for omitting the names.[33]

5. Raffles [New Topic]

The Board has announced a "bright line" right that bans any employer-sponsored (or union-sponsored) raffle conducted within 24 hours of the polling period of a representation election. In previous cases, the Board conducted a case-by-case analysis to determine if a specific raffle interfered with a representation election given the specific circumstances involved in the case and developed a multifactor test that examined issues such as whether the raffle was used to propagandize about union dues, whether the raffle occurred in conjunction with any electioneering at or near the polls, whether the raffle or prize was contingent on how an employee voted or on the outcome of the election, and whether the value of the prize was so substantial as to induce a vote in favor of the sponsoring party.[34] This analysis, however, led to inconsistency in the Board's raffle decisions.

Recognizing these inconsistencies, the "confusing" nature of the varying cases, and that the "elaborate exercise in line drawing" performed in the Board's previous raffle cases in an effort to separate objectionable raffles from unobjectionable ones created time-con-

---

[32]Special Citizens Futures Unlimited, 331 NLRB No. 19 (2000).

[33]Woodman's Food Market, Inc., 332 NLRB No. 48 (2000); *see also* Merchants Transfer Co., 330 NLRB No. 165 (2000).

[34]Hollywood Plastics, Inc., 177 NLRB 678, 71 LRRM 1397 (1969), Buzza-Cardozo, 177 NLRB 578, 71 LRRM 1390 (1969), Sony Corp. of Am., 313 NLRB 420, 145 LRRM 1242 (1993).

suming litigation, divided Board decisions, confusing and inconsistent results, and unwarranted delays in completion of representation proceedings, the Board overruled its previous line of election-day raffle cases and announced a bright-line test for determining whether a raffle during an election period is objectionable conduct.[35] The Board held that raffles will now be prohibited if "(1) eligibility to participate in the raffle or win prizes is in any way tied to voting in the election or being at the election site on election day or (2) the raffle is conducted at any time during a period beginning 24 hours before the scheduled opening of the polls and ending with the closing of the polls." "Conducting a raffle" was defined by the Board to include "(1) announcing a raffle; (2) distributing raffle tickets; (3) identifying the raffle winners; and (4) awarding the raffle prizes."[36] If a raffle is shown to have been conducted during the proscribed period, the election will be set aside.

6. Videotaping [New Topic]

The Board also clarified its position regarding employer request for employees to appear in election campaign video materials. In *Allegheny Ludlum*,[37] a case on remand from the D.C. Circuit, the Board held that an employer, unlike unions, cannot lawfully solicit employees to appear in campaign video presentations, because such requests would unlawfully pressure employees to make an observable choice for or against union representation. An employer may lawfully solicit employees to appear in a campaign video, according to the Board, if (1) solicitation is in the form of a general announcement that discloses the purpose of the filming, (2) assurances are given that participation is voluntary, (3) participation will not result in rewards and benefits, (4) nonparticipation will not result in reprisals, (5) employees are not pressured into making a decision in the presence of a supervisor, (6) the employer has not engaged in serious or pervasive unfair labor practice concerned with the organizing campaign, and (7) the employer's solicitation of consent does not exceed legitimate video participation purposes.

The Board concluded by clarifying its holding in *Sony Corp. of America*,[38] that an employer does not have to have employees' explicit consent before including their images when (1) the video in

---

[35]Atlantic Limousine, Inc., 331 NLRB No. 134, 165 LRRM 1001 (2000).

[36]*Id.*, 165 LRRM 1006.

[37]320 NLRB 484, 152 LRRM 1142 (1995).

[38]313 NLRB 420, 145 LRRM 1242 (1993).

question does not represent employee views regarding union representation, (2) employees were not misled about the uses of their images at the time of filming, (3) the video contains a predominant disclaimer stating that it is not intended to reflect the views of the employees appearing in it, and (4) nothing in the video contradicts this disclaimer.

C. Union Conduct

2. Specific Promises and Grants of Benefits

The Board and the courts continue to disagree in those situations where the union actually grants benefits. In *Comcast Cablevision—Taylor v. NLRB*[39] the Sixth Circuit refused to enforce the Board's bargaining order where the union made a pre-election offer to employees of a free weekend trip to Chicago for a meeting with union officials. The court deemed the trip, consisting of transportation and one night's lodging, together with the union meeting, sufficiently valuable to influence voters. A similar result was reached by the D.C. Circuit in *Freund Baking Co v. NLRB*.[40] In that case, the court held that a union's sponsorship of a lawsuit against an employer on behalf of eligible voters seeking recovery of alleged unpaid overtime violated the Board's rule against providing benefits to voters in the critical period before a representation election.

In *Maremount Corp. v. NLRB*,[41] however, the Sixth Circuit enforced the Board's bargaining order, holding that the union did not unlawfully influence employees to sign a "vote yes" petition by giving out t-shirts. The court relied on the testimony of the employees that they were not obligated to sign the petitions to receive the t-shirts. In addition, the court followed its earlier precedent that a union may distribute inexpensive campaign propaganda, such as t-shirts, at a union meeting.

3. Waiver of Initiation Fees

In assessing whether a promise by a union during an election campaign to either waive or reduce its initiation fees or dues is permissible under *NLRB v. Savair Manufacturing Co.*,[42] the crucial dis-

---

[39]232 F.3d 490, 165 LRRM 2803 (6th Cir. 2000).
[40]165 F.3d 928, 160 LRRM 2299 (D.C. Cir. 1999).
[41]177 F.3d 573, 161 LRRM 2338 (6th Cir. 1999).
[42]414 U.S. 270, 84 LRRM 2929 (1973).

tinction continues to be whether the waiver offer was made across the board to all employees regardless of pre-election union support, a permissible promise, or whether the waiver offer was made only to those employees who manifested preelection union support or who voted for the union, an impermissible promise. Thus, an across-the-board waiver offer to all employees is not permissible when the offer is conditioned on all employees signing authorization cards before a certain date.[43]

The Eighth Circuit held that were an impermissible promise is later corrected by a permissible one, a substantial material issue of fact is raised, necessitating a hearing.[44] The court found that the Board erred in certifying the union after only conducting interviews with several employees and concluding that even if the first impermissible statement was made by the union's organizer, it was effectively corrected before the election. Raising the possibility that not all employees who heard the improper offer were present to hear the clarification, the court found that the employer's evidence raised factual issues that required the Board to hold a hearing.

4. Other Union Conduct

a. Interrogation

Courts continue to recognize that unions may lawfully poll eligible voters regarding their union sympathies, despite the fact that employer polls are generally unlawful.[45] However, an employer may successfully challenge such polling if the employer can demonstrate that the union's polling activities were, in fact, coercive.[46] One court, however, has held that the Board must conduct an evidentiary hearing to determine the propriety of union polling activities where prima facie evidence of coercion is presented.[47]

---

[43]Gulf Caribe Maritime, Inc., 330 NLRB No. 120 (2000).

[44]NLRB v. Superior of Mo., Inc., 233 F.3d 547, 165 LRRM 2785 (8th Cir. 2000).

[45]Keeler Die Cast v. NLRB, 185 F.3d 535, 162 LRRM 2028 (1999), *cert. denied*, 529 U.S. 1018 (2000) (pre-election polling by union not inherently coercive); Maremont Corp. v. NLRB, 177 F.3d 573, 161 LRRM 2338 (6th Cir. 1999) (union's circulation of "vote yes" petition during pre-election period not per se objectionable conduct).

[46]NLRB v. Gormac Custom Mfg., Inc., 190 F.3d 742, 162 LRRM 2156 (6th Cir. 1999); *Keeler Die Cast, supra* note 45, 185 F.3d at 539.

[47]*Gormac, supra* note 46, 190 F.3d at 750–751.

c. Videotaping [New Topic]

Photographing or videotaping of employees by unions during the preelection period generally will not constitute grounds for setting aside the results of a representation election. The Board overruled its decision in *Pepsi Cola Bottling Co.*[48] and held that a union's photographing or videotaping of employees engaging in protected election campaign activities, on its own, does not interfere with employee free choice.[49]

D. Third-Party Conduct

The Board continues to hold that ordinary pro-union employees are judged under a third-party standard.[50] In a case involving an election in a U.S. territory,[51] the D.C. Circuit held that newspaper reports about legislation seeking to curtail the rights of nonresidents to remain did not create an atmosphere of fear, although 77 percent of the employees involved in the election were nonresidents. The court held that the reports were not coercive because they eventually identified that the legislation would affect all nonresidents alike rather than disadvantage union nonresidents in particular, and the report did not tie the passage of the legislation to the outcome of the election.[52]

The Board held that a rumor concerning an ethnic slur did not create an atmosphere of fear or confusion, even though the rumor was repeated by employees several times.[53]

E. Violence and Threats

An employee's free and uncoerced choice in an election may be interfered with by actions that create an impression that an employer is not in control of its own facilities and that it is not capable of standing up to the union. Following the rationale of the Board in *Phillips Chrysler Plymouth, Inc.*,[54] the D.C. Circuit refused to validate

---

[48]289 NLRB 736, 128 LRRM 1275 (1988).
[49]Randell Warehouse of Ariz., Inc., 328 NLRB No. 153, 161 LRRM 1265 (1999).
[50]Cal West Periodicals, 330 NLRB No. 87, 163 LRR 1155 (2000).
[51]Pacific Micronesia Corp. v. NLRB, 219 F.3d 661, 164 LRRM 2720 (D.C. Cir. 2000).
[52]*See also* Associated Rubber Co., 332 NLRB No. 165 (2000).
[53]Cross Pointe Paper Corp., 330 NLRB No. 101 (2000).
[54]304 NLRB 16, 138 LRRM 1025 (1991).

an election where there was a direct challenge by the union on the day of the election of the employer's assertion of its property rights, resulting in an impression that it was helpless to control the situation.[55] The union officials walked around the facility and into patient examination rooms without the employer's permission, and repeatedly disagreed with the employer's executive director as to when employees were entitled to vote. The court held that this behavior had the purported imprimatur of the Board because the Board agent conducting the election had delegated to union officials the task of telling employees when to vote.[56] As a result, the court remanded the case to the Board to, at a minimum, conduct a hearing on the employer's objections.

The Board in *Cal-West Periodicals, Inc.*[57] further distinguished between pre-election threats by a party to engage in violence and such threats by employees who are not agents of either party, finding that "employees reasonably have a greater concern about threats emanating from the union that may become their exclusive representative than they would have from threats uttered by a single nonagent individual." The Board refused to set aside the election.

The Seventh Circuit held that "pushy lobbying" by an employee who later appeared at the election as a union observer did not constitute intimidation in *NLRB v. Americold Logistics.*[58]

III. REMEDIES

The Board in *Baker Victory Services, Inc.*[59] changed the standard to be used for determining whether an election should be set aside because of severe weather conditions on the day of the election. The issue is whether the conditions "reasonably denied eligible voters an adequate opportunity to vote and a determinative number did not vote." The Board's decision abandoned the test used by the plurality in *Glass Depot, Inc.*,[60] namely whether a "representative complement"

---

[55]North of Market Senior Servs. Inc. v. NLRB, 204 F.3d 1163, 163 LRRM 2711 (D.C. Cir. 2000).

[56]*Phillips Chrysler Plymouth, supra* note 54.

[57]330 NLRB No. 87, 163 LRRM 1155 (2000).

[58]214 F.3d 935, 164 LRRM 2636 (7th Cir. 2000).

[59]331 NLRB No. 146, 165 LRRM 1057 (2000).

[60]318 NLRB 766, 150 LRRM 1055 (1995).

of employees voted, and adopted the position taken by the dissent in *Glass Depot* and by the Board's decision in *V.I.P. Limousine, Inc.*[61]

A party to an election is generally estopped from profiting from its own misconduct.[62]

---

[61]274 NLRB 641, 118 LRRM 1399 (1985).
[62]*See* Elizabethtown Gas v. NLRB, 212 F.3d 257, 164 LRRM 2257 (4th Cir. 2000).

Chapter 10

REPRESENTATION PROCEEDINGS AND ELECTIONS

I. QUESTIONS CONCERNING REPRESENTATION

A. Petitions by Labor Organizations and Employees

1. *Showing of Interest*

It is the Board's established policy not to require a current showing of interest when an election is set aside because of a meritorious objection. In *Freund Baking Co.*[1] the Board rejected the argument that the showing of interest was stale when it ordered a second election.

When the unit found appropriate differs from that of the petitioned for unit, the union is to be given reasonable time to procure additional showing of interest.[2]

In *Perdue Farms*[3] the Board restated its policy that evidence that a showing of interest was obtained by fraud or duress should be submitted to the regional director.

The Board has indicated that fraud or duress in obtaining the showing of interest may also be considered as objectionable conduct.[4]

---

[1]330 NLRB No. 13 (2000).

[2]Alamo Rent-A-Car, 330 NLRB No. 147 (2000). *See also* Brown Transp. Corp., 296 NLRB 1213, 133 LRRM 1170 (1989); Casale Indus., 311 NLRB 951, 143 LRRM 1291 (1993); and CHM section 11031.2.

[3]328 NLRB No. 130 (1999).

[4]St. Peter More v. NLRB, 327 NLRB No. 152 (1999). *See also* Millsboro Nursing & Rehabilitation Ctr., Inc., 327 NLRB No. 153, 160 LRRM 1209 (1999).

B. Petitions by Employers

2. History Under the Taft-Hartley Act

a. Unrecognized Unions

The Board holds that a mere request for a Section 8(f) agreement does not amount to a present demand for recognition. In *Western Pipeline, Inc.*[5] the Board further concluded that an unsubstantiated claim that the employer was an alter ego of the signatory contractor and obligated to sign the contract was nothing more than a request to sign a Section 8(f) agreement and therefore did not raise a QCR.

Informational picketing under the second proviso to Section 8(b)(7)(c) that truthfully advises the public that an employee does not have a contract with the union is not a claim for recognition within the meaning of Section 9(c)(1)(B).[6]

b. Incumbent Unions

In *Raven Government Services*[7] the Board found that an employer fails to meet the *Allentown Mack*[8] test when it commits and fails to remedy serious unfair labor practices and bases its withdrawal of recognition on a hearsay report of a decertification petition and the alleged inactivity of the union.

3. Disclaimer of Interest

A regional director has the discretion to allow a petitioner to withdraw its petition while objections are pending when the petitioner agrees, in writing, that it will not seek a new election within 1 year after the last election, even when the employer objects to the withdrawal.[9]

---

[5]328 NLRB No. 138 (1999).
[6]New Otani Hotel, 331 NLRB No. 159 (2000).
[7]331 NLRB No. 84 (2000).
[8]Allentown Mack Sales & Serv., 316 NLRB 1199, 149 LRRM 1051 (1995), *enforced*, 83 F.3d 1483, 152 LRRM 2257 (D.C. Cir. 1996), *rev'd and remanded*, 522 U.S. 359 (1998).
[9]Baltimore Gas & Elec. Co., 330 NLRB No. 9 (2000).

II. TIMELINESS OF PETITIONS

A. The One-Election-per-Year Rule

2. The Certification Year

An employer cannot withdraw recognition from a union after the expiration of the certification year on the basis of an antiunion petition circulated and presented to the employer during the certification year. The Board expressly affirmed its holding in *United Supermarkets*[10] and overruled its holding in *Rock-Tenn Co.*,[11] to the extent that it "suggests that, based on evidence received during the certification year, an employee may announce that it intends to withdraw recognition from the union at the end of the certification year."[12]

B. Pendency of Unfair Labor Practice Charges

The Board continues to hold that petitions filed during the posting period of a settlement agreement will be dismissed.[13]

E. Contract-Bar Doctrine

The Board continues to follow its *Briggs Indiana* rule[14] that a union will be barred from seeking representation of employees if it has agreed with the employer not to seek during the life of the agreement. In *Lexington House*,[15] the Board held that such an agreement does not have to be part of the collective-bargaining agreement.

1. Requisites of the Contract

The absence of an execution date in a contract does not remove it as a bar if the date of execution was before the petition and that date can be established.[16]

3. Unlawful Clauses

The Board holds that a finding of unlawful contract limitation on employee free choice, which is sufficient to remove the contract's

---

[10]287 NLRB 119, 127 LRRM 1210, *enforced,* 862 F.2d 549 (5th Cir. 1989).
[11]315 NLRB 670 (1994).
[12]Chelsea Indus., 331 NLRB No. 184 (2000).
[13]Hertz Equip. Rental Corp., 328 NLRB No. 5 (1999).
[14]63 NLRB 1770 (1945).
[15]329 NLRB No. 124 (1999).
[16]Cooper Tank & Welding Corp., 328 NLRB No. 97 (1999).

bar status, must be made solely from the face of the contract and not with the use of extrinsic evidence.[17]

A union-security clause was not illegal on its face and therefore did not lose its bar status. In finding that the clause was not illegal on its face the Board noted that the clause did not require payment of "assessment." It also noted that an alleged denial of the 30-day grace period did not appear on the face of the agreement nor was the contract effective retroactively so as to preclude a 30-day grace period.[18]

The negotiation of a contract intended to resolve outstanding unfair labor practice charges operates as a bar to a petition by a rival union, where there was no evidence that the underlying charges were frivolous.[19]

F. Clarification of Units

Explicitly reaffirming the relitigation rule it implicitly established in *I.O.O.F. Home of Ohio,*[20] the Board panel dismissed an employer's unit clarification petition and held that the employer was estopped from challenging the nonsupervisory status of certain employees following its voluntary stipulation to include them in the bargaining unit and its failure to reserve the issue for postelection determination.[21]

III. Election Procedures

A. Preelection Matters

2. Details of the Election

c. Place

The decision to conduct an election on or off the employer's premises or by mail or manual ballot is within the discretion of the regional director.[22]

---

[17]Four Seasons Solar Prods. Corp., 332 NLRB No. 9 (2000).

[18]*Id.*

[19]Supershuttle of Orange County, Inc., 330 NLRB No. 138, 163 LRRM 1275 (2001).

[20]322 NLRB 921, 154 LRRM 1122 (1997).

[21]Premier Living Center, 331 NLRB No. 9, 164 LRRM 1296 (2000).

[22]San Diego Gas & Elec., 325 NLRB No. 218 (1998).

3. Voter List and Eligibility

a. The *Excelsior* List of Eligible Voters' Names and Addresses

An analysis that focuses solely on the percentage of omissions from the *Excelsior* list relative to the number of employees in the unit fails to effectuate the purposes of the *Excelsior* rule. The Board, reexamining the substantial compliance analysis, held that although it will continue to consider the percentage of names omitted, it also will consider whether the number of omissions is determinative in the election as well as the employer's reasons for the omissions.[23]

b. Eligibility

Bargaining-unit employees who have been selected for a promotion to management that is not effective until after the election still share a community of interest with the bargaining-unit employees and are eligible to vote.[24]

B. The Election Proper

1. Observers

The Board announced a new rule prohibiting both employers and unions from using statutory supervisors as observers, finding that such use by either party calls into question the integrity of the election process.[25]

The Board set aside an election where a Board agent allowed the voting to proceed with two employer observers present but no union observers, despite a stipulated election agreement providing for an equal number of observers from both sides.[26]

2. Balloting

c. Mail Ballots

It is not an abuse of a regional director's discretion to refuse to allow an employee who will be on vacation to vote by absentee ballot.[27]

---

[23]Woodman's Food Mkts., 332 NLRB No. 48 (2000).
[24]Nichols House Nursing Home, 332 NLRB No. 157 (2000).
[25]Family Serv. Agency, 331 NLRB No. 103, 164 LRRM 1305 (2000).
[26]Browning-Ferris Indus., 327 NLRB No. 130, 160 LRRM 1145 (1999).
[27]NLRB v. Cedar Tree Press, 169 F.3d 794, 160 LRRM 2685 (3d Cir. 1999).

C. Standards for the Conduct of Elections

1. The Opportunity to Vote

An election will be set aside where severe weather conditions on election day reasonably denied an adequate opportunity to vote and a determinative number of eligible voters did not vote.[28]

2. Conduct In and Around the Polling Areas

The Board continues to hold that elections should be held in an atmosphere free from improper influence. Following this principle, it determined that a union's use of a sound truck, which broadcasted pro-union music that could be heard by anyone entering the employer's premises all day on election day, interfered with the election and violated the *Peerless Plywood* rule.[29]

The Board has also adopted a new bright-line rule prohibiting election-day raffles.[30] Reversing its earlier case-by-case analysis, the Board determined that raffles are unlawful if (1) eligibility to win is tied to voting in the election or presence at the election site on election day, or (2) they are conducted during the time that the polls are open or in the 24-hour period before the beginning of the election.[31]

3. The Integrity of the Ballots and the Ballot Box

The Board continues to hold that it will uphold challenges to the integrity of the election process only where the facts "raise a 'reasonable doubt as to the fairness and validity of the election.'"[32] Applying this standard, the Board declined to set aside an election where the Board agent took a break during the election and left the ballot box in the voting room "under the watchful eyes" of both election observers.[33]

---

[28]Baker Victory Servs., 331 NLRB No. 146, 165 LRRM 1057 (2000) (rejecting "representative component" test of *Glass Depot, Inc.*, 318 NLRB 766, 150 LRRM 1055 (1995)).

[29]Bro-Tech Corp., 330 NLRB No. 7, 162 LRRM 1399 (1999).

[30]Atlantic Limousine, Inc., 331 NLRB No. 134, 165 LRRM 1001 (2000).

[31]*Id. See also* Beverly Enterprises-Tennessee, Inc., 331 NLRB No. 144, 165 LRRM 1370 (2000) (applying the new rule).

[32]Sawyer Lumber Co., 326 NLRB No. 137, 160 LRRM 1140 (1998).

[33]*Id. See also* Elizabethtown Gas Co. v. NLRB, 212 F.3d 257, 164 LRRM 2257 (4th Cir. 2000) (upholding Board decision that election need not be set aside where Board agent required employees to vote with eraserless pencils, Board agent briefly left ballot box unattended except for election observers, and Board agent

4. Conduct of Board Agents

In *NLRB v. Superior of Missouri, Inc.*[34] the Eighth Circuit denied enforcement of a Board decision involving a Board agent who overslept on the day of the election. In *Superior of Missouri*, an election had been scheduled at the employer's facility beginning at 6:00 a.m. The Board agent assigned to oversee the election overslept and did not arrive at the time the polls were scheduled to open. The employer kept its voters, who were truck drivers, at the facility until 6:45 a.m., when, having heard nothing from the Board agent, the employer released them to begin their routes. The Board unilaterally rescheduled the election for the following week, and the Board agent delivered new election notices that did not explain why he had failed to appear the previous week.[35]

Before the rescheduled election, the employer distributed a letter apologizing to employees for any inconvenience, stated that the employer was not at fault, and urged the employees to vote in the rescheduled election. The employees were never told why the Board agent had failed to show up for the first election. The employer filed objections to the conduct of the election based on sworn affidavits submitted by bargaining unit and nonbargaining unit employees that stated that the employees were upset and blamed the employer when they could not start work on time because the Board agent failed to appear for the original election. The sworn affidavits also recounted a rumor that spread among the employees that the employer had paid off the Board so that the Board would not show up to hold the election. The objections were overruled without an evidentiary hearing. The Eighth Circuit denied enforcement of the Board's order, holding that the employer was entitled to a hearing on its objections because it had made a prima facie showing of objectionable conduct that may have affected the outcome of the election.[36]

---

allowed observers to take unescorted breaks, because acts did not raise a reasonable doubt about the fairness or validity of the election). *See also* Sir Francis Drake Hotel, 330 NLRB No. 98, 163 LRRM 1173 (2000) (Board denied employer's objection where union observer ignored Board agent's instructions and spoke to 5 or 6 of the approximately 100 voters in polling area—conversations were brief and lasted from few seconds to 1 minute, and evidence established that conversations were innocuous and in no way suggested to voters that it was union rather than Board that was conducting election).

[34]233 F.3d 547, 165 LRRM 2785 (8th Cir. 2000).
[35]*Id.* at 550, 165 LRRM at 2786.
[36]*Id.* at 551–52, 165 LRRM at 2787–88.

Board agents cannot delegate official election tasks to observers, where doing so would compromise the integrity of the election.[37] Applying this rule, the D.C. Circuit held that an employer presented a prima facie case that the integrity of an election was impugned where union agents were allowed to walk through the plant, in union regalia, announcing that the Board had sent them to tell employees when they could vote.[38]

Like Board agents, Board interpreters must not influence employees' wishes.[39] Thus, the Board set aside an election where an interpreter asked employees, "Do you know where to put your yes vote?"[40]

D. Resolution of Challenges and Objections to the Election

3. Resolution of Challenges and Objections

Parties may request subpoenas from the regional director or the hearing officer.[41] On proper motion, subpoenas may be revoked.[42] Parties are not entitled to subpoenas that result in mere fishing expeditions.[43] For purposes of subpoena-enforcement proceedings, the Board has held that parties need not prove that a subpoena was actually received.[44] Instead, an attorney's affirmation of service of a subpoena by mail "was sufficient to establish service of the subpoena."[45]

Parties seeking the testimony of a Board agent in a representation hearing must request general counsel approval.[46] Absent "unusual circumstances," Board employees are typically not involved as witnesses in Board litigation.[47]

---

[37]North of Market Senior Servs. v. NLRB, 204 F.3d 1163, 163 LRRM 2711 (D.C. Cir. 2000).

[38]*Id.*

[39]Renco Elecs. Inc., 330 NLRB No. 52, 163 LRRM 1053 (1999).

[40]*Id.*

[41]Rules & Regs. §102.66(c).

[42]*Id.*

[43]Millsboro Nursing & Rehabilitation Ctr., 327 NLRB No. 153 n.2, 160 LRRM 1209 (1999).

[44]Best Western City View Motor Inn, 327 NLRB 468, 160 LRRM 1221 (1999).

[45]*Id.* at 469.

[46]Rules & Regs. §102.118.

[47]*See Millsboro, supra* note 43, 327 NLRB No. 153 at n.2, and cases cited therein for discussion of the policy reasons behind such decisions. *See also* Brinks, Inc., 331 NLRB No. 10 n.2, 164 LRRM 1040 (2000) (concluding that regional director did not abuse his discretion in denying request for Board agent testimony where both parties presented witnesses and matter was fully litigated without agent's testimony).

E. Runoff and Rerun Elections

Rerun elections are not new elections; they are subsequent phases of the first election.[48] Accordingly, the Board has held that unions that were not on the ballot in the original election cannot intervene and appear on the ballot in a rerun election.[49]

---

[48]W.M. of New York, 326 NLRB 1126, 161 LRRM 1064 (1998).
[49]*Id.*

APPROPRIATE BARGAINING UNITS

I. Background

In *Allen Health Care Services*[1] the Board held that it has an affirmative, statutory obligation to determine the appropriate unit and cannot simply close a hearing because there was no employer position presented on the appropriateness of the unit. Because the unit in *Allen* was not presumptively appropriate, the case was remanded to the regional director for hearing.

In *Overnite Transportation Co.*[2] the Board ordered an election in the smallest appropriate unit containing the employees sought by the petition and rejected the employer's request for a wall-to-wall unit.

II. General Factors in Unit Determinations

A. Community of Interest Among Employees

The Board has rejected the argument that it has a special per se rule for unit determinations in the research-and-development industry. Instead, it used a community-of-interest standard for deciding the unit in that industry.[3]

D. Bargaining History

In *Red Coats, Inc.*[4] the Board decided unit issues based in part on bargaining history.

A long history of collective bargaining for two facilities in a single contract has been deemed insufficient to rebut the presumption of the appropriateness of a single-facility unit.[5]

E. Employer's Organizational Structure

The presence of centralized administration and control of some labor relations policies and procedures is not inconsistent with a finding that there exists sufficient local autonomy to support a single-location presumption.[6]

---

[1]332 NLRB No. 134 (2000).
[2]331 NLRB No. 85 (2000).
[3]The Aerospace Corp., 331 NLRB No. 74 (2000).
[4]328 NLRB No. 28, 161 LRRM 1100 (1999).
[5]U.S. Tsbaki, Inc., 331 NLRB No. 47 (2000).
[6]New Britain Transp. Co., 330 NLRB No. 57 (1999). *Cf.* Waste Mgmt. Northwest, 331 NLRB No. 51 (2000).

The Board continues to apply a multifactor test in deciding between multi- and single-facility unit contentions.[7]

Overruling longstanding precedent, the Board will now include temporary workers in the same bargaining unit with an employer's regular workers without the mutual consent of the employer and the temporary agency.[8] However, the petitioned-for unit must still meet the Board's traditional analysis applied to determining appropriate units.[9]

III. Types of Units

A. Unit Classifications Required by the Act

1. Professionals

Following its decision in *Group Health Association*[10] the Board uses a rebuttable presumption that medical technologists are professional employees.[11]

In *Pratt & Whitney*[12] the Board explained that the *Sonotone*[13] voting procedures for professional/nonprofessional elections do not alter the unit after the election has taken place.[14] The Board reaffirmed its use of the *Sonotone* procedures and ordered the hearing officer to take evidence on the professional issue to determine whether a *Sonotone* election should have been held.

2. Guards

In one recent decision, the Seventh Circuit declared that, according to Section 9(b)(3), the only limitation on the Board's power with regard to "mixed" guard/nonguard units is that the Board may

---

[7]*See, e.g.,* Alamo Rent-A-Car, 330 NLRB No. 147 (2000) (transfers, supervisors); *New Britain Transp. Co., supra* note 6 (geographic separation, interchange of employees); and *Waste Management Northwest, supra* note 6 (supervision, plant integration, and similarity of skills).

[8]M.B. Sturgis, Inc., 331 NLRB No. 173, 165 LRRM 1017 (2000) (reaffirming and clarifying *Greenhoot, Inc.,* 205 NLRB 250, 83 LRRM 1656 (1973)), *overruling* Lee Hosp., 300 NLRB 947, 136 LRRM 1348 (1990) and Hexacomb Corp. & W. Temporary Servs., 313 NLRB 983, 145 LRRM 1338 (1984).

[9]*Id.*

[10]317 NLRB 238, 149 LRRM 1129 (1995).

[11]Pontiac Osteopathic Hosp. & Serv. Employees Int'l Union, 327 NLRB 1172, 161 LRRM 1003 (1999). The Board also held that when it has sufficient notice that there is an issue of professional status in a case, it must conduct an inquiry, and it cannot rely on the failure of the parties to raise the issue.

[12]327 NLRB No. 199, 160 LRRM 1241 (1999).

[13]Sonotone Corp., 90 NLRB 1236, 26 LRRM 1354 (1950).

[14]*Pratt & Whitney, supra* note 12, citing Hamilton Test Sys. v. NLRB, 743 F.2d 136, 117 LRRM 2248 (2d Cir. 1984). *See also* NLRB v. Lorimar Prod., 771 F.2d 1294, 120 LRRM 2425 (9th Cir. 1985).

not certify unions to represent guard employees if the union also includes nonguards.[15] As a consequence, the duty of collective bargaining imposed by Section 8(a)(5) still applies to an existing unit of guard and nonguard employees.[16]

Assigning firefighters to property protection duties during a strike will not result in a finding that the firefighters are guards.[17]

In *Corrections Corp. of America*,[18] the Board applied *Monsanto Chemical Co.*,[19] and found that an agreement covering a mixed guard/nonguard unit does not bar a petition for a guard-only unit.

B. Unit Classifications in General

3. Plant and Employer Units

Notwithstanding its tendency to find systemwide units in the oceanic transport industry, the Board found a less-than-fleetwide unit in *Keystone Shipping Co.*[20]

C. Specialized Units

1. Units in Health Care Institutions

b. Development of the Law: Application of Community of Interest Standard and the Eight-Unit Result

(1) Physicians, Excluding Interns and Residents

In *Boston Medical Center Corp.*[21] the Board overruled *Cedars-Sinai Medical Center*[22] and held that residents and interns are employees under the Act.

---

[15]General Serv. Employees Local 73 v. NLRB, 230 F.3d 909, 165 LRRM 2580 (7th Cir. 2000), *reversing* 328 NLRB 87 (1999).

[16]*Id. See also* New CF&I, Inc., 2000 NLRB LEXIS 316 (May 17, 2000). Notably, a contract covering a mixed guard/nonguard bargaining unit does not serve as a bar to a petition for a guard-only unit. Corrections Corp. of Am., 327 NLRB 577, 160 LRRM 1165 (1999), *following* Monsanto Chem. Co., 108 NLRB 870, 34 LRRM 1099 (1954).

[17]Boeing Co., 328 NLRB No. 25 (1999).

[18]327 NLRB No. 127, 160 LRRM 1165 (1999).

[19]108 NLRB 870, 34 LRRM 1099 (1954).

[20]327 NLRB No. 163, 160 LRRM 1225 (1999).

[21]330 NLRB No. 30, 162 LRRM 1329 (1999); *see also* New York Univ., 332 NLRB No. 111, 165 LRRM 1241 (2000) (teaching assistants, graduate assistants, and research assistants are employees within the meaning of the Act), discussed *infra* pp. 111–12. *Cf.* Ameri Health Inc./Ameri Health HMO, 329 NLRB No. 76 (1999), finding that a unit of primary care physicians were independent contractors.

[22]223 NLRB 251, 91 LRRM 1398 (1976).

(2) Registered Nurses

In *Crittenton Hospital*[23] the Board rejected the argument that its eight-unit standard required that all RNs be included in a petitioned-for unit, and held that a nonconforming unit of RNs that excluded certain specialty RNs was appropriate because of the 25-year representation of the unit by another union.

e. Application of the Rule

In *St. Mary's Duluth Clinic*[24] the Board held that a nonincumbent union could seek to represent a nonconforming unit consisting of some, but not all, of a hospital's employees who would otherwise constitute an appropriate unit under the eight-unit rule. Under the bargaining rule, where nonconforming units exist, additional units are appropriate only if they conform "insofar as practicable" to an enumerated unit.[25] The Board ruled that to require an incumbent union with a longstanding bargaining relationship to represent additional employees with possible conflicting interests would ignore the importance of labor stability and collective-bargaining history.

f. Units in Nonacute Health Care Institutions

Under the *Park Manor Care Center*[26] analysis, the Board does not apply the health care bargaining-unit rule in nonacute health care facilities, and instead uses a "pragmatic or empirical community of interest" analysis to decide bargaining units. The Board has now applied this analysis in connection with RN units,[27] home health care and hospice facilities,[28] and a medical equipment and services facility.[29]

2. Units in College and Universities

b. Development of the Law: Basic Structure of Professional Units and the Impact of *Yeshiva*

(4) Other Specific Inclusions and Exclusions

k. *Graduate Students.* Applying the rules established in *Boston Medical Center Corp.*,[30] the Board, in *New York University*,[31] held that

---

[23]328 NLRB No. 120, 161 LRRM 1022 (1999).
[24]332 NLRB No. 154, 166 LRRM 1057 (2000).
[25]29 C.F.R. §103.30.
[26]305 NLRB 872, 139 LRRM 1049 (1991).
[27]South Hills Health Sys., 330 NLRB No. 170 (2000).
[28]Jefferson Health Sys., 330 NLRB No. 107, 163 LRRM 1185 (2000); Health Acquisition Corp., 332 NLRB No. 134, 165 LRRM 1378 (2000).
[29]CGE Caresystems, Inc., 328 NLRB No. 103, 161 LRRM 1299 (1999).
[30]330 NLRB No. 30, 162 LRRM 1329 (1999).
[31]332 NLRB No. 111, 165 LRRM 1241 (2000).

teaching assistants, graduate assistants, and research assistants are employees within the meaning of the Act. The Board reasoned that although graduate students are indeed students, they are also paid to perform services under the direction and control of the employer.[32]

D. Multi-Employer Bargaining Units

2. Establishment of the Multi-Employer Unit: Its Consensual Nature

The Board continues to require employer consent to form a multi-employer unit.[33] However, employer consent is not required when the petitioned-for unit includes temporary and regular employees of a single-user employer.[34] In reaching this conclusion, the Board overruled *Lee Hospital*,[35] which required employer consent before including joint employees in a single unit.

---

[32] *Id.* at 1243.

[33] M.B. Sturgis, Inc., 331 NLRB No. 173, 165 LRRM 1017 (2000) (reaffirming and clarifying *Greenhoot, Inc.*, 205 NLRB 250, 83 LRRM 1656 (1973)).

[34] *Id.*

[35] 300 NLRB 947, 136 LRRM 1348 (1990).

Chapter 12

RECOGNITION AND WITHDRAWAL OF RECOGNITION WITHOUT AN ELECTION

III. ELEMENTS OF A BARGAINING OBLIGATION IN THE ABSENCE OF AN ELECTION

A. Majority Representation

The initial inquiry in cases of majority representation is whether a majority of the employees in an appropriate unit have signed authorization cards as of the date of the employer's alleged refusal to bargain. In one case, the Ninth Circuit held that a district court abused its discretion by finding insufficient evidence of majority status to support an interim injunctive bargaining order.[1] Ruling that the district court applied an erroneous legal standard and based its decision on clearly erroneous findings of fact, the Ninth Circuit concluded that the regional director established a sufficient likelihood of success on the issue of majority status. The court found that the employer did not refute the validity of an unambiguous union authorization card on which the majority turned. In this regard, there was no showing that the employee card signer was told that the card would be used for any purpose other than to call for an election. Rather, the employee testified that she was told that the card would be used for the purpose of an election, and could not recall whether she had been told anything more.

The Board continues to hold that an employer has no obligation to forego an election and accept a card count as proof of majority status, absent a clear agreement to do so.[2] The Board has declined to reconsider its 1984 decision that majority support for a union is a prerequisite for a remedial bargaining order.[3]

---

[1]Scott ex rel. NLRB v. Stephen Dunn & Assocs., 241 F.3d 652, 662–64, 166 LRRM 2385 (9th Cir. 2001).

[2]Jefferson Smurfit Corp., 331 NLRB No. 80, 165 LRRM 1219 (2000) (examining and copying cards does not constitute clear agreement by employer to accept card count as proof of majority status).

[3]Nabors Alaska Drilling, 325 NLRB 574, 158 LRRM 1004 (1998) (Board declined to reconsider propriety of its earlier holding in *Gourmet Foods, Inc.*, 270 NLRB 578, 116 LRRM 1105 (1984)).

1. Form of Designation

Even in the face of contrary solicitation, unambiguous single-purpose cards remain valid for purposes of establishing majority support absent affirmative proof that the signer was explicitly told that the card would be used *solely* to obtain an election.[4]

2. Name of Union

It remains unchanged that a union designation indicated in general terms, without identifying either a particular local or the international union, is sufficient.

3. Status of the Solicitor

The Board continues to find that union authorization cards solicited directly by a manager or supervisor are usually invalid.[5] Incidental and noncoercive involvement by a supervisor, however, is not found to invalidate the cards.[6] In *Waldinger Corp.*[7] the Board held that cards were not tainted by a supervisor's statements in support of a union or by his presence at a union meeting while cards were distributed and signed. The Board explained that, to find supervisory taint, the supervisor's conduct must either imply that the employer favored the union or coercively induce employees to sign the cards because of fear of supervisory retaliation.[8]

4. Time of Execution

To count in determining a union's majority status, a card must have been signed during the union's current organizing campaign. Majority status at a new employer facility can be established by counting union authorization cards signed by employees while working at another employer facility, prior to their transfer to the new facility. The authorization cards remain valid as to the emerging bargaining

---

[4]Overnite Transp. Co. v. NLRB, 240 F.3d 325, 339–40, 166 LRRM 2577 (4th Cir. 2001), *enforcing* 329 NLRB No. 91, 166 LRRM 1101 (1999) (union obtained valid authorization cards from majority of employees, even if solicitors told employees that purpose of cards was to have election); *Scott ex rel. NLRB v. Stephen Dunn & Assocs., supra* note 1.

[5]Planned Bldg. Servs., Inc., 330 NLRB No. 116, nn.4, 14 (2000), *citing* Sara Neuman Nursing Home, 270 NLRB 663, 116 LRRM 1447 (1984).

[6]Debbie Reynolds Hotel, Inc., 332 NLRB No. 46, 2000 WL 1475576, *7 (2000).

[7]331 NLRB No. 70, 2000 WL 895098, *3, *4, 164 LRRM 1280 (2000).

[8]*Id.*, 2000 WL 895098, at *3.

unit at the new facility, even though the employees signed while not formally employed at the new facility.[9] The Board and Fourth Circuit distinguished the situation of transferring employees, who are invested in a company and its unionization status, from that of job applicants, who have not been hired and whose knowledge of the terms and conditions of employment is extremely limited.[10]

5. Authentication

The Board continues to hold that an authorization card can be properly authenticated by a person other than the signer or a witness to the card signing.[11] A judge or handwriting expert may authenticate a signature on a union authorization card by comparing the signature on the card with signatures on subpoenaed employment documents.[12] In *Traction Wholesale Center Co.*[13] the Board entered a bargaining order based on a card majority where a dispositive union authorization card was authenticated by an ALJ who compared the card signature with signatures on the employee's employment application and work-rules form. The Board found that the ALJ's conclusion was reinforced by its own independent comparison of the employee's signature on a W-4 form with the other signatures in evidence. The Board rejected the employer's purported lack of knowledge about the authenticity of the signatures on business records that it maintained and relied on in the course of employment.[14]

B. Demand for Recognition in an Appropriate Unit

Typically, a union need not demonstrate proof of majority status when it makes a demand for recognition; it is sufficient that the union possesses signed authorization cards from a majority of em-

---

[9]Overnite Transp. Co. v. NLRB, 240 F.3d 325, 340–41, 166 LRRM 2577 (4th Cir. 2001), *enforcing* 329 NLRB No. 91 (1999).

[10]*Id.*, at 341 n.10, citing Koons Ford of Annapolis, Inc., 282 NLRB 506 (1986).

[11]*See, e.g.*, Douglas Foods Corp., 330 NLRB No. 124, 2000 WL 284304, *35, 163 LRRM 1201 (2000) (card properly authenticated by solicitor who received signed card from signatory but did not witness execution of card).

[12]Traction Wholesale Ctr. Co., 328 NLRB No. 148, 1999 WL 1186753, *2–*4, 164 LRRM 1266 (1999), *enforced*, 216 F.3d 92, 164 LRRM 2769 (D.C. Cir. 2000); Parts Depot, Inc., 332 NLRB No. 64 (2000) (judge or handwriting expert may determine genuineness of signatures on authorization cards by comparing them to W-4 forms in employer's records).

[13]*Traction*, *supra* note 12, 1999 WL 1186753, at *2–*4.

[14]*Id.*

ployees in an appropriate unit. With regard to the construction industry, the Board continues to hold that a union is not required to present authorization cards from a majority of the unit to support its demand for recognition under Section 9(a) of the Act. Rather, an employer's acknowledgment of majority support in a recognition agreement, without proof, is sufficient to satisfy the "contemporaneous-showing" requirement and to preclude the employer from challenging majority status.[15] However, the Tenth Circuit has declined to accept the Board's view. In *NLRB v. Oklahoma Installation Co.*[16] the Tenth Circuit held that where a recognition agreement does not explicitly recite that the union submitted proof of majority status in support of its demand or that the employer acknowledged the proof of majority support as the basis for Section 9(a) recognition of the union, the presumption that a Section 8(f) rather than a Section 9(a) relationship was formed governs.[17]

C. Employer Unfair Labor Practices

1. Conduct Warranting a Gissel Bargaining Order

b. "Hallmark" Violations: Invasive Employer Conduct

The Board and courts continue to hold that an employer's discharge of union supporters constitutes "hallmark" violations that justify bargaining orders. Recent "hallmark" violations cited by the Board have included a combination of improper actions, such as discharges and layoffs, and threats, such as those involving plant closures and pay cuts.[18]

---

[15]HY Floors & Gameline Painting, Inc., 331 NLRB No. 44, 164 LRRM 1185 (2000); Oklahoma Installation Co., 325 NLRB 741, 158 LRRM 1081 (1998).

[16]219 F.3d 1160, 1164–66, 164 LRRM 2841 (10th Cir. 2000), *denying enforcement and remanding* 325 NLRB 741, 158 LRRM 1081 (1998).

[17]*Id.; Cf.* NLRB v. Triple C Maintenance, Inc., 219 F.3d 1147, 164 LRRM 2785 (10th Cir. 2000), *enforcing* 327 NLRB No. 15, 163 LRRM 1048 (1998) (§9(a) relationship found where recognition agreement explicitly stated that "recognition is predicated on clear showing of majority support for [the Union] indicated by [the] bargaining unit employees"); Sheet Metal Workers Local 19 v. Here Bros., Inc., 201 F.3d 231, 163 LRRM 2133 (3d Cir. 1999) (§9(a) relationship found where recognition agreement explicitly stated, "the union has submitted proof and the Employer is satisfied that the union represents a majority of its employees").

[18]*See, e.g.*, Douglas Foods Corp., 330 NLRB No. 124, 163 LRRM 1201 (2000) (employer discharged two union supporters, conducted sham sale of business operation, and threatened to eliminate work and impose pay cuts if employees organized a union); Debbie Reynolds Hotel, Inc., 332 NLRB No. 46 (2000) (employer subcontracted out most of unit work, laid off and discharged employees, and threat-

c. Other Specific Employer Unfair Labor Practices

(1) Threats

The Board has issued bargaining orders where the employer threatened employees with adverse consequences if they honored Board subpoenas or testified in Board proceedings;[19] threatened discharge, loss of work, or plant closing because of union activity;[20] threatened to refuse to permit the union to represent employees;[21] or threatened to deny work uniforms.[22]

(2) Promise or Grant of Benefits

The Board has granted bargaining orders where, among other unfair practices, the employer granted an employee a pay raise before an election, while suggesting that the employee vote against the union;[23] or promised wage and benefit increases if an employee voted against the union.[24]

(3) Unlawful Efforts to Undermine or Discourage Union Support

The Board has issued bargaining orders where, in retaliation for union support or in an effort to undermine or discourage such support, the employer refused to recognize or bargain with the union, or withdrew recognition from the union;[25] solicited employee sentiment about matters that are mandatory subjects of bargaining;[26] so-

---

ened job loss and plant closing); M.J. Metal Prods., Inc., 328 NLRB No. 170, 163 LRRM 1164 (1999) (employer discharged 4 union supporters out of a unit of 15 and threatened to sell business and shut down operations); General Fabrications Corp., 328 NLRB No. 166, 162 LRRM 1100 (1999) (employer discharged, laid-off, and suspended employees who engaged in union activity and made threats of job loss, plant closure, and futility in event of union victory), *enforced*, 222 F.3d 218, 164 LRRM 2974 (6th Cir. 2000).

[19]Parts Depot, Inc., 332 NLRB No. 64 (2000); *Douglas Foods Corp.*, *supra* note 18.

[20]*Debbie Reynolds Hotel, Inc.*, *supra* note 18; Kajima Eng'g & Constr. Co., 331 NLRB No. 175 (2000); Traction Wholesale Ctr., 328 NLRB No. 148, 164 LRRM 1266 (1999), *enforced*, 216 F.3d 92, 164 LRRM 2769 (D.C. Cir. 2000); L.S.F. Transp., Inc., 330 NLRB No. 145 (2000).

[21]*Debbie Reynolds Hotel, Inc.*, *supra* note 18.

[22]*Traction Wholesale Ctr.*, *supra* note 20.

[23]Douglas Foods Corp., 330 NLRB No. 124, 163 LRRM 1201 (2000).

[24]*Kajima Eng'g*, *supra* note 20; *Douglas Foods supra* note 23.

[25]Ryan Iron Works, Inc., 332 NLRB No. 144 (2000); Debbie Reynolds Hotel, 332 NLRB No. 46 (2000); Traction Wholesale Ctr., 328 NLRB No. 148, 164 LRRM 1266 (1999); L.S.F. Transp., Inc., 330 NLRB No. 145 (2000).

[26]*Ryan Iron Works*, *supra* note 25.

licited employee grievances;[27] refused to reinstate unfair labor practice strikers on their unconditional offers to return to work;[28] unilaterally altered wages, hours, and other terms and conditions of employment, except for the terms and conditions of replacement workers hired during a strike;[29] suggested that it would be futile for employees to select the union as their bargaining representative;[30] changed work assignments or refused to assign work to union supporters;[31] discontinued a practice of extending cash advances to employees;[32] instituted new work rules;[33] imposed onerous working conditions;[34] decreased overtime;[35] discharged employees;[36] subcontracted bargaining-unit work;[37] or laid off employees.[38]

(4) Interrogation

The Board has issued bargaining orders where the employer coercively interrogated employees about their union activities and the union activities of other employees.[39]

(5) Other Offenses

The Board has issued bargaining orders where the employer created the impression of surveillance of employees who supported the union.[40]

Although a bargaining order is more likely in the case of a small-sized bargaining unit, where the effects of employer unfair labor practices are less likely to be dissipated, a bargaining order may none-

---

[27] *Debbie Reynolds Hotel, supra* note 25.

[28] *Ryan Iron Works, supra* note 25.

[29] *Id.*

[30] Kajima Eng'g & Constr. Co., 331 NLRB No. 175 (2000); Douglas Foods Corp., 330 NLRB No. 124, 163 LRRM 1201 (2000).

[31] L.S.F. Transp., Inc., 330 NLRB No. 145 (2000).

[32] *Id.*

[33] *Id.*

[34] Parts Depot, Inc., 332 NLRB No. 64 (2000).

[35] Douglas Foods Corp., 330 NLRB No. 124, 163 LRRM 1201 (2000).

[36] Debbie Reynolds Hotel, Inc., 332 NLRB No. 46 (2000); Kajima Eng'g & Constr. Co., 331 NLRB No. 175 (2000); Traction Wholesale Ctr., 328 NLRB No. 148, 164 LRRM 1266 (1999), *enforced*, 216 F.3d 92, 164 LRRM 2769 (D.C. Cir. 2000); *L.S.F., supra* note 31.

[37] *Debbie Reynolds Hotel, supra* note 36.

[38] *Id.*; *Kajima Eng'g, supra* note 36; L.S.F. Transp., Inc., 330 NLRB No. 145 (2000).

[39] *Debbie Reynolds Hotel, Inc., supra* note 36; *Kajima Eng'g & Constr., supra* note 36; *Traction Wholesale Ctr., supra* note 36; *Douglas Foods Corp., supra* note 35.

[40] Douglas Foods Corp., 330 NLRB No. 124, 163 LRRM 1201 (2000); *L.S.F., supra* note 38.

theless be appropriate in a large unit where the impact of the employer's unfair practices is felt through the bargaining unit.[41] The Board continues to be more likely to issue a bargaining order where unfair labor practices are committed by the employer's highest officials.[42]

2. Conduct Not Warranting a Gissel Bargaining Order

The Board continues to refuse to issue *Gissel* bargaining orders in situations in which traditional Board remedies would lead to a fair election.[43] In addition, bargaining orders continue to be inappropriate in situations in which the unfair labor practices have been extended to only one or a few employees.[44] The Board in *Burlington Times, Inc.*[45] declined to enter a bargaining order recommended by a judge. The Board determined that the noneconomic benefits granted by the employer had less direct significance to employees than wage increases, and were therefore unlikely to have such an enduring effect on election conditions.

The Board has also refused to issue *Gissel* orders in more fact-specific situations. For example, the Board held that a bargaining order was improper when the Board had unjustifiably delayed the case for more than 4 years.[46] The Board held that such a delay would likely render a bargaining order unenforceable. In an attempt to avoid further unnecessary litigation, the Board ordered the parties to proceed directly to a second election.[47]

Although the Board's traditional view is that the validity of a *Gissel* bargaining order should be determined at the time of the commission of the unfair labor practices, the Board has stated that a bargaining order should also be appropriate at the time of the

---

[41] *See* Scott ex. rel. NLRB v. Stephen Dunn & Assocs., 241 F.3d 652, 166 LRRM 2385 (9th Cir. 2001) (granting interim bargaining order pursuant to §10(j), despite large size of unit, where employer's unfair labor practices affected entire unit).

[42] Rankin & Rankin, Inc., 330 NLRB No. 148, 165 LRRM 1221 (2000).

[43] *See generally,* Canned Foods, Inc., 332 NLRB No. 160 (2000); Aqua Cool, 332 NLRB No. 7 (2000); Willamette Indus., Inc., 331 NLRB No. 73 (2000).

[44] Mid-Mountain Foods, Inc., 332 NLRB No. 19 (2000) (holding bargaining order to be inappropriate in situation in which handbill containing threat of plant closure was only distributed to one employee).

[45] 328 NLRB No. 96, 163 LRRM 1281 (1999).

[46] Wallace Int'l de Puerto Rico, 328 NLRB No. 3, 161 LRRM 1123 (1999).

[47] *Id.*

issuance of the order.[48] In addition, the Board has considered employee turnover to determine whether a bargaining order is warranted.[49]

D. The Bargaining Order as an Extraordinary Remedy

The Board has continued to issue *Gissel* bargaining orders where an employer engages in conduct that is seriously coercive even in the absence of a Section 8(a)(5) violation. In *General Trailer, Inc.*[50] the Board issued a bargaining order to remedy serious Section 8(a)(1) violations, including the employer's use of armed guards, the locking of its gate on the day of the election, and the prevention of discharged employees from casting challenged ballots.

In addition to the requirement that an employer comply with the standards of *Struksnes Construction Co.*[51] the Board has ruled that polling concerning union representation without giving the union advance notice violates Section 8(a)(1).[52] In its decision on remand, the Board also distinguished the Supreme Court's holding in *Allentown Mack Sales & Service v. NLRB*,[53] noting that the only employee statement alleged to evidence union disaffection did not meet the *Allentown Mack* test, however phrased.

V. DEFENSES TO THE REMEDIAL BARGAINING ORDER

B. Change of Circumstances

The Board continues to hold that the validity of a *Gissel* bargaining order depends on "an evaluation of circumstances when the unfair labor practices were committed."[54] In *Audubon*, the Board found that the unfair labor practices were so "serious and substantial in character" that the possibility of correcting these practices by traditional

---

[48]Charlotte Amphitheater Corp. dba Blockbuster Pavilion, 331 NLRB No. 165 (2000) (holding that order must be justified at time of its issuance).

[49]Research Fed. Credit Union, 327 NLRB 1051, 161 LRRM 1156 (1999).

[50]330 NLRB No. 150 (2000).

[51]165 NLRB 1062, 65 LRRM 1385 (1967).

[52]Henry Bierce Co. v. NLRB, 307 NLRB 622, 141 LRRM 1089 (1992), *enforced as modified*, 23 F.3d 1101, 146 LRRM 2419 (6th Cir. 1994), *supplemental order*, 328 NLRB No. 85, 163 LRRM 1209 (1999).

[53]522 U.S. 359 (1998).

[54]Audubon Regional Medical Ctr., 331 NLRB No. 42 (2000); Overnite Transp. Co., 329 NLRB No. 91 (2000).

remedies was slight, and therefore a bargaining order was appropriate. The Board recognized, however, that high levels of turnover among employees made it unlikely that the courts would enforce a bargaining order. The Board, therefore, ordered a second election.[55]

In those circumstances where the Board has not issued a bargaining order because it would likely be unenforceable in the court of appeals, the Board has found that the employees' rights would be better served by proceeding directly to another election and ordering special remedies.[56] For example, on union request, the employer is required to supply the names and addresses of the current unit employees, provide access to employee bulletin boards, and allow reading of the Board notices by an employer official or NLRB agent.[57]

Where the Board does enter a *Gissel* order, the courts require an explanation as to why traditional remedies are insufficient to remedy the unfair labor practices.[58]

C. Union Discrimination or Misconduct

In *Comcast Cablevision*[59] the court set aside a union certification where, before the election, the union offered a free weekend trip to Chicago to attend a 2-hour union meeting. Applying the test articulated in *NLRB v. Savair Manufacturing Co.*,[60] the court held that the inducement was "sufficiently valuable and desirable in the eyes of the person to whom it was offered to have the potential to influence that person's vote."[61]

---

[55]*Cf.* Parts Depot, Inc., 332 NLRB No. 64 (2000) (lingering effect of employer misconduct warranted bargaining order despite employer turnover).

[56]*Audubon, supra* note 54; Wallace Int'l of P.R., 328 NLRB No. 3, 161 LRRM 1123 (1999).

[57]In other cases, the special remedy was limited to supplying names and addresses. *See, e.g.,* Cooper Hand Tools, 328 NLRB No. 21 (1999); Regal Recycling Inc., 329 NLRB No. 38, 163 LRRM 1245 (1999); *see also* Comcast Cablevision of Philadelphia, 328 NLRB No. 74, 161 LRRM 1166 (1999); Research Fed. Credit Union, 327 NLRB No. 182, 161 LRRM 1156 (1999).

[58]Traction Wholesale Ctr. Co. v. NLRB, 216 F.3d 92, 164 LRRM 2769 (D.C. Cir. 2000); Vincent Indus. Plastics, Inc. v. NLRB, 209 F.3d 727, 164 LRRM 2039 (D.C. Cir. 2000); Charlotte Ampitheater Corp., 331 NLRB No. 165 (2000).

[59]232 F.3d 490 (5th Cir. 2000).

[60]414 U.S. 270 (1973).

[61]*Comcast Cablevision, supra* note 59.

VI. WITHDRAWAL OF RECOGNITION

Recently, the Board overruled its long-held view in *Celanese Corp.*,[62] that an employer could withdraw recognition from an incumbent union when it had a good-faith doubt about the union's continuing majority status. In *Levitz Furniture Co. of the Pacific, Inc.*[63] the Board ruled that an employer may unilaterally withdraw recognition from an incumbent union only where the employer can demonstrate that "the union has actually lost the support of the majority of the bargaining unit employees. . . ." According to the Board, this new standard will foster elections that are the preferred method of resolving questions concerning representation. In consideration of this new standard, the Board discontinued its practice of a unitary standard for withdrawal and RM petitions. For RM petitions, the Board adopted the *Allentown Mack Sales and Service v. NLRB*[64] standard of reasonable uncertainty about the union's continued majority status to obtain such an election.

The Seventh Circuit set aside the Board's decision in *Temple Security*,[65] where the Board found that the employer acted lawfully when it withdrew recognition from the union on the termination of the contract solely on the ground that the unit was a mixed-guard unit.[66] The court declined to create an exception to the application of Section 8(a)(5) for mixed unions and remanded the cases "for consideration of the Union's section 8 claims."

Not only is an employer prohibited from withdrawing recognition during the year after certification, an employer may not withdraw recognition outside the certification year on the basis of evidence of loss of majority status acquired within the certification year.[67]

Where an employer extends voluntary recognition to a union, a presumption of majority status arises and continues for a reasonable period of time.[68] The Board, in seeking to enable bargaining rela-

---

[62]95 NLRB 664, 28 LRRM 1362 (1951).

[63]333 NLRB No. 105 (2001).

[64]522 U.S. 359 (1998).

[65]328 NLRB No. 87, 161 LRRM 1129 (1999).

[66]General Servs. Employees Union v. NLRB, 230 F.3d 909, 165 LRRM 2580 (7th Cir. 2000).

[67]Chelsea Indus., Inc., 331 NLRB No. 184, 165 LRRM 1118 (2000) (antiunion petition was circulated and presented to employer during certification year).

[68]*See* Main Edition, Chapter 12, "Recognition and Withdrawal of Recognition Without an Election," Section VI. [Withdrawal of Recognition].

tionships to become productive, does not measure a "reasonable time" by the number of days or months but by what transpired and what was accomplished in the bargaining sessions.[69] The Board examines the factual circumstances to determine if the parties have had sufficient time to reach an agreement. In so doing, the Board considers the degree of progress made in negotiations, whether the parties were negotiating for an initial contract, and whether or not the parties were at an impasse.[70]

In *St. Elizabeth Manor, Inc.*[71] the Board held that once a successor's obligation to recognize an incumbent union attaches, the union is entitled to bargain for a reasonable period of time without a challenge to its majority status. The Board overruled *Southern Mouldings, Inc.*,[72] and held that a "successor bar" will preclude challenges to the incumbent union during this period.

B. Activity or Inactivity by the Union

In *Henry Bierce Co.*[73] the Board held that the employer unlawfully withdrew recognition because it lacked a good-faith belief based on objective evidence that the union lacked majority support. The Board rejected the employer's contentions regarding employee and union activity, where the employer had violated its contractual obligations to pay negotiated wages and benefits and to notify the union of job openings and new hires. The fact that the union did not file grievances, replace a steward who had retired, or submit a contract to its members for ratification did not support a good-faith doubt, because, the Board held, these were purely internal union matters. Moreover, the union had actively negotiated successor labor agreements during this time.

The Board ruled in *Avery Dennison*[74] that the lawfulness of an employer's withdrawal of recognition is not an appropriate subject for deferral to arbitration because the withdrawal involves "the very existence of the collective bargaining relationship between the parties."

---

[69]Ford Center for the Performing Arts, 328 NLRB No. 1, 161 LRRM 1037 (1999).
[70]MGM Grand Hotel Inc., 329 NLRB No. 50, 162 LRRM 1202 (1999).
[71]329 NLRB No. 36, 162 LRRM 1146 (1999).
[72]219 NLRB 119, 89 LRRM 1623 (1975).
[73]328 NLRB No. 85, 163 LRRM 1209 (1999).
[74]330 NLRB No. 56, 163 LRRM 1033 (1999).

C. Filing of Decertification Petition

In *Vincent Industrial Plastics*[75] the Board found that the employer's unremedied unfair labor practices had tainted the filing of a decertification petition, and the employer could not rely on the petition as the basis for its withdrawal of recognition and refusal to bargain.[76]

E. Miscellaneous Factors

The employer in *Red Coats, Inc.*[77] voluntarily recognized the union as bargaining representative in three separate single-location units. After the parties bargained to impasse, the employer claimed that the single-location units were inappropriate and withdrew recognition. The Board found that the employer was equitably estopped from challenging the appropriateness of the units it had agreed to through voluntary recognition. Under these circumstances, where the unit had been agreed to by the parties and is not prohibited by the Act, the unit is appropriate regardless of whether the Board would have certified it ab initio.

---

[75]328 NLRB No. 40, 163 LRRM 1123 (1999), *enforced,* 209 F.3d 727, 164 LRRM 2039 (D.C. Cir. 2000).

[76]*See also* Eby-Brown Co., 328 NLRB No. 75 (1999); Sheridan Manor Nursing Home, 329 NLRB No. 71 (1999), *aff'd,* 225 F.3d 248, 165 LRRM 2132 (2d Cir. 2000); California Portland Cement, 330 NLRB No. 27 (1999); V&S Progalv, Inc. v. NLRB, 168 F.3d 270, 280–82, 160 LRRM 2518 (6th Cir. 1999). *But see* Americare Pine Lodge Nursing v. NLRB, 164 F.3d 867, 160 LRRM 2201 (4th Cir. 1999), and Mathews Readymix v. NLRB, 165 F.3d 74, 160 LRRM 2353 (D.C. Cir. 1999) (reversing findings by Board that decertification petitions were tainted and withdrawal of recognition was illegal).

[77]328 NLRB No. 28, 161 LRRM 1100 (1999).

Part IV

THE COLLECTIVE BARGAINING PROCESS

THE DUTY TO BARGAIN

I. INTRODUCTION

B. Elements of the Bargaining Obligation

1. The Duty to Meet, Confer, and Negotiate

There is still no per se standard to determine whether the parties have met their Section 8(d) obligation to meet and confer in good faith.[1]

2. The Obligation to Deal in Good Faith

The Board and the courts continue to take a case-by-case approach in determining whether a party's conduct at the bargaining table constitutes bad faith bargaining.[2]

---

[1] See, e.g., Altofer Mach. Corp., 332 NLRB No. 12 (2000) ("[A]ttention must be paid to the [party's] 'conduct in the totality of the circumstances in which bargaining took place.'"); Fleischut v. Burrows Paper Corp., 162 LRRM 2719 (S.D. Miss. 1999) (employer violated Act by "[f]ailing and refusing to meet and confer at reasonable times and intervals with the Union as the exclusive collective-bargaining representative.").

[2] See, e.g., TNT USA Inc. v. NLRB, 208 F.3d 362, 163 LRRM 2989 (2d Cir. 2000) (employer who repudiated tentative agreement after union "threw in the towel" to reach agreement did not bargain in good faith); NLRB v. Waymouth Farms Inc., 172 F.3d 598, 160 LRRM 3018 (8th Cir. 1999) (employer engaged in bad faith bargaining by misleading union regarding potential relocation sites, thus impeding union's ability to bargain over effects of relocation); Fleischut, supra note 1 (employer who withheld customary across-the-board raises and never had any intention of reaching agreement with union refused to bargain in good faith); Gadsden Tool Inc., 327 NLRB No. 46, 163 LRRM 1302 (2000) (bad faith bargaining exists when employer enters negotiations with no intention of reaching agree-

3. The Subjects of Bargaining

The Board and the courts continue to apply the *Borg-Warner*[3] distinctions between mandatory, permissive, and illegal subjects of bargaining.[4]

II. PER SE VIOLATIONS

A. Unilateral Changes

An employer's unilateral change of a mandatory subject of bargaining during the course of a collective bargaining relationship remains a per se violation of the Act.[5] In *Duffy Tool & Stamping v.*

---

ment); Reading Rock Inc., 330 NLRB No. 132, 164 LRRM 1325 (2000) (repeated proposal to change scope of bargaining unit is evidence of overall bad faith bargaining).

[3]NLRB v. Borg-Warner Corp., Wooster Div., 356 U.S. 342, 42 LRRM 2034 (1958).

[4]*See, e.g.,* Woodland Clinic, 331 NLRB No. 91, 164 LRRM 1289 (2000) (stating that a pay-for-performance wage proposal that confers on employer broad discretionary powers is mandatory subject of bargaining); *Reading Rock Inc., supra* note 2 (reiterating that proposal to change scope of bargaining unit is permissible subject of bargaining).

[5]BP Amoco Corp. v. NLRB, 217 F.3d 869, 164 LRRM 2889 (D.C. Cir. 2000) (modifications to health plan). *See also* Vincent Indus. Plastics v. NLRB, 209 F.3d 727, 164 LRRM 2039 (D.C. Cir. 2000) (changes in attendance policy, working hours, work duties, and time-keeping method); Alwin Mfg. Co. v. NLRB, 192 F.3d 133, 162 LRRM 2385 (D.C. Cir. 1999) (institution of minimum production standards and change in vacation scheduling policy); Loral Defense Sys.-Akron v. NLRB, 200 F.3d 436, 162 LRRM 3025 (6th Cir. 1999) (change in health care plans); Visiting Nurses Servs. of W. Mass. v. NLRB, 177 F.3d 52, 161 LRRM 2326 (1st Cir. 1999), *cert. denied*, 528 U.S. 1074, 163 LRRM 2192 (2000) (increase in wage rate and alteration to vacation policy); Cotter & Co., 331 NLRB No. 94, 164 LRRM 1307 (2000) (new work rules); WWOR-TV Inc., 330 NLRB No. 180, 164 LRRM 1358 (2000) (new terms and conditions of employment); Vincent Indus. Plastics, 328 NLRB No. 40, 163 LRRM 1123 (2000) (change in attendance policy); Grinnell Fire Prot. Sys. Co., 328 NLRB No. 76 (1999), *enforced*, 236 F.3d 187, 166 LRRM 2065 (4th Cir. 2000) (implementation of current contract offer); Traction Wholesale Ctr., 328 NLRB No. 148, 164 LRRM 1266 (2000) (change in lunch time "punch in and out" policy and practice of allowing employees to take company vans home); Leisure Knoll Assoc., 327 NLRB No. 93, 165 LRRM 1359 (2000) (change in paid vacation days and elimination of double-time pay for Sundays and holidays); Richard Mellow Elec. Contractors Corp., 327 NLRB No. 171, 161 LRRM 1018 (1999) (increase in wage rate); Kurdziel Iron of Wauseon Inc., 327 NLRB No. 44, 163 LRRM 1285 (2000) (discontinuance of practice of granting October wage increase); Consec Sec., 328 NLRB No. 171, 162 LRRM 1046 (1999) (imposition of a rule requiring employees to obtain approval from main office for all time off); United Refining Co., 327 NLRB No. 143, 161 LRRM 1292 (1999) (changes in wage rates, health

NLRB[6] the Seventh Circuit rejected the Fifth Circuit's view that an employer may unilaterally implement a mandatory subject of bargaining if impasse was reached on that particular issue.[7] Instead, the court adopted the position favored by the Board and other circuits, and held that impasse is not reached until the parties are "deadlocked in the negotiation as a whole."[8] Thus, an employer violates the Act when it unilaterally implements a mandatory subject of bargaining if impasse is reached only on that issue.[9]

B. Bargaining Directly With Employees

An employer violates Section 8(a)(5) by circumventing the union and bargaining directly with the employees.[10]

---

plans, cafeteria privileges, sick privileges, and seniority system). *Cf.* Chicago Local No. 458-3m v. NLRB, 163 LRRM 2833 (D.C. Cir. 2000) (parties had reached impasse when employer implemented final offer).
[6]233 F.3d 995, 165 LRRM 2929 (7th Cir. 2000).
[7]*Id.* at 2930–31.
[8]*Id.* at 2932.
[9]*Id.*
[10]*See, e.g.,* Leisure Knoll Assoc., 327 NLRB No. 93, 165 LRRM 1359 (2000) (employer negotiated wage rate with individual employee whom it wanted to come to work earlier); Grinnell Fire Protection Sys. Co., 328 NLRB No. 76 (1999), *enforced,* 236 F.3d 187, 166 LRRM 2065 (4th Cir. 2000) (employer engaged in direct dealing by offering some employees higher wage rate than offered in last contract proposal); O'Dovero & O'Dovero Constr. Inc., 325 NLRB No. 187, 160 LRRM 1071 (1999) (employer violated Act by dealing directly with employees regarding their wages and benefits); ABF Freight Sys. Inc., 325 NLRB No. 93, 160 LRRM 1027 (1999) (employer acted unlawfully when manager demanded that employee withdraw her grievance). *Cf.* Kurdziel Iron of Wauseon Inc., 327 NLRB No. 44, 163 LRRM 1285 (2000) (conversation between member of union negotiating committee and employer, initiated by union member, about whether employees would receive a raise if union was voted out was not employer's attempt to bargain directly with employee). In *American Pine Lodge Nursing & Rehab. Ctr. v. NLRB,* 164 F.3d 867 (4th Cir. 1999), the court reversed the Board holding that there was no support for a rule requiring employers to delay informing its employees of a proposal until after the union has had some period of time to consider the proposal. Further, contrary to the Board, the court held that the employer did not engage in unlawful direct dealing when a supervisor had a brief conversation with an employee about a proposal the employer had sent to the union offering to extend the existing contract for one year in return for wage increases, where the supervisor did not go beyond reporting the employer's proposal in one conversation.

C. Refusal to Execute Written Contract

The Board and the courts continue to follow the rule that a party's refusal to reduce to writing or sign a written memorandum of the agreement made is a per se refusal to bargain.[11]

D. Refusal to Meet at Reasonable Times

A party who refuses to meet at reasonable times, or causes unreasonable delay, unlawfully refuses to bargain.[12]

F. Insisting on Nonmandatory Subjects of Bargaining

The Board and the courts continue to follow the rule that a party unlawfully refuses to bargain by insisting to impasse on the addition of a permissive subject of bargaining to the contract.[13] Recently, the Ninth Circuit added to the ever-growing category of permissible subjects when it held that the negotiation of personal service contracts was not a mandatory subject of bargaining.[14]

---

[11]*See, e.g.*, Gadsden Tool Inc., 327 NLRB No. 46, 163 LRRM 1302 (2000) (employer violated Act by refusing to sign collective bargaining agreement after union surprised employer by accepting employer's position on several subjects); Flying Dutchman Park Inc., 329 NLRB No. 46, 162 LRRM 1283 (1999) (employer committed unfair labor practice by refusing to sign collective bargaining contract containing unlawful union-security clause after it learned that decertification petition had been filed).

[12]*See, e.g.*, Richard Mellow Elec. Contractors Corp., 327 NLRB No. 171, 161 LRRM 1018 (1999) (employer unlawfully refused to bargain where it rejected union's proposed meeting dates and failed to respond to union's request for meetings on at least three occasions).

[13]*See, e.g.*, Dunbar ex rel. NLRB v. Carrier Corp., 66 F. Supp. 2d 346, 161 LRRM 2112 (N.D.N.Y. 1999) (employer committed an unfair labor practice by insisting to impasse on a proposal to deny bumping and bidding between plants). *Cf.* Reading Rock Inc., 330 NLRB No. 132, 164 LRRM 1325 (2000) (employer who repeatedly proposed to change the scope of the bargaining unit, a permissible subject of bargaining, did not insist on it to impasse or signal it was the price the union would have to pay for an agreement).

[14]Retlaw Broad. Co. v. NLRB, 172 F.3d 660, 160 LRRM 2909 (9th Cir. 1999).

III. THE GOOD FAITH REQUIREMENT

A. Totality of Conduct Assessed: *General Electric* and the Proper Role of the Parties

The Board continues to evaluate allegations of employer bad faith based on the totality of the employer's conduct, including the employer's conduct at and away from the bargaining table.[15] For example, in *Burrows Paper Corp.*[16] the Board adopted the ALJ's finding that the employer engaged in surface bargaining based on the employer's proposals, as well as its statements, during negotiations. The employer proposed, among other things, (1) that employees would be paid the minimum wage, which was substantially less than their current pay rate; (2) that the contract would remain effective for only 1 year from the date of the representation election; and (3) that it would retain sole discretion to make annual adjustments to wage rates of unit employees without any role for the union. The employer also refused to agree to include a grievance and arbitration procedure, while at the same time insisting on a no-strike, no-lockout clause and a management rights clause that gave it complete discretion to hire, fire, discipline, and so forth. The Board noted that the bargaining positions of the employer were to be viewed in light of the employer's chief executive officer's disparaging statements about the union. In concluding that the employer had violated Section 8(a)(5), the Board emphasized that its decision was based on the totality of the circumstances.

Likewise, in *Summa Health System, Inc.*,[17] the Board based its holding, that the employer had not engaged in good-faith bargaining, on more than just the substantive proposals of the employer. The Board noted that in addition to the employer's continued insistence on sweeping proposals concerning work transfer, job classification, and wages, other factors indicated bad faith, including unlawful unilateral conduct and failing to comply with the union's request for information relevant to the negotiations.

---

[15]332 NLRB No. 15 (2000); Altorfer Mach. Co., Lift Truck Div., 332 NLRB No. 12 (2000) ("good faith or the lack of it depends upon a factual determination based on overall conduct"); U.S. Ecology Corp., 331 NLRB No. 23, 165 LRRM 1197 (2000) ("In order to determine whether a party has bargained in good faith, it is necessary to examine its overall conduct, both at the bargaining table and away from it."); Summa Health Sys., Inc., 330 NLRB No. 197 (2000).

[16]332 NLRB No. 15 (2000).

[17]*Supra* note 15.

B. Indicia of Good or Bad Faith

1. Surface Bargaining

No substantial changes in the Board's position on surface bargaining occurred during the period of this supplement. Nevertheless, the Board's position on the impact of conduct away from the bargaining table was highlighted in its decision in *U.S. Ecology Corp.*[18] In that case, the employer and the union met more than 60 times but were unable to reach an agreement, even after a strike. According to the Board, the employer engaged in regressive bargaining. Significant to the Board was the credited testimony by the union vice president that a company manager told him that the plant manager had stated that there would be no contract, regardless of what the union did. The Board decided to affirm the ALJ's finding that the employer violated Section 8(a)(5) by engaging in surface bargaining.

In *Richard Mellow Electrical Contractors Corp.*,[19] the Board held that the employer's good faith defense was not relevant to determining if it violated Section 8(a)(5) where, among other things, it failed to respond to the union's request for meetings on numerous occasions, it failed to provide disclosable information requested by the union, and it unilaterally granted wage increases before reaching an impasse in bargaining.

2. Concessions, Proposals, and Demands

a. Concessions

The Board and the courts continue to consider whether a party has made concessions in bargaining in analyzing the totality of the party's bargaining conduct.[20]

b. Proposals and Demands

Application of the principles laid out in *Reichhold Chemicals II*[21] has continued to be the subject of numerous Board cases.[22]

---

[18]331 NLRB No. 23, 165 LRRM 1197 (2000).

[19]327 NLRB No. 171, 161 LRRM 1018 (1999).

[20]United States Ecology Corp., 331 NLRB No. 23, 165 LRRM 1197 (2000).

[21]288 NLRB 69, 127 LRRM 1265 (1988), *rev'd on other grounds sub nom.* Teamsters Local 515 v. NLRB, 906 F.2d 719, 134 LRRM 2481 (D.C. Cir. 1990), *cert. denied*, 498 U.S. 1053, 136 LRRM 2152 (1991).

[22]Ryan Iron Works, 332 NLRB No. 49 (2000); Oklahoma Fixture Co., 331 NLRB No. 145, 165 LRRM 1122 (2000); Summa Health Sys., Inc., 330 NLRB No. 197

The Board also continues to apply the rule that the making of regressive proposals are permissible when based on changed circumstances, particularly if the party provides a reasoned explanation for the modification at the time it is presented to the other side. In *Oklahoma Fixture Co.*[23] the Board found that the employer's regressive proposals on hiring hall and union security could not be viewed as being offered in an effort to frustrate the negotiating process given that the employer explained the reasons for them. However, regressive proposals will still be considered as evidence of general bad faith bargaining where the employer fails to provide a reasoned explanation.[24]

The Board also continues to find bad faith bargaining on the basis of employer demands that the union accept proposals in the area of management rights that would leave the employees in a worse position than if there was no contract at all.[25]

3. Dilatory Tactics: Refusing to Confer at Reasonable Times and Intervals

The rule that a party may not engage in dilatory bargaining tactics to frustrate agreement continues to be applied by the Board.[26]

4. Representative With Inadequate Authority to Bargain

The Board and the courts continue to apply the rule that a party must confer adequate authority on its representative to allow meaningful collective bargaining to occur at the table, even if the representative does not have ultimate authority to enter into an agreement on behalf of the principal.[27]

5. Imposing Conditions

The Board found that a party had engaged in a general refusal to bargain when it conditioned bargaining on an initial agreement to a nonmandatory subject.[28]

(2000); Grinnell Fire Protections Sys. Co., 328 NLRB No. 76, 161 LRRM 1146 (1999), *enforced*, 236 F.3d 187, 166 LRRM 2065 (4th Cir. 2000); Richard Mellow Elec. Contractors Corp., 327 NLRB 1112, 161 LRRM 1018 (1999); People Care Inc., 327 NLRB 814 (1999).

[23]331 NLRB No. 145, 165 LRRM 1122 (2000).
[24]*U.S. Ecology, supra* note 20.
[25]Burrows Paper Corp., 332 NLRB No. 15 (2000); *Summa Health, supra* note 22.
[26]Health Care Servs. Group, Inc., 331 NLRB No. 94 (2000).
[27]*Id.*
[28]Reading Rock, Inc., 330 NLRB No. 132 (2000).

6. Unilateral Changes

The Board and the courts continue to regard an employer's unilateral implementation of new terms and conditions of employment without first bargaining to an impasse as evidence of bad-faith bargaining.[29] Moreover, impasse on one or more subjects will not excuse piecemeal implementation of the items on which impasse has been reached unless the items are so crucial to the negotiations that they create impasse in the negotiations as a whole or the exceptions discussed in *Bottom Line Enterprises*[30] are present.[31]

7. Bypassing the Representative: Individual Contracts of Employment

Continuing to apply the rule that bypassing the union and negotiating individual agreements with employees is an indicia of bad-faith bargaining, the Board in *Grinnell Fire Protection Systems Co.*[32] found evidence of bad faith where the employer directly offered its employees higher wages than contained in its last contract proposal to the union.[33] Additional recent cases in which the Board relied on direct dealing with employees in finding general bad-faith bargaining include *Lexus of Concord*[34] and *Summa Health Systems*.[35]

8. Commission of Unfair Labor Practices

The Board continues to consider evidence of other unfair labor practices in assessing whether the party has engaged in bad faith bargaining conduct.[36]

---

[29]Lexus of Concord, Inc., 330 NLRB No. 98 (2000); Summa Health Sys., 330 NLRB No. 197 (2000); Visiting Nurse Servs. of W. Mass. v. NLRB, 177 F.3d 52, 161 LRRM 2326 (1st Cir. 1999); Anderson Enters., 329 NLRB No. 71 (1999); Grinnell Fire Protection Sys. Co., 328 NLRB No. 76 (1999); Vincent Indus. Plastics Inc., 328 NLRB No. 40, 163 LRRM 1123 (1999); Richard Mellow Elec. Contractors Corp., 327 NLRB No. 171, 161 LRRN 1018 (1999).

[30]302 NLRB 373, 137 LRRM 1301 (1991).

[31]CalMat Co., 331 NLRB No. 141 (2000); Detroit Newspapers, 330 NLRB No. 78 (2000).

[32]328 NLRB No. 76, 161 LRRM 1146 (1999).

[33]*See also* Anderson Enters., 329 NLRB No. 71 (1999).

[34]330 NLRB No. 198 (2000).

[35]330 NLRB No. 197 (2000).

[36]Burrows Paper Corp., 332 NLRB No. 15 (2000); United States Ecology Corp., 331 NLRB No. 23, 165 LRRM 1197 (2000); *contra* Quirk Tire, 330 NLRB No. 137 (2000).

IV. The Duty to Furnish Information

B. Nature of the Duty to Furnish Information

An employer is required, on request, to supply the union with necessary and relevant information.[37] If the information sought by the union is private or confidential,[38] the employer is required to bargain in good faith with the union to seek an accommodation that resolves the conflicting interests of the employer and the union.[39]

---

[37]Naperville Ready Mix, Inc., 329 NLRB No. 19 (1999) (employer must provide union with information concerning sale of trucks that had been driven by employees); Washington Beef Inc., 328 NLRB 612, 163 LRRM 1223 (2000); Retlaw Broadcasting Co. v. NLRB, 172 F.3d 660, 160 LRRM 2909 (9th Cir. 1999) (employer must furnish union with copies of personal service contracts offered to some of its employees); Atlas Concrete Constr. Co. Inc., 329 NLRB No. 1, 162 LRRM 1423 (1999) (names and dates of hire of replacement workers hired during strike were necessary for union to perform its duties as representative); Fleming Co., 332 NLRB No. 99, 165 LRRM 1309 (2000) (employer unlawfully refused to provide union with complete copy of employee's personnel file, copies of any work rules applicable at time of employer's discharge, and list of names, addresses, and telephone numbers of all bargaining-unit members employed by the predecessor employer from which employee was discharged so that union could process grievance of employee); Beverly Cal. Corp. fka Beverly Enters. v. NLRB, 227 F.3d 817, 165 LRRM 2257 (7th Cir. 2000) (employer unlawfully failed to furnish union with attendance and disciplinary records of nonunion employees at its nursing home, where union, which was concerned that unit employees were being treated differently than nonunion employees, had valid reason to request such records); Supervalu Inc., Pittsburgh Div. v. NLRB, 184 F.3d 949, 161 LRRM 3115 (8th Cir. 1999) (employer must provide a copy of its sales agreement with buyer that reopened a store with nonunion work force. The information was necessary to assess employer's compliance with its WARN obligations.); Beverly Health & Rehabilitation Servs., Inc., 328 NLRB 959, 162 LRRM 1093 (1999) (nursing home had an obligation to provide union with certain patient data, including average number of Medicare patients); Conagra, Inc., 328 NLRB No. 24, 161 LRRM 1067 (1999) (Board, after court's reversal of contrary decision, can conclude as law of case that employer did not have to provide financial data. Therefore, any conditions for its provision imposed by employer were lawful).

[38]An employer must present evidence to support its claim of confidentiality. See Woodland Clinic, 331 NLRB No. 91, 164 LRRM 1289 (2000), and Retlaw Broadcasting Co. v. NLRB, 172 F.3d 660 (9th Cir. 1999).

[39]Metropolitan Edison Co., 330 NLRB No. 21, 163 LRRM 1001 (1999) (employer violated §8(a)(5) by its blanket refusal to provide union with names of informants who provided information related to workplace theft); Green Bay Area Visitor & Convention Bureau, 327 NLRB No. 150, 163 LRRM 1152 (1999) (although employee Social Security numbers need not be supplied, employer must furnish union with employee dates of hire, rates of pay, job classifications, addresses, telephone numbers, and company personnel policies, fringe benefits, job descriptions, discipline, and wage and salary plans); GTE Southwest, Inc., 329 NLRB

5. Employer Defenses

An employer's bare denial of the relevance of information requested by a union does not assert a defense warranting an NLRB hearing.[40]

D. Information That Must Be Furnished

2. Other Information

Information on impending subcontracting must be provided to a union where necessary to negotiate a new agreement and to police existing agreements.[41]

V. ECONOMIC PRESSURE DURING BARGAINING

An employer may lock out employees in response to an "inside-game" strategy under which members of the union agreed, among other things, to refuse to work voluntary overtime and to "work to rule."[42] Even assuming that inside-game tactics constitute protected activity, a lockout in response to such an economic weapon is not inherently destructive of employees' rights, where legitimate and substantial business justification for the lockout exists. Such justification may exist even if the only purpose is to force the union to cease its inside-game tactics.

VI. BARGAINING IMPASSES

A. Elements of Impasse

In addition to the factors set forth in *Taft Broadcasting Co.*[43] for determining whether impasse has been reached, the Board also con-

---

No. 57, 164 LRRM 1389 (1999) (because testing information may involve trade secrets, bargaining was required about conditions for providing information).

[40]Beachview Care & Rehabilitation Ctr., 328 NLRB No. 36 (1999).

[41]ATC/Vancom of Nevada, 326 NLRB No. 155, 162 LRRM 1424 (1998).

[42]Central Ill. Public Serv. Co., 326 NLRB 928, *aff'd*, 215 F.3d 11, 164 LRRM 2193 (D.C. Cir. 2000). The court affirmed a Board decision that an employer did not commit an unfair labor practice when it locked out its employees during contract negotiations, because the Board determined that lockout was not instituted out of antiunion animus but with the legitimate and substantial business justification of countering the effects of an "inside game strategy." Electrical Workers Local 702 v. NLRB, 215 F.3d 11 (D.C. Cir. 2000).

[43]163 NLRB 475 (1967), *enforced sub nom.* Television and Radio Artists, Kansas City Local, 395 F.2d 622 (D.C. Cir. 1968).

siders as a factor the parties' demonstrated flexibility and willingness to compromise in their efforts to reach agreement.[44]

B. Effect on the Bargaining Obligation

The Board and the courts continue adhering to the rule that an employer may not unilaterally change the terms and conditions of employment as soon as parties reach deadlock on any issue in negotiations. Rather, the parties must reach deadlock in negotiations as a whole.[45] An exception to that rule is that unilateral change is not unlawful if economic exigencies compel prompt action.[46]

---

[44]NLRB v. Beverly Enter., 174 F.3d 13, 160 LRRM 2935 (1st Cir. 1999) (no impasse even though no bargaining for 6 months and union indicated it would be difficult to sell employer's offer and made no counter offer, because this is not same as an assertion that union will not move from its bottom line); Grinnell Fire Protection, 328 NLRB No. 76, 161 LRRM 1146 (1999) (impasse issues are decided on basis of totality of circumstances, notwithstanding that employer had asserted that it had reached its final position and union had not yet offered specific concessions where union declared its intention to be flexible and had made previous concessions); Anderson Enters. dba Royal Motor Sales, 329 NLRB No. 71 (1999) (although union adamantly opposed employer's flat-rate compensation system, union accepted concept of compensating employees based on flat-rate hours and demonstrated required flexibility to avoid impasse); Cotter & Co., 331 NLRB No. 94 (2000) (no impasse even though union told employer that it could not recommend employer's last, best, and final offer, because it is common place that experienced negotiators make concessions cautiously and that negative initial reactions are later reconsidered to achieve agreement).

[45]Duffy Tool & Stamping LLC, 330 NLRB No. 36, 165 LRRM 1372 (1999), *enforced*, 233 F.3d 995, 165 LRRM 2929 (7th Cir. 2000). The First Circuit upheld a Board decision that it was a violation of §8(a)(5) for an employer during negotiations to unilaterally implement certain of its proposals where impasse had not been reached on the proposals as a whole, even though the union had rejected the proposals that were implemented. Such implementation would vitiate the role of the bargaining representative and preclude meaningful effective collective bargaining. Visiting Nurse Servs. of W. Mass. Inc. v. NLRB, 177 F.3d 52, 161 LRRM 2326 (1st Cir. 1999), *enforcing* 325 NLRB No. 212, 159 LRRM 1298 (1998).

The Sixth Circuit enforced a Board finding that two employers violated §8(a)(5) by unilaterally implementing final contract offers. Changes to employee health insurance plans were not reasonably comprehended within the employer's final preimpasse offers. Loral Defense Sys.-Afran v. NLRB, 200 F.3d 436, 162 LRRM 3025 (6th Cir. 1999), *enforcing* 320 NLRB 755, 151 LRRM 1233 (1996).

[46]Vincent Indus. Plastics, Inc., 320 NLRB No. 40, 163 LRRM 1123 (2000) (no economic exigencies were present to privilege employer's unilateral implementation of new attendance policy where absentee problem was strictly internal matter and was not beyond respondent's control to correct. Problem was also not one of absenteeism unforeseen or not reasonably foreseeable, because it had existed for long period of time.).

Unremedied unfair labor practices will also preclude a good-faith impasse and preclude unilateral action.[47]

VII. DEFENSES AND EXCEPTIONS: WAIVER, SUSPENSION, AND TERMINATION OF BARGAINING RIGHTS

A. Waiver of Bargaining Rights

The Board continues finding a waiver of the statutory right to bargain based on language contained in a collective-bargaining agreement if that language is specific regarding the waiver of the right to bargain regarding the particular subject at issue. Thus, the Board looks to the precise wording of the contract provision to determine whether there has been a clear and unmistakable waiver.[48] In addition, the Board continues applying the clear and unmistakable waiver analysis,[49] notwithstanding the D.C. Circuit Court of Appeals' decision in *NLRB v. U.S. Postal Service*.[50] In this case, the court, in considering whether an employer must bargain over a mandatory subject of bargaining, looked to whether the matter was covered by the collective-bargaining agreement, and not to whether the union had clearly and unmistakably waived its right to bargain. The court viewed

---

[47] *Cf.* Alwin Mfg. Co., 326 NLRB 646, 162 LRRM 1120 (1998) (it was unlawful for employer to unilaterally implement its final proposal where it had not yet remedied previous unfair labor practices) with Quick Tire, 330 NLRB No. 137 (2000) (there was no evidence that previous unfair labor practices adversely affected bargaining and therefore precluded good-faith impasse).

[48] *See* Allison Corp., 330 NLRB No. 190 (2000) and CII Carbon, L.L.C., 331 NLRB No. 155 (2000), where the Board found that collective bargaining agreement gave the employer the specific right to take the action at issue.

[49] Mt. Sinai Hosp., 331 NLRB No. 111, 2000 WL 1126752, *2 (2000) (management rights clause, which permitted employer to "discontinue, reorganize, or combine any operation even if the effect is a reduction in the unit work or in the number of unit employees", did not privilege the employer's reclassification of sous chefs as Assistant Culinary Managers, a new supervisory position); Ryder/Ate, Inc., 331 NLRB No. 110 (2000) (union did not clearly and unmistakably waive its right to bargain about new attendance policy, notwithstanding management rights clause that permitted employer to make reasonable work rules and rules of conduct and make amendments to these rules); Dorsey Trailers, Inc., 327 NLRB 835 (1999) (union did not clearly and unmistakably waive its right to bargain new attendance policy, "the exclusive right to manage the plant and its business and to exercise customary functions of management in all respects and to make fair and reasonable rules for the purpose of maintaining order, safety, and effective operation").

[50] 8 F.3d 832, 144 LRRM 2691 (D.C. Cir. 1993).

the "covered by" and "waiver" inquiries as analytically distinct, thus holding,

> A waiver occurs when a union knowingly and voluntarily relinquishes its right to bargain about a matter; but where the matter is covered by the collective bargaining agreement, the union has exercised its bargaining right and the question of waiver is irrelevant.[51]

---

[51]*Id.* at 836, 144 LRRM at 2694.

CHAPTER 14

EFFECT OF CHANGE IN BARGAINING REPRESENTATIVE DURING THE TERM OF A COLLECTIVE BARGAINING AGREEMENT

I. CONTEXT IN WHICH ISSUE ARISES

A majority of the Board in *VFL Technical Corp.*[1] again reiterated that a union's disclaimer of representational interest would be rejected only where collusion between the parties (the incumbent, disclaiming union, and union seeking an election or the employees) to avoid the contract was shown. A disclaimer predicated on an umpire's "no raid" decision[2] was not grounds to reject the disclaimer.

---

[1]332 NLRB No. 159 (2000) (decision affirming regional director's supplemental decision following remand in 329 NLRB No. 29, 162 LRRM 1257 (1999)).

[2]Occurring under Article XX of the AFL-CIO's constitution.

III. Mergers and Transfers of Affiliation

A. Due Process

The Board has continued to consider due process in addressing mergers and affiliations,[3] although only a negative vote[4] has been found sufficient for the Board to refuse to recognize the affiliation. Although the Board has continued not to review adherence to internal union procedures in determining due-process issues,[5] the LMRDA has been used effectively by dissident union members opposed to the merger in challenging the internal procedures used.[6]

B. Continuity of Representation

The Board has continued to apply the *Western Commercial*[7] factors in assessing whether the new representative has sufficient continuity with the former union.[8] In *Defiance Hospital, Inc.*,[9] the Board found continuity was established where "the maintenance of traces

---

[3]*See, e.g.*, RCN Corp., 333 NLRB No. 45 (2001); King Soopers, Inc., 332 NLRB No. 5 (2000); Defiance Hosp., Inc., 330 NLRB No. 70 (2000) (fact that members of union jointly representing bargaining unit with affiliating union not allowed to vote insufficient).

[4]Cold Heading Co., 332 NLRB No. 84 (2000). The facts showed the employer had contended for a year that "leaders" were now supervisory employees and no longer in the bargaining unit. The leaders were allowed to vote by a separate ballot. Their votes, if counted, would be determinative of the negative vote total against affiliation. The employer then declared it no longer considered leaders to be supervisors and refused to recognize the affiliation. The Board found that the employer did not violate the Act by refusing to bargain with the affiliated union because a majority of the unit, as specified in the collective bargaining agreement, had voted against affiliation. The dissent argued the employer should be equitably estopped from arguing that leaders were in the appropriate unit. The majority found it unnecessary to address the estoppel issue, because it was not raised by the general counsel, but left open for future consideration whether an estoppel doctrine should be applied.

[5]*See, e.g.*, Mike Basil Chevrolet, Inc., 331 NLRB No. 137, 165 LRRM 1063 (2000) (fact that vote did not comply with bylaws of affiliating independent union not sufficient; secret ballot vote occurred after notice and opportunity to discuss issue).

[6]*See, e.g.*, Richardson v. Robinson, 2000 US Dist. LEXIS 9903 (N.D. Ga. 2000); Gee v. Textile Processors, 2000 US Dist. LEXIS 5121 (N.D. Ill. 2000).

[7]288 NLRB 214, 127 LRRM 1313 (1988).

[8]*See, e.g.*, USA Polymer Corp., 328 NLRB 1242 (1999) (burden of proof to show discontinuity of representation is on party asserting it).

[9]330 NLRB No. 70 (2000) (quoting News/Sun Sentinel v. NLRB, 90 F.3d 430, 432, 132 LRRM 2988 (D.C. Cir. 1989)).

of a pre-existing identity and retention of autonomy over the day-to-day administration of bargaining agreements" was found.

The Board continues to emphasize the day-to-day administration factor.[10] For example, in *Mike Basil Chevrolet*,[11] a small independent labor organization affiliated with a local of the United Autoworkers Union requested a certification amendment from the Board. The Board found adequate continuity of representation because the independent union would continue to be able to participate in basic labor relations decisions at the local level, even though it had lost much of its autonomy as a result of the affiliation.

---

[10]*See* King Soopers, Inc., 332 NLRB No. 5 (2000); Mike Basil Chevrolet, Inc., 331 NLRB No. 137, 165 LRRM 1063 (2000).
[11]*Id.*

CHAPTER 15

EFFECT OF CHANGE IN THE EMPLOYING UNIT: SUCCESSORSHIP

III. Successorship and the Bargaining Obligation

A. Continuity of the Work Force: "The Concept of Majority"

In *Daufuskie Island Club & Resort*[1] the Board adopted the ALJ's decision that where an employer discriminates against the employees of its predecessor, the Board will presume that "the union's status as the majority representative of the employees would have continued."[2] Immediately after its purchase, the new owner in *Daufuskie* engaged in an active campaign to bar employees of the predecessor owner—who months before the purchase had voted to be represented by a union and entered into a contract with the union—from being hired, thereby preventing the new owner from becoming the legal successor of the previous owner. Finding that the new owner's unfair labor practices created a presumption of successorship, the Board held that the new owner had an obligation to recognize and bargain with the union as the representative of the employees. The new owner also was barred from establishing initial terms and conditions of employment and was bound initially by the contract negotiated between the union and the predecessor employer.[3]

1–2. *The Applicable Yardstick*
The Appropriate Time for Measuring Majority Status

In *St. Elizabeth Manor, Inc.*[4] the Board overruled *Southern Mouldings, Inc.*,[5] where the Board held that, absent the successor's adopting the existing contract, the union has only a "rebuttable presumption of continuing majority status."[6] *Southern Mouldings* permitted the successor employer to challenge the majority status of the union representing its employees within days of its recognizing the union,

---

[1]328 NLRB No. 56, 1999 WL 318900 (1999).
[2]*Id.*, 1999 WL 318900, at *14.
[3]*Id.*
[4]329 NLRB No. 36, 1999 WL 798923, 162 LRRM 1146 (1999).
[5]219 NLRB 119, 89 LRRM 1623 (1975).
[6]*Id.*

so long as it had a good faith doubt of the union's continuing majority status. In its *St. Elizabeth* decision, the Board balanced the competing goals of giving employees the right to choose who, if anyone, will represent them versus achieving labor stability by giving the union a reasonable period to bargain without challenge to its majority status. Then the Board overruled *Southern Mouldings* after reasoning that the policies favoring labor stability for a reasonable period of time after an employer has voluntarily recognized a particular union for the first time—the new union and new employer engaging in first-time bargaining—apply with equal force to the relationship between a successor employer and union it had voluntarily recognized.[7]

3. Presumption of the Union's Continued Majority Status

In its *St. Elizabeth Manor, Inc.* decision,[8] overruling *Southern Moldings, Inc.,*[9] the Board established a new "successor bar." The "successor bar" presumes that a successor collective bargaining representative retains majority support of the employees in the bargaining unit until at least a reasonable period for bargaining between the union and successor employer has expired. Shortly thereafter in *MGM Grand Hotel, Inc.,*[10] the Board held that a "reasonable time" is not measured by the number of days or months spent in bargaining, but by what has transpired and what was accomplished in the bargaining sessions.

In a pre-*St. Elizabeth Manor* pre-"successor bar" case, the Ninth Circuit agreed with the Board that a successor employer could not rely on the union's representation that it was planning an "old-fashioned" organizing campaign, and the union's collecting of authorization cards, as supporting a good-faith doubt that the union lacked majority status. Rather, during a change in ownership, a union's attempt to strengthen its support is not necessarily evidence that the union lacks majority support; such activity is consistent with what a prudent union, with majority support, would do under the circumstances.[11]

---

[7]*St. Elizabeth, supra* note 4, 1999 WL 798923, *3–*6. Members Hurtgen and Braeme dissented, asserting that the majority ignored the priority that they believed that the Board should accord to employees in having the freedom to select their bargaining representative. *Id.* at *10.

[8]329 NLRB No. 36, 162 LRRM 1146 (1999).

[9]219 NLRB 119, 89 LRRM 1623 (1975).

[10]329 NLRB No. 50, 162 LRRM 1202 (1999).

[11]Northern Mont. Health Care Ctr. v. NLRB, 178 F.3d 1089, 1097, 161 LRRM 2469 (9th Cir. 1999).

4. Discriminatory Refusals to Hire Predecessor's Employees

The Board continues to hold that where the new owner engages in discriminatory refusals to hire its predecessor's employees, it will infer that all of the former employees would have been retained, absent the unlawful discrimination. For example, in *Daufuskie Island Club & Resort*,[12] the Board found that the following employment practices were evidence of discriminatory animus toward predecessor union employees:

> requiring special approval for hiring predecessor employees; hiring new employees instead of predecessor employees, even though the employer told predecessor employees that it was keeping their applications on file, and the employer had a continuous need for workers; and considering supervisory ratings and discipline with respect to predecessor employees, but not with respect to new applicants.[13]

The Board then lists the factors that should be considered in analyzing the lawfulness of a successor's motives in undertaking actions such as those just described:

> Within the *Wright Line* framework, there are several factors which the Board has considered in analyzing the lawfulness of the alleged successor's motive: expressions of union animus; absence of a convincing rationale for the failure to hire the predecessor's employees; inconsistent hiring practices or overt acts or conduct demonstrating a discriminatory motive; and evidence supporting a reasonable inference that the new owner conducted its hiring in a manner precluding the predecessor's employees from being hired in a majority of the new owner's overall work force.[14]

The facts and factors combined convinced the Board that the new owner's unlawful motives required the owner to offer employment to the predecessor's employees.

In two cases the Board applied the *Wright Line*[15] analysis in arriving at the conclusion that the new owners of two businesses had not discriminated against the predecessor's employees when they did not

---

[12]328 NLRB No. 56, 1999 WL 318900 (1999).
[13]*Id.* at *7.
[14]*Id.* at *13, citing Galloway School Lines, 321 NLRB 1422, 1423–24 (1966).
[15]251 NLRB 1083 (1980).

hire them shortly after their purchases. In *Global Industrial Servs.*[16] after analyzing the new owner's actions that appeared to smack of antiunion motivation, the Board concluded that what most likely led to the predecessor's employees not being hired is that they did not want to work for the substantially reduced wages being offered by the new owner. Then in *GFS Building Maintenance, Inc.*,[17] although the new owner harbored and demonstrated antiunion animus, the Board rejected the discrimination claim, because the new owner had, for an extended period of time, not hired predecessor employer's employees when it had purchased competitors.

B. Continuity of Identity in the Business Enterprise or Employing Industry

The Board and courts continue to hold that an employer is a "successor" if there is "substantial continuity" of the operations after the new employer takes over from the predecessor.[18] Although the Board continues to refer to the "totality of the circumstances" when determining whether an employer is a successor, the hiring of a majority of the former work force remains the focus of this analysis.[19]

In *Tree-Free Fiber Co.*[20] a divided Board held that the "substantial continuity analysis in successor cases is to be taken primarily from the perspective of the employees." The employer, which purchased a paper mill employing 500 workers and commenced producing after a 16-month hiatus one of several products previously produced by the predecessor with a work force of only 50 workers, satisfied the "substantial continuity" test. The Board relied on the fact that the affected employees employed by the successor did the same work in essentially the same manner as they did for its predecessor.

C. Continuity of the Appropriate Bargaining Unit

The Board and the courts continue to examine when and whether changed circumstances that are a result of the shift in pro-

---

[16]328 NLRB No. 34 (1999).

[17]330 NLRB No. 115, 165 LRRM 1304 (2000).

[18]N.K. Parker Transp., Inc., 332 NLRB No. 54 (2000); NLRB v. Onyx Precision Servs., Inc., 129 F. Supp. 2d 230 (W.D.N.Y. 2000) (relocation of facility will not defeat a finding of "substantial continuity").

[19]Pennsylvania Transformer Tech., Inc., 331 NLRB No. 151 (2000); National Metal Processing, Inc., 331 NLRB No. 105 (2000).

[20]328 NLRB No. 51, 161 LRRM 1081 (1999).

prietary control are sufficient to render a bargaining unit no longer appropriate. In *Deferiet Paper Co.*[21] the Board granted the general counsel's motion for summary judgment and found that the new employer had violated Sections 8(a)(2) and (5) of the Act by recognizing only one of two unions that had represented separate units of the predecessor. The new employer contended that, because of its newly implemented working conditions, the unit represented by the IAM had accreted to the unit represented by PACE and that a separate IAM unit was no longer appropriate. In rejecting this argument, the Board found that the redesignation of job classifications and the issuance of an employee handbook that announced that employees might be required to work in areas other than their traditional craft did not constitute significant changes in the structure and operation of the facility. The Board emphasized that the affected employees continued to perform their various duties in essentially the same manner as before the sale. Thus, the two units had not merged and remained separately appropriate.

On review, the D.C. Circuit determined that the Board applied an incomplete test in reaching its determination that the IAM unit remained separately appropriate.[22] Quoting from *Trident Seafoods*,[23] the court wrote, "Although the Board places a heavy evidentiary burden on a party attempting to show that historical units are no longer appropriate, this burden can be met if historical units no longer conform reasonably well to other standards of appropriateness." The court said the Board could not simply judge whether the changes implemented by the new employer were "so significant, or so major, or so fundamental that the old unit had been replaced by a new and different one." Instead, the Board must go further and determine whether compelling evidence showed that under the new enterprise the old unit no longer conformed to the Board's contemporaneous standards of appropriateness.

However, a mere negligible, cosmetic, or inconsequential change in the unit by a new employer will not destroy its continued appropriateness. The Board and the courts have also found consistently that the continued appropriateness of a unit is usually unaffected by a diminution in the unit size, particularly where the successor acquired only a fraction of the workplaces in a multisite bargaining unit, reduced the size of a single homogeneous unit, or took over

---

[21]330 NLRB No. 89, 166 LRRM 1040 (2000).
[22]235 F.3d 581, 166 LRRM 2107 (3d Cir. 2000).
[23]101 F.3d 111, 153 LRRM 2833 (D.C. Cir. 1996).

only a discrete portion of its predecessor's heterogeneous bargaining unit. In *NLRB v. Simon DeBartelo Group*[24] the court upheld the Board's order that the new owner of a mall was obligated to bargain with the union, notwithstanding the fact that it contracted out the work previously performed by 35 housekeeping employees and retained only the four maintenance mechanics from the predecessor's unit. The employer contended that, as a consequence, the new unit was dramatically smaller than the old one and was significantly more homogeneous (i.e., only one job classification versus multiple job classifications); therefore, continuity of the unit no longer existed. The court, in line with the Board, found that diminution of the unit through subcontracting did not warrant applying a different standard than the one used in those circumstances where the unit was otherwise downsized. According to the court, the change in the size of the bargaining unit would not lead the continuing employees to perceive their job situations as substantially altered, let alone indicate a loss of support for the union.[25]

D. The Effect of Hiatus

In line with the Supreme Court's decision in *Fall River Dyeing Corp. v. NLRB*,[26] the Board and the courts have continued to view hiatus in a successorship scenario as having a limited effect on the bargaining obligation of the new employer. In *Tree-Free Fiber Co.*[27] a split panel found that a hiatus of 16 months between the cessation of the predecessor's operation and the commencement of the successor's operations lacked significance in the "substantial continuity" analysis. Therefore, such hiatus could not be relied on by a successor as a basis for refusal to recognize the incumbent union.

---

[24]241 F.3d 207, 166 LRRM 2608 (2d Cir. 2001).

[25] *See also* Tree-Free Fiber Co., 328 NLRB No. 51, 161 LRRM 1081 (1999) (where the Board restated its position that when new employer's employees constitute appropriate unit—and majority of those unit employees were employees of the predecessor—new employer's successor obligation is not defeated simply because new unit is substantially smaller—only 50 employees, compared with predecessor's 500); Northern Mont. Health Care Ctr. v. NLRB, 178 F.3d 1089, 161 LRRM 2469 (9th Cir. 1999) (enforcing Board's ruling that successor bargaining unit made up of both predecessor's employees and employees of new owner constituted only negligible change in bargaining unit, and therefore did not provide successor employer with defense for refusing to bargain with union representing predecessor's employees).

[26]482 U.S. 27, 125 LRRM 2441 (1987).

[27]328 NLRB No. 31, 161 LRRM 1081 (1999).

In *NLRB v. F & A Food Sales, Inc.*[28] the Tenth Circuit considered the effect of a hiatus as a result of contracting out of unit work rather than of the cessation of that work. In *F & A Food*, the employer contracted out its trucking operations with the union's acquiescence. The union did not seek to continue to represent the trucking employees after they converted to the control of the subcontractor. About 2 years later, the subcontractor terminated the arrangement, and the trucking operations reverted to the employer. The employer rebuffed the union's bargaining demand on behalf of those returned employees. The employer argued that any bargaining obligation had terminated because it was now a successor employer to a nonrepresented group of employees and that the union waived its right to represent the employees because it did not seek to represent them during the subcontracting hiatus. The court found, in agreement with the Board, that the successorship doctrine was inapplicable in this case, because "F & A simply returned to its status as original employer after a short hiatus, agreed to by the union, with no substantial changes in the original employment relationship."[29] Moreover, the court concluded that because the union had acquiesced to the subcontracting arrangement expressly contemplated by the collective bargaining agreement, it had not waived its right to resume representation of that group of employees once the subcontract was terminated.

E. Determining When the Bargaining Obligation Attaches

The principle that a bargaining obligation attaches upon the union's valid demand for recognition remains unchanged. In *Tree-Free Fiber Co.*[30] the union submitted its written request to bargain 41 days before the successor employer had hired a substantial and representative complement of its employees. Citing *Fall River Dyeing Corp. v. NLRB*,[31] the Board held that the request to bargain remained in effect under the "continuing demand" rule.[32]

---

[28]202 F.3d 1258, 163 LRRM 2327 (10th Cir. 2000).

[29]*Id.* at 1262.

[30]328 NLRB No. 51, 161 LRRM 1081 (1999).

[31]482 U.S. 27, 52–63 (1987).

[32]The Board also noted that the validity of a written bargaining request was not affected by the fact that, in a joint bargaining representative context, only one union was formally identified. The Board noted that the president of the joint representative had signed the bargaining request. That labor organizations sharing joint representation rights may act on behalf of others and that to the extent that there was ambiguity in the request, the employer was obliged to seek clarification. *Supra* note 30, 161 LRRM at 1082.

However, in *Pennsylvania Transformer Technology, Inc.*[33] the Board addressed the question of when a demand for bargaining is premature. In January 1997, the employer began operation following the purchase of the predecessor's facilities and assets. The employer scaled back the business from that of the predecessor, building only one of the two transformers and occupying approximately one half the space formerly used. At the time of the union's demand for bargaining in April 1998, the employer had hired 68 production employees, nearly 80 percent of whom were from the ranks of the predecessor's bargaining unit. By the time of the trial, the employer had added another 32 employees, a majority of whom were also employees of the predecessor. The employer claimed that the union's bargaining demand was premature, because the employer would not reach its full complement of 400 employees for another 2 years. The Board rejected the employer's defense, and concluded that, based on all the circumstances at the time of the demand for bargaining, the employer was in a normal production phase and had hired a substantial and representative complement of employees. The Board noted that it had historically dismissed the argument that a successor need not honor a bargaining demand until it had reached its "full" employee complement and that "it would unduly frustrate existing employees' choice to delay selection of a bargaining representative for months or years until the very last employee is on board."[34]

In general, a new owner may unilaterally establish initial terms and conditions of employment before the attachment of the bargaining obligation. The Board and the courts have recognized two exceptions to that right: where it is "perfectly clear" that the new owner plans to hire all of the employees in the predecessor's unit and where the successor forfeits that right by refusing to hire union employees or informing the employees to be hired that union representation will not be accepted. On its initial review of the Board's decision in *Advance Stretchforming Int'l, Inc.*,[35] the Ninth Circuit agreed with the Board's ultimate conclusion that the employer had breached its duty to bargain with the union by unilaterally setting the initial terms and conditions of employment. However, the court analyzed the case as one controlled by the "perfectly clear" exception, whereas the Board had analyzed it under the forfeiture doctrine based on

---

[33] 331 NLRB No. 151, 2000 WL 1258390 (2000).
[34] 2000 WL 1258390, at *3 (quoting Clement-Blythe Cos., 182 NLRB 502 (1970)).
[35] 208 F.3d 501, 164 LRRM 2001 (9th Cir. 2000).

the statement made to the predecessor's employees that there would be "no union, no security, no nothing."[36]

On rehearing,[37] the court issued an amended opinion in which it adopted the Board's forfeiture analysis. Although enforcing the Board's order in part, it remanded the case for the Board to reconsider its remedy. The court declared that the Board's remedy, requiring the employer to provide backpay at the earlier contract rate from the time the bargaining obligation attached until a new contract was reached, was punitive. The court said that the employer could only be required to pay the contract wages "for a reasonable time that would allow for bargaining," provided the employer could show that it would have lawfully rejected the contract rates.[38]

Applying the Sixth Circuit's "more restrictive" view of the *Burns* "perfectly clear" caveat than the Board in *Spruce Up* and it's progeny,[39] the Board in *DuPont Dow Elastomers LLC*[40] found that the employer waited until 17 days after it formally tendered unconditional offers of hire to the predecessor's employees to announce significant changes in terms and conditions. As a consequence, the Board found the perfectly clear exception was applicable, particularly where the employees were misled by "tacit inference" to believe that they would be employed without significant changes to their terms and conditions of employment.[41]

IV. SUCCESSORSHIP AND THE CONTRACTUAL OBLIGATION

A. The "Alter Ego" Employer

The Board continues to apply the alter ego doctrine to impose the union agreements and obligations of one enterprise on another where ostensibly separate business enterprises are in fact operated as one or where a supposed new employer is really a disguised continuance of or a conduit for a diversion of work from the old. Two or more entities are alter egos if they have substantially identical management, business purposes, operation, equipment, customers, supervision, and ownership. If the Board holds that the employer is an

---

[36]*Id.*, 164 LRRM at 2004–05.
[37]233 F.3d 1176, 165 LRRM 2890 (9th Cir. 2001).
[38]*Id.*, 165 LRRM at 2874–75.
[39]332 NLRB No. 98, 2000 WL 1679480 (2000).
[40]*Id.*, 2000 WL 1679480, at *5.
[41]*Id.*

alter ego, then the alter ego employer will be held jointly and severally responsible for remedying the unfair labor practices committed
by the "prior employer." Prospectively the alter ego employer has a
duty to bargain with the union, and an alter ego's refusal to meet
and bargain with the union is a violation of Sections 8(a)(1) and (5)
of the Act.[42] There is no single factor that is controlling for the Board
to find an alter ego situation.[43]

1. Alter Ego Status Compared With Single-Employer Status

In *NYP Acquisition Corp.*[44] the Board clarified the alter ego/single-
employer distinction, stating that under the *Johnstown Corp.*[45] line of
decisions, alter ego is not a subset of the single-employer concept.
Instead, alter ego and single-employer are separate but related con-
cepts. The single-employer analysis is inapplicable where the case
does not involve two ongoing businesses being operated by a common person.[46]

The Board went on to state that where the two enterprises had
"markedly different business purposes"—one to serve as an interim
manager of the business to preserve its assets and the other solely a
purchaser—and lacked antiunion motive, they are not alter egos.[47]

2. The Defining Factors of the Alter Ego Employer

a. The Factor of Common Ownership

The Board has gradually been whittling down the requirement
that there be common ownership to find an alter ego relationship.
In *Standard Commercial Cartage, Inc.*[48] the Board held that it was of no
great significance that the new employer did not have an ownership
interest in the previous company, where he was an active manager
with an owner who joined him in an ownership capacity in the second company.

---

[42]Concourse Nursing Home, 328 NLRB No. 51 (1999).
[43]*See, e.g.*, Standard Commercial Cartage, Inc., 330 NLRB No. 12 (1999).
[44]332 NLRB No. 97, 2000 WL 1643528, 165 LRRM 1281 (2000).
[45]322 NLRB 818, 154 LRRM 1053 (1997).
[46]*NYP, supra* note 44, 165 LRRM at 1281–82 n.1.
[47]*Id.*, 2000 WL 1643528, *5.
[48]Standard Commercial Cartage, Inc., 330 NLRB No. 12 (1999).

b. The Factor of Employer Motive to Evade Labor Obligations

Although the existence of an unlawful motive to avoid the union remains a strong factor in determining whether an alter ego relationship exists, it is not essential to prove such a motive for the Board to find an alter ego relationship.[49]

In the same way, the presence of a legitimate reason for a change in ownership does not preclude a finding of alter ego status. In *Metalsmith Recycling Co.*[50] the Board found that despite the fact that the employer had a number of "legitimate" reasons for ceasing operations (e.g., avoidance of the enforcement of hazardous waste ordinances), if one of those reasons was an effort to escape further dealings with the union, that reason was enough to find an alter ego relationship.[51]

3. Alter Ego Status Based on the "Disguised Continuance of the Old Employer"

In *Oil Workers Local 7-517 v. Uno-Ven Co.*[52] the court affirmed a grant of summary judgment against the union, which had sought to have a labor contract applied to a "successor." There had been a dissolution of a partnership that had signed a contract covering an oil refinery. The assets of the refinery were then transferred to a subsidiary of the same parent corporation, which was owned by one of the two original partners. That subsidiary then hired yet another subsidiary of the same parent corporation to operate the refinery. The court concluded that the case did not fall into any of the exceptions to the principle of respecting the formal separateness of affiliated corporations identified by the court—not following corporate formalities, improper purpose behind the split, an unlawful act authored by a corporate affiliate, and the affiliate assuming by assignment or otherwise the labor contract.[53]

---

[49]*Id.* (Board continues to examine whether purpose in setting up alter ego was to evade responsibilities under Act); Metalsmith Recycling Co., 329 NLRB No. 15 (1999) ("evidence of unlawful antiunion motive in the creation of a corporation is relevant, but not essential, to a finding of alter ego status.")

[50]*Supra* note 49 (holding that unlawful motivation is not a required element of alter ego finding).

[51]*Id.*

[52]170 F.3d 779, 160 LRRM 2788 (7th Cir. 1999).

[53]*Id.*, at 781, 160 LRRM at 2790.

6. Application of Alter Ego Test in Bankruptcy Settings

Rejecting a collective bargaining agreement in bankruptcy does not affect the agreement's continued existence. The alter ego will be bound to the contract made by its ego corporation and cannot avoid liability as an alter ego by claiming as an affirmative defense the protection that the ego corporation received in the bankruptcy proceeding.[54]

C. Adoption of Predecessor's Contract

The case-by-case approach continues to be applied in determining whether a successor employer had adopted or assumed the labor contract of its predecessor.[55]

The reason for providing a presumption of majority support to a union beginning a new relationship is particularly pertinent in successorship situations, because this is a period of uncertainty. Therefore, in *St. Elizabeth Manor, Inc.*[56] the Board overruled *Southern Moldings*,[57] to hold that once a successor's duty to recognize an incumbent union has attached, pursuant to its newly created "successor bar," the union is entitled to a reasonable period of bargaining without challenge to its majority status through a decertification petition, an employer petition, or a rival union petition. As has been its custom, the Board did not define "reasonable period of time" for bargaining under the new-successor bar rule. Rather, it will analyze each case on its facts.

---

[54]Metalsmith Recycling Co., 319 NLRB No. 15 (1999).

[55]*Cf.* Chartier v. 3205 Grand Concourse Corp., 202 F.3d 89, 163 LRRM 2149 (2d Cir. 2000), *on remand*, 100 F. Supp. 2d 210, 165 LRRM 2749 (S.D.N.Y. 2000) (no adoption where purchaser rebuffed union's efforts to discuss assumption and demonstrated belief that it was not bound by contract of sale to assume seller's obligations under CBA); Balanoff v. 83 Maiden LLC, 2000 WL 16947, 163 LRRM 2337 (S.D.N.Y. 2000) (court enforced arbitrator's award that purchaser of a building was bound by agreement entered into by its predecessor, because, as part of the purchase agreement, purchaser assumed the contract between its predecessor and union).

[56]329 NLRB No. 36, 162 LRRM 1146 (1999).

[57]219 NLRB 119, 89 LRRM 1623 (1975).

CHAPTER 16

SUBJECTS OF BARGAINING

III. DEVELOPMENT OF THE DISTINCTION BETWEEN "MANDATORY" AND "PERMISSIVE"

B. *Pittsburgh Plate Glass*—The "Vitally Affects" Test

In *Pall Biomedical Products Corp.*[1] an employer's revocation of a letter agreement with the union in which it agreed to extend recognition to the union at a newly acquired facility if unit work was performed there by employees and to provide the union with access to the facility and certain information was reviewed by the Board to determine whether the revocation was a mandatory subject of bargaining within the "vitally affects" test articulated by the Supreme Court in *Allied Chemical & Alkali Workers Local 1 v. Pittsburgh Plate Glass Co.*[2] The union represented employees at the employer's two other locations. When the employer purchased the new facility, the union sought to include it in the contractual unit. After a strike, the matter was resolved by the letter of agreement, which the employer subsequently repudiated. The ALJ found that the letter of agreement was a nonmandatory subject of bargaining that the employer was not obligated to honor. The Board reversed the ALJ, finding that the employer's revocation of the letter of agreement, including the recognition clause, violated Section 8(a)(5). Characterizing the recognition clause in the letter of agreement as one specifically directed at the concerns of the employees that had prompted them to strike over the possible transfer of bargaining-unit work to the new facility, the Board found that the clause indeed vitally affected the unit employees under the *Pittsburgh Plate Glass* test. The Board likened the recognition clause at issue to the "after-acquired store" clause at issue in *Kroger Co.*,[3] which was designated a mandatory subject of bargaining and interpreted to include, as a matter of law, a requirement of majority support. The Board distinguished the recognition clause

---

[1]331 NLRB No. 192 (2000).
[2]404 U.S. 157, 78 LRRM 2974 (1971).
[3]219 NLRB 388, 89 LRRM 1641 (1975) (providing for voluntary recognition of union in stores acquired after execution of collective bargaining agreement).

from a broader "application of contract" clause held to be a permissive subject of bargaining by the Tenth Circuit.[4]

E. Application of *First National*: From *Otis Elevator* to *Dubuque Packing*

With a split decision in *Eby-Brown Co.*,[5] the Board viewed relocation "labor costs" broadly to include both direct and indirect costs. Thus, even though the employer's decision to relocate to a recently acquired nonunionized facility was based on factors linked solely to geographical considerations (i.e., lower costs because of closer proximity to customers), the Board agreed with the ALJ that the employer's decision was ultimately based on labor costs because labor costs could affect those other costs; concessions by the union might have changed those other costs enough to cause the employer to reconsider the move. As a result, an employer may be required to bargain if negotiating a decrease in current labor costs might make keeping operations in place more economical than moving the operations.

The law in this area continues to remain "unruly," as evidenced by the Fourth Circuit's decision in *Dorsey Trailers, Inc. v. NLRB*.[6] The court considered an employer's decision during a union strike to close its trailer manufacturing plant and relocate the work to a newly purchased facility without bargaining over the decision. The ALJ had found inter alia that the decision to relocate the work was a mandatory subject of bargaining, that the employer had not bargained in good faith, and that no bargaining impasse existed. Concluding that the employer's failure to bargain over the relocation decision was motivated by its desire to retaliate against the union for striking, the ALJ found violations of Sections 8(a)(3) and (5), and ordered the employer to reopen the plant, reinstate employees terminated because of the closing, and repay lost earnings. The Board affirmed the ALJ's decision and adopted his order. The Fourth Circuit disagreed and denied enforcement of a portion of the Board's order.[7]

The Fourth Circuit noted that *First National Maintenance Corp. v. NLRB*[8] did not address the issue of whether relocation of work is a

---

[4]Mine Workers (Lone Star Steel), 231 NLRB 573, 96 LRRM 1083 (1977), *enforced in part and denied in part*, 639 F.2d 545 (10th Cir. 1980).

[5]328 NLRB No. 75 (1999).

[6]233 F.3d 831, 165 LRRM 3003 (4th Cir. 2000).

[7]*Id.*

[8]452 U.S. 666, 107 LRRM 2705 (1981).

term or condition of employment. The court concluded that the decision to relocate, like the decision to partially close a facility, was "not amenable to resolution through the bargaining process."[9] Given the limited benefits of bargaining, balanced against the employer's loss of "freedom to decide where to locate its business and where to invest its finite capital resources," the court determined that the decision to relocate was not a mandatory subject of bargaining.

IV. MANDATORY SUBJECTS OF BARGAINING

A. Wages

2. *Specific Forms of Compensation*

Section 8(a)(5) was violated by an employer's unilateral termination of merit pay increases, despite the contention that regular merit pay increases were never a condition of employment, having been previously awarded at the employer's "whim." In *NLRB v. Dynatron/Bondo Corp.*,[10] the court upheld the Board and found convincing the fact that the employees had had merit reviews and that the majority of employees had received annual merit pay increases in each of the preceding 13 years.

c. Health and Welfare, and Insurance Plans

In *Maurer v. Joy Technologies*[11] the Sixth Circuit reaffirmed that although active employee benefits such as a health insurance plan are a mandatory subject of bargaining, retirement benefits are not.

The employer in *Brook Meade Health Care Acquirors*[12] violated the Act when it unilaterally increased the employees' contribution to health insurance premiums. The Board held that even if the employer had given the union sufficient notice and an opportunity to bargain over the proposal, the employer would not have been able to implement the proposal unilaterally where the union did not engage in delaying tactics simply by insisting on getting legal advice, and increased premiums affecting only about ten employees were not "economic exigencies" compelling prompt action. In *Amoco Corp. v. NLRB*[13] the employer did not violate Section 8(a)(5) when it uni-

---

[9]*Dorsey Trailers, supra* note 6, 233 F.3d at 842.
[10]176 F.3d 1310, 161 LRRM 2394 (11th Cir. 1999).
[11]212 F.3d 907, 164 LRRM 2344 (6th Cir. 2000).
[12]330 NLRB No. 121, 164 LRRM 1020 (2000).
[13]217 F.3d 869, 164 LRRM 2889 (D.C. Cir. 2000).

laterally implemented its modified medical plan following an impasse in collective bargaining negotiations. The plan's reservation-of-rights provision was incorporated into the collective bargaining agreement, and, therefore, the employer's authority to modify the plan without mandatory bargaining was "covered by" the agreement.

f. Merit Wage Increases

The Board continues to examine a number of factors to determine whether an employer's unilateral grant or discontinuance of a merit wage increase to unit employees is an unfair labor practice. For example, in *News Journal Co.*,[14] the Board held that the employer did not commit an unfair labor practice by discontinuing its practice of granting wage increases to employees after successful completion of their 90-day probationary periods, without first giving the union an opportunity to bargain. The Board held that there was no evidence that a practice ever existed that employees automatically received wage increases after completion of their probationary period; rather, a wage increase was given at the discretion of the employer.

The Board still adheres to the principle, established in *McClatchy Newspapers*,[15] that an employer cannot unilaterally implement a merit wage increase program, even after bargaining to impasse over the issue, because to do so would give the employer complete discretion in determining all aspects of the wage increase.[16] The courts, however, have suggested that the *McClatchy* rule is limited only to situations where an employer implements a merit pay plan but provides no details about the plan.[17] In *The Edward S. Quirk Co., Inc. dba Quirk Tire v. NLRB*[18] the First Circuit granted enforcement in part[19] and

---

[14]331 NLRB No. 177, 164 LRRM 1129 (2000).

[15]321 NLRB 1386, 153 LRRM 1137 (1996), *enforced,* 131 F.3d 1026, 157 LRRM 2023 (D.C. Cir. 1997). *See also* McClatchy Newspapers, 322 NLRB 812, 154 LRRM 1086 (1996).

[16]Quirk Tire, 330 NLRB No. 137 (2000), *enforced in part, vacated in part,* 241 F.3d 41, 166 LRRM (1st Cir. 2001). The Board also held that an employer's proposal for a merit wage increase that gives the employer complete discretion in determining wage rates is indicative of unlawful "surface bargaining." *But see* Woodland Clinic, 331 NLRB No. 91, 164 LRRM 1289 (2000) (Board refused to find unfair labor practice where there was no evidence that employer actually granted any merit wage increases to its employees).

[17]Detroit Typographical Union No. 18 v. NLRB, 216 F.3d 109, 164 LRRM 2797 (D.C. Cir. 2000) (employer's merit wage that provided for raises—averaging 4% in first year and 3% in second and third years)—based on employee evaluations and subject to grievance procedure did not violate *McClatchy*).

[18]241 F.3d 41, 166 LRRM 2666 (1st Cir. 2001).

[19]Order enforced where substantial evidence supported finding that the discharge of the union shop steward was an unfair labor practice.

vacated in part the Board's order finding that the employer had engaged in an unfair labor practice by unilaterally implementing a new merit wage increase plan. The First Circuit was not convinced that the *McClatchy* rule should have been applied in that case, because the employer provided some standards for merit increases, including allowing the employees to grieve the decision. In the absence of an articulated rationale, the court remanded to allow the Board to give a reasoned explanation of why the employer's unilateral implementation of the wage plan was an unfair labor practice.

g. Housing, Meals, Services and Discounts Supplied by Employer

Both the Board and courts continue to hold that meal monies and other benefits provided by the employer are mandatory subjects of bargaining.[20]

B. Hours

The Board found violations of Section 8(a)(5) where the employers failed to bargain or give notice before replacing time clocks with the manual recording of time by supervisors and requiring an additional 15 minutes of overtime,[21] moving employees' start time up by 15 minutes, limiting telephone usage to emergency calls, limiting employees' break time to two 15-minute breaks, and altering employees lunch periods,[22] implementing a new attendance policy,[23] and imposing a monetary charge for lost time cards.[24] In *Beverly Cali-*

---

[20]Dunbar v. Onyx Precision Serv., Inc., 129 F. Supp. 2d 230 (W.D.N.Y. 2000) (employer violated NLRA by refusing to bargain with union and unilaterally changing amount of meal monies); Traction Wholesale Ctr. Co., Inc. v. NLRB, 216 F.3d 92, 164 LRRM 2769 (D.C. Cir. 2000) (employer committed unfair labor practice by unilaterally changing its policy on employees' personal use of company vans); Kurdziel Iron of Wauseon, Inc., 327 NLRB 155, 163 LRRM 1285 (1998) (employer violated §8(a)(5) by threatening unilateral reduction in lunch-break time).

[21]Vincent Indus. Plastics, 328 NLRB No. 40, 163 LRRM 1223 (1999), *enforcement granted in part, denied in part,* 209 F.3d 727, 164 LRRM 2039 (D.C. Cir. 2000).

[22]Pepsi-Cola Bottling of Fayetteville, Inc., 330 NLRB No. 134 (2000), *aff'd,* 330 NLRB No. 153 (2000).

[23]*Vincent Indus. Plastics, supra* note 21; Duffy Tool & Stamping, 330 NLRB No. 36, 165 LRRM 1372 (1999), *aff'd,* 233 F.3d 995, 165 LRRM 2929 (7th Cir. 2000); Dorsey Trailers, Inc., 327 NLRB 835, 165 LRRM 1392 (1999).

[24]NLRB v. Beverly Enterprises—Mass., Inc., 174 F.3d 13, 160 LRRM 2935 (1st Cir. 1999).

fornia v. NLRB[25] the Seventh Circuit affirmed the Board's determination that the employer's unilateral reduction in employees' hours and modification of employees' break time and refusal to provide attendance records of nonunit employees violated Section 8(a)(5). Although the contract gave the employer the right to "schedule its operations work force," the contractual language was general, and the court found that it did not constitute a clear and unmistakable waiver of the employees' statutory rights.

C. Other Terms and Conditions of Employment

2. *Specific Terms and Requirements*

c. Union-Security Provisions and Hiring Halls

The Board has recently reaffirmed that Section 8(a)(5) is not violated by an employer who unilaterally ceases giving effect to a union dues checkoff provision in a contract on its expiration, because such provisions are, as explained in the Fourth Edition, a creature of contract.[26]

e. Plant Rules and Discipline

An employer's unilateral implementation of or changes to plant rules without notice to or consultation with the union may constitute a violation of Section 8(a)(5) where such new rules or changes constitute material, significant, and substantial changes to terms and conditions of employment.[27] An employer, therefore, violates the Act by converting a previous informal and occasional rule into a written policy statement that includes discipline and applies at all times.[28]

---

[25]227 F.3d 817, 165 LRRM 2257 (7th Cir. 2000), *enforcing in relevant part* 326 NLRB 153, 159 LRRM 1049 (1998), *aff'd*, 326 NLRB 232, 159 LRRM 1033 (1998).

[26]Hacienda Hotel Inc. Gaming Corp., 331 NLRB No. 89, 164 LRRM 1273 (2000) (affirming ALJ dismissal of §8(a)(5) and (1) charges based on employers' discontinuance of the checkoff procedure following expiration of contract). *See also* Wilkes Tel. Membership Corp., 331 NLRB No. 98, 164 LRRM 1338 (2000) (finding that dues checkoff expired with contract as a matter of law).

[27]Pepsi Cola Bottling Co., 330 NLRB No. 134 (2000) (changes to telephone use policy, lunch and break periods, and new restrictive conditions on conversations between employees). *See also* Consec Sec., 328 NLRB No. 171, 162 LRRM 1046 (1999) (rule proscribing procedure for exchanging shifts with other employees); Cotter & Co., 331 NLRB No. 94, 164 LRRM 1307 (2000) (absent valid impasse in negotiations, employer's unilateral implementation of new work rules was violation of §8(a)(5)).

[28]*In re* Scepter Ingot Casting, Inc., 331 NLRB No. 153 (2000) (employer required to afford earlier notice and opportunity to bargain concerning decision to

In *Pacific FM, Inc.*[29] the Board held that an employer is not required to bargain over procedural changes to timekeeping policies. The employer issued a memorandum informing employees of a new time clock system and procedures for using it.[30] The Board based its holding on *The Bureau of National Affairs, Inc.*[31] and found that the employer had the right to track employees' hours and that employees were not prejudiced by the new system.[32]

In *Consec Security*,[33] the Board affirmed an ALJ's decision that an employer's rule prescribing the procedure for exchanging shifts with other employees affected the unit employees' terms and conditions of employment and, therefore, could not be implemented unilaterally.

g. Grievance Procedures and Arbitration

In *Wire Products Manufacturing Corp.*[34] the arbitration provision in the collective bargaining agreement required that the arbitration panel contain "experienced arbitrators." During the selection of the panel, the employer insisted on "special requirements" that the arbitrators be selected only from certain out-of-state regions and that they all be accredited by the American Arbitration Association. The Board found that such insistence unilaterally altered the arbitration provision in the collective bargaining agreement, and thus violated Section 8(a)(5).

m. Major Business Changes

(2) Partial Closure, Sale, or Merger of Business, or Plant Relocation

The Board found an employer's argument unpersuasive that closure of a facility was motivated by production and scheduling problems exacerbated by the collective bargaining agreement because the employer had failed to seek relief from the union before closing

---

require employees to sign policy statement reflecting unilateral change in work rules).

[29]332 NLRB No. 67 (2000).

[30]*Id.*

[31]235 NLRB 8, 97 LRRM 1447 (1978).

[32]*Pacific FM, supra* note 29. If the modification in time-keeping procedures affects a mandatory subject such as hours, then the employer may not unilaterally implement the change. *See* Section IV.B. [Mandatory Subjects of Bargaining; Hours], *supra.*

[33]328 NLRB No. 171, 162 LRRM 1046 (1999).

[34]329 NLRB 23, 165 LRRM 1014 (1999).

the facility. Earlier threats of closure were sufficient to establish anti-union animus in the decision to subcontract work.[35]

In *Dorsey Trailers v. NLRB*[36] the Fourth Circuit, following *First National Maintenance v. NLRB*[37] and *Arrow Automotive Industries v. NLRB*,[38] held that a decision to relocate a plant was a business decision, not a "term or condition of employment," and thus not a mandatory subject of bargaining. As a consequence, the Fourth Circuit held that the Board erred when it ordered the employer, which had transferred work to a new plant following the union's strike, to transfer work back to the original plant. The court also held that a restoration order exceeded the Board's authority, because closure of the employer's facility did not evidence discriminatory animus by the employer. According to the court, the union could protect its members' interests through bargaining over the effects of a decision to relocate work, which is a mandatory subject of bargaining.

n. Successorship and "Application of Contract" Clauses

In *Pall Biomedical Products Corp.*[39] the Board held that a letter of agreement between the union and the employer providing that the employer would recognize the union at a designated new facility if it employed "one or more employees performing bargaining unit work," was valid, and a mandatory subject of bargaining. Relying on *Kroger Co.*,[40] and distinguishing *Lone Star Steel*,[41] the Board found that the clause at issue was more limited in scope than the "application-of-contract" clause at issue in *Lone Star Steel*, because it specifically pertained to bargaining-unit work at only one other facility in the same geographical area. In addition, the agreement was directed at the concerns of the unit employees and "vitally affect[ed]" the terms and conditions of their employment. The record showed that just before the letter of agreement, the union went on strike over the

---

[35]Westchester Lace, Inc., 326 NLRB No. 119, 163 LRRM 1181 (1998).

[36]233 F.3d 831, 165 LRRM 3003 (4th Cir. 2000).

[37]452 U.S. 666, 107 LRRM 2705 (1981).

[38]853 F.2d 223, 128 LRRM 3137 (4th Cir. 1988).

[39]331 NLRB No. 192, 165 LRRM 1137 (2000).

[40]219 NLRB 388, 89 LRRM 1641 (1975) (collective bargaining clause that required employer to recognize union in any newly acquired store held valid by Board where application of clause depended on union's majority status).

[41]Mine Workers (Lone Star Steel Co.), 231 NLRB 573, 96 LRRM 1083 (1977), *enforcement granted in part, denied in part and remanded*, 639 F.2d 545, 104 LRRM 3144 (10th Cir. 1980), *cert. denied*, 450 U.S. 911, 106 LRRM 2513 (1981).

issue of bargaining-unit work being transferred to the other facility, and that strike did not end until the employer executed the letter of agreement.

V. PERMISSIVE SUBJECTS OF BARGAINING

A. In General

Where a party links a mandatory and a permissive subject in a proposal, the Board continues to permit the withdrawal or modification of the mandatory subject if the permissive subject is rejected.[42]

The Board also continues to follow the rule that a party may not conclude negotiations by agreeing only to the proposals of the other party that constitute mandatory subjects of bargaining.[43] In addition, where the employer was found not to have bargained in good faith because it impermissibly insisted to impasse on a permissive subject, the Board ordered the withdrawal of the permissive proposal and the resumption of bargaining as a remedy.[44]

B. Specific Subjects

1. Definition of Bargaining Unit

A proposal to transfer bargaining-unit employees outside the bargaining unit remains a permissive subject of bargaining.[45]

Similarly, an employer may not insist to impasse on a clause in the collective bargaining agreement denying employee status to certain bargaining unit members because it is a permissive subject of bargaining.[46] The D.C. Circuit enforced the Board's ruling that the implementation after impasse of a proposal to change the union's work jurisdiction was not unlawful.[47]

---

[42]Dependable Storage, Inc., 328 NLRB No. 6, 164 LRRM 1286 (1999).

[43]California Pie Co., Inc., 329 NLRB No. 88, 162 LRRM 1390 (1999).

[44]Id.

[45]California Portland Cement, 330 NLRB No. 27 (1999); Dunbar v. Carrier Corp., 66 F. Supp. 2d 346, 161 LRRM 2112 (N.D.N.Y. 1999).

[46]Reading Rock, 330 NLRB No. 132, 164 LRRM 1325 (2000).

[47]Detroit Typographical Union v. NLRB, 216 F.3d 109, 164 LRRM 2797 (D.C. Cir. 2000), enforcing in relevant part 326 NLRB 700, 159 LRRM 1065 (2000).

3. Selection of Bargaining Representative

A proposal for a "most favored nations clause" that included not only the local union that was the certified bargaining representative but also the local's international union and any affiliated local unions in a four-state area constituted a permissive subject of bargaining because it sought to sweep away basic safeguards provided to employees under the Act concerning the selection of their representatives for the purposes of collective bargaining.[48] The Board indicated that this clause was also unlawful under the circumstances, because it could subject the employees' terms and conditions of employment to the unrelated bargaining result of entities (parent and sister locals) that the employees had not selected as their bargaining representatives.

7. Interest Arbitration and Bi-Level Bargaining

The Board and the courts continue to hold that interest arbitration is a permissive subject of bargaining.[49]

8. Internal Union Affairs

The Board and the courts continue to follow the rule that procedures relating to adoption, ratification, or acceptance of a collective bargaining agreement are permissive subjects of bargaining.[50]

12. Settlement of Unfair Labor Practice Charges

The Board continues to hold that an employer may not condition bargaining on the withdrawal of unfair-labor practices or other litigation.[51]

---

[48]California Pie Co., Inc., 329 NLRB No. 88, 162 LRRM 1390 (1999).

[49]Electrical Workers (IBEW) Local 666 v. Stokes Elec. Serv., Inc., 225 F.3d 415, 164 LRRM 3089 (4th Cir. 2000); Summa Health Sys., Inc. (AFSCME, Local No. 684), 330 NLRB No. 197 (2000).

[50]Longshoremen (ILA) Local 1575 (Navieras, NPR, Inc.), 332 NLRB No. 139, 165 LRRM 1377 (2000). NLRB v. Concordia Electric Coop., Inc., 163 LRRM 2300, 2320 (5th Cir. 1999) (special magistrate recommended employer be found in contempt of court order, enforcing Board bargaining order for failure to execute agreement and instead unlawfully insisting that union follow particular ratification process, a permissive subject of bargaining).

[51]WWOR-TV, Inc., 330 NLRB No. 180, 164 LRRM 1358 (2000).

14. Miscellaneous

An employer's proposal of "personal service contracts" to be negotiated directly with current and prospective employees is permissive rather than mandatory and may not be implemented on impasse.[52]

VI. ILLEGAL SUBJECTS OF BARGAINING

B. Specific Illegal Subjects

The Board, consistent with its holding in *Carpenters District Council of Northeast Ohio (Alessio Construction)*,[53] continues to scrutinize contract clauses that fall within the literal proscription of Section 8(e) under a two-step analysis, including: (1) whether the clause is secondary in nature or has the primary objective of preserving bargaining unit work for the employees of the signatory employer;[54] and (2) whether the clause has a secondary purpose and is saved from illegality by the construction industry proviso.[55] In *Southwestern Materials* the Board considered two separate contractual provisions and determined that both had secondary objectives.[56] With respect to the first provision—a cease-doing-business clause—the Board found that it was not sheltered by the construction industry proviso because it fell outside the "categories of secondary activity that Congress intended to be tolerated in the construction industry."[57] The second provision was found to be lawful under Section 8(e) pursuant to the construction industry proviso because there was no evidence that the clause was intended to be applied to work other than at a construction site.[58]

The Board continues to find union-security clauses obligating an employer to hire only union members and to obtain approval

---

[52]Retlaw Broadcasting Co. v. NLRB, 172 F.3d 660, 160 LRRM 2909 (9th Cir. 1999), *enforcing* 324 NLRB 138, 158 LRRM 1135 (1997).

[53]310 NLRB 1023, 143 LRRM 1049 (1993).

[54]29 U.S.C. §158(e).

[55]Iron Workers (Southwestern Materials & Supply), 328 NLRB No. 42, 161 LRRM 1258 (1999).

[56]*Id.* at 1261–62.

[57]*Id.; see also* Operating Eng'rs, Local 520 (Massman Constr. Co.), 327 NLRB No. 208, 161 LRRM 1001 (1999) (Board found no evidence that joint venture clauses, unlike subcontracting agreements of sort previously found lawful by Board, were part of the pattern of bargaining in construction industry at time of proviso's enactment in 1959).

[58]*Southwestern Materials, supra* note 55, 161 LRRM at 1262.

from the union even for employees hired without the union's assistance as unlawful.[59] However, an employer who had orally agreed to the entire contract, including the unlawful provision, may not refuse to execute the contract where the employer's refusal to sign the contract is motivated by reasons other than the presence of the unlawful provision.[60]

In *Oxy USA, Inc.*[61] the Board found that the employer's proposal that the union replace the employer as sole sponsor and administrator of the health insurance plan covering unit employees did not contemplate payments to the union and therefore did not violate Section 302(a) of the Labor-Management Relations Act.[62] Accordingly, the employer's insistence to impasse on this bargaining proposal was not a violation of Section 8(a)(5).

---

[59]Flying Dutchman Park, Inc., 329 NLRB No. 88, 162 LRRM 1390 (1999).
[60]*Id.*
[61]329 NLRB No. 26, 162 LRRM 1113 (1999).
[62]29 U.S.C. §186(a).

Part V

ARBITRATION AND THE ACT

CHAPTER 17

RELATION OF BOARD ACTION TO ENFORCEMENT OF AGREEMENTS UNDER SECTION 301

III. SCOPE AND PURPOSE OF SECTION 301

B. A Source of Federal Substantive Law

Courts continue to require an allegation that a collective bargaining agreement was breached to invoke jurisdiction pursuant to Section 301. In *Food & Commercial Workers v. Albertson's, Inc.*[1] the Tenth Circuit addressed a union's attempt to use Section 301 as a basis for declaring a collective bargaining agreement invalid because it violated the Fair Labor Standards Act (FLSA). Citing the Supreme Court's decision in *Textron Lycoming Reciprocating Engine Division, Avco Corp. v. Auto Workers*[2] the Tenth Circuit held that the mere contention that a collective bargaining agreement violated the FLSA was insufficient to give rise to Section 301 jurisdiction in the absence of a claim that the employer had actually breached the agreement.[3] The court did note, however, that had the union alleged that a strike was imminent and that the invalidity of the agreement under the FLSA would be the union's defense to a Section 301 suit by the employer, federal jurisdiction might in fact exist.[4]

Courts continue to use Section 301 jurisdiction to enforce agreements referring to or incorporated in collective bargaining agreements. The Second Circuit issued a permanent injunction barring an employer from transferring work until it made every reasonable effort to preserve the work.[5] This ruling was based on a letter agreement incorporated within a collective bargaining agreement that required the employer to make "every effort" to preserve work done by the employees covered by the collective bargaining agreement.[6]

The Tenth Circuit held that Section 301 provides federal courts with jurisdiction over a claim by an employee against his or her employer and union for the breach of a conciliation agreement resolving an earlier employment discrimination claim.[7] The court found that the conciliation agreement itself did not confer any rights on the employee; rather, the independent source of the rights the employee sought to enforce was the collective bargaining agreement itself.[8]

---

[1]207 F.3d 1193, 163 LRRM 2903 (10th Cir. 2000).
[2]523 U.S. 653, 158 LRRM 2193 (1998).
[3]*Albertson's, supra* note 1.
[4]*Id.*
[5]Machinists District Lodge 91 v. United Techs. Corp., 230 F.3d 569, 165 LRRM 2641 (2000).
[6]*Id.*, at 579.
[7]Cisneros v. ABC Rail Corp., 217 F.3d 1299, 164 LRRM 2780 (10th Cir. 2000).
[8]*Id.* at 1303.

The Third Circuit held that Section 301 jurisdiction extends to a strike settlement agreement.[9] The court determined that the agreement was negotiated by the employer and unions, and that it served the dual purpose of providing striking union members with employment rights and ending their strike against the employer, thereby distinguishing it from a series of individual employment contracts.[10] Moreover, the court ruled that the unions and employers entered into the agreement to establish labor peace and to resolve a controversy, thus bringing the agreement within Section 301.[11]

In *Rock-Tenn Co. v. Paperworkers*[12] the Fourth Circuit addressed the issue of whether a corporation, rather than merely one of its divisions, may be bound by a collective bargaining agreement. An employer brought a Section 301 action seeking a declaratory judgment that it was not bound by a collective bargaining agreement because it was between one of its divisions and the union. The court held that the employer's voluntary participation in the arbitration process without objection precluded it from later arguing that it was not bound by the collective bargaining agreement.[13] In addition, the court held that the collective bargaining agreement could be reasonably interpreted to bind the corporation and not merely its division and, therefore, the arbitrator's decision should not be vacated.[14]

F. Overlapping Jurisdiction: Conflict or Accommodation?

1. Federal and State Courts

a. Concurrent Jurisdiction

The Eighth[15] and Ninth[16] Circuits hold a state's procedural rules govern Section 301 suits commenced in state court, and before any removal to federal court, without regard to the effect those procedural rules may have on the federal substantive law concerning the

---

[9]Beidleman v. Stroh Brewery Co., 182 F.3d 225, 161 LRRM 2656 (3d Cir. 1999).

[10]*Id.* at 231.

[11]*Id. See also* Rollie Winter & Assocs., Ltd. v. Fox River Valley Bldg. & Constr. Trades Council, 59 F. Supp. 2d 807, 161 LRRM 3159 (E.D. Wis. 1999) (holding that federal court jurisdiction exists based on §301 over claim seeking to enforce oral agreement because agreement was significant to maintenance of labor peace).

[12]184 F.3d 330, 161 LRRM 2862 (4th Cir. 1999).

[13]*Id.* at 336.

[14]*Id.* at 337.

[15]Winkels v. George A. Hormel & Co., 874 F.2d 567, 131 LRRM 2338 (8th Cir. 1989).

[16]Prazak v. Bricklayers Local 1, 233 F.3d 1149, 165 LRRM 2853 (9th Cir. 2000).

statute of limitations. However, the Fourth Circuit has held to the contrary.[17]

b. Statutes of Limitations

In *Prazak v. Bricklayers Local 1*[18] the Ninth Circuit held that a federal district court, on removal of a hybrid Section 301 suit commenced in state court, could not dismiss the suit based on the 6-month statute of limitations if the suit was commenced within that limitations period as prescribed under the state's procedural rules. Finding that state procedural rules govern hybrid Section 301 actions brought in state court, the court found that the dismissal of the action by the state court for lack of progress, and the subsequent refiling of the action in state court within 1 year in accordance with state procedural rules, did not provide the federal district court, on removal, with the right to apply the limitations period as if the action had been originally commenced in federal court.

The courts continue to find that the limitations period of a Section 301 suit is not tolled by pursuit of a Board action;[19] nor is it tolled while an employee informally seeks help from successive union stewards.[20] Likewise, the courts continue to find that the hybrid Section 301 6-month limitations period is not tolled absent evidence of positive misconduct by the union or employer that was deliberately designed to lead employees not to bring their challenges within the limitations period.[21] Finally, in *Bailey v. Boilermakers Local 374*,[22] a nonhybrid Section 301 action by employees against their union-employer, the Seventh Circuit held that the employer's unfulfilled promise to rehire employees did not toll the statute of limitations, absent something more, such as an offer to rehire coupled with a request not to sue.

---

[17]Cannon v. Kroger Co., 832 F.2d 303, 126 LRRM 2968 (4th Cir. 1987).

[18]*Supra* note 16; *Cannon, supra* note 17.

[19]Glass & Pottery Workers Local 421 v. A-CMI Mich. Casting Ctr., 191 F.3d 764, 162 LRRM 2290 (6th Cir. 1999).

[20]Christiansen v. AVP Crepaco, Inc., 178 F.3d 910, 161 LRRM 2333 (7th Cir. 1999) (limitations period began to run when union initially failed to file timely grievance and subsequent union action on same grievance did not restart limitations period).

[21]Barlow v. American Nat'l Can Co., 173 F.3d 640, 161 LRRM 2222 (8th Cir. 1999).

[22]175 F.3d 526, 161 LRRM 2074 (7th Cir. 1999).

2. The Board and the Courts

In *Pace v. Honolulu Disposal Services, Inc.*[23] the Ninth Circuit found that the hybrid Section 301 action brought by a group of employees claiming wrongful denial of pay and benefits provided in a series of collective bargaining agreements was primarily contractual in nature and that the district court had jurisdiction despite the claim of the employer and union that the case involved representational issues within the Board's primary jurisdiction.

IV. INJUNCTIONS IN AID OF ARBITRATION: SECTION 301 VERSUS NORRIS-LAGUARDIA

B. The *Boys Market* Injunction: Halting the Strike Over an Arbitrable Grievance

1. The Prerequisites for Issuance of Injunctive Relief

a. In General

According to the Second Circuit, "where a case does not concern either conduct enumerated in §4 or a dispute subject to mandatory arbitration, the proper approach is to allow injunctive relief provided the policies of both §301 and the NLA are thereby advanced."[24] The union sued for specific performance of the employer's nonarbitrable, contractual undertaking to make "every effort" to preserve certain bargaining-unit work. The employer had resisted injunction, arguing that injunctions may issue only where the underlying dispute is subject to mandatory bargaining and an injunction is essential to prevent undermining of the arbitration process. The court disagreed, asserting these are merely exceptions to the "general rule" that "an injunction may issue only where the dispute is subject to judicial resolution and the conduct to be enjoined is not included within the letter or spirit of §4 of the NLA."[25] In upholding the injunction, the court concluded that "[w]here a grievance is not

---

[23]227 F.3d 1150, 165 LRRM 2385 (9th Cir. 2000); *accord* Journeyman v. Valley Engineers, 975 F.2d 611, 141 LRRM 2326 (9th Cir. 1992).

[24]Aeronautical Indus. Dist. Lodge 91 v. United Techs. Corp., Pratt & Whitney, 230 F.3d 569, 580, 165 LRRM 2641, 2648 (2d Cir. 2000) (upholding the injunction).

[25]*Id.* at 580, 165 LRRM at 2648.

subject to arbitration or any other final and binding dispute resolution procedure, litigation is presumptively available under §301, and courts may issue injunctions consistently with the provisions of the NLA."[26]

c. Strike Over an Arbitrable Dispute

For there to be a finding that there is an arbitrable dispute, the employer must allege that the dispute is subject to a contractual arbitration clause and that it is ready to proceed with arbitration.[27] The arbitrability of the dispute must be "clear" and "undisputed."[28]

d. Irreparable Injury and the Balance of Equities

An employer was enjoined from liquidating certain assets because doing so would cause irreparable harm by rendering meaningless any arbitral award of backpay or other damages and the arbitration process itself.[29] Conversely, the court found that allowing the employer to close the facility in question would not cause irreparable harm. The court reasoned that the relevant market in the local area was "reasonably fluid," and that if the arbitrator ordered the facility reopened and the employees reinstated, the employer could regain its customers "over a reasonable period of time."

Although a dispute was subject to arbitration, the court found it lacked jurisdiction to grant an injunction where failure to do so would not render arbitration "a 'meaningless ritual.'"[30] In that case, the union sought to enjoin an employee's forced transfer. The court found that the employee had options other than injunction that would preserve the value of arbitration. Specifically, the employee had the option of refusing the transfer and being disciplined or terminated. The union could then arbitrate the discipline or termination.

Although courts must hear the evidence and balance the equities, a court need not find a threat of "unlawful acts" to issue an

---

[26]*Id.* at 580–81, 165 LRRM at 2648.

[27]Pickens-Kane Moving & Storage Co. v. Teamsters Local 705, 161 LRRM 2159, 2162 (N.D. Ill. 1999); Stuart Dean Co., Inc. v. Metal Polishers Local 8A-28A, 121 F. Supp. 2d 399 (S.D.N.Y. 2000).

[28]Allied Sys. Ltd. v. Teamsters Local 327, 179 F.3d 982, 989, 161 LRRM 2493, 2498 (6th Cir. 1999); *accord* Earthgrains Baking Cos. v. Teamsters Local 78, 35 F. Supp. 2d 1203, 160 LRRM 2638 (E.D. Cal. 1999).

[29]Teamsters Local 299 v. U.S. Truck Co. Holdings, Inc., 87 F. Supp. 2d 726, 163 LRRM 2412 (E.D. Mich. 2000).

[30]Chicago Typographical Union No. 16 v. Daily Racing Form, Inc., U.S. Dist. LEXIS 3370 (N.D. Ill. 1999).

injunction.[31] Section 301 allows suits for breach of contract, for example, which usually does not involve unlawful conduct.

f. Limitations on Prospective Relief; Mootness

In *Pace Mechanical Services v. Journeymen Plumbers Local 98*[32] the court granted the employer's motion for prescriptive injunctive relief where the union's threat to refuse to perform certain work, coupled with its past acts, was indicative of future strike activity. The union had already engaged in work slowdowns, vandalism, and failure to provide adequate numbers of workers.

4. Injunctions Against Employers to Preserve the Status Quo

In a "reverse *Boys Markets*" case, an employer was enjoined from liquidating certain of its assets to prevent the employer from evading the duty to arbitrate or otherwise undermining the integrity of the arbitral process.[33] Allowing the employer to liquidate the assets would have rendered any arbitral award of backpay or other damages meaningless. Enjoining liquidation of the assets was therefore held necessary to ensure meaningful relief through the arbitral process.

V. NLRB INTERPRETATION OF THE COLLECTIVE BARGAINING AGREEMENT

B. Cases Where the Board Interprets Contract Provisions

1. Interpretation of Lawful Contract Clauses

Provided the right to strike is interrelated with ambiguity in a contract, the federal courts are without jurisdiction to issue a *Boys Markets* injunction.[34] Where the contract excepts from its arbitration requirement certain types of contract violations and provides that the union retains the right to strike with respect to such violations, a court may not enjoin a strike where the union presents a colorable claim that such violations have occurred.[35]

---

[31]Aeronautical Indus. Dist. Lodge 91 v. United Techs. Corp., Pratt & Whitney, 230 F.3d 569, 582, 165 LRRM 2641, 2649 (2d Cir. 2000).

[32]U.S. Dist. LEXIS 7635 (E.D. Mich. 1999).

[33]*U.S. Truck Co., supra* note 29 at 736–37, 163 LRRM at 2420–21.

[34]Allied Sys. Ltd. v. Teamsters Local 327, 179 F.3d 982, 989, 161 LRRM 2493, 2498 (6th Cir. 1999).

[35]*Id.*

Chapter 18

ACCOMMODATION OF BOARD ACTION TO THE ARBITRATION PROCESS

II. Prearbitral Deferral: Applying the *Collyer* Doctrine

A. The Parties' Relationship

The Board continues to refuse to defer under *Collyer* when an employer's conduct evidences an enmity toward the principle of collective bargaining.[1] Where an employer engages in bad faith bargaining with an intent to avoid a contract, the Board also continues to refuse to defer.[2]

B. The Parties' Willingness to Arbitrate and Arbitrability

The Board has refused to defer under *Collyer* where an employer has rejected the underlying grievance[3] or has prevailed upon the arbitrator to decide the case on a procedural ground, and not on the merits.[4] The Board has also refused to defer when no arbitration agreement exists.[5]

C. Whether the Dispute Centers on the Collective Bargaining Agreement

1. *Matters Incidentally Related to the Collective Bargaining Agreement*

The Board has found deferral unwarranted where an employer transferred work previously performed by bargaining-unit employees to employees at a different facility. Subsequent to the transfer of work, the employer laid off the bargaining-unit employees, withdrew its recognition of the union, terminated the contract, and implemented new terms and conditions of employment. The Board found that while the decision to transfer may have been subject to arbitration standing alone, the subsequent issues (withdrawal of recogni-

---

[1]Budrovich Constr. Co., 331 NLRB No. 178 (2000); Wire Prods. Mfg. Corp., 329 NLRB No. 23 (1999); and Wire Prods. Mfg. Corp., 329 NLRB No. 115 (1999).

[2]United States Ecology Corp., 331 NLRB No. 23, 165 LRRM 1197 (2000).

[3]Wire Prods. Mfg. Corp., 328 NLRB No. 115 (1999).

[4]Pepsi-Cola Co., 330 NLRB No. 69 (2000) (employer initially prevailed upon arbitrator to decide case on procedural ground, and not merits, and arbitrator thereafter refused to decide case on merits, even though employer ultimately requested that arbitrator decide case on merits).

[5]Resco Prods., 331 NLRB No. 162 (2000) (successor employer not party to collective bargaining agreement); Edward S. Quirk Co., 330 NLRB No. 137 (2000) (collective bargaining agreement had expired).

tion, termination of the collective bargaining agreement, and changing terms and conditions of employment) were not. Reiterating its policy against bifurcated proceedings, the Board refused to defer.[6]

3. Matters Involving the Contract: Unilateral Action

The Board will defer a charge of a Section 8(a)(5) violation based on a unilateral change in terms and conditions of employment, if the employer's action arises from its interpretation of a contractual term covering the issue and the contract can plausibly be interpreted to allow the change made by the employer.[7] If, however, the contractual language will not necessarily resolve the issue, and there is not a clear and unmistakable waiver by the union of its right to negotiate over that term of employment, the Board will find a violation of Section 8(a)(5) and not defer the issue to arbitration.[8]

4. Demands for Information

The Board continues to exclude alleged refusals to furnish information from *Collyer* deferral.[9]

III. POST-ARBITRAL DEFERRAL: APPLYING THE *SPIELBERG* STANDARDS

A. The Issue Under the Act Was Presented and Considered in Arbitration

3. Application of the "Factual Parallelism" Standard

The Board continues to hold that it is inappropriate to defer to an arbitral award if the arbitrator did not adequately consider the unfair labor practice issue,[10] or if the arbitrator did not address the same issue that was before the Board.[11]

---

[6]Avery Dennison, 330 NLRB No. 56, 163 LRRM 1033 (1999).

[7]Charles S. Wilson Mem. Hosp., 331 NLRB No. 154, 2000 WL 1268771 at *3 n.4 (2000).

[8]*Id.*

[9]Mt. Sinai Hosp., 331 NLRB No. 111 (2000).

[10]Kohler Mix Specialties, Inc., 332 NLRB No. 61 (2000).

[11]New Orleans Cold Storage Warehouse, 326 NLRB 1471 (1998), *enforced*, 201 F.3d 592, 163 LRRM 2330 (5th Cir. 2000).

B. Fair and Regular Proceedings

1. The Arbitral Procedure

The Board in *Laborers International Union of North America*[12] adhered to precedent and deferred to two arbitration decisions when it found that the arbitrator had been given all relevant records and all of the affected grievants were represented by independent counsel.

D. The Award Is Not Repugnant to the Policies of the Act

The Board continues to refuse to defer to an arbitration award when it considers the result repugnant to the Act. For example, in *United States Postal Service*,[13] the Board refused to defer when employees engaged in protected activity and the arbitrator ignored Board precedent.[14]

IV. Other Factors Affecting the Board's Post-Arbitral Deferral Policy

B. Certain Unfair Labor Practices: Sections 8(a)(2) and 8(a)(4)

The Board continues to find that allegations of violation of Section 8(a)(4) may not be deferred to arbitration. In *Nationsway Transp. Serv.*,[15] the Board affirmed the ALJ's refusal to defer to the parties' settlement of a grievance where "the contractual issue resolved by the grievance settlement [was] not factually parallel to the unfair labor practice issues raised by the complaint and . . . therefore, deferral to the settlement [was] not warranted under *Postal Service*."[16]

---

[12]331 NLRB No. 28, 164 LRRM 1169, 2000 WL 718227 (2000).

[13]332 NLRB No. 28 (2000).

[14]*See also* Mobil Exploration & Producing U.S. v. NLRB, 200 F.3d 230, 163 LRRM 2387 (5th Cir. 1999), *enforcing* 325 NLRB 176, 156 LRRM 1279 (1997) (NLRB properly found that arbitration award—upholding employee's discharge and finding that his remarks to co-worker in lunchroom that employer was trying to fire him and had security guard after him for trying to "right a wrong" and assert his opposition to union president were delivered in insubordinate manner, stripping him of protection—was "clearly repugnant" to the purposes and policies of the Act).

[15]327 NLRB No. 184, 164 LRRM 1339 (1999).

[16]300 NLRB No. 23, 135 LRRM 1209 (1990).

V. RESPONSE OF THE REVIEWING COURT TO THE BOARD'S DEFERRAL STANDARDS

The courts continue to uphold the Board's refusal to defer to an arbitration award where the Board is found to have properly applied the applicable standards to the facts of the particular case.[17]

---

[17] *Mobil Exploration, supra* note 14 (Board's refusal to defer to arbitration decision upholding employees' discharge for allegedly breaching duty of confidentiality had sound basis in precedent; Board applied well-established balancing test for determining award was "clearly repugnant" to the Act and found that employees' substantial §7 right to engage in the activity in question was not outweighed by employer's "superficial claim of a confidentiality interest.") New Orleans Cold Storage & Warehouse Co. v. NLRB, 201 F.3d 592, 163 LRRM 2330 (5th Cir. 2000), *enforcing* 326 NLRB 1471, 163 LRRM 1095 (1998) (Board properly applied *Speilberg* factors in refusing to defer to award, where arbitrator limited his decision to the question of whether employer was obligated to assign employee to specific job he previously held, and did not consider employee's claim before Board that he had been discriminatorily assigned to different job upon reinstatement and later discharged for engaging in protected activity).

PART VI

ECONOMIC ACTION

CHAPTER 19

THE PRIMARY STRIKE

I. INTRODUCTION: THE RIGHT TO STRIKE

B. Preemption

Courts have continued holding that state statutes that infringe on an employer's right to replace strikers are preempted by the NLRA. For example, in *State v. Labor Ready, Inc.*[1] the Washington state Court of Appeals held that a strike-breaker statute that provided that employers could not use services of third parties in securing replace-

---

[1]103 Wash. App. 775, 14 P.3d 828 (2001).

ment personnel was preempted. Courts have been much less willing, however, to conclude that breach-of-contract claims brought by individuals hired as strike replacements are preempted,[2] relying on the Supreme Court's decision in *Belknap, Inc. v. Hale*.[3]

II. Strikes Protected Under the Act

B. Economic and Unfair Labor Practice Strikes

1. *Unfair Labor Practice Strikes*

In reaffirming the principle that unfair labor practice strikers cannot be permanently replaced, the Board and the courts have grappled with the issue of whether an economic dispute or an unfair labor practice actually caused a work stoppage. For example, in *Alwin Manufacturing Co. v. NLRB*,[4] the court found that unremedied unfair labor practices caused the bargaining impasse at issue, and held, therefore, that the resulting strike was properly classified as an unfair labor practice strike requiring the reinstatement of strikers who had been replaced. The Board has reached similar results, even when there was a substantial delay between the commencement of a strike and the occurrence of unfair labor practices[5] or when the unfair labor practices were just one of the reasons for the work stoppage.[6]

The Board continued to hold that unfair labor practice strikers who make an unconditional offer to return to work are entitled to immediate reinstatement, even if the employer purported to hire permanent replacements.[7]

---

[2]*See* Baldwin v. Pirelli Armstrong Tire Corp., 3 S.W.3d 1, 160 LRRM 2541 (Tenn. Ct. App. 1999) (holding that NLRA did not preempt breach of contract claim of replacement workers who were allegedly promised permanent employment but then discharged at conclusion of strike).

[3]463 U.S. 491, 113 LRRM 3057 (1983).

[4]192 F.3d 133, 162 LRRM 2385 (D.C. Cir. 1999).

[5]RGC (USA) Mineral Sands, Inc., 332 NLRB No. 172 (2000).

[6]Boydston Elec., Inc., 331 NLRB No. 194 (2000) (an unfair labor practice strike was found where employer's unlawful conduct at least partially caused employees' decision to strike, regardless of whether unfair labor practices were flagrant, serious, or pervasive); Ryan Iron Works, Inc., 332 NLRB 49 (2000) (employer's unfair labor practices will convert economic strike into unfair labor practice strike).

[7]Dorsey Trailers, Inc., 327 NLRB No. 55, 165 LRRM 1392 (1999) (ordering reinstatement of unfair labor practice strikers who made unconditional offer to return to work).

2. Economic Strikes

Although the Mackay[8] doctrine, allowing an employer to permanently replace economic strikers, retains its vitality, the Board has continued placing the burden on the employer to demonstrate that it is justified in refusing to reinstate a striker who seeks to return to work.[9]

III. UNPROTECTED AND PROHIBITED STRIKES

A. Unlawful or Wrongful Means

3. Partial and Intermittent Strikes

The Board continues holding that employees who engage in partial or intermittent strikes lose the protection of the Act. For example, the Board found no violation of the Act where an employer discharged a customer service representative who asked co-workers not to interact with a vendor whose employees were striking. This, the Board reasoned, was solicitation to participate in an intermittent, partial work stoppage, which was unprotected activity.[10] Similarly, the Board approved an ALJ's recommendation that a "grade strike" by teaching fellows at Yale University was unprotected activity because it was a partial strike and the strikers had effectively misappropriated property of the university as a result of this activity.[11]

4. Picket Line Misconduct; Strike Violence

The Board has continued to recognize that an employer may discharge employees who engage in picket line misconduct during

---

[8]NLRB v. Mackay Radio & Tel. Co., 304 U.S. 333, 2 LRRM 610 (1938).

[9]TNS, Inc., 329 NLRB No. 61, 166 LRRM 1018 (1999) (work stoppage to protest abnormally dangerous working conditions is not economic strike, and employer may not permanently replace employees engaged in such a work stoppage); Erman Corp., 330 NLRB No. 26, 163 LRRM 1042 (1999) (to disenfranchise striking employee, employer cannot rely on temporary economic downturn; rather, it must show that employee's job was permanently eliminated); Pirelli Cable Corp., 331 NLRB No. 158 (2000) (unlawful for employer to condition reinstatement of economic strikers on submission of letter expressing their desire and availability for reinstatement).

[10]Electronic Data Sys. Corp., 331 NLRB No. 52, 164 LRRM 1211 (2000).

[11]Yale Univ. & Graduate Employees & Students Orgs., 330 NLRB No. 28, 162 LRRM 1393 (1999); see also Forsyth Elec. Co., Inc., 332 NLRB No. 68 (2000) (employees engaged in a covert work slowdown may be lawfully discharged).

the course of a strike. For example, in *Siemens Energy & Automation, Inc.*,[12] the Board held that the discharge of a striker who kicked cars and threw roofing tacks onto the roadway at the vehicular entrance to the employer's plant did not violate the Act. The Board found that such conduct may reasonably tend to coerce or intimidate employees in the exercise of their right to refrain from participating in the strike. In *Patrick Media Group*,[13] however, the Board concluded that the employer's discharge of a striker for provoking and engaging in a fight with the employer's security guard violated Section 8(a)(1) because the evidence did not establish that anything more than a verbal altercation had taken place. In *CalMat Co.*[14] the Board found no Section 8(a)(1) violation where an employer told a striker—who was retired—that he was not eligible for rehire. In this case, the striker had threatened a security guard with physical harm and carried a collapsible night stick on the picket line. In the same case, another striker was lawfully discharged for stepping in front of a slow-moving truck as it attempted to cross the picket line, and then trying to assault the truck driver.[15]

B. Unlawful or Wrongful Ends

1. *Strikes in Violation of the Act*

The Board has continued holding that a strike or other economic action in support of a proposal on a nonmandatory bargaining subject is unlawful.[16]

2. *Strikes in Breach of Contract*

The Fourth Circuit has held that where picketing regarding grievable matters is intended to cause a work stoppage, it is not informational picketing, no matter how few workers participate.[17] Such picketing is not, therefore, protected by Section 7 of the Act.

---

[12]328 NLRB No. 164, 162 LRRM 1083 (1999).

[13]326 NLRB 1287, 163 LRRM 1064, *enforced*, 203 F.3d 53 (D.C. Cir. 1999).

[14]326 NLRB No. 21, 161 LRRM 1016 (1998).

[15]*Id.*

[16]Detroit Newspaper Agency, 327 NLRB No. 146, 160 LRRM 1193 (1999), *rev'd on other grounds*, 216 F.3d 109, 164 LRRM 2797 (D.C. Cir. 2000).

[17]Mine Workers v. Island Creek Coal Co., 179 F.3d 133, 161 LRRM 2463 (4th Cir. 1999).

IV. RIGHTS OF EMPLOYEES RESPECTING PICKET LINES: SYMPATHY STRIKES

B. Effect of Contractual Waiver of Rights

The Sixth Circuit has held that a union was not enjoined from striking over an employer's decision that one facility's pay rate would govern when it was merged with another, despite the presence of a no-strike clause in the collective bargaining agreement, because the issue of whether the strike was covered by the provision of the agreement was itself arbitrable.[18] Meanwhile, the Seventh Circuit held that a collective bargaining agreement's no-strike clause was meant to apply to sympathy strikes for the signatory union's own picket lines, where the agreement's sympathy-strike exception explicitly referred only to the picket lines of other unions and not to the those of the signatory union.[19]

C. Sympathy Strikes Not Enjoinable: *Buffalo Forge*

The Eleventh Circuit held that a union lawfully called a pilots' sympathy strike where the procedures it followed were consistent with the union's strike policy, and the union constitution had not been changed and had been consistently applied since 1966.[20]

---

[18]Allied Sys. Ltd. v. Teamsters Local 327, 179 F.3d 982, 161 LRRM 2493 (6th Cir. 1999), *cert. denied*, 528 U.S. 963 (1999). *See also* Earthgrains Baking Cos. v. Teamsters Local 78, 35 F. Supp. 2d 1203, 160 LRRM 2638 (E.D. Cal. 1999) (court denied employer's request for preliminary injunction where it found that issue of whether no-strike clause of collective bargaining agreement was applicable would have to be addressed before any ruling on injunctive relief).

[19]R.L. Coolsaet Constr. Co. v. Engineers, 177 F.3d 648, 161 LRRM 2195 (7th Cir. 1999).

[20]Dunn v. Airline Pilots Ass'n, 193 F.3d 1185, 162 LRM 2577 (11th Cir. 1999).

CHAPTER 20

THE LOCKOUT

I. INTRODUCTION: HISTORICAL PERSPECTIVE

C. Evolution of Justifiable Lockouts: The Defensive Lockout

1. The Single-Employer Defensive Lockout

The Board and the courts continue to adhere to the principle that defensive lockouts are permissible where an employer's actions are not motivated by a purpose to interfere with and defeat its employees' union activities,[1] and where such actions were intended to avoid several economic hardships caused by a union's use of economic weapons.[2]

In *Electrical Workers (IBEW) Local 702 v. NLRB*[3] the D.C. Circuit denied a request for review of the Board's decision in *Central Illinois*

---

[1] 72 NLRB 601, 602, 19 LRRM 1208 (1947).

[2] *See, e.g.*, Tanco Communications, 220 NLRB 636, 90 LRRM 1321 (1975), *enforcement denied*, 567 F.2d 871, 97 LRRM 2660 (9th Cir. 1978), and other cases cited in the Main Edition, Chapter 20, "The Lockout."

[3] 215 F.3d 11, 164 LRRM 2193 (D.C. Cir. 2000), *cert. denied*, 121 S. Ct. 654, 165 LRRM 3056 (2000).

Public Service Co.[4] The court affirmed the Board's conclusion that the employer did not act unlawfully when it locked out its employees in response to the unions' "inside game" tactics such as working to the rule and refusing voluntary overtime, as well as to pressure from the union to reach agreement. The court agreed with the Board that because the lockout was not inherently destructive of employee rights, it was necessary to establish that the employer's motivation for the lockout was improper to find the lockout to be unlawful. The court held that the employer had the right to engage in the lockout as a defensive measure to counteract the union's "inside game" tactics, even assuming that such tactics were protected activity.

In *CII Carbon*[5] the employer locked out only those employees who worked at a location where an act of sabotage occurred. The Board held that the employer had a legitimate and substantial business justification for the lockout because sabotage was an unprotected activity, the employer acted out of a concern for safety, and the employer's preliminary investigation revealed that the sabotage could have occurred only with the complicity or knowledge of the unit employees at that particular location. Moreover, the Board found no probative evidence that the employer had an antiunion motivation in locking out the employees.

II. Contemporary Law of Lockouts

A. The Offensive Economic Lockout—In General

The Board continues to apply the standards set forth in *American Ship Building v. NLRB*[6] and *NLRB v. Brown Food Store*[7] in evaluating whether the use of the lockout as an offensive weapon in the collective bargaining process is lawful.

1. *Lockouts Occurring in Conjunction With Employer Unfair Labor Practices*

In *Eddy Potash, Inc.*[8] the employer bargained to impasse and insisted, as a condition of reaching any final collective bargaining agree-

---

[4]326 NLRB 928, 159 LRRM 1217 (1998).
[5]331 NLRB No. 155 (2000).
[6]380 U.S. 300, 58 LRRM 2672 (1965).
[7]380 U.S. 278, 58 LRM 2663 (1965).
[8]331 NLRB No. 71, 2000 WL 895102 (2000).

ment, that the unions agree to 12-hour shifts for employees working in underground mines. The employer locked out its employees to pressure the unions to agree to this proposal. The Board concluded that the 12-hour-shift proposal was an illegal subject of bargaining because it violated the Mineral Lands and Mining Act of 1920, and that therefore, it was unlawful for the employer to insist to impasse on that proposal. As a consequence, the employer's offensive lockout to force agreement to that proposal was also found to be unlawful.

In *Graphic Communications Local 458-3M (Chicago) v. NLRB*[9] the D.C. Circuit affirmed the Board's conclusion that the employer's offensive lockout was lawful because its purpose was to apply economic pressure on the employees to support its legitimate bargaining position. The court agreed with the Board that although the employer's bargaining position may have been regressive, it did not amount to bad faith bargaining. Therefore, the lockout in support of the position was not unlawful.[10]

Anderson Enterprises, dba Royal Motor Sales[11] involved two lockouts that failed to satisfy the standard of *American Ship Building* for a permissible offensive lockout. Regarding the first lockout, the employer claimed it had a substantial business justification, because the lockout was necessitated by contractual provisions as a prerequisite to lawful implementation of the employer's final proposal. The Board rejected this argument, and held that the lockout was unlawful because the union had waived any such contractual requirements, and the lockout merely served as a preliminary step to an unlawful implementation because the parties were not at impasse, given the context of serious unremedied unfair labor practices.

Regarding the second lockout, the employer implemented its final offer at a time when it had neither reached a lawful impasse nor asserted the existence of economic exigencies. The Board found that the employer locked out its employees with the intent of retaliating against them because their bargaining representative insisted on good-faith collective bargaining. Moreover, the Board found that the employer locked out its employees with the intent of coercing

---

[9]206 F.3d 22, 163 LRRM 2833 (D.C. Cir. 2000), *denying petition for review*, 325 NLRB 1166, 158 LRRM 1241 (1998).

[10]*See also* Electrical Workers (IBEW) Local 702 v. NLRB, 215 F.3d 11, 164 LRRM 2193 (D.C. Cir. 2000), *cert. denied*, 121 S. Ct. 654, 165 LRRM 3056 (2000), in which the Court affirmed the Board's findings that the lockout was lawful under both defensive and offensive criteria.

[11]329 NLRB No. 71, 166 LRRM 1123 (1999), *enforced*, 2001 WL 59043 (D.C. Cir. 2001).

the union to accept its unilaterally implemented final offer. Because the employer's unilateral, pre-impasse implementation of its final offer constituted an unfair labor practice, the final offer was held to be an illegitimate bargaining position that the employer was not free to pursue through the use of a lockout.[12]

3. The Pre-Impasse Lockout

Although the existence of an impasse is still not a prerequisite for a finding of a lawful offensive lockout,[13] the impasse and lockout doctrine continue to intersect in cases arising under Sections 8(a)(1), (3), and (5).[14]

---

[12]*Id.*

[13]Darling & Co., 171 NLRB 801, 68 LRRM 1133 (1968) *enforced sub nom.* Lane v. NLRB, 418 F.2d 1208, 72 LRRM 2439 (D.C. Cir. 1969).

[14]*See, e.g., Anderson Enters., supra* note 11.

Chapter 21

PICKETING FOR ORGANIZATION
AND RECOGNITION

III. PROSCRIBED ORGANIZATIONAL OR RECOGNITIONAL OBJECTIVE

A. Evidence of Proscribed Object

The Board continues to determine whether or not picketing is for organizational or recognitional purposes based on an analysis of the union's overall conduct, including events preceding the picketing, as well as those that accompany the picketing.[1]

---

[1]Electrical Workers (IBEW) Local 3 (Genmar Elec. Contracting, Inc.), 332 NLRB No. 123 (2000); Roofers, Waterproofers and Allied Workers Local 11 (Funderburk Roofing, Inc.), 331 NLRB No. 4 (2000) (signs that say employer "does

C. Area-Standards Picketing

The Board found no present demand for recognition, and therefore dismissed an employer's election petitions, where the union's placards advised the public that the employer did not have a contract with the union and requested a boycott and where union handbills alleged that working conditions at a nonunion hotel were substandard compared with union hotels. In addition, nothing in the record indicated that the union acted contrary to a letter from the union president disclaiming any immediate recognitional objective.[2]

In *Petrochem Insulation*[3] the Board held that petitioning state governmental agencies with objections to environmental standards of employer contracts is protected area-standards activity within the meaning of the mutual aid or protection provision of Section 7 of the Act. According to the Board, working conditions may include the safety and health of all employees who may eventually be employed at a particular worksite.

The Board continues to adhere to its view that an employer violates the Act by regularly allowing nonunion organizations to use its premises for solicitation, while denying unions that same access to its property.[4] In *Sandusky Mall*[5] the Board addressed the issue of whether a mall owner had discriminated against union agents in connection with access to mall property. The mall owner refused to permit union agents to engage in "area-standards" handbilling on mall property while at the same time the mall owner had allowed charitable, civic, and other organizations to solicit on the same property. The Board majority found unlawful discrimination because the owner had unlawfully distinguished between union activity and other activity.

---

not employ members of" are often construed as having organizational objective). *See also* NLRB v. Calkins dba Indio Grocery Outlet, 187 F.3d 1080, 161 LRRM 3121 (9th Cir. 1999), *enforcing* 323 NLRB 1138, 155 LRRM 1210 (1997), *cert. denied,* 120 S. Ct. 1831, 164 LRRM 2256 (2000).

[2]Hotel & Restaurant Employees Local 11 (New Otani Hotel & Garden), 331 NLRB No. 159 (2000) (finding that the union engaged in only informational picketing as defined in the second proviso to §8(b)(7)(C)).

[3]330 NLRB No. 10, 163 LRRM 1276 (1999), *enforced,* 240 F.3d 26, 166 LRRM 2433 (D.C. Cir. 2001).

[4]Albertson's Inc., 332 NLRB No. 104, 166 LRRM 1003 (2000) (finding unlawful discrimination in exclusion of nonemployees seeking access to employer property to engage in area-standards handbilling).

[5]329 NLRB No. 62, 162 LRRM 1191 (1999), *enforcement denied,* 166 LRRM 2641 (6th Cir. 2001). Relying on its decision in *Cleveland Real Estate Partners v. NLRB,* 95

IV. PICKETING WHEN ANOTHER UNION IS CURRENTLY RECOGNIZED

The Board continues to hold that a Section 8(b)(7)(A) violation will be found if only one of the objectives of picketing is recognitional or organizational.[6] Whether picketing is for organizational or recognitional purposes is a question of fact to be determined from the union's overall conduct.[7]

D. Inapplicability of Informational Proviso

The informational nature of a picket is not a defense to a Section 8(b)(7)(A) charge in a case where the picket also has an organizational or recognitional objective.[8]

V. PICKETING WITHIN TWELVE MONTHS OF A VALID ELECTION

A. Validity of the Election

2. *Other Assertions of Invalidity*

The Board continues to adhere to its "no-relitigation" rule.[9]

VII. THE INFORMATIONAL PICKETING PROVISO

The Board and courts continue to hold that truthful picketing to inform customers that an employer does not employ members of a labor organization is protected Section 7 conduct.[10]

F.3d 457 (6th Cir. 1996), the Sixth Circuit held that the mall owner lawfully enforced its general no-solicitation rule against union nonemployees, although it occasionally allowed limited charitable activities in the mall, which were deemed beneficial to the owner and the tenants.

[6] *See* Roofers, Waterproofers & Allied-Workers Local 11 (Funderburk Roofing, Inc.), 331 NLRB No. 4 (2000).

[7] *See* Electrical Workers (IBEW) Local 3, 332 NLRB No. 123 (2000) (citing Teamsters Local 618 (S&R Auto Parts), 193 NLRB 714 (1971)).

[8] *See Roofers, supra* note 6 (finding that recognition was "at the least, an objective" of picketing despite union's claim that picketing was solely informational and union's use of disclaimers of any recognitional objective).

[9] United Health Care Employees (FPA Med. Mgmt., Inc.), 331 NLRB No. 117, 165 LRRM 1009 (2000) ("the Board has traditionally applied its 'no relitigation' rule in cases where the bargaining unit in both the unfair labor practice case and the representation case are the same").

[10] *See, e.g.*, NLRB v. Calkins dba Indio Grocery Outlet, 187 F.3d 1080, 161 LRRM 3121 (9th Cir. 1999), *enforcing* 323 NLRB 1138, 155 LRRM 1210 (1997) (California

A. Scope of the Proviso: Dual-Purpose Picketing

The Board continues to permit picketing with an object of recognition or organization when the statements made on signs are limited to language that is expressly sanctioned by the second proviso to Section 8(b)(7)(C). Furthermore, picketing to advise the public that an employer does not employ members of, or have a contract with, a union does not, without more, establish that the union has made a present demand for recognition as required by Section 9(c)(1)(B).[11]

---

state law does not protect shopping mall or supermarket owners' interest in excluding speech activity from their adjacent sidewalks and parking lots, so nonemployees may lawfully inform customers that employer did not employ members of labor organization; activity was protected by §8(b)(7)(C)'s second proviso).

[11]*See* New Otani Hotel & Garden, 331 NLRB No. 159 (2000) ("statements made on the Union's placards, advising the public that the Employer does not have a contract with the Union and requesting a boycott, were limited to language that is expressly sanctioned under that proviso . . . [and] such picketing does not constitute evidence of a present demand for recognition that would support the processing of a petition under Section 9(c)(1)(B).").

CHAPTER 22

SECONDARY ACTIVITY: HANDBILLS, PICKETS, AND STRIKES

II. SECTION 8(b)(4)(B): PROHIBITED SECONDARY ACTIVITY DEFINED

A. Definitions of Terms

Courts continue to closely examine picketing[1] and handbilling activities to determine whether the activities "induce or encourage" neutral employees within the meaning of Section 8(b)(4)(i). In *Warshawsky & Co. v. NLRB*[2] the D.C. Circuit reversed the Board's holding and found that the totality of the circumstances established that the union's handbilling was intended to "induce" neutral employees to cease work: The handbilling occurred only at times when neutral employees would be arriving at the job site; the handbillers engaged the neutral employees in conversation as they approached the site; and none of the neutral employees proceeded to work on the days the handbilling occurred.[3]

---

[1]The Board has adhered to the proposition that "picketing" within the meaning of the statute does not require "patrolling." Painters District Council 9 (We're Associates), 329 NLRB No. 17 (1999) (affirming ALJ's conclusion that "milling around," carrying signs, and mounting sign on automobile to confront vehicles constituted "picketing").

[2]182 F.3d 948, 161 LRRM 2772 (D.C. Cir. 1999), *cert. denied,* 529 U.S. 1003, 163 LRRM 2704 (2000).

[3]*Cf.* Electrical Workers (IBEW) Local 98 (Telephone Man), 327 NLRB No. 113 (1999) (violation of §8(b)(4)(i)(B) based on harsh comments by union to neutral employees. "The words 'induce or encourage' are broad enough to include in them every form of influence and persuasion.").

Courts also continue to interpret the terms "threaten, coerce or restrain" under Section 8(b)(4)(ii). In *George v. National Association of Letter Carriers*[4] the Fifth Circuit stated that "the possibility of economic ramifications" does not transform otherwise lawful conduct into "threats, coercion, or restraint" under the statute. The court concluded that a union's dispatch of letters to another union to persuade the latter union's members to join the union's boycott did not violate Section 8(b)(4)(ii)(B). The court noted that letter writing had even fewer potentially coercive, threatening, or restraining characteristics than lawful handbilling or other in-person communication.[5]

The term "doing business" under Section 8(b)(4) has been interpreted to include "continuing long-term negotiation over the purchase of a new asset from a neutral party."[6]

B. The Elusive Distinction Between Primary and Secondary Conduct

Distinguishing primary conduct from secondary conduct remains an issue requiring precise analysis. In *Service Employees Local 525 (General Maintenance Service Co.)*[7] a divided Board held that membership in a trade organization that included both primary and neutral employer-members and that actively assisted the primary employers to lessen the impact of primary activity by unions did not,

---

[4]185 F.3d 380, 162 LRRM 2137 (5th Cir. 1999), *cert. denied*, 528 U.S. 1156, 163 LRRM 2576 (2000).

[5]*Id.*, 185 F.3d at 391. To apply the Act, courts examine the means and tone of the communication. Calmat Co. v. Local 12, 165 LRRM 2628 (C.D. Ca. 1998), *aff'd*, 211 F.3d 1272, 165 LRRM 2639 (9th Cir. 1998) (union unlawfully threatened and coerced customers of primary employer), *cert. denied*, 531 U.S. 943, 165 LRRM 2640 (2000); Moore-Duncan v. Metropolitan Regional Council of Philadelphia & Vicinity, 162 LRRM 2615 (E.D. Pa. 1999) (creating vastly excessive noise levels by broadcasting protest message over loudspeaker constituted coercion), *aff'd*, 225 F.3d 649, 164 LRRM 3024 (3d Cir. 2000); Printpack, Inc. v. Graphic Communications Local 761S, 988 F. Supp. 1201, 161 LRRM 2154 (S.D. Ind. 1997) (refusing motion to dismiss employer's action brought under §303 where language of letter sent by union to employer's customers could be considered threatening).

[6]Taylor Milk Co. v. Teamsters, 167 LRRM 2087 (3d Cir. 2001) (union interfered with primary employer's attempts to purchase business from secondary person; primary intended to transfer work to purchased business and close its existing facility at which union represented employees, rejecting union's argument that it was "within its rights" to engage in secondary conduct, court noted that "we look to the intention of the parties in coercing neutral parties, not to the general rights of parties to take particular actions").

[7]329 NLRB No. 64 (1999).

standing alone, cause the neutral employer-members to lose their neutrality in primary labor disputes involving other members of the trade organization. An otherwise neutral employer remains neutral even if it has an economic interest in the outcome of the primary dispute. The Board explained that a loss of neutrality will be found where the employer has an "ally"[8] relationship or exercises "substantial, actual and active control" over the working conditions of the primary employees.[9]

In *Kim's Trucking Inc. v. Teamsters Local 179*[10] Kim's Trucking, a secondary employer, alleged a violation of Section 8(b)(4)(B) because a union "threatened" Kim's Trucking that it would picket the primary contractor that subcontracted work to Kim's if the subcontracting continued. The court found that the alleged conduct did not violate the Act and also found that the union's single-person picket at the primary employer's work site was a "textbook example" of a proper picket of a primary employer.[11]

In *Electrical Workers (IBEW) Local 98 (Telephone Man)*[12] the Board held that an "observer" at a neutral gate engaged in "signal picketing" undertaken for an impermissible secondary object where the observer engaged in conduct going beyond mere observation, such as flashing the reverse side of the sign containing the primary picketing language, talking to employees of neutrals as they used the gate, and entertaining visits from pickets from the primary gate. The Board also affirmed that conduct that has the foreseeable effect of causing neutral employees to strike, such as a union agent's telling employees of a neutral to "get out of my building" because primary employees were also working there and calling the attention of neutral employees to a primary picket line at a gate not used by them, constitutes Section 8(b)(4)(i)(B) inducement. Finally, the Board held that a strike by employees of a neutral resulting from Section 8(b)(4)(i)(B) conduct also constitutes coercion of the neutral employer within the meaning of Section 8(b)(4)(ii)(B).

---

[8] *See* Fourth Edition, Chapter 22, "Secondary Activity: Handbills, Pickets, and Strikes," Section II.E. [Section 8(b)(4)(B): Prohibited Secondary Activity Defined; The Ally Doctrine], for a discussion of the ally doctrine.

[9] In this case, the Board also held that a law firm that represents a primary employer in its dispute with a union is not, by virtue of its representation, a primary employer. 329 NLRB No. 64.

[10] 13 F. Supp. 2d 715, 162 LRRM 2179 (N.D. Ill. 1998).

[11] *Id.*, 13 F. Supp. 2d at 718.

[12] 327 NLRB No. 113 (1999).

C. The Situs of the Dispute

2. Common and Ambulatory Situs

The Board continues to analyze the lawfulness of secondary picketing under the *Moore Dry Dock* standards.[13] For example, in *Painters District Council 9 (We're Associates, Inc.)*[14] the Board found that the union failed to comply with the *Moore Dry Dock* standards because it picketed at an office building at which the primary employer had not engaged in activities or work for more than 1 month.[15]

Santiago v. Teamsters Local 705[16] involved a union's strike against the operator of a multibuilding complex. The union had picketed at the complex's gate reserved for employees and customers of a movie production company that had leased part of the complex from the operator. Notwithstanding the union's claim that leasing space at the facilities to film and television production companies was one of the regular ongoing aspects of the operator's business, the court held that the operator's regular lease of parts of the complex to others did not transform the lessees' employees into persons whose work contributes to the day-to-day operation of the employer's business.

D. The Reserved Gate and the Related-Work Test

3. Application to the Construction Industry

In *Warshawsky & Co. v. NLRB*[17] the D.C. Circuit held that a union representing a subcontractor's employees engaged in an unlawful secondary boycott by directing handbills at neutral employees of the general contractor and other subcontractors. The handbills' language; the time, place, and manner of their distribution; and the simultaneous conversations between the union agents and the neutral employees established that the union sought to induce the neutral employees to cease work.

---

[13]92 NLRB 547, 27 LRRM 1108 (1950).

[14]329 NLRB No. 17 (1999).

[15]*See also* Electrical Workers Local 98 (Telephone Man), 327 NLRB 593 (1999) (union violated *Moore Dry Dock* by continuing to picket after having received fax notification that primary was not working at site).

[16]166 LRRM 2142 (N.D. Ill. 2000), *rulings on motion in limine,* 166 LRRM 2147 (2001).

[17]182 F.3d 948, 161 LRRM 2772 (D.C. Cir. 1999), *cert. denied sub nom.* Ironworkers Local 386 v. Warshawsky & Co., 529 U.S. 1003, 163 LRRM 2704 (2000).

The Seventh Circuit, applying the Board's "totality of the circumstances" test to determine the motive for the union's conduct, found that the union engaged in unlawful secondary activity when it picketed a gate to a public utility's storage facility reserved for a unionized independent contractor and picketed a main gate that was occasionally used by a nonunion primary employer to retrieve supplies.[18] One of the union's objectives was to pressure the contractor and public utility to cease doing business with the primary employer.

4. Application Generally: The Totality of Conduct Test

Electrical Workers (IBEW) Local 98 (Telephone Man)[19] involved "signal picketing" undertaken for an impermissibly secondary objective—activity short of true picketing that acts as a signal to neutrals that sympathetic action on their part is desired by the union. The observer carried a sign that read "observer" on one side, but had the primary message on the reverse that "conveniently" flipped over from time to time whenever anyone entered the area. The observer stationed himself at the gate and spoke with the neutral's employees, who then turned away and did not report to work. The union also unlawfully picketed in violation of the *Moore Dry Dock* standards by maintaining pickets at a neutral gate for 5 hours after being notified of the reserved gate. Also, the union agent stated to the neutral employer that he should "pay the men what they're worth," thereby evidencing a secondary objective.

The Board held that the union did not violate Section 8(b)(4) at secondary sites by holding gatherings or rallies that did not rise to the level of picketing.[20] Further, the Board held that comments by a union organizer that workers were being treated shabbily were too ambiguous to violate Section 8(b)(4) and that the organizer's attempts to bait a security guard into a fight similarly did not violate Section 8(b)(4), because it was not an appeal to an employee to withhold services or to disrupt business relations.

Applying *Moore Dry Dock*, however, in this case the Board found that the union unlawfully picketed secondary buildings by failing to identify the primary employer on its signs and picketing when the primary's employees were not on site after the union had received

---

[18]R.L. Coolsaet Constr. Co. v. Operating Eng'rs Local 150, 177 F.3d 648, 161 LRRM 2195 (7th Cir.), *cert. denied*, 120 S. Ct. 498, 162 LRRM 2832 (1999).

[19]327 NLRB No. 113 (1999).

[20]Service Employees Local 525 (Gen. Maintenance Serv. Co., Inc.), 329 NLRB No. 64 (1999).

notice that they would not be there.[21] The Board rejected the union's argument that a limitation to picketing late at night when the primary's employees were at the site would deprive the union of the opportunity to appeal to the public. The Board did not find the limitation analogous to the problems of a reserved gate at a remote site, which effectively would eliminate the union's ability to bring the labor dispute to the public's attention. The union also unlawfully picketed private homes of employees of the secondary employers because the object of the picketing was to exert improper influence on a neutral party. Appearing at night with candles was inherently intimidating, despite the fact that the union obtained a parade permit. A divided Board held that the delivery of a sealed envelope to a secondary's manager did not have the "reasonably foreseeable effect" of threatening, coercing, or restraining the manager within the meaning of Section 8(b)(4)(ii)(B).

In *Warshawsky & Co. v. NLRB*[22] the court refused to enforce the Board's ruling that handbilling a neutral employer's employees did not have secondary effects. The court held that the union's conduct had the foreseeable effect of inducing the neutral's employees to walk off the job site; the handbills themselves did not have a sufficiently large disclaimer; the handbilling took place at a time and place when only the neutral employees were present; and there were simultaneous conversations between the union agents and the neutral employees.

The Seventh Circuit held that the union violated Section 303 and was liable for damages because the union engaged in secondary picketing in violation of Section 8(b)(4) by the following activities:[23] picketing a gate reserved for another unionized contractor's employees and a main gate occasionally used by the nonunion primary employer, using employees of the unionized secondary employer on the picket line, maintaining a picket regardless of whether the primary employer was on site, failing to target the primary employer but focusing instead on areas where the unionized secondary employer worked, and telling the secondary employers that it would

---

[21] *See also* Painters District Council 9 (We're Associates, Inc.), 329 NLRB No. 17 (1999) (union picketed at the common situs when the primary employer was not at the site, failed to follow a valid reserve gate, and failed to identify the primary employer on its picket signs).

[22] 182 F.3d 948, 161 LRRM 2772 (D.C. Cir. 1999), *cert. denied,* 529 U.S. 1003, 163 LRRM 2704 (2000).

[23] R.L. Coolsaet Constr. Co. v. Operating Eng'rs Local 150, 177 F.3d 648, 161 LRRM 2195 (7th Cir.), *cert. denied,* 120 S. Ct. 498, 162 LRRM 2832 (1999).

remove the pickets only if the primary nonunion employer ceased work at the job site.

In *NLRB v. Ironworkers Local 433* [24] the union was found to be in contempt of a 7-year-old consent decree when it engaged in secondary picketing. The court found unpersuasive that the current union officers were unaware of the existence of the consent decree because they were not in office at the time the decree was issued and that the union's attorney simply forgot about the decree.

F. Applying the Primary-Secondary Tests

1. *Conduct Other Than Picketing*

The District Court granted a Section 10(l) injunction against a union that deliberately used vastly excessive noise volumes in broadcasting its protest that a contracting firm working at an apartment complex was compensating its carpenters at wage rates below those prevailing in the area.[25] The extreme noise levels could constitute coercive action, constituting a violation of Section 8(b)(4)(B).

The Board found that a grocery store union violated the Act by filing a grievance and demanding arbitration about the store's Cinnabon bakery operation.[26] The union claimed that its members should have performed the work of preparing and selling Cinnabon's products, which was being done by Cinnabon employees at leased premises within the store. The Board concluded that the union's grievance and demand for arbitration had an unlawful secondary objective of forcing the store to cease doing business with Cinnabon. It held that the union had "failed to present a colorable contractual claim to the work in controversy."[27] The work was not "fairly claimable" by the union, because union members had never performed baking duties similar to those done by Cinnabon employees. Finally, the Board concluded that the grocery store did not have the "right to control" the work of handling and selling Cinnabon's products.[28]

---

[24]169 F.3d 1217, 160 LRRM 2736 (9th Cir. 1999) (fines for violations of a consent decree did not trigger the need for criminal procedural safeguards).

[25]Moore-Duncan v. Metropolitan Regional Council of Philadelphia and Vicinity, 162 LRRM 2615 (E.D. Pa. 1999), *aff'd*, 164 LRRM 3024 (3d Cir. 2000).

[26]Food & Commercial Workers Local 367 (Quality Food Centers, Inc.), 333 NLRB No. 84, 166 LRRM 1377 (2001).

[27]*Id.*, 166 LRRM at 1378.

[28]*Id.* at 1379.

In *Taylor Milk Co. v. Teamsters*[29] the union violated the Act by interfering with the primary employer's attempts to purchase a business from a secondary person; the primary employer intended to transfer work to the new business and close its existing facility at which the union represented the employees. On the other hand, the court held that a union did not violate Section 8(b)(4)(ii)(B) where it threatened to write to other affiliated locals asking them to boycott a company that sold uniforms.[30] The court found the proposed letter-writing campaign did not constitute coercive, threatening, or restraining behavior under the Act.

3. Location of the Picketing

Unlawful secondary activity occurs when a union pickets a gate reserved for a contractor whose employees are unionized and pickets a main gain that the nonunion primary contractor has used only occasionally, where the union's object is to force the primary employer off the site.[31]

In *Kobell v. African American Workers*[32] the court entered a 10(l) injunction against a union that had a primary dispute with a city, county, and public auditorium authority. The injunction barred picketing at a stadium construction site. The union claimed that the picketing was informational, but the signs did not identify with whom the union had the dispute. Some of the signs read: "Picket Line Crossing Is Union Busting AAWU." The court found that the government agencies were not engaged in their normal business at the site. The union's objective was to enmesh the contractors in the dispute between the government agencies and the union.

Where the union's picketing satisfies the *Moore Dry Dock*[33] standards about the location of the picketing, the union does not violate the Act's prohibition against secondary activity.[34]

---

[29]2001 WL 456698 (3d Cir. 2001).

[30]George v. National Ass'n of Letter Carriers, 185 F.3d 380, 162 LRRM 2137 (5th Cir. 1999), *cert. denied*, 163 LRRM 2576 (2000).

[31]R.L. Coolsaet Constr. Co. v. Operating Eng'rs Local 150, 177 F.3d 648, 161 LRRM 2195 (7th Cir.), *cert. denied*, 120 S. Ct. 498, 162 LRRM 2832 (1999).

[32]1999 WL 734129, 162 LRRM 2235 (W.D. Pa. 1999).

[33]Sailors' Union (Moore Dry Dock), 92 NLRB 547, 27 LRRM 1108 (1950).

[34]Kim's Trucking v. Teamsters Local 179, 13 F. Supp. 2d 715, 162 LRRM 2179 (N.D. Ill. 1998) (union picketed only at times primary asphalt contractor's trucks were on site, and were engaged in contractor's regular business, picketed only in immediate vicinity of asphalt contractor's trucks, and clearly disclosed on its signs that dispute was with asphalt contractor).

III. HANDBILLING

A. *DeBartolo II*: Consumer Handbilling Not Prohibited by Section 8(b)(4)(B)

As discussed in the Fourth Edition, in *DeBartolo II*,[35] the Supreme Court held that Section 8(b)(4)(ii)(B) does not prohibit peaceful handbilling, unaccompanied by picketing, that urges customers and consumers not to patronize a neutral employer. In *George v. National Association of Letter Carriers*[36] the Fifth Circuit held that publicity, such as letter writing—unconnected with picketing, patrolling, or violence—is not "coercion, threats or restraint," even if it effectively persuaded consumers not to patronize a secondary employer.

On the other hand, the D.C. Circuit distinguished *DeBartolo II* and denied enforcement of the Board's decision in *Warshawsky & Co. v. NLRB*,[37] finding the evidence to "fairly demand" an inference that the union sought to induce neutral employees to refuse to work through the distribution of handbills unconnected with picketing or patrolling. The court concluded that *DeBartolo II* was fundamentally different because it involved Section 8(b)(4)(ii)(B) and not conduct that sought to directly induce or encourage a secondary strike under Section 8(b)(4)(i)(B).

In *Petrochem Insulation, Inc.*,[38] the Board followed *DeBartolo II* and held that petitioning of state governmental agencies by unions, seeking denial of environmental permits to nonunion construction companies, did not constitute "coercion" under Section 8(b)(4)(ii)(B). The Board stated that governmental lobbying by a union, like handbilling, is activity protected by the First Amendment.

B. Standards for Lawful Handbilling

1. *The Conduct of Handbilling*

Handbilling activity directed at the employees of a neutral employer, rather than consumers, may violate Section 8(b)(4). In

---

[35]Edward J. DeBartolo Corp. v. Building & Constr. Trades Council (Florida Gulf Coast) (*DeBartolo II*), 485 U.S. 568, 128 LRRM 2001 (1988).

[36]185 F.3d 380, 162 LRRM 2137 (5th Cir. 1999), *cert. denied*, 528 U.S. 1156, 163 LRRM 2576 (2000).

[37]182 F.3d 948, 161 LRRM 2772 (D.C. Cir. 1999), *denying enforcement to* Iron Workers Local 386, 325 NLRB 748, 158 LRRM 1180 (1998), *cert. denied*, 529 U.S. 1003, 163 LRRM 2704 (2000).

[38]330 NLRB No. 10, 163 LRRM 1276 (1999), *enforced*, 240 F.3d 26, 166 LRRM 2433 (D.C. Cir. 2001).

Warshawsky & Co. v. NLRB[39] the union had a labor dispute with a subcontractor on a construction site. The union distributed area-standards handbills in proximity to a road used primarily by persons going to and from the construction site. The site was not open to members of the general public. The D.C. Circuit held that the protections afforded by *DeBartolo II* do not extend to area-standards handbilling directed at neutral employees.

2. Location of Handbilling

a. *Lechmere*: Nonemployee Access to Employer Property Curtailed

The Board and the courts continue to examine state law to determine whether an employer has sufficient property rights to exclude union representatives from private property. In *Farm Fresh, Inc.*,[40] the Board held that under Virginia law a lease that did not specifically include sidewalks among the leased areas but that did impose an obligation on the lessee to clean and maintain the sidewalks created a sufficient property interest to permit the lessee to exclude union representatives.[41] The D.C. Circuit found that the Board had misinterpreted Virginia law and remanded the case to the Board for further proceedings.[42] On remand, the Board concluded that the maintenance provisions in the lease agreements did not create a sufficient property interest to permit exclusion of union representatives.[43]

b. Limitations on Nonemployee Handbilling on Employer Property After *Lechmere*

The Board maintains the position that where an employer allows nonemployee solicitation but does not allow union solicitation, the fact that the allowed solicitation is charitable or not controversial does not preclude a finding of discrimination. In *Albertson's, Inc.*[44]

---

[39] *Supra* note 37.
[40] 326 NLRB 997, 159 LRRM 1201 (1998), *enforcement denied in part*, 222 F.3d 1030 (D.C. Cir. 2000), *on remand*, 332 NLRB No. 156 (2000).
[41] *Id.*
[42] *Id.*, 222 F.3d at 1036.
[43] *Supra* note 40, 332 NLRB No. 156, at 4–5.
[44] 332 NLRB No. 104, 166 LRRM 1003 (2000). *See also* Sandusky Mall Co., 329 NLRB No. 62, 162 LRRM 1191 (1999) (violation of §8(a)(1) where employer allowed other groups to solicit in the mall concourse but did not allow union handbillers), *enforcement denied*, 242 F.3d 682, 166 LRRM 2641 (6th Cir. 2001). *But*

the Board held that the employer violated Section 8(a)(1) by allowing the Salvation Army, youth and student groups, and veterans groups to solicit on the employer property and not allowing union handbilling. The Board found that the solicitation permitted by the employer exceeded "the small number of isolated beneficent acts that the Board regards as a narrow exception to an otherwise valid, nondiscriminatory no-solicitation policy."[45]

IV. Consumer Picketing

B. Development of the Law After *Tree Fruits*

1. *"Merged Products" and Other Problems of the Economic Setting*

The Fifth Circuit set forth a detailed analysis and explanation of the *Tree Fruits*, *Safeco*, and *DeBartolo I* and *II* decisions and cited the Third Edition (Developing Labor Law, 3d Edition, Hardin, Ed.) in concluding that a union official's threats to write letters to other union locals urging a consumer boycott were not prohibited by Section 8(b)(4)(B), because such conduct alone did not constitute coercion within the meaning of Subsection (ii).[46] In so doing, the court noted that the *Safeco* principle prohibits only consumer *picketing* or similar coercive conduct that has the effect of urging a total boycott of a business,[47] and that letter writing has even fewer potentially coercive characteristics than does handbilling.[48]

3. *Specificity of the Union's Appeal: Location and Timing*

The Ninth Circuit enforced a Board decision that a supermarket committed an unfair labor practice by threatening to have union representatives arrested for handbilling and picketing on a privately

---

see 6 West Ltd. Corp., 237 F.3d 767, 780 (7th Cir. 2001), *denying enforcement to* 330 NLRB No. 77, 163 LRRM 1113 (2000) (finding no violation where employer allowed solicitations for girl scout cookies, Christmas ornaments, and raffle tickets but did not allow union solicitations, stating, "A restaurant in the United States of America should be free to prohibit solicitations on the premises that interfere with or bother employees or customers, and allow those solicitations which neither interfere with nor bother employees or customers").

[45]332 NLRB No. 104, 166 LRRM at 1008.

[46]George v. National Ass'n of Letter Carriers, 185 F.3d 380, 162 LRRM 2137 (5th Cir. 1999).

[47]*Id.*, 185 F.3d at 389.

[48]*Id.* at 391–92.

owned walkway and parking lot in furtherance of a consumer boy-cott.[49] Initially, the court rejected the supermarket's assertion that because the union representatives' conduct was improperly located on its private property, such conduct was not protected by Section 7 of the NLRA. The court indicated that *whether* conduct is protected by Section 7 and *where* it may be exercised are distinct inquiries.[50] The court determined that the union representatives' handbilling and picketing, which was designed to truthfully inform customers that the supermarket did not employ members of a labor organiza-tion, was clearly protected by Section 7.[51] The court also found that inasmuch as California law prohibited owners of shopping malls and general-access supermarkets from excluding speech on their private sidewalks and parking lots, the union representatives were legally entitled to engage in protected activity on the supermarket's pri-vately owned sidewalk and parking lot.[52]

V. ACTIONS FOR DAMAGES UNDER SECTION 303

A. Nature of the Action

1. *Relationship to Section 8(b)(4)*

Regardless of the application of the *Moore Dry Dock* standards, the ultimate inquiry to determine whether unlawful secondary activ-ity has occurred is the union's state of mind.[53] Intent can be "in-ferred from the nature of the conduct, evaluated in light of the prac-tical realities of a given situation."[54]

---

[49]NLRB v. Calkins dba Indio Grocery Outlet, 187 F.3d 1080, 161 LRRM 3121 (9th Cir. 1999), *cert. denied*, 529 U.S. 1098, 164 LRRM 2256 (2000).

[50]*Id.*, 187 F.3d at 1088–89.

[51]*Id.*

[52]*Id.*, at 1089–93. The court distinguished its holding in this matter from its decision in *Sparks Nugget, Inc. v. NLRB*, 968 F.2d 991, 140 LRRM 2747 (9th Cir. 1992), in which it found that a casino owner *could* prohibit conduct similar to that in the instant case from its private sidewalk and parking lot, on the grounds that Nevada law, unlike California law, does not extend special protection to free-speech interests at the expense of a store owner's property interests. 187 F.3d at 1093–94.

[53]R.L. Coolsaet Constr. Co. v. Operating Eng'rs Local 150, 177 F.3d 648, 161 LRRM 2195 (7th Cir.), *cert. denied*, 120 S. Ct. 498, 162 LRRM 2832 (1999).

[54]Intercity Maintenance Co. v. Service Employees Local 254, 62 F. Supp. 2d 483, 494, 162 LRRM 2099 (D. R.I. 1999), *remanded*, 166 LRRM 2656 (1st Cir. 2001) (trial court should have submitted claim to jury regarding loss of business because sufficient evidence existed to raise issue of causal relationship between union's conduct and loss).

2. Who Can Sue and Be Sued?

Because the Act does not apply to unions representing public employees, an employer cannot sue a union representing public employees for conduct that violates Section 8(b)(4)(B).[55]

A union is liable under Section 303 for its agent's threats that, unless the neutral ceased doing business with the primary employer, the neutral would experience strike action, property damage, and assaults against the neutral's employees.[56] Section 303 does not create a claim against union officers in their individual capacity.[57] An international union is not liable for the conduct of its local union unless the international instigated, supported, ratified, encouraged, or was aware of the local union's conduct.[58]

An employer may be required to arbitrate its Section 303 damage claim if an applicable collective bargaining agreement provides for an arbitration procedure with an extremely broad scope.[59]

C. The Measure of Damages

In *Taylor Milk Co. v. Teamsters*[60] the employer claimed that its damage was the lost opportunity to purchase another facility in which it expected to save its failing business. The union contended that the labor agreement did not permit the employer to move the work from the existing business to the new facility. The employer stated that, even if the labor agreement prohibited the transfer of the work, it would have purchased the new facility. The district court stated that it could not award damages because it would have to interpret the labor agreement, which only an arbitrator could do. The court of appeals held that the district court must interpret the labor agreement as part of the process of determining damages. The court of appeals outlined what damages would be awarded if the district court

---

[55]Pacific N. Maritime Ass'n v. Longshoremen (ILWU) Local 63, 198 F.3d 1078, 162 LRRM 3037 (9th Cir. 1999), *cert. denied,* 164 LRRM 2576 (2000).

[56]American Dev., Inc. v. Operating Eng'rs Local 150, 1999 WL 543207 (N.D. Ill. 1999).

[57]Intercity Maintenance Co. v. Service Employees Local 254, 62 F. Supp. 2d 483, 162 LRRM 2099 (D. R.I. 1999), *remanded,* 241 F.3d 82, 166 LRRM 2656 (1st Cir. 2001).

[58]*Id.*; Santiago v. Teamsters Local 705, 166 LRRM 2142 (N.D. Ill. 2000), *rulings on motion in limine,* 166 LRRM 2147 (2001).

[59]Interstate Brands Corp. v. Bakery Drivers & Bakery Goods Vending Machines Local 550, 167 F.3d 764, 160 LRRM 2404 (2d Cir.), *cert. denied,* 162 LRRM 2448, 120 S. Ct. 68 (1999).

[60]2001 WL 456698 (3d Cir. 2001).

concluded either that the labor agreement permitted the work transfer or prohibited the work transfer.[61]

Prejudgment interest may be ordered in a Section 303 action even though the damages award could not be calculated with absolute precision.[62]

Where a Section 303 action constitutes retaliation against a union's conduct that the Act protects, the court may order the employer to pay the union's legal fees and expenses for defense of the Section 303 action.[63]

D. Limitations, Federal Preemption, and Supplemental Jurisdiction

1. Statutes of Limitations

In Rhode Island, the 10-year statute of limitations for tortious interference with business relationships is applicable to Section 303 claims.[64]

2. Federal Preemption

Section 303 generally preempts state law tortious interference claims based on secondary activity unless the claims concern the union's actual or threatened violence. However, to avoid preemption, the claim must be based on actual or threatened violence that occurred during the period of the alleged tortious interference.[65]

---

[61]*Id.*, at *8. If the labor agreement did not permit the work transfer, there would not be damages because the employer admitted that the purchase of the new facility alone would not generate a profit. If the labor agreement permitted the work transfer and it would have led to a profit, the employer could recover future profits. However, the payment for a purchase option and the out-of-pocket expenses in connection with the purchase would be offset against the recoverable future profits.

[62]R.L. Coolsaet Constr. Co. v. Operating Eng'rs Local 150, 177 F.3d 648, 161 LRRM 2195 (7th Cir.), *cert. denied*, 120 S. Ct. 498, 162 LRRM 2832 (1999) (interest allowed on equipment expenses for employer-owned equipment).

[63]BE&K Constr. Co. v. NLRB, 246 F.3d 619 (6th Cir. 2001).

[64]Intercity Maintenance Co. v. Service Employees Local 254, 62 F. Supp. 2d 483, 162 LRRM 2099 (D. R.I. 1999), *remanded*, 241 F.3d 82, 166 LRRM 2656 (1st Cir. 2001).

[65]Pickens-Kane Moving & Storage Co. v. Teamsters Local 705, 1999 WL 89649, 161 LRRM 2159 (N.D. Ill. 1999).

CHAPTER 23

SECTION 8(e): THE "HOT-CARGO" AGREEMENT

III. INTERPRETATION AND APPLICATION

A. Definitions and Coverage

In *Teamsters Local 166 (Shank/Balfour Beatty)*[1] the Board affirmed the ALJ's uncontested finding that the parties entered into an agreement within the meaning of Section 8(e) based on a letter written by the employer in response to repeated statements by union officials that the union would file a grievance under its project labor agreement if the employer hired certain owner-operators to haul concrete. The ALJ noted that the employer's letter, in which it agreed to use haulers according to the terms of the PLA, was never disavowed by the union.[2]

---

[1]327 NLRB 449, 160 LRRM 1147 (1999).
[2]*Id.* at 454.

D. Subcontracting and Work-Allocation Clauses

3. *Application of* National Woodwork

a. Work-Preservation Clauses Generally

The Second Circuit held that Section 8(e) was not violated by a provision prohibiting the employer from relocating to a port that did not employ longshoremen represented by the union.[3] The employer was a member of a multi-employer association, which had negotiated the collective bargaining agreement with a union representing longshoremen on the Atlantic and Gulf coasts. The court found that the agreement defined both the bargaining unit and the primary-employment relationship on a coastwide basis, and thus the provision was a valid work preservation agreement.

E. Construction Industry Proviso Allowing Agreements Concerning Job-Site Work

2. *Job-Site Work*

The Board continues to apply its long-standing rule when interpreting contract clauses under the Section 8(e) construction industry proviso. In *Southwestern Materials & Supply Inc.,*[4] the Board considered the lawfulness of two contract clauses against the charge that both violated Section 8(e). The Board concluded that the first—an anti–dual-shop clause—violated Section 8(e) because it bound neutral employers related to the signatory employer but not a party to the labor contract in the circumstance where the signatory employer had no control over the work assignments of these related neutral employers. The Board held that anti–dual-shop clauses fall outside of the "categories of secondary activity that Congress intended to be tolerated in the construction industry."

The second clause prohibited the signatory employer "from subcontracting work within the union's jurisdiction to any person or entity that does not have a contract with the union." This was found to have a secondary, rather than a primary, work preservation objective, in violation of Section 8(e).[5] However, even though the clause

---

[3]Bermuda Container Line Ltd. v. Longshoremen, 193 F.3d 250, 162 LRRM 2257 (2d Cir. 1998).

[4]328 NLRB No. 142, 161 LRRM 1258 (1999).

[5]*Id.*

was not limited to the particular job sites at which both union and nonunion workers are employed, the Board held that it fell within the construction industry proviso of Section 8(e), because there was no showing that the clause had been or was intended to be applied to offsite work.[6]

3. Obtaining and Enforcing Subcontracting Agreements

In *Massman Construction Co.*[7] the Board found that a joint-venture clause violated Section 8(e), because the clause attempted to control the signatory employer's business relations even where the signatory employer had no control over the labor relations of the joint venture. In addition, the clause was not protected by the construction industry proviso because the clause went beyond the specific exemptions envisaged by Congress when it passed the proviso in 1959.

Where a union entered into an agreement with the employer prohibiting the employer from employing owner-operators to deliver materials to one of two entrances to a construction site, the Board ordered the union to cease and desist from enforcing the prohibition at both entrances because in either case the transportation and delivery of materials was not jobsite work.[8]

4. Clauses Prohibiting Double Breasting

The Board continues to apply the two-part test articulated in *NLRB v. Longshoremen (ILA)*[9] for determining whether an anti-double breasting clause is a valid work-preservation clause. If the clause does not meet this test, and thus falls within the general proscription of Section 8(e), the Board will determine whether the clause is saved by the construction industry proviso.[10] In this regard, the Board con-

---

[6]*Id.*

[7]327 NLRB No. 208, 161 LRRM 1001 (1999).

[8]Teamsters Local 166 (Shank/Balfour Realty), 327 NLRB No. 84, 160 LRRM 1147 (1999).

[9]447 U.S. 490, 104 LRRM 2552 (1980).

[10]International Ass'n of Bridge Structural & Ornamental Iron Workers (Southwestern Materials & Supply, Inc.), 328 NLRB No. 142, 161 LRRM 1258 (1999) (subcontracting clause was lawful absent evidence that it was intended to be applied offsite).

tinues to strictly construe the construction industry proviso to shelter only those clauses common to the construction industry when the proviso was adopted in 1959.[11]

---

[11]*Id.*; Operating Engineers Local 520 (Massman Constr. Co.), 327 NLRB 1257, 161 LRRM 1001 (1999) (finding that anti–dual-shop clause covering joint ventures was not part of pattern of bargaining in construction industry at time of construction proviso's enactment).

CHAPTER 24

JURISDICTIONAL DISPUTES AND "FEATHERBEDDING"

II. JURISDICTIONAL DISPUTES

B. Enactment of Sections 8(b)(4)(D) and 10(k)

3. Scope of Section 8(b)(4)(D)

The basic principles stated in the Main Edition regarding the scope of Section 8(b)(4)(D) of the Act remain the same. Unions often defend against a Section 8(b)(4) allegation by claiming that they have engaged in picketing for recognition or work-preservation purposes. However, such claims fail where at least one of the objectives of the picketing is for the purpose of forcing the target employer to assign the work to the picketing union.[1]

The Board continues to find that a jurisdictional dispute cannot exist unless there are two competing claims to a particular work assignment.[2] A competing claim for disputed work exists even if the claim is made by separate groups of workers who are represented by the same union local.[3] In addition, the Board has found that an active competing claim to work exists when union employees employed by a subcontractor have a collective bargaining agreement assigning work to the union and employees of the employer at issue also claim the work in question.[4]

The Board continues to hold that an active competing claim to a work assignment does not exist when the dispute merely involves a question about which union will represent a group of employees performing the work at issue and no objection exists about the employees performing the work:[5]

> There must, in short, be either an attempt to take a work assignment away from another group, or to obtain the assignment rather than have it given to the other group.
>
> . . .
>
> A demand for recognition as bargaining representative for employees doing a particular job, or in a particular department, does

---

[1]Carpenters Local 13 (First Chicago NBD Corp.), 331 NLRB No. 37, 164 LRRM 1263 (2000) (union's claim that picketing was for recognition purposes failed where only one truck driver was asked to sign recognition card and union never approached company about recognition); Operating Eng'rs Local 150 (Diamond Coring Co.), 331 NLRB No. 179, 166 LRRM 1084 (2000) (union not engaging in recognitional picketing when previously it threatened work stoppage. *See* Main Edition, Chapter 24, "Jurisdictional Disputes and 'Featherbedding,'" Section II.B.3. [Jurisdictional Disputes; Enactment of Sections 8(b)(4)(D) and 10(k); Scope of Section 8(b)(4)(D)].

[2]*See* Main Edition, Chapter 24, "Jurisdictional Disputes and 'Featherbedding,'" Section II.B.3. [Jurisdictional Disputes; Enactment of Sections 8(b)(4)(D) and 10(k); Scope of Section 8(b)(4)(D)].

[3]Electrical Workers (IBEW) Local 98 (Honeywell, Inc.), 332 NLRB No. 51, 165 LRRM 1338 (2000).

[4]*Carpenters Local 13 (First Chicago NBD Corp.), supra* note 1, 164 LRRM at 1265 (2000).

[5]Carpenters Local 1307 (Dearborn Village LLC), 331 NLRB No. 27, 164 LRRM 1283 (2000). *But see* Graphic Communications Workers Local 508M (Joseph Berning Printing Co.), 331 NLRB No. 102 (2000) (dispute not merely over which union would represent employees currently performing work because union sought to have work reassigned to employee whom it represented).

not to the slightest degree connote a demand for the assignment of work to particular employees rather than to others.[6]

A bona fide disclaimer of jurisdiction of disputed work by a labor organization that originally claimed the work will eliminate an active competing claim to the work. As a result, the Board will not find reasonable cause to believe that a jurisdictional dispute exists in such circumstances. The party asserting that a disclaimer has occurred that negates the existence of a jurisdictional dispute has the burden of proving "a clear, unequivocal, and unqualified disclaimer of all interest in the dispute."[7]

C. Procedure in Jurisdictional Dispute Cases

1. Generally

The Board's authority to decide jurisdictional disputes under Section 10(k) requires it to consider whether there is reasonable cause to believe that a Section 8(b)(4)(D) violation has occurred. The Board has used this approach to determine the appropriateness of its subpoena power. In *Plumbers Local 562 (C&R Heating & Serv. Co., Inc.)*[8] the Board quashed a union subpoena seeking employer-association testimony to prove that a rival union's threats were collusive and not genuine. According to the Board, the union failed to meet the threshold requirements for Section 10(k) proceedings that there be reasonable cause to believe that Section 8(b)(4)(D) has been violated. In the absence of evidence that threats were not genuine or were made in collusion with the employer, the Board declined to permit the union "to engage in a fishing expedition."[9]

---

[6]*Carpenters Local 1307 (Dearborn Village L.L.C.)*, *supra* note 5, 164 LRRM at 1285, citing Laborers Local I (DEL Constr.), 285 NLRB 593, 595, 127 LRRM 1099, 1101 (1987) (quoting Food & Commercial Workers Local 1222 (FedMart Stores), 262 NLRB 817, 819, 110 LRRM 1383, 1385 (1982)).
[7]Plumbers Local 562 (Grossman Contracting Co.), 329 NLRB No. 53, 164 LRRM 1313, 1317 (1999) (quoting Machinists (Hudson Gen. Hosp.), 326 NLRB 62, 65, 159 LRRM 1017, 1020 (1981)). *See* Main Edition, Chapter 24, "Jurisdictional Disputes and 'Featherbedding,'" Section II.B.3. [Jurisdictional Disputes; Enactment of Sections 8(b)(4)(D) and 10(k); Scope of Section 8(b)(4)(D)].
[8]328 NLRB No. 176, 1999 WL 671776, 162 LRRM 1300 (1999).
[9]*Id.*, 1999 WL 671776 at 5, 162 LRRM at 1301.

2. Voluntary Adjustment

The Board continues to find that an agreement that constitutes "an agreed method of voluntary adjustment," and thus deprives the Board of Section 10(k) jurisdiction to hear and determine the underlying dispute, must be one to which all parties to the dispute, including the employer, are bound.[10]

3. Disclaimer

The Board continues to rule that the party asserting that a disclaimer negates the existence of a jurisdictional dispute has the burden to prove a clear, unequivocal, and unqualified disclaimer of all interest in the work in dispute.[11] Moreover, the Board continues to hold that a disclaimer is insufficient where the union engages in behavior that is inconsistent with its professed intent to disclaim the disputed work.[12]

D. Factors Determining Jurisdictional Disputes

The Board continues to follow the factors from *Jones Construction*[13] in determining which employees should be assigned disputed work.[14] Although it is unable to establish the weight to be given the various factors, the Board continues to assert that "[e]very decision will have to be an act of judgment based on experience and common sense rather than on precedent."[15] In a majority of the cases,

---

[10]*See* Operating Eng'rs Local 150 (Diamond Coring Co.), 331 NLRB No. 179, 166 LRRM 1084 (2000).

[11]*See* Teamsters Local 295 (Emery Freight Corp.), 332 NLRB No. 105 (2000); Carpenters Local 558 (Joyce Bros. Storage & Van Co.), 331 NLRB No. 131 (2000).

[12]Teamsters Local 259 (Globe Newspaper Co.), 327 NLRB 117, 160 LRRM 1195 (1999) (union's pursuit of contract grievance and arbitration was inconsistent with its asserted disclaimer).

[13]Machinists Lodge 1743 (J.A. Jones Constr. Co.), 135 NLRB 1402, 49 LRRM 1684 (1962). For the list of *Jones Construction* factors, see Fourth Edition, Chapter 24, "Jurisdictional Disputes and 'Featherbedding.'"

[14]*See, e.g.,* Carpenters Local 624 (T. Equip. Corp.), 332 NLRB 428, 154 LRRM 1057 (1996); Iron Workers Local 1 (Fabcon, Inc.), 311 NLRB 87, 144 LRRM 1047 (1993); Elevator Constructors Local 5 (Stuart-Dean Co.), 310 NLRB 1189, 143 LRRM 1283 (1993).

[15]*Machinists Lodge 1743, supra* note 13; Electrical Workers (IBEW) Local 98 (NFF Constr., Inc.), 332 NLRB No. 121 (2000); Carpenters Local 1006 (J.P. Patti Co.), 332 NLRB No. 69, 166 LRRM 1194 (2000); Electrical Workers (IBEW) Local 98 (Honeywell, Inc.), 332 NLRB No. 51, 165 LRRM 1338 (2000); Operating Eng'rs Local 12 (Winegardner Masonry, Inc.), 331 NLRB No. 189 (2000); Operating Eng'rs

the Board's analysis of the facts and application of the factors continue to lead to awards that support the employer's assignment of the work.[16]

When making a determination, one of the factors the Board continues to consider is the certification and collective bargaining agreements between employers and unions. Where two collective bargaining agreements both arguably cover disputed work, the Board will favor the agreement currently in effect over an expired agreement.[17] Furthermore, the Board has ruled that where there are two extant collective bargaining agreements covering the disputed work, neither will be considered in a Section 10(k) proceeding because the agreements favor neither group of employees.[18] In the same case, the Board ruled that an interunion agreement does not favor an award of the disputed work to either group of employees where there is no conclusive evidence about whether the interunion agreement applies to the disputed work or that the area and industry practice conforms to the terms of the agreement.[19]

E. Post-Hearing Procedure

In jurisdictional dispute cases, the Board also declines to issue broad prospective awards in the absence of evidence that similar work disputes are likely to arise in the future or that the offending union has a proclivity to engage in unlawful conduct to obtain similar work to that in the dispute.[20]

Local 150 (Diamond Coring Co., Inc.), 331 NLRB No. 179, 166 LRRM 1084 (2000); Electrical Workers (IBEW) Local 98 (AIMM, Inc.), 331 NLRB No. 156, 165 LRRM 1155 (2000); Graphic Communications Local 508 (Joseph Berning Printing Co.), 331 NLRB No. 102 (2000); Electrical Workers (IBEW) Local 1049 (Asplundh Constr. Corp.), 331 NLRB No. 90, 166 LRRM 1036 (2000); Carpenters Local 13 (First Chicago NBD Corp.), 331 NLRB No. 37, 164 LRRM 1263 (2000); Laborers Local 320 (N.W. Natural Gas. Co.), 330 NLRB No. 86, 163 LRRM 1133 (2000).

[16]See Electrical Workers (IBEW) Local 1049 (Asplundh Constr. Corp.), 331 NLRB No. 90, 166 LRRM 1036 (2000).

[17]See Laborers Local 210 (Concrete Cutting & Breaking), 328 NLRB No. 182, 162 LRRM 1117 (1999).

[18]See Plumbers Local 562 (Charles E. Jarrell Contracting), 329 NLRB No. 54, 163 LRRM 1056 (1999).

[19]Id.

[20]See Operating Eng'rs Local 12 (Winegardner Masonry), 331 NLRB No. 189 (2000) (finding that evidence failed to show that union had proclivity to engage in unlawful conduct to obtain similar work); Operating Eng'rs Local 150 (Diamond Coring Co.), 331 NLRB No. 179, 166 LRRM 1084 (2000) (concluding that requisite showing that similar disputes are likely to arise in future had not been made);

F. Relationship of Section 8(b)(4)(D) Proceedings to Other Actions and Unfair Labor Practice Proceedings

Joining other circuits, the Eighth Circuit ruled it was appropriate to stay a Section 301 action to enforce an arbitration award pending the Board's determination in a Section 10(k) or 8(b)(4)(D) proceeding.[21] The Board's decision overrides that of an arbitrator in the event of a conflict.[22]

III. "FEATHERBEDDING"

C. Application of the Law

The Board continues to adhere to *American Newspaper*,[23] which interpreted Section 8(b)(6) narrowly. In *Teamsters Local 282 (TDX Construction Corp.)*,[24] the Board reversed the ALJ's finding that the union had violated Section 8(b)(6) by picketing the employer's job site in an effort to force the employer to hire an onsite steward that it did not need or want. The Board held that there was no violation of the Act because the union "did not seek payment for an employee to stand idly by" or for work that was "not relevant" to the employer's general activities on the work project.

Electrical Workers (IBEW) Local 98 (AIMM, Inc.), 331 NLRB No. 156 (2000) (holding employer's request for award covering all installation work exceeded defined work in dispute, and therefore was overly broad); Electrical Workers (IBEW) Local 1049 (Asplundh Constr. Corp.), 331 NLRB No. 90, 166 LRRM 1036 (2000) (finding broad award inappropriate); Carpenters Local 13 (First Chicago NBD Corp.), 331 NLRB No. 37, 164 LRRM 1263 (2000) (concluding that broad order was inappropriate where evidence fell short of establishing proclivity); Plumbers Local 562 (C&R Heating & Serv. Co., Inc.), 328 NLRB No. 176, 162 LRRM 1300 (1999) (declining to grant broad prospective award even though work-jurisdiction dispute between two unions was ongoing, where each of disputes involved distinct type of work and thus work likely to be disputed in future could be anticipated); Laborers Local 210 (Concrete Cutting & Breaking), 328 NLRB No. 182, 162 LRRM 1117 (1999) (declining to issue area-wide award without evidence that offending union had proclivity to engage in unlawful conduct to obtain similar work).

[21]Sheet Metal Workers Local 36 v. Murphy Constr. Co., 191 F.3d 909, 910–11, 162 LRRM 2334 (8th Cir. 1999).

[22]*Id.*; T. Equip. Corp. v. Massachusetts Laborers' Dist. Council, 166 F.3d 11, 160 LRRM 2257 (1st Cir. 1999).

[23]American Newspaper Publishers Ass'n v. NLRB, 345 U.S. 100, 31 LRRM 2422 (1953).

[24]332 NLRB No. 82, 165 LRRM 1305 (2000).

Part VII

RELATIONS BETWEEN EMPLOYEE
AND UNION

Chapter 25

THE DUTY OF FAIR REPRESENTATION

II. Jurisdiction and Procedures to Enforce the Duty

A. The Courts

1. Exhaustion of Contractual Remedies

Before an individual employee may bring an action alleging breach of a labor agreement, the employee must exhaust the available grievance procedure.[1] However, if the employee can fully dem-

---

[1]Republic Steel Corp. v. Maddox, 379 U.S. 650, 652–53, 58 LRRM 2193 (1965).

onstrate the futility of completing the grievance process, either because of the employer's repudiation of contractual procedures or because the employee's union (which has exclusive authority to invoke higher levels of the procedure) wrongfully refuses to process the grievance, then the employee may be permitted to proceed with a Section 301 claim against the employer and/or the union.[2] Although there have been no changes in the law underlying exhaustion of contractual remedies, two cases have applied these principles to different situations, arriving at different results.

In *Duerr v. Minnesota Mining & Manufacturing Co.*[3] the plaintiff initially filed his case in state court for breach of contract and violation of Illinois's Wage Payment Act. The federal court upheld removal of the suit, because both of the plaintiff's claims required interpreting a collective bargaining agreement, as well as a subsequent agreement entered into between the employer and union based on an interpretation of the overtime-payments clause of the collective bargaining agreement. The plaintiff–employee made no claim that the employer had repudiated the contract's grievance process or that the union had wrongfully refused to process his grievance. Instead, he claimed, in part, that at the time he pursued his lawsuit against the employer, he was no longer employed and was no longer a member of the union, and the union, therefore, could not invoke the grievance process on his behalf.[4]

The court rejected the plaintiff's defense for not exhausting the grievance process, because he *had* been employed at the time that the union's president informed him that he would not receive additional overtime payments following his resignation.[5] The court cited a case with analogous facts to support its decision, and distinguished another case where the employees could not pursue the grievance procedure because the change in their employment status and subsequent inability even to file a grievance was beyond their control.[6]

---

[2]Vaca v. Sipes, 386 U.S. 171, 185, 64 LRRM 2369 (1967).

[3]101 F. Supp. 2d 1057 (N.D. Ill 2000); *see also* Bennefield v. Hoechst Celanese Corp., 230 F.3d 1351 LRRM (4th Cir. 2000) (where court, in per curiam decision, dismissed employee's age discrimination and retaliation claims against employer, because employee had not filed her lawsuit within 90 days after receiving right-to-sue letter, and her duty of fair representation claim against union, because she failed to exhaust contractual grievance and arbitration procedure).

[4]*Id.* at 1059–60, 1062–63.

[5]*Id.* at 1063.

[6]*Id.* at 1063–64, citing Roman v. United States Postal Serv., 821 F.2d 382 (7th Cir. 1987) (where court dismissed employee's lawsuit for backpay allegedly owed

The court in *Meredith v. Louisiana Federation of Teachers*[7] reached the opposite result where the plaintiff's employer repudiated the grievance-arbitration process, and the plaintiff was not in a position to effectively pursue her contractual rights. The plaintiff was employed as a field representative with the Louisiana Federation of Teachers when she negotiated an individual contract to work for the local St. Tamany Federation under the same terms of employment she enjoyed with the Louisiana Federation. The St. Tamany Federation subsequently terminated the plaintiff's employment; the state federation took the position that the plaintiff no longer worked for it, making her ineligible to use the grievance procedure, and the united professional staff association ignored the plaintiff's requests for assistance.

On these facts, and citing *Vaca v. Sipes*,[8] the court overruled the Louisiana Federation's motion to dismiss for lack of subject-matter jurisdiction, because the federation had taken the position that the plaintiff was not covered by its collective bargaining agreement with the professional staff association and would not "consider the Plaintiff's grievance."[9]

2. Exhaustion of Internal Union Remedies

The U.S. Supreme Court decided the basic issue of exhausting available internal union review procedures providing for possible reinstatement of an employee's grievance in *Clayton v. Auto Workers*.[10] The Court determined that three factors must be considered in determining whether the plaintiff–employee must exhaust internal union procedures: (1) whether the union's officers are so hostile to the employee as to eliminate any hope for a fair hearing on the employee's claim; (2) whether the internal union procedures would have been inadequate to restore the employee's grievance or to award the employee full relief under Section 301; and (3) whether exhausting the internal union remedies would have unreasonably delayed

---

him, because employee had resigned his job without first filing grievance seeking backpay) and distinguishing Anderson v. AT&T Corp., 147 F.3d 4657 (6th Cir. 1998) (where employees were permitted to sue employer without exhausting contractual procedures after being transferred to another plan at same company whose employees were in another bargaining unit).

[7]209 F.3d 398, 164 LRRM 2099 (5th Cir. 2000).
[8]386 U.S. 171, 64 LRRM 2369 (1967).
[9]*Id.* at 402–03.
[10]451 U.S. 679, 107 LRRM 2385 (1981).

the employee's opportunity for a judicial hearing on the merits of his or her claim.[11]

There have been no changes in the law requiring exhaustion of internal union remedies. In two cases before the same trial judge,[12] the court sustained union motions to dismiss for failure to exhaust internal union remedies. In *Moore v. Auto Workers Local 598*[13] the plaintiff–employee sued both the employer and the union after the union decided not to pursue his grievance. Before the incident that led to the employee's final termination, he had already been terminated once for using a co-worker's time card to clock out of the plant. On that occasion, he had been reinstated a week later. He had also received a number of disciplinary reprimands and suspensions over the next 5 years of his employment. Then, beginning in May 1981 and continuing over the next 11 years, the employee was classified 15 times as a voluntary quit for failing to report to work after taking a vacation or being on sick leave.[14] On June 12, 1987, after being threatened with severe discipline for taking off for a year following his failure to report for work, the employee was reinstated only because of the union's intercession. Then, after a series of additional voluntary quit–reinstatements, the employee took off from work on September 14, 1992, and did not return to work.[15]

On these facts, the union shop committee chair decided in 1992 that the employee did not have a good case and chose not to pursue his grievance to arbitration, but did set it aside for inclusion in a bargaining proposal at an appropriate time. About 4 years later, in 1995 to 1996, the employee decided that he was dissatisfied with the union's approach to his grievance but still waited another 4 years before filing his hybrid Section 301 case on October 1, 1999.[16]

In addition to the employee's failure to meet the 6-month statute of limitations within which to file his duty-of-fair-representation case, and his failure on the merits to show a breach of the contract by the employer or breach of the duty of fair representation by the union, the court held that he also failed to exhaust the internal union procedures provided for in the UAW constitution.[17] The employee

---

[11]*Id.* at 689.

[12]Honor. Gerald E. Rosen of the U.S. District Court for the Eastern District of Michigan, Southern Division.

[13]2000 U.S. Dist. LEXIS 20368, 165 LRRM 3016 (E.D. Mich. 2000).

[14]*Id.* at 3017.

[15]*Id.* at 3018.

[16]*Id.* at 3019.

[17]*Id.* at 3022.

made no showing that the union was hostile to him, that the review procedures were unfair or unreasonable, that the internal review process could not have reactivated his grievance or awarded him full and final relief, or that the UAW's internal review procedures would have unduly delayed his access to the courts for a judicial hearing of his claims. On these facts, the court granted the union summary judgment.[18]

In *Cotter v. Daimler-Chrysler*[19] following the plaintiff–employee's numerous instances of tardiness for work and lengthy absences from work, the employer and union entered into a "last-chance" agreement, which the employee signed.[20] After the employee's numerous post–last-chance-agreement "salary continuation" absences extended the terms of the 1-year agreement, the company discharged the employee for accruing seven more absences during the extended period of the last-chance agreement.[21]

The union filed a grievance for the employee. Once it confirmed that key words of the last-chance agreement did apply to the employee and did in fact extend the terms of the last-chance agreement up to the time of the last of his seven absences, however, the union withdrew the grievance. The employee knew that he could appeal the union's withdrawal decision through the union's internal review process, but claimed that he took no action because he had heard a rumor that it was too late to pursue an appeal.[22]

Instead, almost 2 years later, the employee filed a lawsuit in state court, after which the employer removed the case to federal court. The federal court dismissed the case, in part, because the employee failed to exhaust internal union remedies. The court rejected the employee's futility defense, which was based on statements that he allegedly heard from others, because such a subjective belief did not excuse him from attempting to use an available procedure.[23] Applying *Clayton* to the facts before it, the court found: no evidence of hostility by the union toward the employee; if the employee had successfully pursued his internal remedies, his grievance could have been reactivated; and the internal appeals procedure would not have unduly delayed the plaintiff's pursuit of a judicial hearing.[24]

---

[18]*Id.* at 3022–23.
[19]87 F. Supp. 2d 746, 164 LRRM 2111 (E.D. Mich. 2000).
[20]*Id.* at 748–49.
[21]*Id.* at 749.
[22]*Id.* at 749–50.
[23]*Id.* at 752–54.
[24]*Id.* at 755.

B. The Labor Board

3. Preemption and Accommodation

The courts continue to hold that contract, tort, or other claims and theories nominally derived from state law are preempted when in fact they are premised on the duty of fair representation or a related breach of contract. That rule blocked actions by the plaintiffs based on state law claims of: (1) fraudulent misrepresentation, tortious interference, and civil conspiracy;[25] (2) breach of a settlement agreement, covenant of good faith and fair dealing, promissory estoppel, breach of fiduciary duties, and retaliation and gender discrimination;[26] and (3) discrimination against one for the exercise of his religious beliefs, state wrongful discharge, and civil conspiracy claims.[27] In these cases, the courts found that the claims were based on, centered around, or importantly affected by labor contracts, labor-based settlement agreements, or a local labor memorandum of understanding. As a consequence, these claims entwined the union in employees' disputes with the employer and turned the issue into what duty the unions owed to the employees. As one of the courts observed, "Where a plaintiff's allegations fall within the scope of the duty of fair representation, federal labor law governs and ordinarily preempts any state law claims based on those allegations."[28] In the cases, the courts granted the unions' motions under Rule 12(b)(1) and (6), asserting lack of jurisdiction and failure to state a claim, because the plaintiffs had failed to bring their lawsuits within 6 months of the action complained of and therefore were time-barred.[29] In *Bergeron v. Henderson*[30] the court found a state law claim of sex discrimination wholly preempted and entered judgment for the union on the pleadings.

---

[25]Beidleman v. Stroh Brewing Co., 182 F.3d 225, 161 LRRM 2656 (3d Cir. 1999).

[26]Audette v. Longshoremen Local 24, 195 F.3d 1107, 162 LRRM 2705 (9th Cir. 1999).

[27]Thomas v. National Ass'n of Letter Carriers, 225 F.3d 1149, 1158 (10th Cir. 2000).

[28]*Id.* at 1158. *See also* Enoch v. Continental General Tire, No. 5: 99 CV-174-5 (W.D. Ky. 2000 and 2001).

[29]*See Beidleman, supra* note 25, 161 LRRM at 2663; *Audette, supra* note 26, 162 LRRM at 2707; *Thomas, supra* note 27, at 169–70.

[30]52 F. Supp. 2d 149, 161 LRRM 2705, 2763–65 (D. Me. 1999).

III. Nature of the Duty

B. The Nature of the Duty in Grievance Handling and Contract Administration

There has been no change in the showing that an employee claiming a breach in the duty of fair representation must make to establish a "hybrid" claim. The union, with its exclusive statutory authority to represent all members of the designated unit, has the "statutory obligation to serve the interests of all members without hostility or discrimination toward any, to exercise its discretion with complete good faith and honesty, and to avoid arbitrary conduct."[31] Thus, to prove a breach of the duty of fair representation, the plaintiff–employee must show that the union's conduct was "arbitrary, discriminatory, or in bad faith."[32] To prevail against either an employer or union, an employee must show not only that the discharge or other action against the employee violated the collective bargaining agreement but also that the union breached its duty of fair representation.[33] Proof that the union breached the duty of fair representation is necessary even to raise the question of whether the employer violated the collective bargaining agreement.[34]

Unions breach their duty when they discriminate among employees in a bargaining unit based on their membership status in the union or their participation in its governance. Thus, in *Electrical Workers (IBEW) Local 724 (Albany Electrical Contractors Ass'n)*[35] the Board held that the union violated its duty of fair representation by routinely failing to operate a referral hall in conformity with the requirements of its collective bargaining agreement and by arbitrarily requiring only one of many registrants to comply fully with the application requirements of the collective bargaining agreement to the detriment of that individual. Another union violated its duty of fair representation by refusing to process a grievance for an employee because the employee had opposed the incumbent union officers in internal union matters.[36]

---

[31]Vaca v. Sipes, 386 U.S. 171, 177 (1967).
[32]*Id.* at 190.
[33]United Parcel Serv. v. Mitchell, 451 U.S. 56, 62 (1981).
[34]*Id.*
[35]327 NLRB No. 137, 160 LRRM 1177 (1999).
[36]Communications Workers Local 3410 (BellSouth Telecommunications), 328 NLRB No. 135 (1999).

When a union asked about the membership status of an employee who wanted to initiate a grievance, thereby giving the message that membership in the union was a precondition to obtaining union assistance in the grievance process, the union breached its duty of fair representation and also violated Section 8(b)(1)(A) of the Act by restraining or coercing the employee in the exercise of rights guaranteed by Section 7.[37] In *Letter Carriers Branch 758 (Postal Service)*[38] the union breached its duty of fair representation by denying employees access to their grievance files and by refusing to provide those employees copies of their grievance files at a reasonable copying cost.

Although the *Vaca* standard makes unions liable for arbitrary conduct toward employees they represent, it permits unions wide latitude in making judgments about grievances and does not punish unions for simple negligence in the discharge of their duties. Thus, where a union accepted the strict terms of an employer's "zero-tolerance" drug policy, it did not act irrationally or unreasonably in its handling of an employee's grievance based on its opinion that it was unlikely that it would prevail in arbitration of the employee's claims.[39] Before rejecting the employee's request to take his grievance to arbitration, the union consulted two experts to test the employee's claims that various over-the-counter medicines he had been taking produced a false-positive result in the urine sample collected by the employer's testing laboratory. Once the union learned that the over-the-counter medicines were not likely to produce false-positive results, the court concluded that having "accepted the terms of [the employer's] 'zero tolerance' drug policy," the union would have had little likelihood of success in arbitration.[40]

In a significant decision, *Steamfitters Local 342*,[41] the Board overruled *Iron Workers Local 118 (California Erectors)*,[42] which had imposed liability on unions for ordinary errors in operating referral halls. Reasoning that the Supreme Court's holding in *Steelworkers v. Rawson*,[43] that "mere negligence" by a union in the exercise of its obligations does not breach the duty of fair representation, applies in the con-

---

[37]American Postal Workers, 328 NLRB No. 37, 161 LRRM 1237 (1999).

[38]328 NLRB No. 144, 162 LRRM 1091 (1999).

[39]Wilder v. GL Bus Lines, 164 LRRM 2906 (2000).

[40]*Id.* at 2914.

[41]329 NLRB No. 65, 162 LRRM 1156 (1999). *See also* Plumbers Local 375 (H.C. Price Constr.), 330 NLRB No. 55, 163 LRRM 1041 (1999).

[42]309 NLRB 808 (1992).

[43]499 U.S. 362, 134 LRRM 2153, 2157 (1990).

text of an exclusive referral hall, the Board held the union did not breach its duty to an applicant who lost an employment opportunity as a result of the union's honest, inadvertent mistake.

C. The Duty in Collective Bargaining

Since the Supreme Court's decision in *Air Line Pilots v. O'Neill*,[44] there have been no changes in the legal standards governing unions' obligations to the employees they represent in their handling of the basic obligations of collective bargaining, including negotiating and settling of agreements. A union is entitled to a "wide range of reasonableness" in its actions; this "'wide range of reasonableness' gives the union room to make discretionary decisions and choices, even if those choices are ultimately wrong." As a consequence, "a settlement is not irrational (and thus arbitrary) simply because it turns out in retrospect to have been a bad settlement."[45]

Thus, in *Fay v. Teamsters Local 553*[46] a Section 301 hybrid action arising from the merger of bargaining units of combined companies, the district court held that the union did not breach its duty of fair representation by deciding to dovetail rather than endtail the seniority lists. Similarly, in *White v. White Rose Food*[47] the court held that a union was not required under the Act or its own constitution or bylaws to submit an amendment to the collective bargaining agreement to its membership for ratification, even though the original agreement had been so ratified.

In *Longshoremen Local 1575*[48] employees charged that their union denied them the right to vote on whether to ratify a contract. The union and employer had negotiated a new contract. In a membership meeting held to ratify the new contract, 80 percent of the membership stood in protest to a new contract provision. The union president then requested that all those in favor of the new contract stand up, then announced that the contract had been ratified by those who were actually standing in protest. The Board found that the union had not breached its duty of fair representation on the grounds that the union was not required to request a vote of its membership to ratify the contract. Membership ratification is a permissive subject

---

[44]499 U.S. 65, 67, 136 LRRM 2721 (1991).
[45]*Id.* at 79, quoting Ford Motor Co. v. Huffman, 345 U.S. 330, 338 (1953).
[46]67 F. Supp. 2d 86 (E.D.N.Y. 1999).
[47]237 F.3d 174, 166 LRRM 2281 (2d Cir. 2001).
[48]332 NLRB No. 139, 165 LRRM 1377 (2000).

of bargaining, and the parties had not agreed that such a vote was required to make the contract effective.[49]

In *Williams v. Molphus*[50] the Sixth Circuit reversed the grant of summary judgment and, applying the Supreme Court's *O'Neill* standard, remanded for further proceedings to determine whether a union acted in bad faith or with discriminatory intent when it endtailed seniority pursuant to a negotiated rider to a national agreement.

IV. Statute of Limitations

There is continuing disagreement among the courts over the application of the Section 10(b) 6-month statute of limitations adopted for hybrid actions in *DelCostello v. Teamsters*.[51] On the question of whether an employee can sue only the employer for breach of a collective bargaining agreement, and not the union for breach of duty more than 6 months after the act giving rise to the claim, two courts held that the employee could not avoid the 6-month statute of limitations by bringing only the breach of contract action against the employer.[52] In *Scott*, the court reasoned that, because the class was time-barred from proving that the union had breached a duty of fair representation, summary judgment for the employer with respect to the Section 301 claim was also appropriate. Both decisions appear to be in direct conflict with the language of *DelCostello*, which stated, "the employee may, if he chooses, sue one defendant and not the other; but the case he must prove is the same whether he sues one, the other, or both."[53]

However, in *White v. White Rose Food*[54] the court held that the fact that the plaintiffs are barred by the statute of limitations from bringing a suit against the union does not mean that they are precluded from bringing suit against the employer in a separate Section 301 action. In a later decision arising out of the same dispute, the

---

[49]*Id.*, 165 LRRM at 1378.

[50]171 F.3d 360, 160 LRRM 2803 (6th Cir. 1999).

[51]462 U.S. 161, 169–70, 172, 113 LRRM 2737 (1983).

[52]Carrion v. Enter. Ass'n, 227 F.3d 29, 165 LRRM 2280 (2d Cir. 2000); Scott v. Auto Workers Local 879, 242 F.3d 837, 166 LRRM 2615 (8th Cir. 2001).

[53]*DelCostello, supra* note 51, 462 U.S. at 165. *See* Lyon v. Continental General Tire Co., Civil Action No. 5: 99-CV-354-R (W.D. Ky. 2001) (court dismissed Section 301 action in part because employee failed to prove that his union, although not a party to suit, breached duty of fair representation).

[54]128 F.3d 110, 156 LRRM 2680 (2d Cir. 1997).

court relied on its previous decision to allow the action to proceed against the employer and the court ruled that, although the union's joinder in the suit was time-barred, the plaintiffs nevertheless had to prove both that the employer breached a collective bargaining agreement and that the union breached its duty of fair representation to the plaintiff employees.[55]

In *Prazak v. Bricklayers Local 1*[56] the Ninth Circuit held that an employee who initially files a hybrid Section 301/fair representation claim in state court within the 6-month statute of limitations is not barred by the statute of limitations rule set forth in *DelCostello* and *West v. Conrail*[57] if the case is subsequently removed to federal court. The court stated that *DelCostello* and *West* did not seek to create strict uniformity in federal court responses to application of state versus federal jurisdictional rules, but rather both decisions "crafted limited rules in order to facilitate the filing of hybrid actions."[58] *Prazak* directly conflicts with the Fourth Circuit's decision in *Cannon v. Kroger*,[59] that "the statute of limitations applicable to 'hybrid' actions runs until the action is properly commenced under the dictates of the Federal Rules of Civil Procedure."[60]

V. REMEDIES

A. The Board

1. Unfair Labor Practice Cases

The Board ordered a backpay make-whole remedy, to be determined at the compliance stage of the proceedings, for the class of unidentified applicants subject to a union's hiring hall referral practices in contravention of contractual referral rules. The Board also ordered the union to refer the one identified discriminated applicant in conformity with the hiring-hall rules and to make him whole

---

[55]White v. White Rose Food and Teamsters Local 138, 237 F.3d 174, 166 LRRM 2281 (2d Cir. 2001).

[56]233 F.3d 1149, 165 LRRM 2853 (9th Cir. 2000).

[57]481 U.S. 35 (1987).

[58]*Prazak, supra* note 56, at 1152.

[59]832 F.2d 303, 126 LRRM 2968, 2970 (4th Cir. 1987).

[60]*Id.*, 832 F.2d at 305–06. *But see* Winkels v. George A. Hormell & Co., 874 F.2d 567, 131 LRRM 2338 (8th Cir. 1989); Gorwin v. Teamsters Local 282, 838 F. Supp. 116, 145 LRRM 2888 (S.D.N.Y. 1993) decided like *Prazak,* and Mitchell v. Joseph's Supermarkets, Inc., 712 F. Supp. 59, 133 LRRM 2116 (W.D. Pa. 1989) (criticizing holding in *Cannon* as it applies to hybrid §301/fair representation cases).

for any losses from its previous failure to treat him in the same manner as its other applicants.[61]

In *Communications Workers Local 3410 (BellSouth Telecommunications)*[62] the Board applied the evidentiary burdens as reallocated in *Iron Workers Local 377 (Alamillo Steel Corp.)*.[63] The reallocation requires the general counsel, in a case alleging a union's mishandling of a grievance, to demand make-whole relief in the complaint and to show not only that the union breached its duty of fair representation but also that the grievant would have prevailed in the grievance–arbitration procedure had the union not breached its duty. The showing that the grievant would have prevailed, however, is postponed to the compliance stage of the proceeding, and that affords the union an opportunity to resolve the grievance through the contractual machinery. If the union is unable to secure resolution, the general counsel then must establish in the compliance proceeding that the grievance was meritorious. The principal effect of the change is to avoid litigation of the merits of the grievance in the initial unfair labor practice proceeding.

B. The Courts

3. Injunctions and Other Equitable Remedies

In *Commer v. City of New York, District Council 37, Local 375*[64] an individual employee of the city of New York sued unions that represented the plaintiff and certain other city employees for an injunction to compel the submission of an extant collective agreement to a ratification vote, presumably so that it could be rejected. Federal jurisdiction of the action was established under the Labor-Management Reporting and Disclosure Act (LMRDA) on the ground that the defendants were "mixed" unions, representing both "statutory" employees (covered by the NLRA or Railway Labor Act), and also "nonstatutory" city employees (excluded from coverage by those statutes). In a proceeding that occurred after the dismissal of all statutory claims under the LMRDA, the court denied the union's motion for summary judgment, and observed in dictum that the complaint could not be taken to allege violations of the unions' breach of the

---

[61]Electrical Workers (IBEW) Local 724 (Albany Elec.), 327 NLRB No. 137 (1999).

[62]328 NLRB 135 (1999).

[63]326 NLRB No. 54, 159 LRRM 1097 (1998).

[64]163 LRRM 2432 (S.D.N.Y. 1999).

duty of fair representation. The court did not address the question of whether federal—as opposed to state—law would be the source of the unions' supposed obligation of fair representation to the plaintiff, who was not a statutory employee.

4. *Apportionment of Liability*

The Eighth Circuit suggested that where an employee files a claim for retaliation based on the exercise of his or her LMRDA Section 431 free-speech rights, just as in duty-of-fair-representation cases, an employer may be held liable for that portion of the employee's loss that was caused by its breach of contract. In *Kinslow v. Postal Workers*,[65] the postal service denied an employee overtime, and the union did not file a grievance despite the employee's request that it do so. The employee claimed, and the court found, that the union's decision not to file the grievance was based on his request to examine the union's financial records after the local president was indicted for embezzling union funds. The court held that the union was liable only for the loss of overtime pay that it caused by failing to file the grievance that would have rectified the employer's withholding of overtime in violation of the agreement. In dictum, the court stated that if the employee had sued it, the Postal Service could have been held liable for lost overtime wages resulting from its violation of the collective bargaining agreement up to the time when the union should have processed the employee's complaint by filing the grievance.

---

[65]222 F.3d 269, 164 LRRM 3025 (7th Cir. 2000).

Chapter 26

UNION SECURITY

II. Required Membership—The Union Shop

A. In General

In three cases[1] involving union conduct undertaken before the Board's *California Saw*[2] decision, the Board held that the union vio-

---

[1]Painters (Meiswinkel/RFJ, Inc.), 327 NLRB 1020, 162 LRRM 1173 (1999); Teamsters Local 435 (Mercury Warehouse), 327 NLRB 458, 160 LRRM 1130 (1999); and Carlon-Lamson & Sessions Co., 328 NLRB 983, 162 LRRM 1019 (1999).

[2]California Saw & Knife Works, 320 NLRB 224, 151 LRRM 1121 (1995), *enforced sub nom.* Machinists v. NLRB, 133 F.3d 1012, 157 LRRM 2287 (7th Cir.), *cert. denied sub nom.* Stang v. NLRB, 525 U.S. 813 (1998).

lated the Act by continuing to charge nonmember employees for nonrepresentational activities after the nonmember employees had filed a *Beck* objection. In *Meiswinkel*[3] and *Carlon-Lamson*[4] the Board held that the union was still entitled to collect dues related to representational activities even if notice of *General Motors* and *Beck* rights had not been given employees as required by *California Saw.*

Regarding notice requirements, the D.C. Circuit held that a union violated its duty of fair representation by providing *Beck* objectors with only general categories of expenditures; failing to disclose payments to affiliates and how those affiliates used those funds; and not informing employees who had not yet exercised their *Beck* rights of what percentage of dues was spent on non-representational activities.[5] In so doing, the court refused to enforce the contrary position of the Board, and remanded the case to the Board. The Board has not yet considered the case on remand.

The Board found in *Kroger, Inc.*[6] that a union violates Section 8(b)(1) by requiring *Beck* objectors to adhere to internal union procedures as a condition precedent to protesting the union's calculation of the appropriate fee reduction for activities not germane to collective bargaining.

Expenditures for organizing within the same competitive market as bargaining-unit employees may be charged to objecting nonmember employees, and dues and fees collected from nonmember employees may be expended for such activities.[7]

B. Enforcement Procedures

In *Yellow Freight Systems of Indiana*[8] the Board held that the union violated its duty of fair representation by failing to inform employees, represented under a collective bargaining agreement containing a union-security clause, of their *General Motors* and *Beck* rights.

Likewise, in *Incisa, U.S.A., Inc.*[9] the Board concluded that a union violated the Act by failing to notify an employee of his *Beck* rights when it first sought to obligate him to pay dues, and by causing the employer to terminate the employee for not joining the union.

---

[3]*Supra* note 1.
[4]*Id.*
[5]Penrod v. NLRB, 203 F.3d 41, 163 LRRM 2513 (Cal. Ct. App. 2000).
[6]327 NLRB 1237, 1238 (1999).
[7]Meijer, Inc., 329 NLRB No. 69, 162 LRRM 1177 (1999).
[8]327 NLRB 996, 997 (1999).
[9]327 NLRB 563, 564 (1999).

An employer commits an unfair labor practice by refusing to execute an agreed on contract because of the inclusion of an unlawful union-security clause, where the employer was in fact motivated by a decertification petition filed by some of its employees between agreement to final terms of a collective bargaining agreement and the union's request that it execute the contract. The clause at issue required an employee to obtain a "referral from the union before starting to work," but the collective bargaining agreement in question did not contain an exclusive hiring-hall clause.[10]

D. Uniform Periodic Dues and Fees

A union violates the Act by using the dues-checkoff provision to collect either dues or fees for nonrepresentational activities from *Beck* objectors.[11]

E. The Belated Tender

Unions are expected to provide members with a reasonable period, of not less than 30 days after their resignation, to tender reduced dues and fees based on *Beck* before employees can be terminated for failure to tender dues or agency fees.[12]

F. The Contract Bar

1. *Representation Elections*

In *Four Seasons Solar Products Corp.*[13] the regional director decided the contract did not serve to bar a representation petition due to an unlawful union-security provision because it appeared to require, as a condition of employment, the payment of assessments. The Board disagreed, reasoning that the contract language regarding certain payments to the union did not operate to remove the contract bar to the petition. The contract contained no express requirement that an employee pay assessments as a condition of employment. The Board observed that *Paragon Products Corp.*[14] delineates three instances where a contract will not bar the processing of

---

[10]Flying Dutchman Park, Inc., 329 NLRB No. 46, 162 LRRM 1283 (1999).
[11]Kroger, Inc., 327 NLRB 1237, 1238 (1999).
[12]Polymark Corp., 329 NLRB No. 7, 162 LRRM 1033 (1999).
[13]332 NLRB No. 9, 2000 WL 1369713, 165 LRRM 1177 (2000).
[14]134 NLRB 662, 49 LRRM 1160 (1961).

a petition because of an unlawful union-security provision: (1) those that expressly and unambiguously require the employer to give preference to union members (a) in hiring, (b) in laying off, or (c) for purpose of seniority; (2) those that specifically withhold from incumbent nonmembers or new employees the statutory 30-day grace period; and (3) those that expressly require, as a condition of continued employment, the payment of sums of money other than "periodic dues and initiation fees uniformly required."

In *Four Seasons*[15] the dues-checkoff clause contained no statement that payment of "uniform assessments" was a condition of employment or was even required. Moreover, the union-security clauses that did contain "condition of employment" language mentioned only dues and initiation fees and required only that employees "be and remain members of the Union in good standing." Under those circumstances, the board concluded that the contract did not expressly require the payment of assessments as a condition of employment and thus did not fall within the ban set forth in *Paragon Products*.

IV. SECTION 14(b) AND STATE "RIGHT-TO-WORK" LAWS

In *NLRB v. Pueblo of San Juan*[16] the court approved a finding that the Pueblo of San Juan, a federally recognized Indian tribal government, had the authority to enact and enforce a right-to-work tribal ordinance prohibiting union security agreements for companies engaged in commercial activity on tribal lands. The case arose after a 27-year lessee, Duke City Lumber Company, which had a collective bargaining agreement for its entire term, sold the sawmill to Idaho Timber. The Pueblo and Idaho Timber negotiated a new lease containing a preferential-employment hiring provision for Pueblo members and a provision forbidding the company from entering into a collective bargaining agreement requiring union membership.[17] The District Court held that, because federal law does not preempt local regulation of contracts that require union membership as a condition of employment, and because the text of the NLRA and the leg-

---

[15]*Four Seasons, supra* note 13, 2000 WL 1369713, at *3.
[16]228 F.3d 1195, 165 LRRM 2321 (10th Cir. 2000).
[17]Labor Organization Ordinance Number 96-63 provided that no person shall be required to become or remain a member of a labor organization or pay dues, fees, assessments, or other charges of any kind to a labor organization. It also prohibited in-lieu payments to a charity or other third party.

islative history of the statute failed to mention or discuss Indian tribes, the Pueblo's ordinance could stand. Moreover, Indian tribes and the federal government are dual sovereigns. The Tenth Circuit concluded that lease provisions that restrict closed shops and give preferential hiring to tribal members are internal economic matters that directly effect a sovereign's right of self-government.

In *Wilkes Telephone Membership Corp.*[18] the general counsel argued that the line of cases establishing that dues checkoff clauses expire with the contract should not be considered controlling where state law prohibits union-security provisions.[19] The Board rejected that argument and held that, even in right-to-work states, such provisions were ordinary creatures of contract.

A union policy, which establishes a fee schedule for all union nonmembers for grievance representation, does not violate a state's right-to-work law. This is so because payment of a service fee for representation is not a condition of employment.[20]

Section 14(b) only gives states the right to make their own laws that are more restrictive than federal law of union security agreements. Accordingly, Colorado's union-security law, which allows deauthorization petitions to be filed only during a 15-day window 4 months before the end of a contract or its 3-year anniversary, was found preempted by the NLRA, which allows deauthorization petitions at any time.[21]

In *Teamsters Local 435 (Mercury Warehouse)*[22] the Board also held that Colorado could not authorize union-security clauses that allow unions to charge nonmembers for nonrepresentational activities, contrary to the Supreme Court's interpretation of the NLRA in *Beck*. Although Section 14(b) of the Act allows states to regulate union security, they are only free to pursue their own more *restrictive* poli-

---

[18]331 NLRB No. 98, 164 LRRM 1338 (2000).

[19]Since 1962, the Board has held that an employer's checkoff obligation, and union security clauses in general, terminate with the contract's expiration. Bethlehem Steel, 136 NLRB 1500, 50 LRRM 1013 (1962), *remanded on other grounds sub nom.* Marine and Shipbuilding Workers v. NLRB, 320 F.2d 615, 53 LRRM 2878 (3d Cir. 1963). *Accord* Hacienda Hotel Inc., 331 NLRB No. 89, 164 LRRM 1273 (2000) (no §8(a)(5) violation where an employer notified union that it intended to cease checking off dues 6 months after expiration of collective bargaining agreement, even where contract contained no union-security provisions, because they were affirmatively prohibited by Nevada law).

[20]Cone v. Nevada Serv. Employees Union, 998 P.2d 1178, 164 LRRM 2202 (Nev. 2000) (per curiam).

[21]Albertson's/Max Food Warehouse, 329 NLRB No. 44, 162 LRRM 1169 (1999).

[22]327 NLRB 458, 460, 160 LRRM 1130 (1999).

cies in matters of union security agreements, and state law cannot sanction a more expansive union security arrangement than that permitted by federal law.[23] The Board rejected the union argument that under Section 14(b), Colorado law controlled all union security clauses and, therefore, if a contract ratified in Colorado did not adopt federal protections for dues dissenters, *Beck* would not apply.

V. Hiring-Hall and Job-Referral Practices

A. General Rules

A union's negligence in handling referrals from an exclusive hiring hall, even without discriminatory intent, may violate the union's duty of fair representation. In *Jacoby v. NLRB*[24] the employee, a member of the union, registered for employment through the union's hiring hall and was placed on the highest priority list.[25] However, because of negligence, the union mistakenly dispatched lower priority employees before the employee with higher priority.[26] The Board had held that the union's negligence did not violate the duty of fair representation or the Act.[27] The D.C. Circuit disagreed, holding that the Board misinterpreted case law and reasoning that the fact that the deviation was merely negligent did not mandate a finding that the union did not breach its duty of fair representation. Rather, the Board was directed to consider on remand "whether, given the union's heightened duty of fair dealing in the context of a hiring hall, the union's negligent failure to adhere to its referral standards was an unfair labor practice."[28]

It remains the case that a union's arbitrary actions may violate its duty of fair representation owed to those individuals who seek to

---

[23]The union alleged that a contract negotiated between it and an employer and ratified by employees allowed a union to charge nonmember objectors for nonrepresentational activities under *Beck*. *Id.*, 327 NLRB at 459.

[24]233 F.3d 611, 165 LRRM 2993 (D.C. Cir. 2000).

[25]*Id.* at 613.

[26]*Id.*

[27]Steamfitters Local 343 (Contra Costa Elec.), 329 NLRB No. 65, 162 LRRM 1156 (1999) (holding that union does not violate Act when its actions in regard to exclusive hiring hall are result of mere negligence).

[28]*Jacoby, supra* note 24, 233 F.3d at 617. *But see* Pipefitters & Steamfitters Local 247, 332 NLRB No. 95, n.1 (2000) (Board acknowledged that "union does not violate the Act when its actions in regard to an exclusive hiring hall are a result of mere negligence.").

use the union's hiring hall.[29] In addition, in hiring-hall cases where a union prevents an employee from being hired or causes an employee's discharge, the Board still holds that the union may rebut the presumption that it has "encouraged union membership" by showing that its action "was necessary to the effective performance of its function of representing its constituency."[30] The Board also reiterated its prohibition of discrimination based on an employee's engagement in protected activity or lack of union membership or local membership.[31]

In *Carpenters Local 370*[32] a case involving a nonexclusive hiring hall, the Board held that

> [a]bsent either a finding that the Union owed the [employee] a duty of fair representation in these circumstances, or a finding that the Union was retaliating against the [employee] because he engaged in Section 7 activity, there is no basis to conclude that the Union violated the Act by failing to provide [the employee] with the requested information [regarding the Union's operation of the nonexclusive hiring hall].[33]

Courts continue to recognize that an employee may sue a union under Title I of the LMRDA.[34] In *Laborers Local 294*[35] the Board de-

---

[29]Theatrical Stage Employees, 332 NLRB No. 3, 165 LRRM 1163 (2000) (union did not act arbitrarily where it legally denied former member's reapplication to its hiring hall because of former member's history of misconduct); Electrical Workers (IBEW) Local 3 (White Plains), 331 NLRB 150 (2000) (union's actions not arbitrary or discriminatory).

[30]*Theatrical Stage Employees, supra* note 29 (union demonstrated that its denial of former member's reapplication to its hiring hall because of former member's history of misconduct was necessary to protect representative role that union performs in administering exclusive hiring hall).

[31]Newspaper and Mail Deliverers' Union of New York City & Vicinity (City & Suburban Delivery Sys.), 332 NLRB No. 77 (2000) (union discriminated in refusing to refer employees who engaged in protected activity); Electrical Workers (IBEW) Local 3 (White Plains), 331 NLRB 150 (2000) (union violated Act when it required employees who use its exclusive hiring hall to comply with its constitution and bylaws, and in refusing to register nonmember on its out-of-work list and refer him for employment because of his nonmember status); Pipefitters & Steamfitters, 332 NLRB No. 95 (2000) (union discriminatorily failed to place employee who was not a member of local on out-of-work list, although union did not unlawfully fail to refer employee to work).

[32]332 NLRB No. 25, 165 LRRM 1211 (2000).

[33]*Id.*, 165 LRRM at 1212.

[34]Kaufman v. Electrical Workers (IBEW), 124 F. Supp. 2d 1127, 166 LRRM 2025 (N.D. Ill. 2000) (court denied union's motion for summary judgment on employees' claim that union brought charges against them in retaliation for their support of changes to union's job-referral system).

[35]331 NLRB No. 27, 164 LRRM 1169 (2000).

ferred to arbitrators' rulings regarding the legality of a union's dispatch of three individuals, allegedly in violation of contract and hiring-hall rules.

Discrimination in the use of an exclusive hiring hall based on race violates Sections 8(b)(1)(A) and 8(b)(2) of the Act. In a case brought pursuant to Title VII and Section 1981, and not alleging unfair labor practices under Section 8(b) of the Act, the Sixth Circuit Court of Appeals, in *Alexander v. Laborers Local 496*,[36] affirmed a district court's ruling that a union hiring hall's referral practice was unlawful because of its discriminatory disparate treatment of African Americans. The plaintiffs, nonunion referral applicants for jobs at a power plant, established a prima facie case of disparate-treatment racial discrimination by demonstrating that they were African American, that they were available for referral by the union, that there were job opportunities available, that they were not referred by the union to such job opportunities, and that white nonunion members were referred for work. The union's proffered legitimate nondiscriminatory reason for its selection of individuals for referral was that the employer requested only those persons "working-in-the-calling." Finding that this reason was a pretext for disparate-treatment race discrimination, the Sixth Circuit reasoned that the "working-in-the-calling" policy had been routinely waived for white applicants but not for African American applicants.

B. Remedies

The Board continues to provide an order to cease and desist from further discrimination and to provide backpay for the discriminatee as its basic relief.[37]

VI. The Dues Checkoff

A. The LMRA and the Courts

Once a checkoff authorization form with a portability clause is executed, it may allow deductions when the employee leaves employment and returns to the same employer. In *Food & Commercial Workers District Local 540 v. Pilgrim's Pride Corp.*[38] several employees

---

[36] 177 F.3d 394 (6th Cir. 1999), *cert. denied*, 528 U.S. 1154 (2000).

[37] *See, e.g.*, Electrical Workers (IBEW) Local 3 (White Plains), 331 NLRB No. 150 (2000).

[38] 195 F.3d 328, 162 LRRM 2513 (5th Cir. 1999).

had signed checkoff authorization forms, subsequently left employment, and then were later rehired. The union requested that the company deduct union fees from the employees' paychecks, and the company complied. The company later refused to continue withholding the dues after some of the employees objected. An arbitrator ruled that the employer was obligated to honor the earlier authorization forms when the employees returned to work with the same employer. The District Court enforced the ruling, and the Fifth Circuit affirmed.

C. The NLRB

It continues to be an unfair labor practice to pay assessments by checkoff without employee authorization. In addition, the Board has found that a union violated Section 8(b)(1)(A) of the Act by threatening employees with discharge for failing to pay dues under the union's "market recovery program," owing from their employment on Davis-Bacon projects.[39]

The Board found an unfair labor practice where the union accepted and retained dues deducted from the wages of an employee who resigned from the union, and it continued to demand payment of such dues after the employee sought information about the "financial core" minimum demanded of a nonmember, and requested termination of his dues checkoff authorization.[40]

Similarly, the Board has held that a union unlawfully charged an employee a service fee equal to full union dues when it spent a portion of the fee for purposes unrelated to collective bargaining after the employee resigned his membership in the union and filed a *Beck* objection.[41] The Board has also held that a union violates its duty of fair representation by failing to grant employees, who resign their union membership, a separate window period following resignation in which to file a *Beck* objection.[42]

---

[39]Electrical Workers (IBEW) Local 48 (Kingston Constructors, Inc.), 332 NLRB No. 161 (2000).

[40]Graphic Communications Local 735-S (Quebecor Printing Hazelton, Inc.), 330 NLRB No. 11 (1999).

[41]Paperworkers Local 987 (Sun Chem. Corp. of Mich.), 327 NLRB 1011, 161 LRRM 1028 (1999).

[42]Polymark Corp., 329 NLRB No. 7, 162 LRRM 1033 (1999), *rev'd in part on other grounds sub nom.*, Mohat v. NLRB, 166 LRRM 2256 (6th Cir. 2000) (unpublished disposition).

The Board has held that an employer does not violate Sections 8(a)(5) and (1) by unilaterally ceasing a checkoff arrangement, because the employer's duty to continue a checkoff arrangement ends when the contract creating the checkoff expires.[43]

VII. Constitutional Dimensions and Other Statutory Requirements

B. Effect of Political Expenditures

As prescribed in *Lehnert*,[44] courts continue to determine which expenses may be charged to nonmembers on a case-by-case basis.[45] Courts continue to apply the principles set forth in *Chicago Teachers Union v. Hudson*[46] and *Ellis v. Brotherhood of Railway, Airline & Steamship Clerks*,[47] when determining whether proper notice of the right to object to the imposition of fees used for purposes other than collective bargaining, in both substance and form, was provided to employees, and identifying which union activities properly may be charged to dissenters.[48] In *Lutz v. Machinists*[49] the court addressed the issue of whether a union operating under the Railway Labor Act[50] could, consistent with the First Amendment, prohibit nonmember employees from filing a "continuing objection" to the payment of union dues unrelated to the costs associated with collective bargaining and contract administration.[51] Pursuant to the union's proce-

---

[43]Hacienda Resort Hotel, 331 NLRB No. 89, 164 LRRM 1273 (2000); Wilkes Tel. Membership Corp., 331 NLRB No. 98 (2000).

[44]Lehnert v. Ferris Faculty Ass'n, 500 U.S. 507, 137 LRRM 2321 (1991).

[45]*See* Otto v. Pennsylvania State Educ. Ass'n, 107 F. Supp. 2d 615, 623, 165 LRRM 2466, 2472 (M.D. Pa. 2000) (holding that union's extra-unit litigation expenses were not related to collective bargaining or contract administration and could not constitutionally be charged to objectors); Belhumeur v. Labor Relations Comm'n, 432 Mass. 458, 471, 165 LRRM 2458, 2465 (2000) (expenses incurred by teachers' union in advocating public education funding held to be political speech and therefore nonchargeable to dissenting employees, whereas article published in union publication characterized as "informational support services" did not constitute political speech and was chargeable).

[46]475 U.S. 292, 121 LRRM 2793 (1986).

[47]466 U.S. 435, 116 LRRM 2001 (1984).

[48]*See, e.g.*, Tavernor v. Illinois Fed'n of Teachers, 226 F.3d 842, 846–47, 165 LRRM 2193, 2195–96 (7th Cir. 2000) (analyzing whether union's "fair share fees" collection procedure violated First Amendment rights of objectors).

[49]121 F. Supp. 2d 498, 166 LRRM 2032 (E.D. Va. 2000).

[50]46 U.S.C. §151 et seq.

[51]*Lutz, supra* note 49, at 499–500, 166 LRRM at 2033.

dure, objectors were required to submit such objections on an annual basis, and failure to do so resulted in waiver of any earlier objection for the forthcoming year and precluded fee reduction.[52] The court held that the procedure contravened *Chicago Teachers Union v. Hudson*,[53] and that mandating an annual objection to dues was not "carefully tailored to minimize the infringement" on nonmembers' constitutional rights.[54] As the court observed, the D.C. Circuit, the Sixth Circuit, and the District Court of Maryland have upheld union procedures requiring annual objections of private-sector employees under the more deferential duty of fair-representation standard.[55]

Rejecting the contrary position of the NLRB, the U.S. Court of Appeals for the District of Columbia ruled, in *Penrod v. NLRB*,[56] that unions have an affirmative obligation pursuant to their duty of fair representation to inform all "potential objectors," including new employees and financial core payers as well as those who had not objected to the payment of certain union dues as permitted under *Beck*,[57] of the percentage of dues spent on nonrepresentational union activities.[58] Specifically, the court concluded that unions must "give employees 'sufficient information to gauge the propriety of the union's fee'—i.e., the percentage reduction."[59]

Several class actions have been approved in California concerning union collection and retention of fair-share payments under public employee collective bargaining agreements. In California, the state government code was amended, effective January 1, 2000, to require fair-share payments by all employees in represented bargaining units in the California state university and University of California systems.[60] In each of the cases, employees claimed their bargain-

---

[52]*Id.* at 500, 166 LRRM at 2034.

[53]475 U.S. 292, 121 LRRM 2793 (1986).

[54]Lutz v. Machinists, 121 F. Supp. 2d 498, 506, 166 LRRM 2032, 2038 (E.D. Va. 2000).

[55]*Id.* at 502, 166 LRRM at 2035 (citing Abrams v. Communications Workers, 59 F.3d 1373, 1381, 149 LRRM 2928, 2935 (D.C. Cir. 1995); Tierney v. City of Toledo, 824 F.2d 1497, 1506, 125 LRRM 3217, 3222 (6th Cir. 1987); Kidwell v. Transportation Communications Int'l Union, 731 F. Supp. 192, 205, 133 LRRM 2692, 2702 (D. Md. 1990)).

[56]203 F.3d 41, 163 LRRM 2513 (D.C. Cir. 2000).

[57]487 U.S. 735, 128 LRRM 2729 (1988).

[58]*Penrod, supra* note 56, at 47–48, 163 LRRM at 2517. *Accord* Thomas v. NLRB, 213 F.3d 651, 653, 655–56, 164 LRRM 2577, 2578, 2580 (D.C. Cir. 2000).

[59]*Penrod, supra* note 56, at 48, 163 LRRM at 2517 (quoting Hudson, 475 U.S. at 306, 121 LRRM at 2799).

[60]CAL. GOV'T. CODE §3583(5)(a)(1) (2000).

ing representative did not provide proper *Hudson* procedural safe-guards.[61]

The Seventh Circuit struck down the system used to collect fair-share fees from certain university clerical employees.[62] Under that system, the union denoted more than 80 percent of full union dues as the estimated fair-share fee. However, the union collected and escrowed an amount equal to 100 percent of union dues. In addition, nonmember objections to the proposed fair share were not processed until 6 months after the initial deduction was made, and a determination was not made until at least 1 year after the deduction was first made.

In *Whitley County Teachers Association v. Bauer*[63] the court examined a collective bargaining agreement's fair-share provision. Teachers were given three options at the start of the school year: Pay a fair-share fee equivalent to full dues; pay an estimated amount for only those expenses germane to the collective bargaining function; or pay nothing pending an arbitrator's determination. In light of the third option, which was imposed if the two payment options were not chosen, the fair-share provision was held constitutional. Furthermore, even though *Hudson* safeguards were not set out in the collective bargaining agreement, their existence protected the fair-share provision.

C. Religious Objectors

In January 2000, the California government code was amended to require union security payments by represented employees in the California state university and University of California systems. Section 3584 of the code provides an exception to payment of the fair-share fee by members "of a bona fide religion, body, or sect that has historically held conscientious objections to joining or financially supporting public employee organizations."[64] In lieu of dues, the employee pays a sum "equal to the amount of the fair share fee . . . to a religious, nonlabor charitable fund. . . ."[65]

[61]Murray v. Local 2620, State, County & Municipal Employees, 192 F.R.D. 629, 164 LRRM 2359 (N.D. Cal. 2000); Friedman v. California State Employees Ass'n (CSEA), 163 LRRM 2924 (E.D. Cal. 2000); Cummings v. Connell, 163 LRRM 2086 (E.D. Cal. 1999); Wagner v. Professional Eng'rs, 163 LRRM 2715 (E.D. Cal. 1999).

[62]Tavernor v. Illinois Fed'n of Teachers & Univ. Professionals Local 4100, 226 F.3d 842, 165 LRRM 2193 (7th Cir. 2000).

[63]718 N.E.2d 1181, 163 LRRM 2875 (Ind. Ct. App. 1999).

[64]Cal. Gov't Code §3584 (2000).

[65]Cal. Gov't Code §3584(a) (2000).

Part VIII

ADMINISTRATION OF THE ACT

Chapter 27

JURISDICTION:
COVERAGE OF THE ACT

I. CONSTITUTIONALITY

B. The Shadow of the First Amendment: Jurisdiction Over Religious Organizations

In *Ukiah Adventist Hospital dba Ukiah Valley Medical Center & California Nurses Ass'n*[1] citing earlier decisions[2] and assuming that the Religious Freedom Restoration Act of 1993 (RFRA)[3] was constitutional, the Board asserted jurisdiction over a hospital operated by the Seventh Day Adventist Church. The Board held that its assertion of jurisdiction did not violate the First Amendment or the RFRA because assertion of such jurisdiction is in furtherance of a compelling interest in preventing labor strife and protecting employees' rights to organize and bargain and is the "least restrictive means of accomplishing the goals of the Act."[4]

II. STATUTORY JURISDICTION

A. Basic Coverage: "Commerce" and "Affecting Commerce"

Federal courts have continued to decide NLRA questions that arise as collateral issues in cases brought under other federal statutes. In *Albany Specialties v. Board of Education*[5] the court held that because the plaintiff raised antitrust claims in addition to labor claims relating to enforcement of a project labor agreement, the plaintiff was entitled to seek injunctive and declaratory relief in federal court rather than before the Board.

E. Nonprofit Organizations

The Board and the courts continue to find NLRA jurisdiction over nonprofit community service organizations. For example, in *NLRB v. Young Women's Christian Association*[6] the court enforced a Board decision asserting jurisdiction over a private, not-for-profit

---

[1]332 NLRB No. 59, 165 LRRM 1258 (2000).
[2]University of Great Falls and Mont. Fed'n of Teachers, 331 NLRB No. 188, 165 LRRM 1150 (2000).
[3]42 U.S.C. §2000bb-1.
[4]*University of Great Falls, supra* note 2.
[5]162 LRRM 3071 (N.D.N.Y. 1999).
[6]192 F.3d 1111, 162 LRRM 2268 (8th Cir. 1999).

corporation engaged in administering a federal Head Start Program, despite the fact that the program was subject to extensive governmental control. Similarly, in *FiveCAP, Inc.*[7] the Board asserted jurisdiction over a nonprofit community action agency that administers various state and federal antipoverty programs and that received annual gross revenues in excess of $1 million and received federal funds from outside the state of Michigan in excess of $50,000. In doing so, it rejected the employer's contention that it was a political subdivision.

F. Relation to Jurisdictions of Other Agencies

1. Railway Labor Act

The Board has continued to focus on whether an employer meets the definition of "carrier" under the Railway Labor Act when assessing if the employer is exempt from coverage under the NLRA. As part of its deliberations, the Board will usually seek the views of the National Mediation Board. In *D & T Limousine Service Inc.*[8] the employer had contracted with a railroad to provide transportation services to railroad employees. The Board adopted the ALJ's finding that the employer's retention of a wide range of control in operating the business (i.e., hiring, firing, setting wages, and setting policies) established that it was not "controlled" by the railroad and was, therefore, subject to the NLRA.[9]

III. DEFINITIONS AND LIMITATIONS ON COVERAGE

B. Employer

1. Single-Employer Status

In *Beverly California*[10] the Seventh Circuit affirmed a Board finding of single-employer status. Where two corporations were a single employer at the time of termination but not during the unfair-labor

---

[7]332 NLRB No. 83 (2000). *See also* FiveCAP, Inc., 331 NLRB No. 157 (2000).
[8]328 NLRB 769, 769 (1999).
[9]*Cf.* Evergreen Aviation Ground Logistics, 327 NLRB 869, 162 LRRM 1014 (1999) (after referral to NMB, Board held employer that provided ground services and ground equipment maintenance for airlines was "carrier" and not subject to NLRA).
[10]227 F.3d 817, 165 LRRM 2257 (7th Cir. 2000).

practice proceeding, due process requires notice of those proceedings to both companies.[11]

The D.C. Circuit has rejected an employer's argument that a union was estopped from asserting single-employer status against unionized and nonunion construction companies operated by same family, despite a contention that the union had been aware of the relationship for 20 years.[12]

The Board continues to hold that to establish that two or more employers are joint employers, the two entities "must share or codetermine matters governing essential terms and conditions of employment."[13]

In *M.B. Sturgis Inc.*[14] the Board found that a shipbuilder (user employer) and a second employer that supplied it with employees (supplier employer) were joint employers of the supplied or contingent employees, where the two employers meaningfully affected and codetermined numerous conditions of employment, including supervision, assignment, direction, and discipline. In so holding, the Board rejected an argument that jointly employed contingent employees could not be combined with solely employed workers of the user employer to form a multi-employer unit, absent the consent of both employers. Rather, the Board chose to apply traditional community-of-interest principles to determine appropriateness of the bargaining unit. In its ruling, the Board clarified long-standing precedent initially established in *Greenhoot Inc.*[15] and overruled its decision in *Lee Hospital.*[16] The Board now holds that the requirement of employer consent for bargaining does not apply to units that combine jointly employed and solely employed employees of a single user employer.

2. Agents

The Seventh Circuit has held that where a known antiunion employee expressed antiunion views at captive-audience meetings and where such employee could be construed as having actual or apparent authority to speak as the employer's agent, the employer is properly held to have violated Section 8(a)(1) of the Act by the

---

[11]Viking Indus. Sec. v. NLRB, 225 F.3d 131, 165 LRRM 2129 (2d Cir. 2000).
[12]O'Dovero v. NLRB, 193 F.3d 532, 162 LRRM 2618 (D.C. Cir. 1999).
[13]Bultman Enters., 332 NLRB No. 31, 165 LRRM 1341 (2000).
[14]331 NLRB No. 173, 165 LRRM 1017 (2000).
[15]205 NLRB 250, 83 LRRM 1656 (1973).
[16]300 NLRB 947, 136 LRRM 1348 (1990).

employee's statements.[17] The Sixth Circuit reversed a Board finding that an assistant bookkeeper was an "agent" of the employer because employees reasonably believed the bookkeeper was speaking to employer policies in four antiunion meetings held by the employees.[18] The court found insufficient evidence that employees could reasonably believe the bookkeeper was acting for management where the meetings were not on the employer's premises and she was off the clock.[19] Where an employer openly aligns itself with a third party's statements and actions, the Board will find agency status.[20]

3. Exclusions From Coverage of the Act

In *Yukon Kuskokwim Health Corp.*[21] the Board rejected an employer's contention that it should be excluded from NLRA coverage because the business was a wholly owned tribal enterprise operating on a reservation. The Board found no merit in the argument that the hospital was excluded from coverage because of its proximity to a treaty reservation where there was no evidence that the facility was located on an area subject to a treaty.

The Board continues to apply the two-part standard for determining whether an organization is exempt as a "political subdivision." In *Hinds County Human Resources Agency*[22] the Board noted that an employer is a political subdivision if it is either: (1) created directly by the state to constitute a department or an administrative arm of government, or (2) administered by persons who are responsible to public officials or the general public. In that case, the Board found the agency was exempt because it was created by the county pursuant to state statute, the state statute specifically provided for local government control of the agency, and the agency received all funds from state and federal government sources.

---

[17]Beverly Cal. v. NLRB, 227 F.3d 817, 165 LRRM 2257 (7th Cir. 2000), *petition for cert. filed* (Apr. 9, 2001).

[18]National Health Care, L.P. v. NLRB, 234 F.3d 1269, 166 LRRM 2768 (6th Cir. 2000), *enforcing* 327 NLRB 1175, 161 LRRM 1152 (1999).

[19]*Id.*

[20]*Id. Compare Monastra v. NYNEX Corp.*, 165 LRRM 2500 (S.D.N.Y. 2000), where the court held that a union business agent could not be sued as a discharged employee's employer under the Act, despite a contention that the business agent had so aligned himself with management as to become the employer.

[21]328 NLRB 761, 762, 161 LRRM 1161, *vacated on other grounds*, 234 F.3d 714, 166 LRRM 2012 (D.C. Cir. 2000).

[22]331 NLRB No. 186, 165 LRRM 1172 (2000).

In *Kentucky River Community Care, Inc. v. NLRB*[23] the Sixth Circuit rejected an argument for political subdivision status by a private, nonprofit organization operating as regional mental health board because the organization was established by an individual person in his capacity as citizen of Kentucky.[24]

In *NLRB v. Young Women's Christian Ass'n*[25] the Eighth Circuit joined the Fourth, Sixth, and Tenth Circuits in upholding the Board's *Management Training*[26] standard on the ground that it was a valid exercise of the Board's discretion in exercising its statutory jurisdiction. The Board rejected arguments that it lacked jurisdiction over a daycare center, because the federal government maintained pervasive control over its employees' terms and conditions of employment and it was therefore prevented from engaging in meaningful collective bargaining.

C. Employee

1. In General

Volunteers are not employees and, therefore, they fall outside the coverage of the Act. In *Seattle Opera Ass'n*[27] the Board considered whether auxiliary choristers were statutory employees or volunteers. Applying the analytical framework of *WBAI Pacifica Foundation*,[28] the Board concluded that the choristers were employees. The focus of the Board's analysis is the presence or absence of some economic relationship between the individuals-at-issue and the employer. If there is an economic relationship, the Board will find employee status. In *Seattle Opera*, remuneration in the amount of $214 at the end of the production constituted an economic relationship, and the Board noted that it will not find volunteer status simply because the individuals are "compensated at less than a minimum wage or because their compensation is less than a living wage."[29]

---

[23]193 F.3d 444, 162 LRRM 2449 (6th Cir. 1999), aff'd, ___ U.S. ___, 167 LRRM 2164 (2001).

[24]*See also* FiveCAP, Inc., 331 NLRB No. 157 (2000) (Head Start program not political subdivision where not created directly by state and its Board not directly responsible to electorate).

[25]192 F.3d 1111, 162 LRRM 2268 (8th Cir. 1999).

[26]317 NLRB 1355, 149 LRRM 1313 (1995).

[27]331 NLRB No. 148, 165 LRRM 1273 (2000).

[28]328 NLRB 1273 (1999).

[29]*Seattle, supra* note 27.

The Board has also held that graduate students[30] working in teaching positions and residents[31] employed by a hospital are statutory employees under the Act.

2. Excluded Categories of Employees

a. Supervisors

The criteria for determining supervisory status is set out at Section 2(11) of the Act. The burden of establishing that status rests on the party asserting it.[32] The authority to use independent judgment in effecting any of the statutory contents is sufficient to establish that an individual is a supervisor.[33] But the assessment of an applicant's technical ability to perform required work is not an effective recommendation to have.[34] Routine work assignments are not an exercise of independent judgment sufficient to warrant a finding of supervisory authority.[35]

In *Allstate Insurance Co.*[36] the Board considered whether a Neighborhood Office Agent (NOA), who sold insurance policies from a storefront office, was a supervisor. The employer's NOA program was essentially a commission-based employment system that left entrepreneurial decision making up to the NOA. The Board found that, because the NOA had complete discretion over how to run her office, including whether to staff her office with assistants, her exercise of authority over the assistants was not "in the interest of the employer" but was instead in her own interest.[37] Because her exercise of authority over the assistants was not "in the interest of the employer," the NOA did not meet the Section 2(11) definition of supervisor or of a manager.

---

[30]New York Univ., 332 NLRB No. 111, 165 LRRM 1241 (2000).
[31]Boston Med. Ctr. Corp., 330 NLRB No. 30, 162 LRRM 1329 (1999).
[32]NLRB v. Kentucky River Community Care, Inc., ___ U.S. ___, 167 LRRM 2164 (2001); Freeman Decorating Co., 330 NLRB No. 160 (2000).
[33]Westwood Health Care Ctr., 330 NLRB No. 141 (2000).
[34]*Id.*
[35]Health Resources of Lakeview, 332 NLRB No. 81 (2000) (accommodating employee break routine); Arlington Elec., Inc., 332 NLRB No. 74 (2000) (routine work assignment); Fleming Co., Inc., 330 NLRB No. 32 (1999) (issuance of warranty letter found to lack requested independent judgment). *See also* PROBLEM OF LAW AND PROCEDURE IN REPRESENTATION CASES (1999). Available on NLRB website at www.nlrb.gov.
[36]332 NLRB No. 66, 165 LRRM 1293 (2000).
[37]*Id.*, 165 LRRM at 1296.

The status of nurses as statutory supervisors continues to be a contentious and fact-intensive issue.[38] In a number of recent cases, the Board found that the nurses were not supervisors,[39] and in other cases the Board reached the opposite conclusion.[40] Although the reviewing courts sometimes affirm the Board's determination about the supervisory status of nurses,[41] it is not uncommon for the reviewing court to decide the issue differently.[42] Where the reviewing court rejects the Board's conclusion, this almost always results from the application of a different legal standard rather than a differing analysis of the facts. A conflict in the circuits with respect to the Board's interpretation and meaning of the term "independent judgment," has

---

[38]This issue has been the topic of several law review articles. *See* Patrick M. Kuhlmann, *Comment, The Enigma of NLRA Section 2(11): The Supervisory Exclusion and the Case of the Charge Nurse,* 2000 WIS. L. REV. 157 (2000); Jennifer Claire Leisten, *Note, Independent Judgment Day: The Fourth Circuit Deems Nurses to be Supervisors in* Glenmark Associates v. NLRB, 78 N.C. L. REV. 508 (2000). In addition, the NLRB Office of the General Counsel has issued a Guideline Memorandum on Charge Nurse Supervisory Issues (Mem. OM 99-44, Aug. 24, 1999).

[39]Loyalhanna Care Ctr., 332 NLRB No. 86 (2000) (holding that nurses did not exercise independent judgment with regard to any of indicia of supervisory authority); Coventry Health Center, 332 NLRB No. 13, 165 LRRM 1181 (2000) (holding that charge nurses' role in employer's evaluation procedure did not establish that they were supervisors); Harborside Healthcare, Inc., 330 NLRB No. 191, 164 LRRM 1160 (2000) (concluding that charge nurses' authority to evaluate and call in employees failed to establish that they were supervisors); Elmhurst Extended Care Facilities, 329 NLRB No. 55, 162 LRRM 1317 (1999) (finding that nurses were not supervisors because there was insufficient link between their performance evaluations and retention of nursing assistants or the pay increases that they received); Vencor Hosp.-Los Angeles, 328 NLRB 1136, 1139–40, 162 LRRM 1001 (1999).

[40]Trevilla of Golden Valley, 330 NLRB No. 193, 164 LRRM 1053 (2000) (holding that LPNs exercised independent judgment in completing annual evaluations of nursing assistants, which were relied on by employer to award specific merit increases); Cape Cod Nursing & Retirement Home, 329 NLRB No. 28, 162 LRRM 1213 (1999) (concluding that LPNs were supervisors because their performance evaluations of nursing assistants were used as basis for merit increases); Health Care & Retirement Corp., 328 NLRB 1056, 161 LRRM 1291 (1999).

[41]*See* NLRB v. Hilliard Dev. Corp., 187 F.3d 133, 161 LRRM 2966 (1st Cir. 1999); Northern Mont. Health Care Ctr. v. NLRB, 178 F.3d 1089, 161 LRRM 2469 (9th Cir. 1999); NLRB v. GranCare, Inc., 170 F.3d 662, 160 LRRM 2661 (7th Cir. 1999); Beverly Enters.-Mass, Inc. dba East Village Nursing & Rehabilitation Ctr. v. NLRB, 165 F.3d 960, 160 LRRM 2342 (D.C. Cir. 1999); VIP Health Servs., Inc. v. NLRB, 164 F.3d 644, 160 LRRM 2269 (D.C. Cir. 1999).

[42]Schnurmacher Nursing Home v. NLRB, 214 F.3d 260, 164 LRRM 2531 (2d Cir. 2000); Integrated Health Servs. of Mich. v. NLRB, 191 F.3d 703, 162 LRRM 2273 (6th Cir. 1999); NLRB v. Attleboro Assocs. Ltd., 176 F.3d 154, 161 LRRM 2139 (3d Cir. 1999); Beverly Enters., W. Va., Inc. v. NLRB, 165 F.3d 307, 160 LRRM 2231 (4th Cir. 1999).

resulted in a resolution by the Supreme Court. In *NLRB v. Kentucky River Community Care, Inc.*[43] the Supreme Court rejected the Board's test for determining supervisory status as inconsistent with the Act. According to the Court, the Board rejected the employer's proof of supervisory status on the ground that employees do not use "independent judgment" under Section 2(11) when they exercise "ordinary professional or technical judgment in directing less-skilled employees to deliver services in accordance with employer-specified standards."[44] The Supreme Court found that this interpretation by the Board, by distinguishing different kinds of judgment, introduces a categorical exclusion into the Act that does not exist. The Supreme Court held that the Act permits questions regarding the degree of discretion an employee exercises, but the Board's interpretation renders determinative factors that have nothing to do with degree.

b. Managerial Employees

In *Allstate Insurance Co.*[45] the Board found that although an employee insurance agent exercised considerable discretionary authority, it was not the type of authority that involved formulating or effectuating company policies on behalf of her employer because the risks assumed by such actions ran to the employee. Thus, there was no risk of divided loyalty and no basis for finding the employee functioned in a managerial role. In *Boston Medical Center Corp.*[46] the Board affirmed the regional director's conclusion that chief residents are not statutory supervisors or managerial employees.

c. Confidential Employees

On remand from the Seventh Circuit decision in *E & L Transport Co. v. NLRB*,[47] discussed in the Main Edition, the Board accepted as "the law of the case" that a confidential secretary to the terminal manager was a "confidential" position under the Act because the position involved a labor nexus and because the manager for whom the secretary worked was responsible for formulating the company's labor relations policies. The secretary prepared confidential documents and had regular access to confidential information relating to labor relations policies.[48]

---

[43] ___ U.S. ___, 167 LRRM 2164 (2001).
[44] *Id.*, 167 LRRM at 2173.
[45] 332 NLRB No. 66, 165 LRRM 1293 (2000).
[46] 330 NLRB No. 30, 162 LRRM 1329 (1999).
[47] 85 F.3d 1258, 152 LRRM 2449 (7th Cir. 1996).
[48] E & L Transp. Co., 327 NLRB No. 76, 160 LRRM 1115 (1998).

d. Agricultural Laborers

The Board continues to recognize the existence of both a primary and secondary component to the application of the agricultural exception to NLRB jurisdiction, as set forth in *Farmers Reservoir & Irrigation Co. v. McComb.*[49]

e. Independent Contractors

(3) Owner-Operators in the Trucking Industry

In *Corporate Express Delivery Systems*[50] the Board found that owner-operators were not independent contractors where owner-operators and company drivers performed similar functions for the company. These functions were an integral part of the company's operation and the owner-operators worked for the company on a full-time basis. They were not free to add or delete customers, were required to use insurance recommended by the company, and could not independently negotiate compensation rates with the company. In *Douglas Foods Corp.*[51] the Board found that lease-route operators were employees despite factors suggesting an independent contractor relationship, including a significant degree of control over their compensation, ownership of the product on their trucks from which they kept their daily profit, and assumption of risk of waste or theft. The Board concluded that these factors were outweighed by various indications of employee status, including employer control over the assignment of customers and delivery times, periodic checks by the employer to see if the drivers made deliveries on time and kept their product hot, employer authority to add or subtract customers from drivers' routes without their consent, the use of the employer's "suggested pricing," and the need for employer approval for drivers to sell or assign their lease routes.

In *Slay Transportation Co., Inc.*[52] the Board reversed the regional director's finding of independent contractor status for owner-operators who leased their trucks to the employer. The Board disagreed with the regional director's finding that limited entrepreneurial opportunities, including the ability to hire other drivers to operate their

---

[49]337 U.S. 755 (1949). *See also* United Foods, Inc., 329 NLRB No. 73, 162 LRRM 1278 (1999) (where the Board held that employees involved in an employer's mushroom-slicing operation are agricultural employees engaged in secondary agricultural activity).

[50]332 NLRB No. 144, 166 LRRM 1017 (2000).

[51]330 NLRB No. 124, 163 LRRM 1201 (2000).

[52]331 NLRB No. 170, 165 LRRM 1213 (2000).

vehicles and to control their costs and income, warranted the conclusion that the owner-operators were independent contractors. Instead, the Board focused on the fact that the owner-operators, like company drivers, drove tractors leased by the employer, were trained and tested by the employer, used the company's dispatchers, and were subject to a compensation system established and controlled by the employer.

(6) Taxicab Owner-Operators and Lessees

The Board continues to assess the level of control an employer asserts over drivers in determining whether drivers are independent contractors or employees. In *Stamford Taxi, Inc.*,[53] the Board applied the "right-of-control" test and concluded that the drivers were employees rather than independent contractors when the employer retained title to vehicles, assigned work hours, required the use of its dispatchers, enforced work rules, and linked the employer's income directly to the drivers' fares.

(9) Miscellaneous Classifications

In *AmeriHealth Inc./AmeriHealth HMO*[54] the Board adopted a regional director's conclusion that primary care and specialty physicians who participated in an HMO were independent contractors and not employees within the meaning of Section 2(3) of the Act. Applying the right-of-control test, the Board acknowledged that the HMO had the right to control many details of the services that the physicians delivered to HMO members, but found that other factors, including the physicians' ability to contract with other insurance companies and to provide services not covered by the HMO to HMO members if the members were willing to pay for them, evidenced that the physicians were independent contractors rather than employees of the HMO.

The Board determined that students who serve as graduate assistants are employees under Section 2(3) of the Act in *New York University*.[55] Following the analysis of *Boston Medical Center*,[56] the Board

---

[53]332 NLRB No. 149 (2000).

[54]329 NLRB No. 76, 165 LRRM 1069 (1999).

[55]332 NLRB No. 111, 165 LRRM 1241 (2000).

[56]330 NLRB No. 30, 162 LRRM 1329 (1999) (overruling Cedars-Sinai Med. Ctr., 223 NLRB 251, 91 LRRM 1398 (1976), and holding that medical interns, residents, and fellows are employees under §2(3) of Act, notwithstanding that they are also students).

rejected the university's contention that graduate assistants are not statutory employees because they are "predominantly students" employed by the educational institution in which they are enrolled as students. The Board explained that the comparably low percentage of time that graduate students spend providing services for the university did not change the fact that graduate assistants perform work for the university under the university's control. The Board also reasoned that graduate assistants, unlike students receiving financial aid, perform work and provide services for the university under conditions controlled by the university without receiving academic credit for this work.

f. Family Members and Relationships

The Board continues to exclude relatives of a manager who is not an owner or shareholder from the definition of "employee" under Section 2(3) of the Act if the relative enjoys a "special status" on the job because of the relationship that aligns the interests of the relative more closely with management than with the employees of a unit.[57]

IV. DISCRETIONARY ADMINISTRATIVE JURISDICTIONAL STANDARDS

B. Specific Assertions or Denials of Coverage

8. **National Defense/Federal Funds**—significant amount of revenue from federal funds warrants a finding of Board jurisdiction.[58]

29. **Activities Intimately Connected to Operations of Exempt Employer**—both the Tenth and Eighth Circuits joined the Fourth and Sixth Circuits in upholding the Board's *Management Training* standard. In *Aramark Corp. v. NLRB*[59] the court affirmed the Board's exercise of jurisdiction over a contractor that was substantially controlled by an exempt

---

[57]R & D Trucking, Inc., 327 NLRB 531, 160 LRRM 1113 (1999) (son-in-law of employer's president excluded from unit because his familial relationship afforded him job-related privileges not available to unit members and greater access to management). *See also* Reg'l Home Care, Inc., 329 NLRB No. 6, 166 LRRM 1112 (1999) (sustaining challenges to three ballots because of "special status" resulting from familial relationship).

[58]Kingston Constr., Inc., 332 NLRB No. 161 (2000).

[59]179 F.3d 872, 161 LRRM 2441 (10th Cir. 1999).

governmental entity. The court expressly overruled a contrary line of precedent in finding that the control test is not a prerequisite to the Board's exercise of jurisdiction over a government contractor. Similarly, in *NLRB v. Young Women's Christian Ass'n*[60] the court found that the Board properly asserted jurisdiction over a government contractor without determining whether the contractor could engage in meaningful collective bargaining.

---

[60]192 F.3d 1111, 162 LRRM 2268 (8th Cir. 1999).

Chapter 28

FEDERAL PREEMPTION OF
STATE REGULATION

II. EVOLUTION OF PREEMPTION DOCTRINE

D. Federalism: Recognizing Important Matters of Particular Local Concern

The courts continue to hold that in enacting the NLRA, Congress did not intend to prevent states from establishing minimum employment standards.[1]

In *Dillingham Construction, Inc. v. County of Sonoma*[2] the court held that *Building & Construction Trades Council (San Diego) v. Garmon*[3] did not preempt a state law requiring payment of prevailing wages to employees in apprenticeship programs. The California law was found not to disrupt the right to collective bargaining because it established minimum labor standards that treat all workers equally and neither encourages nor discourages the collective bargaining process. On the other hand, a state labor department's refusal to process an employer group's apprenticeship program application was not enjoined where processing the application may have required the agency to make determinations within the Board's unfair labor practice jurisdiction.[4]

G. A Foundation: *Garmon* Preempts State Regulation of Conduct Arguably Protected or Prohibited by the Act

The courts continue to refine and apply the core principle that matters involving conduct arguably prohibited or protected by the Act are preempted under *Building & Construction Trades Council (San Diego) v. Garmon.*[5]

A supervisor's claims of breach of contract and wrongful discharge in retaliation for his providing testimony unfavorable to the

---

[1]*See* St. Thomas-St. John Hotel & Tourism Ass'n, Inc. v. Government of the U.S. Virgin Islands, 218 F.3d 232, 164 LRRM 2705 (3d Cir. 2000).

[2]190 F.3d 1034, 162 LRRM 2193 (9th Cir. 1999).

[3]359 U.S. 236, 43 LRRM 2838 (1959).

[4]Building Trades Employers' Educ. Ass'n v. McGowan, 166 LRRM 2361 (S.D.N.Y. 2000).

[5]359 U.S. 236, 43 LRRM 2838 (1959).

employer during a contractual grievance arbitration were held pre-empted under *Garmon*.[6] Because the evidence in the state court implicated Sections 7 and 8 of the Act and "would not be distinctly different" from that presented in an unfair-labor-practice proceeding, primary jurisdiction over the matter was vested exclusively in the Board.[7]

H. *Briggs & Stratton* Overruled: States May Not Regulate Economic Weapons Furnished by Congress

In *Dillingham Construction v. County of Sonoma*[8] coverage by California's prevailing wage law of employees in apprenticeship programs was analyzed under the *Machinists* doctrine, which proscribes state regulation of activity intended by Congress to be unregulated.[9] "[B]ecause federal law unequivocally permits regulation of apprenticeship standards" and the California law established nothing more than minimum labor standards for apprentices, the court held *Machinists* preemption inapplicable.[10]

III. *Garmon* Preemption in Specific Situations

B. Trespass

In *NLRB v. Calkins*[11] the court rejected the employer's argument that the need for a uniform national body of law precludes Section 7 rights from being defined by individual state trespass laws. The court enforced the Board's determination that a supermarket committed an unfair labor practice by threatening to have, and by having, nonemployee union representatives arrested for handbilling and picketing in furtherance of a consumer boycott on a privately owned walkway and parking lot, because the union's actions constituted protected activity under Section 7, and California law did not give the employer the right to exclude union organizers from its prop-

---

[6]Ruscigno v. American Nat'l Can Co., Inc., 84 Cal. App. 4th 112, 166 LRRM 3002 (Ct. App. 2000).
[7]*Id.* at 128, 166 LRRM at 3011.
[8]190 F.3d 1034, 162 LRRM 2193 (9th Cir. 1999).
[9]Machinists Lodge 76 v. Wisconsin Employment Relations Comm'n, 427 U.S. 132, 141, 92 LRRM 2881, 2887–88 (1976).
[10]*Dillingham, supra* note 8, at 1038–40, 162 LRRM at 2195–97.
[11]187 F.3d 1080, 161 LRRM 3121 (9th Cir. 1999), *cert. denied,* 529 U.S. 1098, 164 LRRM 2256 (2000).

erty. In enforcing the Board's order, the court rejected the employer's position that *Lechmere, Inc. v. NLRB*[12] created a federal law doctrine that nonemployee union organizers can, with certain limited exceptions not applicable here, be excluded from an employer's private property, and that this federal doctrine preempts state trespass laws such as California's that were at variance with the federal doctrine.[13]

C. Violence, Threats of Violence, and Intimidation

A state law injunction barring picketing at the homes of company employees, including peaceful residential picketing, was not preempted by the Act, on the ground that "regulation of public safety, including preclusion of residential picketing is a matter of local concern," such that it could not be inferred that Congress deprived the state of the power to Act.[14]

In *Terzi Productions, Inc. v. Theatrical Protective Union Local 1*[15] the court found that the plaintiff's state law claim was not preempted under *Garmon*, where there was ample evidence of violence in the record for the jury to have properly found that violence or threats of violence against the plaintiff and neutral parties were a direct cause of the plaintiff's damaged business relations with its clients. Such conduct avoids preemption, because it "touches concerns deeply rooted in local feelings or responsibilities."[16]

D. Other Intentional Torts

1. *Defamation:* Linn v. Plant Guard Workers

The courts continue to hold that under *Linn*,[17] a state law defamation claim concerning utterances made during an organizing campaign is preempted unless the complainant can plead and prove that

---

[12]502 U.S. 527, 139 LRRM 2225 (1992).

[13]*Calkins, supra* note 11, at 1094–95, 161 LRRM at 3131–32.

[14]CF&I Steel, L.P. v. Steelworkers, 990 P.2d 1124, 164 LRRM 2604 (Colo. Ct. App. 1999).

[15]2000 U.S. Dist. LEXIS 12601, 166 LRRM 2485 (S.D.N.Y. 2000).

[16]*Id.*, 166 LRRM at 2489. *Cf.* Intercity Maint. Co. v. Service Employees Local 254, 62 F. Supp. 2d 483, 162 LRRM 2099 (D.R.I. 1999), *aff'd in part, rev'd in part, and remanded on other grounds*, 241 F.3d 82, 166 LRRM 2656 (1st Cir. 2000) (employer's state law tortious interference claims held preempted under *Garmon*, notwithstanding allegations of union threats of violence, because alleged threats were unrelated to tortious interference claims).

[17]Linn v. Plant Guard Workers Local 114, 383 U.S. 53, 61 LRRM 2345 (1966).

the statements were made with "actual malice" and that he or she suffered actual damages.[18]

Of course, in addition to malice, the plaintiff must show there was a false statement of purported fact. Where the evidence showed the plaintiff had in fact crossed picket lines during a lawful sympathy strike so that use of the commonplace epithet "scab" was "literally and factually true," the claim was dismissed.[19]

2. Inflicting Emotional Distress: Farmer v. Carpenters

The lower courts continue to apply the narrow exception to federal preemption of intentional infliction of emotional distress claims established in *Farmer v. Carpenters Local 25*.[20]

3. Fraud, Misrepresentation, and Other Intentional Torts [New Topic]

A state law claim by former employees alleging that the employer had fraudulently induced them into accepting an early retirement package by falsely representing that the plant would close was not preempted by *Garmon* because there was no bargaining obligation with respect to the employer's closure decision, and the employees' claim was solely that the employer committed fraud in a direct communication to them.[21] Conversely, an employer's state law tortious interference claims against a union were preempted under *Garmon*, notwithstanding the employer's assertion that the union threatened violent conduct, because the alleged threats were unrelated to the employer's claims for tortious interference.[22]

E. Internal Union Matters

In *Mitchell-Carr v. McLendon*[23] the New Mexico Supreme Court held that, because Section 8(a)(3) arguably protected the union's

---

[18]Shepard v. Courtoise, 115 F. Supp. 2d 1142, 163 LRRM 2638 (E.D. Mich. 2000). *Accord Intercity Maint. Co., supra* note 16.

[19]Dunn v. Air Line Pilots Ass'n, 193 F.3d 1185, 162 LRRM 2577 (11th Cir. 1999), *cert. denied,* 530 U.S. 1204, 164 LRRM 2448 (2000).

[20]430 U.S. 290, 94 LRRM 2579 (1977). *See, e.g.,* North Am. Roofing & Sheet Metal Co., Inc. v. Building & Constr. Trades Council, 164 LRRM 2367 (E.D. Pa. 2000).

[21]Voilas v. General Motors Corp., 170 F.3d 367, 160 LRRM 2641 (3d Cir. 1999).

[22]Intercity Maint. Co. v. Service Employees Local 254, 62 F. Supp. 2d 483, 162 LRRM 2099 (D. R.I. 1999), *aff'd in part, rev'd in part, and remanded on other grounds,* 241 F.3d 82, 166 LRRM 2656 (1st Cir. 2000).

[23]980 P.2d 65, 161 LRRM 2479 (N.M. 1999).

causing the discharge of employees for nonpayment of dues, their state law claim was preempted by *Garmon*. On the other hand, a prima facie tort claim was not preempted, because the employees' removal from union office and suspension from membership was not an unfair labor practice under Section 8; rather, the allegation concerned internal union matters governed by the Labor-Management Reporting and Disclosure Act, which expressly provides that state law claims are not preempted.[24]

IV. PREEMPTION UNDER SECTION 301

B. The Preemptive Effect of Section 301

Federal and state courts continue to rule that Section 301[25] preempts a variety of state law claims. The five Supreme Court decisions issued in the 1985 to 1990 period[26] and the Court's 1994 *Lividas v. Bradshaw*[27] decision, which are discussed in the Fourth Edition, remain the governing law in shaping judicial resolution of Section 301 preemption issues.

In general, Section 301 is preemptive if the claim is "founded directly on rights created by collective bargaining agreements,"[28] if resolution of the claim is "substantially dependent on analysis of [a collective bargaining agreement],"[29] or if it is "inextricably intertwined" with the terms of the labor agreement.[30] But when the meaning of contract terms is not in dispute, the mere fact that a collective bargaining agreement will be consulted in the course of state law litigation does not invoke the doctrine of federal preemption.[31] Moreover, that the state law analysis involves attention to the same

---

[24]*Id.* at 74–75, 161 LRRM at 2486–87 (citing 29 U.S.C. §413).

[25]29 U.S.C. §185.

[26]Allis-Chalmers Corp. v. Lueck, 471 U.S. 202, 118 LRRM 3345 (1985); Caterpillar Inc. v. Williams, 482 U.S. 386, 125 LRRM 2521 (1987); Electrical Workers (IBEW) v. Hechler, 481 U.S. 851, 125 LRRM 2353 (1987); Lingle v. Magic Chef, Norge Div., 486 U.S. 399, 128 LRRM 2521 (1988); and Steelworkers v. Rawson, 495 U.S. 362, 134 LRRM 2153 (1990).

[27]512 U.S. 107, 146 LRRM 2513 (1994).

[28]*Lingle, supra* note 26, at 410, 128 LRRM at 2525 n.10 (quoting *Caterpillar Inc., supra* note 26, at 394, 125 LRRM at 2524).

[29]*Id.* (quoting *Hechler, supra* note 26, at 859, 125 LRRM at 2356 n.3).

[30]*Allis-Chalmers, supra* note 26, at 213, 118 LRRM at 3350.

[31]*Lividas, supra* note 27, at 123–26, 146 LRRM at 2520.

factual considerations as a determination under the labor agreement does not mandate preemption as long as the state law claim can be resolved without interpreting the agreement itself.[32]

These principles have been applied in cases involving state law claims for breach of contract,[33] breach of a covenant of fair dealing,[34] tortious interference with contract,[35] fraud and misrepresentation,[36] defamation,[37] invasion of privacy,[38] intentional infliction of emotional distress,[39] tortious drug testing,[40] negligence, retaliation

---

[32]Lingle v. Magic Chef, Norge Div., 486 U.S. 362, 409–10, 128 LRRM 2521, 2525 (1988).

[33]Aguilera v. Pirelli Armstrong Tire Corp., 223 F.3d 1010, 165 LRRM 2203 (9th Cir. 2000) (§301 preempted state law claims of breach of individual contracts made by permanent strike replacements who asserted employer promise, on hiring, that they would not be replaced by returning strikers); *but see* Alexander v. UDV N. Am., Inc., 78 F. Supp. 2d 614, 163 LRRM 2606 (E.D. Mich. 1999) (claim for breach of predecessor employer's promise of continued employment to individual employees who were subsequently laid off under terms of labor agreement negotiated by successor was not preempted).

[34]Ortiz v. Prudential Ins. Co., 94 F. Supp. 2d 225, 164 LRRM 2400 (D. Conn. 2000).

[35]Kimbro v. Pepsico, Inc., 215 F.3d 723, 164 LRRM 2449 (7th Cir. 2000); Arnold v. Cabot Corp., 165 LRRM 2179 (N.D. W. Va. 2000) (claim under state's wage act held preempted because threshold issue of whether employee was entitled to pay could be resolved only by interpretation of parties' labor agreement and practices); Beidleman v. Stroh Brewing Co., 182 F.3d 225, 161 LRRM 2656 (3d Cir. 1999).

[36]*Aguilera, supra* note 33; Voilas v. General Motors Corp., 170 F.3d 367, 160 LRRM 2641 (3d Cir. 1999); *Beidleman, supra* note 35.

[37]Caci v. Laborers Int'l Union, 2000 U.S. Dist. LEXIS 4876, 166 LRRM 2232 (W.D.N.Y. 2000) (local union officer's defamation claims preempted where assessing veracity of statements by general executive board's attorney charging organized crime influence could not be assessed without interpreting international union's constitution); Carpenter v. Communications Workers, 163 LRRM 3023 (N.D. Ga. 2000).

[38]Cramer v. Consolidated Freightways, Inc., 167 LRRM 2353 (9th Cir. 2001) (en banc) (claim for invasion of privacy based on surreptitious videotaping by employer of employee restrooms through two-way mirrors not preempted because labor contract did not purport to allow such conduct and in any event employer's use of mirrors was per se unlawful under California penal law), *vacating* 209 F.3d 1122, 164 LRRM 2129 (9th Cir. 2000).

[39]Ortiz v. Prudential Ins. Co., 94 F. Supp. 2d 225, 164 LRRM 2400 (D. Conn. 2000).

[40]Hanson v. DrugScan, Inc., 95 F. Supp. 2d 868, 165 LRRM 2317 (N.D. Ill. 2000) (no preemption under §301 of employee's claim that negligent drug testing caused misidentification of drug sample).

under state workers' compensation and other laws,[41] and violation of state wage and hour laws.[42]

Although a claim that an employer had discriminatorily denied an employee his or her seniority rights would normally be preempted under Section 301, in *Lydon v. Boston Sand & Gravel Co.*[43] the court held that where the parties had previously agreed before an arbitrator that the collective bargaining agreement did not address the issue and that state law provided the employee's exclusive remedy, the employer was estopped from later interposing a federal preemption defense.

In *Voilas v. General Motors Corp.*[44] the Third Circuit found no Section 301 preemption where employees alleged that the company had fraudulently induced them to accept an early retirement severance package by representing to them that the plant was scheduled for closure. The court rejected the employer's contention that resolution of the issue required interpretation of the collectively bargained severance pay plan, noting that the employees were not claiming that the employer misrepresented the plan. Instead, they were claiming it had lied to them about the plant closing to induce them to end their employment and take the severance plan. Accordingly, because the fraud claim was not based on the collective bargaining agreement or the terms of the severance pay plan—nor would its resolu-

---

[41]Trevino v. Levi Strauss & Co., 197 F.3d 777, 163 LRRM 2096 (5th Cir. 1999), *cert. denied*, 165 LRRM 2992 (2000) (retaliation claim under Texas workers' compensation law not preempted because it involved only factual issues concerning employee's conduct and employer's motivation); Naples v. New Jersey Sports & Exposition Auth., 102 F. Supp. 2d 550, 165 LRRM 2476 (D.N.J. 2000) (no preemption of state law claims of disability discrimination and retaliation for filing workers' compensation claim); *but see* Audette v. Longshoremen Local 24, 195 F.3d 1107, 162 LRRM 2705 (9th Cir. 1999) (employees' claim of gender discrimination and retaliation were preempted where premised on alleged breach of settlement agreement by employer association and union).

[42]Firestone v. Southern Cal. Gas Co., 219 F.3d 1063, 164 LRRM 2897 (9th Cir. 2000) (distinguishing *Lividas*, court held claim for overtime compensation under California wage payment law was preempted by §301 because resolution of statutory claim hinged on interpretation of disputed contractual provision); Balcorta v. Twentieth Century-Fox Film Corp., 208 F.3d 1102, 164 LRRM 2071 (9th Cir. 2000) (claim under California wage payment law for waiting time penalties not preempted where all that was required to determine whether employer had violated state law was "a clock or a calculator," not interpretation of labor agreement); Arnold v. Cabot Corp., 165 LRRM 2179 (N.D. W. Va. 2000).

[43]175 F.3d 6, 160 LRRM 2981 (1st Cir. 1999).

[44]170 F.3d 367, 160 LRRM 2641 (3d Cir. 1999).

tion require an interpretation of those agreements—the claim was not preempted under Section 301.[45]

Suits for defamation under state law have received mixed results. In *Graham v. Contract Transportation, Inc.*[46] the Eighth Circuit held that a defamation claim was not preempted under Section 301, where an employee, who was required to take a random drug test by his employer, tested positive, was fired, and later learned that the drug test had not been conducted in accordance with regulations of the federal Department of Transportation. The employer made allegedly defamatory statements about the employee to prospective employers and the agency that processed the employee's unemployment benefits application. Rejecting the employer's preemption argument, the court held that the case turned solely on the factual question of whether the employer lied to others about the employee's use of drugs, a matter that required no analysis of the meaning of the labor contract. In *Reynolds v. Ferguson,*[47] however, a school counselor's defamation claim was held preempted by Section 301 where the alleged defamatory statements were made in a memorandum prepared by the employer regarding his termination. Because the memorandum was intertwined with the termination provisions of the labor contract, the plaintiff could not demonstrate that the memorandum was an unprivileged communication to a third party without resort to an analysis of the contract.

In *Panayi v. Northern Indiana Public Service Co.*[48] Section 301 preemption was found in an employee's invasion-of-privacy suit in a case where his employer had obtained records from a third-party Internet provider of all activity on the employee's account arising from a company telephone number in his work area. The employer obtained those records in the course of an investigation that led to the employee's termination. The court ruled that resolution of the privacy claim depended on whether the management-rights clause of the contract permitted the employer to enforce rules against accessing the Internet through company telephone lines and its right to obtain pertinent records reflecting such use. The determination of whether a person in the plaintiff's position would have any reason-

---

[45]The *Garmon* preemption argument made by the employer is addressed in Section III.D.3. [*Garmon* Preemption in Specific Situations; Other Intentional Torts; Fraud, Misrepresentation, and Other Intentional Torts].

[46]220 F.3d 910, 164 LRRM 3096 (8th Cir. 2000).

[47]73 F. Supp. 2d 841, 163 LRRM 2813 (W.D. Mich. 1999).

[48]109 F. Supp. 2d 1012, 165 LRRM 2125 (N.D. Ind. 2000).

able expectation of privacy thus depended on construing the labor contract and the rules promulgated under it.

C. Relationship to NLRB

1. Introduction: Exclusive Jurisdiction of Board Versus Concurrent Jurisdiction

The courts continue to apply the principle, enunciated in *Smith v. Evening News*,[49] that courts and the Board share concurrent jurisdiction over suits involving conduct that may involve both a contract violation under Section 301 and an unfair labor practice or representation question falling within the Board's exclusive jurisdiction.[50]

Following the Supreme Court's contraction of Section 301 jurisdiction in *Textron Lycoming Reciprocating Engine Division v. Auto Workers*,[51] the Tenth Circuit dismissed a union's declaratory judgment action, where the union asserted that the parties' collective bargaining agreement was invalid to the extent its terms ran afoul of the Fair Labor Standards Act.[52] Jurisdiction did not lie under Section 301 because the union's lawsuit alleged the invalidity—but not the employer's violation—of the collective bargaining agreement. Similarly, in *Hanley v. Lobster Box Restaurant, Inc.*[53] the court lacked Section 301 jurisdiction over the employer's third-party action, which sought invalidation of the labor agreement based on the union's alleged fraud during negotiations. The court explained that the employer could not use the underlying action by trustees of employee benefit funds for the collection of unpaid contributions to "bootstrap" its claim of contract invalidity against the union.

D. Relationship to the Norris-LaGuardia Act

Courts continue to respect the narrowness of the *Boys Market* exception to the Norris-LaGuardia Act's limitations on issuing in-

---

[49]371 U.S. 195, 51 LRRM 2881 (1962).

[50]*See, e.g.*, Pace v. Honolulu Disposal Serv., Inc., 227 F.3d 1150, 165 LRRM 2385 (9th Cir. 2000) (finding that dispute over whether certain employees were covered by labor agreement was "primarily contractual" and therefore properly before District Court and not Board).

[51]523 U.S. 653, 158 LRRM 2193 (1998).

[52]Food & Commercial Workers Local 1564 v. Albertson's, Inc., 207 F.3d 1193, 163 LRRM 2903 (10th Cir. 2000).

[53]35 F. Supp. 2d 366, 161 LRRM 2049 (S.D.N.Y. 1999).

junctions in labor disputes.[54] The Sixth Circuit, in *Allied Systems Ltd. v. Teamsters Local 327*,[55] found that the district court properly denied the employer's request for a preliminary injunction to enjoin the union from striking in response to the employer's decision that one facility's wage rate would govern when two facilities merged. The court limited its holding to a finding that the employer had not demonstrated that its interpretation of the agreement was "so clearly and indisputably correct" to warrant the issuance of a *Boys Market* injunction.[56]

Courts have continued to interpret what it means to safeguard the arbitration process through the grant of a "reverse *Boys Market*" injunction. In *Teamsters Local 299 v. U.S. Truck Co. Holdings Inc.*[57] union sought to enjoin the defendant trucking company and its parent from closing a freight facility pending arbitration of several grievances regarding the closing. The court enjoined the defendants from liquidating the assets of the trucking company because such an action would compromise the arbitration process by rendering a later award meaningless. However, the court declined to enjoin them from closing operations at the facility, because the mere economic injury to the workers was not sufficient to demonstrate irreparable harm.

In *Aeronautical Industrial District Lodge 91 v. United Technologies Corp.*[58] the Second Circuit held that an injunction could properly issue requiring an employer to cease and desist from implementing a plan to transfer bargaining-unit work out of state unless and until the employer made contractually required efforts to preserve the work within the bargaining unit. The labor contract contained an article providing that the company would "make every effort" to preserve the work performed by employees in the bargaining unit, and that the company did not intend to use subcontractors or to transfer work elsewhere. This article, the court found, was explicitly not subject to arbitration under the contract. The employer argued that the district court thus erred in issuing an injunction, because the facts did not fit within the *Boys Market* exception.

Rejecting this approach, the Second Circuit observed that the Norris-LaGuardia Act prohibits issuance of injunctions only in cer-

---

[54] 29 U.S.C. §104.
[55] 179 F.3d 982, 161 LRRM 2493 (6th Cir.), *cert. denied*, 528 U.S. 965, 162 LRRM 2704 (1999).
[56] *Id.* at 990, 161 LRRM at 2499.
[57] 87 F. Supp. 2d 726, 163 LRRM 2412 (E.D. Mich. 2000).
[58] 230 F.3d 569, 165 LRRM 2641 (2d Cir. 2000).

tain targeted arenas. Therefore, it reasoned, federal courts may enforce a collective bargaining agreement via an injunction so long as the dispute is not the type governed by Norris-LaGuardia and so long as judicial relief is otherwise appropriate. Because the contractual provision that the employer make every effort to retain work within the bargaining unit was not among the types of subjects addressed by the Norris-LaGuardia Act, the District Court did not err in issuing an injunction requiring the employer to comply with this obligation.

V. PREEMPTIVE EFFECT OF OTHER STATUTORY PROVISIONS

B. State Power Under Section 14(b) to Regulate Union-Security Agreements

A Colorado state law involving union-security authorization procedures that placed greater limitations than federal law on the ability of employees to seek deauthorization was preempted by the Act.[59] The Board concluded that the clear purpose of Section 14(b) was to permit the states the power to restrict union-security agreements. However, any state law that would require employees to wait longer than the period established by the Act to rescind a union-security agreement would violate federal statutory rights given to employees, and therefore must yield to federal law.[60]

The Act does not preempt an Indian tribal nation from adopting a right-to-work ordinance applicable to employees of a nontribal company engaged in business activities on a reservation.[61] In a case of first impression, the Tenth Circuit rejected the Board's position that because Section 14(b) contains no reference to Indian tribes, parties may enter into a union-security agreement under Section 8(a)(3) in derogation of the ordinance. The court held that the Act is not a statute of general application, and thus in the absence of express statutory prohibition, an Indian tribe has the inherent right to regulate commercial activities on tribal land.[62]

---

[59]Albertson's/Max Food Warehouse, 329 NLRB No. 44, 162 LRRM 1169 (1999), *overruling* City Mkts., Inc., 266 NLRB 1020, 113 LRRM 1105 (1983).
[60]*Id.*
[61]NLRB v. Pueblo of San Juan, 228 F.3d 1195, 165 LRRM 2321 (10th Cir. 2000).
[62]*Id.* at 1202, 165 LRRM at 2326.

E. Fair Representation

1. Concurrent Jurisdiction of Board and Courts

The courts continue to adhere to the general principle that jurisdiction over duty of fair-representation claims is concurrent in the Board and the courts.[63] When the Board interprets the duty of fair representation as part of its unfair labor practice jurisdiction, its decision making is entitled to deference under the *Chevron* doctrine,[64] notwithstanding that the duty is judge-made and court-enforced.[65]

2. Federal Law Governs

Courts continue to hold that state-law fair representation claims against unions, or union agents acting within the scope of their agency, are preempted by the federal duty of fair representation so long as the state law claim is based on rights or obligations analytically indistinguishable from those created by the federal duty of fair representation.[66]

Much of the juridical activity in this area has been in the context of preemption of state antidiscrimination law claims. For example, in *Jackson v. T&N Van Service*[67] an African American employee contended that the union violated the New Jersey Law Against Discrimination (NJLAD) by grieving the employer's decision to discharge three co-workers who allegedly subjected the plaintiff-employee to racial harassment.[68] The court agreed with the union that the NJLAD claim was preempted by the duty of fair representation. The court first observed that "if the state claim creates no new rights for an employee and imposes no duty on a union not already present un-

---

[63]Communications Workers v. Beck, 487 U.S. 735, 128 LRRM 2729 (1988); Marquez v. Screen Actors Guild, 525 U.S. 33, 49, 159 LRRM 2641, 2647 (1998). *Cf.* Dykstra v. Teamsters Local 406, 2000 U.S. Dist. LEXIS 7011, 164 LRRM 2563 (W.D. Mich. 2000) (employee's duty of fair representation claim held preempted under *Garmon* because crux of putative claim was union's alleged refusal to bargain with his employer).

[64]Chevron, USA v. NRDC, 467 U.S. 837 (1984).

[65]Jacoby v. NLRB, 235 F.3d 611, 165 LRRM 2993 (D.C. Cir. 2000).

[66]*See, e.g.*, Thomas v. National Ass'n of Letter Carriers, 225 F.3d 1149 (10th Cir. 2000) (duty of fair representation preempts state law wrongful discharge and civil conspiracy claims); Mamorella v. Derkasch, 276 A.D.2d 152, 716 N.Y.S.2d 211 (4th Dep't 2000) (federal law preempts legal malpractice claim against union attorney for work related to collective bargaining process).

[67]117 F. Supp. 2d 457, 165 LRRM 2402 (E.D. Pa. 2000).

[68]*Id.* at 460, 165 LRRM at 2403.

der the federal duty of fair representation, the state claim is preempted."[69] In applying this standard, courts focus "not on the legal label affixed to the cause of action under state law, but to the conduct that is at the root of the controversy."[70] The plaintiff-employee's NJLAD claim against the union was preempted under this standard because the claim essentially involved the union's role in investigating complaints or grievances of alleged harassers and harassees, activities implicating the duty of fair representation.[71]

Courts also frequently analyze preemption of state law claims against unions under Section 301 preemption principles rather than under the duty of fair representation.[72]

---

[69]*Id.* at 463, 165 LRRM at 2405 (quoting Bergeron v. Henderson, 52 F. Supp. 2d 149, 153, 161 LRRM 2761 (D. Me. 1999)).

[70]*Id.* (quoting *Bergeron,* 52 F. Supp. 2d at 154, 161 LRRM at 2764).

[71]*Id.* at 463–64, 165 LRRM at 2405. *See also* Agosto v. Correctional Officers Benevolent Ass'n, 107 F. Supp. 294, 304, 83 FEP 1042 (S.D.N.Y. 2000) (determining that New York state human rights law claim against union was preempted by duty of fair representation and noting that "[t]he duty of fair representation and Title VII plainly overlap in that they both prohibit discrimination; indeed, some courts essentially equate the two").

[72]*See, e.g.,* Johnson v. Olin Corp., Steelworkers Local 1999-14, 2000 U.S. Dist. LEXIS 14469, 6 WH Cases 2d 941 (S.D. Ind. 2000) (former employee's state-law breach of contract claim, based on allegation of union's breach of its duty of fair representation, held preempted by §301); Black v. National Football League Players Ass'n, 87 F. Supp. 2d 1, 164 LRRM 2566 (D.D.C. 2000) (tortious interference and defamation claims against union preempted by §301); Roach v. Auto Workers, 165 LRRM 2428 (N.D. Okla. 2000) (§301 preempted state law breach of contract and negligence claims against union).

CHAPTER 29

ACCOMMODATIONS TO OTHER FEDERAL ENACTMENTS

I. The NLRA and the Antitrust Law

The Main Edition notes that "union conduct . . . not enjoinable under the Norris-LaGuardia and Clayton Acts [is] immune from criminal prosecution under the Sherman Act." Similarly, union conduct that qualifies as "a labor dispute" is not enjoinable under Norris-

LaGuardia Act even though (1) that conduct violates the antitrust law and (2) the union does not represent or seeks to represent the employees involved.[1]

B. Loss of the Exemption Through Combination With Nonlabor Groups

The courts continue to distinguish between valid "work preservation" clauses and illegal combinations with nonlabor groups intended to create monopolies.[2] In *Sheetmetal Division v. Sheet Metal Workers Local 38*[3] there was evidence that although fabrication of duct work previously had been done mostly onsite, technological changes had shifted much of this fab work to offsite shops (many of which were lower wage shops) outside Local 38's jurisdiction. In response, Local 38 negotiated a collective bargaining agreement with the local multi-employer bargaining association that provided that all sheet metal fabrication work would be performed by Local 38 members, either onsite or in fab shops. Suit was brought by an employer group that did not have a contract with Local 38, alleging that it would be shut out of supplying prefabricated duct work to the Local 38 market by this provision.

The court found that because Local 38 had traditionally performed a substantial portion of this fab work, either onsite or in local shops, this was a valid work preservation clause, not an illegal Section 8(e) hot-cargo clause or an antitrust violation. It was viewed as irrelevant that Local 38 had not historically performed all of this work because it had made no effort to apply the clause to non-signatories to its collective bargaining agreement.

---

[1]Burlington Northern Santa Fe Ry. v. Teamsters Local 174, 203 F.3d 703, 711 n.10, 712 n.12, 163 LRRM 2519 (9th Cir. 2000) (en banc). *Burlington Northern* reversed the panel opinion that had enjoined union picketing to compel the railroad to subcontract solely with employers that had collective bargaining agreements with the union because, according to the panel, it did not constitute a labor dispute within the meaning of the Norris-LaGuardia Act.

[2]*See* Sheetmetal Div. v. Local 38, 208 F.3d 18, 26, 163 LRRM 2910 (2d Cir. 2000).

[3]*Id.*

F. Application of the Statutory and Nonstatutory Exemption After *Connell*

In *Albany Specialties, Inc. v. Board of Education*[4] the District Court denied the plaintiff's motion for a preliminary injunction, holding that a Project Labor Agreement (PLA) for a school district renovation project was protected by the construction industry proviso of Section 8(f).[5] Adhering to *Laborers Local 210 v. Labor Relations Division of Associated General Contractors*[6] the court found that because the PLA was the product of collective bargaining, furthered national labor policy goals, and fell within the ambit of the construction industry proviso of Section 8(f), it was protected from antitrust challenges by the nonstatutory exemption.[7]

At issue in *Sheet Metal Division v. Sheet Metal Workers Local 38*[8] was a clause in an agreement between the defendants Local 38 and Sheet Metal & Roofing Employers Association of Southeastern New York (SENY). This clause provided that all fabrication work performed within Local 38's geographic region would be performed by Local 38 members, but did not forbid contractors from outside Local 38's region from contracting to do work inside the region.[9] The plaintiffs asserted that even though they were not signatories to the agreement between defendants, they were nonetheless bound by the clause because they had their own collective bargaining agreements with other area unions (other than Local 38), which required them to comply with Local 38's work rules while working in Local 38's region.[10] Thus, according to plaintiffs, the clause in the defendants' agreement imposed on them "an unlawful boycott of sheet metal products fabricated outside Local 38's jurisdiction."[11]

The defendant SENY filed an unfair labor practice charge to verify the validity of the clause with respect to Local 38 and itself.[12] The Board's investigation did not reveal a Section 8(e) violation with respect to the agreement, and it therefore declined to issue a com-

---

[4]162 LRRM 3071 (N.D.N.Y. 1999).
[5]*Id.* at 3077.
[6]844 F.2d 69, 79, 128 LRRM 2060, 2068 (2d Cir. 1987).
[7]*Albany Specialties, supra* note 4, at 3079.
[8]208 F.3d 18, 163 LRRM 2910 (2d Cir. 2000).
[9]*Id.* at 20, 163 LRRM at 2912.
[10]*Id.* at 24–25, 163 LRRM at 2915.
[11]*Id.* at 21, 163 LRRM at 2912.
[12]*Id.* 163 LRRM at 2913.

plaint in the matter.[13] However, after the plaintiffs' motion for a preliminary injunction to prevent enforcement of the clause, the District Court found that the clause violated Section 8(e) and, because it did not fall within any exceptions to the Sherman Act, constituted an unlawful restraint on trade.[14]

On appeal, the Second Circuit determined the record was insufficient for the District Court to have found either Section 8(e) or antitrust violations and thus reversed the District Court's declaratory judgement in favor of the plaintiffs.[15] Although the court agreed with Local 38 and SENY that the clause was never intended to be enforced against nonsignatories, it nevertheless determined that it was "hard to see how the likelihood that the clause would be directly enforced against [plaintiffs] was sufficiently concrete to warrant a declaratory judgment."[16]

II. THE NLRA AND THE BANKRUPTCY CODE

A. Power of Bankruptcy Court to Reject College Bargaining Agreement

1. Requirements for Rejection of a Collective Bargaining Agreement

Most courts continue to hold that the nine-step analysis set forth in *American Provision Co.* provides the requisites for determining whether a collective bargaining agreement should be rejected.[17] As set forth in *In re U.S. Truck Co. Holdings, Inc.*, with the exception of the ninth factor of that test (balance of the equities), the debtor has the burden of proof by preponderance of the evidence that the statutory requirements have been met. According to the court, the debtor has the burden of proving the ninth factor by a higher standard than preponderance of the evidence.[18]

With respect to altering obligations under a collective bargaining agreement, the Third Circuit held that "when . . . a debtor in possession . . . binds itself contractually to obtain a change in the

---

[13]Sheet Metal Div. v. Local 38, Sheet Metal Workers, 208 F.3d 18, 21, 163 LRRM 2910, 2913 (2d Cir. 2000).

[14]*Id.* at 22, 163 LRRM at 2913.

[15]*Id.* at 25–26, 163 LRRM at 2917.

[16]*Id.* at 25, 163 LRRM at 2915.

[17]*See In re* U.S. Truck Co. Holdings, Inc., 165 LRRM 2521 (E.D. Mich. 2000).

[18]*Id.* at 2531.

legal relations created by a CBA as a condition precedent to closing a sale of substantially all of the debtor's assets, that constitutes an attempt to effect an alteration of the CBA" under Section 1113, and the debtor is obligated to follow the requirements set forth in Section 1113.[19]

In a case of first impression, in *In re Family Snacks, Inc.*[20] the Eighth Circuit held that Section 1113 permits a debtor to reject a collective bargaining agreement even after the debtor has sold virtually all of its assets. The court analyzed the "reorganization of the debtor" clause of the "necessary to permit the reorganization of the debtor" test set forth in Section 1113(b)(1)(A), and held that "reorganization" should not be equated with the more narrow concept of "rehabilitation" of the debtor. Accordingly, the court concluded that "necessary to permit the reorganization of the debtor" means "necessary to accommodate confirmation of a Chapter 11 plan," and that there was "no principled reason to limit a debtor's right to reject a CBA to a case where the application to reject comes before an asset sale."[21]

B. Priority of Wage and Employee Benefit Plan Contributions

11 U.S.C. §507(a) and subparts amended 1994 as follows:

(a) The following expenses and claims have priority in the following order;

. . .

(3) Third, allowed unsecured claims, but only to the extent of $4,000 for each individual or corporation, as the case may be, earned within 90 days before the date of the filing of the petition on the date of the cessation of the debtor's business, whichever occurs first, for—

(A) wages, salaries or commissions, including vacation, severance and sick leave pay earned by an individual; or

---

[19]American Flint Glass Workers Union v. Anchor Resolution Corp., 197 F.3d 76 (3d Cir. 1999).

[20]257 B.R. 884, 166 LRRM 2400 (8th Cir. 2001).

[21]*Id.* at 2409. Deciding another matter of first impression, the Eighth Circuit in *Family Snacks* also held that the assumption of a collective bargaining agreement does not automatically occur on the bankruptcy court's denial of a debtor's motion to reject. The court emphasized that the assumption of a collective bargaining agreement may not be implied and, instead, the assumption of an agreement by a debtor requires affirmative action by way of a motion seeking assumption. *Id.* at 2415–16.

(B) sales commissions earned by an individual or by a corporation with only one employee, acting as an independent contractor in the sale of goods or services for the debtor in the ordinary course of the debtor's business if, and only if, during the 12 months preceding that date, at least 75 percent of the amount that the individual or corporation earned by acting as an independent contractor in the sale of goods or services was earned from the debtor;

(4) Fourth, allowed unsecured claims for contributions to an employee benefit plan—

. . .

(B) for each such plan, to the extent of—
    (i) the number of employees covered by each such plan multiplied by $4,000; less

The Ninth Circuit's Bankruptcy Panel, in *In re San Rafael Baking Co.*,[22] held that Section 1113 did not give the bankruptcy court the authority to order a Chapter 11 debtor in possession to continue making employee health benefit contributions after expiration of the collective bargaining agreement where no proceedings were initiated before the expiration.

1. Prepetition Claims

The split among the circuits continues with regard to whether unpaid pre-petition workers' compensation insurance premiums are considered contributions to an employee benefit plan (i.e., affording the claim priority status under Section 507(a)(4)). Agreeing with the Eighth and Tenth Circuits on this matter, the court in *In re Perk Development Corp.*[23] held that a claim for unpaid pre-petition workers' compensation insurance premiums is *not* a contribution to an employee benefit plan, which entitled it to priority status under Section 507(a)(4).

With regard to the treatment of claims for vacation pay, the court in *In Re Crafts Precision Industries*[24] reiterated the limitations period under Section 507 and found that vacation pay earned more than 90 days before the debtor filed its petition for bankruptcy is not given priority under Section 507(a)(4). Furthermore, vacation pay is considered a "wage" and not a fringe benefit or a contribution to an

---

[22]219 B.R. 860 (9th Cir. 1998).
[23]246 B.R. 753 (W.D.N.Y. 2000).
[24]244 B.R. 178 (1st Cir. 2000).

employee benefit plan for purposes of determining priority status under Section 507.

3. Priority of Claims for Wages and Benefits Due Under Rejected Agreement

The court in *In re Typocraft Co.*[25] held that regardless of whether a debtor's failure to reject a collective bargaining agreement in accordance with Section 1113(f) had to be treated as an assumption thereof, the debtor was obligated to continue paying pre- and postpetition claims arising under the agreement. Therefore, these claims were entitled to superpriority administrative expense status.

The Fourth Circuit distinguished *In re Unimet Corp.*[26] and concluded that a bankruptcy claim arising from the breach of a collective bargaining agreement may be accorded priority status only to the extent that it fits into one of the exceptions set forth in Section 507.[27]

4. Enforcement of an Unrejected Collective Bargaining Agreement

District courts continue to find that the terms of a collective bargaining agreement should be enforced absent a rejection under Section 1113.[28]

C. Severance Pay and Withdrawal Liability

With regard to the priority of severance pay claims under Section 507, the court in *In re Russell Cave Co.*[29] held (1) such claims are given administrative priority only to the extent that they are earned *after* the bankruptcy petition was filed, (2) severance pay based on seniority is an administrative expense only to the extent it is earned by service during the bankruptcy case, and (3) pre-petition claims for severance pay are given priority only to the extent earned within 90 days of the date of filing of the bankruptcy petition and only up to a limit of $4,300.

---

[25]229 B.R. 685 (E.D. Mich. 1999).

[26]842 F.2d 879 (6th Cir. 1988).

[27]Adventure Resources, Inc. v. Holland, 137 F.3d 786 (4th Cir.), *cert. denied*, 525 U.S. 962 (1998).

[28]*In re* U.S. Truck Co. Holdings, Inc., 2000 Bankr. LEXIS 1376 (E.D. Mich. 2000).

[29]248 B.R. 301 (E.D. Ky. 2000).

The treatment of severance pay provided for in a contract of employment was addressed by the court in *In re Phones For All*.[30] The court found that the agreement to pay severance constituted a conditional right to payment. The creditor, the debtor's former president and CEO, had a contractual right entitling him to a claim against the debtor's estate to receive his severance. However, the creditor was not entitled to receive his severance benefits as an administrative expense under Section 503. Under the terms of his employment contract, the severance pay was earned before the debtor filed bankruptcy and thus was not entitled to treatment as an administrative expense.

---

[30]249 B.R. 426 (N.D. Tex. 2000).

RICO AND LABOR LAW

III. Overview of the Statute

A. Key Elements

1. Racketeering Activity

The plaintiff must plead and prove all the elements of each predicate act, or else that allegation will be dismissed (as will be the RICO claim itself, if all such allegations of predicate acts are dismissed). For example, in *Thornton v. United States Department of Labor*[1] a former official of the Transportation Communications Union alleged that he was wrongfully accused of mismanagement and misappropriation of union funds. His RICO claims were dismissed on defendants' motion for summary judgment because he failed to allege any acts of "racketeering activity" against other union officials or the government.

3. Enterprise

In *Cedric Kushner Promotions, Ltd. v. King*[2] the Supreme Court approved the requirement of "nonidentity" of the person and the enterprise for claims under Section 1962(c). The Court held that the distinctiveness requirement is satisfied "when a corporate employee unlawfully conducts the affairs of the corporation of which he is the sole owner—whether he conducts those affairs within the scope, or beyond the scope, of corporate authority."[3] Basing its decision, in part, on the plain language of Section 1962(c), the Court reasoned that "[t]he corporate owner/employee, a natural person, is distinct from the corporation itself, a legally different entity with different rights and responsibilities due to its different legal status. And we can find nothing in the statute that requires more 'separateness' than that."[4]

5. Causation

Two recent cases demonstrate that individualized determinations of causation can preclude class action treatment for RICO claims. In

---

[1] 2000 WL 1923501 (E.D. Mich. Nov. 17, 2000).
[2] 121 S. Ct. 2087 (2001).
[3] *Id.* at 2092.
[4] *Id.* at 2091.

Patterson v. Mobil Oil Corp.[5] plaintiffs brought a RICO class action alleging that their employer misrepresented its compliance with Texas law requiring procurement of workers' compensation insurance in an attempt to avoid liability for employee injuries caused by negligent acts. The Fifth Circuit reversed class certification because the case required individualized determinations of reliance to prove the underlying predicate acts of fraud that would provide the basis for the RICO claims of each member of the putative class.

Similarly, in *Moore v. Television & Radio Artists*[6] the Eleventh Circuit affirmed the district court's refusal to certify a class of recording artists attempting to establish that record companies improperly interpreted the provision of the union's collective bargaining agreement that determined the amount of contributions to health and retirement funds. The appeals court held that the RICO claims, which were predicated on alleged mail fraud, were inappropriate for class treatment because the claims of the individual plaintiffs did not raise common questions of fact that predominated over individual issues. Although the collective bargaining agreement was common to the RICO claims of the named plaintiffs and putative class members, each singer had one or more different contracts with the record companies that affected the amounts owed. Further, whether each singer relied on the alleged misrepresentations was not susceptible to class treatment.

B. Three Substantive Violations

3. 18 U.S.C. §1962(c) (Conducting an Enterprise's Affairs Through Racketeering)

a. Person/Enterprise Distinction

The Supreme Court has now ruled on whether the RICO "person" (i.e., the defendant) must be distinct from the "enterprise" to state a claim under Section 1962(c). In *Cedric Kushner Promotions, Ltd. v. King*[7] the Court agreed with all the circuits, which previously had determined that Section 1962(c) requires some distinctness between the defendant and the RICO enterprise.

---

[5]241 F.3d 417 (5th Cir. 2001).
[6]216 F.3d 1236 (11th Cir. 2000).
[7]121 S. Ct. 2087 (2001).

(1) Application to Corporate Relationships

In *Cedric Kushner Promotions* the Court endorsed the legal principle that Section 1962(c) "requires no more than [a] formal legal distinction between [the] 'person' and 'enterprise'. . . ."[8] The Court found such a distinction between a corporation and its sole shareholder/employee, reasoning that "[a]fter all, incorporation's basic purpose is to create a distinct legal entity, with legal rights, obligations, powers, and privileges different from those of the natural individuals who created it, who own it, or whom it employs."[9] *Cedric Kushner Promotions* declined to address, among other things, situations involving parent and subsidiary relationships. Even so, the Court's reasoning seems persuasive in such cases. In other words, if Section 1962(c) merely requires a *legal* distinction between the person and the enterprise, then a parent's incorporation of a subsidiary should satisfy that requirement. In such a case, of course, Section 1962(c)'s other requirements still must be met, including the operation or management requirement.[10]

(2) Application to Association-in-Fact Enterprises

A separate issue is raised where there is partial overlap between the RICO person and the alleged association-in-fact enterprise, such as where the defendant is only one member of several, sufficiently distinct, members constituting the enterprise. Most courts have allowed such claims under Section 1962(c), whether or not all of those members have been named as defendants, reasoning that a collective entity is more than the members of which it is comprised. As discussed in the prior section, the Supreme Court's recent decision in *Cedric Kushner Promotions* would seem to support such a result where each member of an association-in-fact enterprise is legally distinct from the other members.

For example, in *Tran v. Tran*[11] the plaintiff was a former hotel employee who alleged that his employer had paid bribes to union representatives, who ignored the employer's violations of a collective bargaining agreement by failing to pay union wages, violating

---

[8]*Id.* at 2092.

[9]*Id.* at 2091.

[10]See Section III.B.3.b. [Overview of the Statute; Three Substantive Violations; 18 U.S.C. §1962(c) (Conducting an Enterprise's Affairs Through Racketeering); Operation or Management Requirement], in Main Edition.

[11]165 LRRM 2142 (S.D.N.Y. 2000).

union work rules concerning duties and maximum hours of employment, failing to provide safe working conditions, failing to enroll employees in the union, and failing to pay for and provide union benefits. After a bench trial, the court held that the plaintiff had established a pattern of racketeering activity, presumably, but without stating, based on multiple violations of 29 U.S.C. §186(b)(1). The court found a proper RICO enterprise comprised of, among others, the individual defendant, certain hotels operated by the defendant, and the union representatives receiving the bribes.

IV. PREDICATE ACTS COMMONLY ALLEGED IN LABOR CASES

C. 29 U.S.C. §186: Restrictions on Payments and Loans to Labor Organizations

Section 186 by its plain language is exceptionally sweeping in its coverage to protect employers from extortion and to ensure honest, uninfluenced representations of employees by stamping out all forms of bribery between management and labor officials. In *United States v. Wilson*[12] the Second Circuit affirmed the RICO conviction of a former local union officer and business manager based on multiple violations of, among other things, 29 U.S.C. §186(b)(1), for accepting payments in exchange for concessions to management over a period of about 20 years.

E. 18 U.S.C. §1951: "Racketeering" Prohibited by the Hobbs Act

3. Application of the Hobbs Act to RICO Cases After Enmons

a. Legitimate Objectives

In *Monterey Plaza Hotel Ltd. Partnership v. Hotel Employees Local 483*[13] the Ninth Circuit affirmed dismissal of a hotel owner's RICO claim against a union for violent picketing, extortion, and intimidation of employees and customers, on, among other grounds, res judicata based on prior state-law actions arising out of the same alleged scheme. Thus, the court of appeals declined to address "the district court's statement that the Hotel's claims were sufficient to allege extortion under the Hobbs Act, 18 U.S.C. §1951."[14]

---

[12]216 F.3d 1074 (2d Cir. 2000) (Table), 2000 WL 778021 (June 15, 2000).
[13]215 F.3d 923 (9th Cir. 2000).
[14]*Id.* at 924–25, 928.

V. ISSUES IN CIVIL LITIGATION

A. Standing

3. *"By Reason of"*

Two recent cases addressed Section 1964(c)'s "by reason of" language in the context of hiring illegal immigrants. In *Commercial Cleaning Services v. Colin Service Systems, Inc.*[15] the court granted the defendant's motion to dismiss because its plaintiff-competitor did not allege facts sufficient to establish that the defendant's alleged RICO violation of hiring illegal immigrants at low wages proximately caused the plaintiff to lose revenue. In *Mendoza v. Zirkle Fruit Co.*[16] lawful employees of the defendant–employer lacked standing to state a RICO claim based on the employer's alleged illegal hiring of undocumented immigrants. Although the plaintiffs were direct victims of the alleged scheme, their alleged injury of depressed wages was too speculative.

In *Mayes v. Operating Engineers Local 106*[17] an individual union member alleged a variety of improprieties by union officials, including unauthorized pension overpayments and receipt of unauthorized pension contributions, improper hiring of retired union members, facilitating an illegal work stoppage, granting union membership to persons not qualified to be in the union, undertaking an improper ballot initiative to create a new union defense fund, and filing inaccurate reports required by the LMRDA. The court granted summary judgment on the plaintiff's RICO claims because, among other reasons, "the injuries he alleges, rather than being unique to him, would be the type suffered by Local 106 as a whole"[18] and because "[u]nquantifiable harm to union membership, as he alleges, is not actionable under civil RICO."[19]

E. Statute of Limitations

In *Forbes v. Eagleson*,[20] a post-*Rotella* case, the Third Circuit affirmed summary judgment on former professional hockey league

---

[15] 2000 WL 545126 (D. Conn. Mar. 21, 2000).
[16] 2000 WL 33225470 (E.D. Wash. Sept. 27, 2000).
[17] 1999 WL 60135 (N.D.N.Y. Feb. 5, 1999).
[18] *Id.*, at *3.
[19] *Id.*, at *4.
[20] 228 F.3d 471, 165 LRRM 2584 (3d Cir. 2000), *cert. denied*, 121 S. Ct. 2551 (2001).

players' class action against their employers and the former executive director of their union on statute of limitations grounds, holding that a civil RICO claim accrues under the "injury discovery" rule.

VI. REMEDIES

B. Criminal Forfeiture

Co-conspirators are jointly and severally liable for forfeiture, including amounts extorted by one member in exchange for his assistance in maintaining labor peace, even if all the defendants did not receive or share in the improper payments.[21]

C. Trusteeships and Other Injunctive Relief

In *United States v. Sasso*[22] the Second Circuit held that RICO's Section 1964(a) authorized the district court to order a retired local union officer to contribute monies for a monitorship that was created to eradicate the possibility of future labor racketeering by local officials.

In *Laborers v. Caruso*[23] the international union reached an agreement with the United States Department of Justice, which included a reform program, to avoid a civil RICO action seeking a receivership. Pursuant to these reforms, the international later brought a trusteeship complaint against the Chicago District Council. The Seventh Circuit affirmed the district court's finding that the international did not act in bad faith or with unclean hands in its efforts to establish the trusteeship.

D. Damages in Private Actions

Former union officers who failed to demonstrate that their union made RICO allegations against them in bad faith cannot recover attorney's fees incurred in successfully defending against the claims.[24]

Where an employer files an unmeritorious RICO claim against unions, the employer's request for treble damages is evidence, in

---

[21]United States v. Corrado, 227 F.3d 543 (6th Cir. 2000).
[22]215 F.3d 283, 164 LRRM 2613 (2d Cir. 2000).
[23]197 F.3d 1195, 163 LRRM 2204 (7th Cir. 1999).
[24]Doyle v. Turner, 90 F. Supp. 2d 311, 165 LRRM 2968 (S.D.N.Y. 2000).

part, of retaliatory purpose to establish an unfair labor practice, thus supporting a Board order to reimburse the unions for all legal and other expenses incurred in defending against the lawsuit.[25]

---

[25]Petrochem Insulation, Inc. v. NLRB, 240 F.3d 26, 166 LRRM 2433 (D.C. Cir. 2001), *enforcing* 330 NLRB No. 10, 163 LRRM 1276 (1999); *cf.* BE&K Constr. Co. v. NLRB, 246 F.3d 619, 166 LRRM 2971 (6th Cir. 2001), *enforcing* 329 NLRB No. 68, 162 LRRM 1217 (1999) (antitrust claims).

CHAPTER 31

NLRB PROCEDURES

I. Organization of Board and Office of General Counsel

B. The Board

As of August 1, 2001, the Board was comprised of Chairman Peter J. Hurtgen, John C. Truesdale, Wilma B. Liebman, and Dennis P. Walsh.[1] Generally, the Board is comprised of two Democrats and two Republicans, with the fifth member coming from the same party as the president. In order to serve a regular term, the nominee must receive Senate confirmation, which is a lengthy process.[2] Therefore, when a Member's 5-year term expires, the next terms begins running immediately, regardless of whether a replacement has been confirmed.[3] After the replacement is confirmed, he or she serves out the remainder of the term.[4]

As of the time of this publication, a replacement had not yet been named for former Member J. Robert Brame. One vacancy remains.

C. The General Counsel

On May 26, 2001, Arthur F. Rosenfeld was confirmed as general counsel to serve a 4-year term. Prior to his confirmation, Mr. Rosenfeld was Senior Labor Counsel to the Senate Committee on Health, Education, Labor and Pensions.

F. Personnel and Budget

In fiscal year 2000, the budget for all agency operations was approximately $205 million.[5] This enabled the agency to do substantial hiring for the first time in 5 years.[6] On December 21, 2000, then-President Clinton signed an omnibus appropriations bill which provided for a 5.2 percent budget increase for fiscal year 2001.[7]

---

[1]Then-President Clinton recess-appointed Walsh on December 29, 2000. 166 Lab. Rel. Rep. (BNA) 20 (Jan. 8, 2001).

[2]165 Lab. Rel. Rep. (BNA) 563 (Aug. 28, 2000).

[3]*Id.*

[4]*Id.*

[5]163 Lab. Rel. Rep. (BNA) 210 (Feb. 21, 2000).

[6]*Id.*

[7]166 Lab. Rel. Rep. (BNA) 21 (Jan. 8, 2001).

II. Procedures in Representation Cases

B. Timeliness of Petitions

The Board found that a contract containing two conflicting termination dates barred a representation petition because at the time the petition was filed it was filed late under either date. The Board concluded that the situation was unlike that in *Bob's Big Boy Family Restaurant*,[8] wherein the union filed its petition within the ambiguous time period and the petition was, therefore, not barred.[9]

A decertification petition will be dismissed if it is filed during the posting period of a settlement agreement that provides for bargaining with employees in the involved petition.[10]

Where an employer hotel had voluntarily recognized a union, the Board required dismissal of three decertification petitions, despite the fact that the collective bargaining process took more than 11 months. The Board found reasonable time to bargain had not yet passed at the time the petitions were filed.[11]

In *Livent Realty*[12] a petition by a rival union was barred by voluntary recognition of the union because a reasonable time to bargain had not yet lapsed.

Applying the rule set forth in *Appalachian Shale Products*[13] the Board held that a contract's failure to set forth specific wage rates is not fatal to the contract acting as a bar, if the contract is complete in other respects.[14]

In *St. Elizabeth's Manor, Inc.*[15] the Board held that once a successor employer's obligation to recognize and bargain with an incumbent union attaches, the union is entitled to a reasonable period of time for bargaining without challenge to its majority status. The case, in effect, creates a *successor bar* to the filing of a petition, and to the withdrawal of recognition by the employer.

---

[8]259 NLRB 153, 158 LRRM 1296 (1981), *enforcement denied*, 693 F.2d 904, 111 LRRM 3132 (9th Cir. 1982).

[9]Suffolk Banana, 328 NLRB No. 157, 162 LRRM 1029 (1999).

[10]Hertz Equip. Rental Corp., 328 NLRB No. 5, 161 LRRM 1126 (1999).

[11]MGM Grand Hotel, Inc., 329 NLRB No. 50, 162 LRRM 1202 (1999).

[12]329 NLRB No. 1, 161 LRRM 1037 (1999).

[13]121 NLRB 1160, 42 LRRM 1506 (1958) (that collective bargaining agreement must contain substantial terms and conditions of employment).

[14]Cooper Tank & Welding Corp., 328 NLRB No. 97, 161 LRRM 1209 (1999).

[15]329 NLRB No. 25 (1999).

Under Case Handling Manual Section 11116.1, the Board, in *Baltimore Gas & Electric Co.*,[16] permitted the withdrawal of a petition during the pendency of objections and challenges proceedings, where the election was held more than 12 months earlier and, thus, any new election based on a new petition would not be held within 12 months of the prior election.

C. Investigation of Petitions

In a case involving allegations of forged authorization cards in support of a representation petition, the Board remanded the case to the regional director for further inquiry.[17] The regional director had previously followed the NLRB Case Handling Manual in making signature comparisons, but felt constrained from conducting a full investigation of the fraud allegations in light of an ongoing criminal investigation by the U.S. Attorney. Upon completion of that investigation, the case was remanded to the regional director to conduct a full inquiry into the allegations of fraud.

In *Supershuttle of Orange County*[18] the Board applied its *Douglas Randall*[19] and *Liberty Fabrics*[20] policies, and dismissed a pending representation case where the parties' agreement to a collective bargaining agreement was intended to resolve a pending Section 8(a)(5) charge. These three cases, thus, present a significant bar to the filing of representation case petitions, where unfair labor practice charges are filed in relation to the conduct of bargaining and result in anything resembling a merit finding.

D. Consent Elections

In *First FM Joint Ventures, dba Hampton Inn & Suites*[21] the Board would not permit an employer to withdraw from a stipulated election agreement on the basis that after entering the stipulation, the union filed a second petition seeking to represent certain other of the employer's employees. This was notwithstanding the employer's

---

[16]330 NLRB No. 9 (2000).
[17]Perdue Farms, Inc., 328 NLRB No. 130, 162 LRRM 1010 (1999).
[18]330 NLRB No. 138 (2000).
[19]320 NLRB 431 (1995).
[20]327 NLRB 38 (1998).
[21]331 NLRB No. 35 (2000).

argument that employees in the stipulated unit shared a community of interest with employees sought in the second petition.

E. Representation Hearings

In *North Manchester Foundry*[22] the Board found that a hearing officer failed to comply with the requirements of the Act or the Board's Rules and Regulations when, because of the small size of the group, he prevented an employer from presenting evidence that a group of employees should be excluded from the bargaining unit.

G. The Election

2. *Eligibility of Voters*

Temporary employees are eligible to vote where there is no date certain for their termination as of the payroll eligibility date.[23]

Undocumented aliens are eligible to vote if they are employed in the bargaining unit during the eligibility period.[24]

An employee is eligible to vote despite the employer's contention that he intended to discharge the employee for absenteeism before the election.[25]

The Board applied the "actual work" rule to exclude from voting in an election employees who had accepted job offers, been entered into the payroll system, and received identification cards, but who had not actually worked at the time of the cutoff period.[26]

I. Amendment, Clarification, and Revocation

Even if timely filed, the Board will dismiss a unit clarification petition where the petition deals with positions that have historically been excluded from the bargaining unit and have not been shown to have undergone recent substantial changes.[27]

The Board continues to hold that, in the absence of newly discovered and previously unavailable evidence or special circumstances,

---

[22]328 NLRB No. 50, 161 LRRM 1065 (1999).
[23]New World Communications, 328 NLRB No. 10, 161 LRRM 1049 (1999).
[24]NLRB v. Kolkka, 170 F.3d 937, 160 LRRM 2810 (9th Cir. 1999).
[25]Leisure Centers, Inc., 326 NLRB No. 117, 163 LRRM 1183 (1999).
[26]NLRB v. Maryland Ambulance Servs., 192 F.3d 430, 162 LRRM 2405 (4th Cir. 1999), *enforcing* 325 NLRB No. 202, 160 LRRM 128 (1998).
[27]Bethlehem Steel Corp., 329 NLRB No. 32, 163 LRRM 1093 (1999).

an employer may not challenge, by a unit clarification petition, the validity of a union's certification based on a belief that unit members are statutory supervisors if it failed to raise the issue during the representation proceeding.[28]

J. Deauthorization and Decertification Elections

The Board has held that state laws regarding union-security authorization procedures that place greater limits on the ability of employees to seek deauthorization are preempted by the LMRA.[29]

However, the Board held in *H.Y. Floors & Gameline Painting, Inc.*[30] that an individual is not estopped from timely challenging a construction industry employer's voluntary Section 9(a) recognition of a union, and thus may file a decertification petition. In so holding, the Board stated that the filing of an unfair labor practice charge is not the only means of challenging majority status in circumstances in which a former Section 8(f) union has been voluntarily granted Section 9(a) recognition. The Board found that a union's majority status may also be challenged by filing a timely representation petition.

III. PROCEDURES IN UNFAIR LABOR PRACTICE CASES

B. The Unfair Labor Practice Charge

1. Time for Filing

The Board held that an amended allegation will not be dismissed as untimely, even though outside the 6-month limitation period, where (1) a new allegation is related to the same legal theory as the allegation contained in the timely filed charge; (2) both allegations were part of the employer's alleged scheme to not hire union employees; and (3) the employer was already required to defend against the same conduct giving rise to the subsequent allegations.[31]

---

[28]Grancare, Inc. dba Premier Living Center, 331 NLRB No. 9, 164 LRRM 1296 (2000).

[29]Albertson's/Max Food Warehouse, 329 NLRB No. 44, 162 LRRM 1169 (1999), *overruling* City Market, Inc., 266 NLRB 1020, 113 LRRM 1105 (1983).

[30]331 NLRB No. 44, 164 LRRM 1185 (2000).

[31]Seven Seventeen HB Denver Corp. dba Adam's Mark Hotel, 325 NLRB No. 91, 160 LRRM 1206 (1999).

In *Outdoor Venture Corp.*[32] the Board held that certain allegations in the complaint were not barred by Section 10(b), even though some of the conduct alleged in the complaint occurred more than 6 months prior to the filing of the charge, because the general counsel was not seeking a remedy for those allegations, and the litigation of those allegations was required only to establish that the strike at issue was an unfair labor practice strike.

Fraudulent concealment will not toll the statute of limitations where "operative facts" have not been concealed.[33]

3. Disposition of Charge

The general counsel's decision not to pursue a charge under one section of the Act does not preclude the prosecution of an unfair labor practice allegation under another section of the Act.[34]

4. Settlement of Unfair Labor Practice Charges

a. Informal Settlements

The Board held that the general counsel was not barred by a settlement agreement from using evidence of presettlement conduct to establish an unfair labor practice in subsequent litigation where the agreement provided that the general counsel reserved the right to use such evidence for any relevant purpose in current or subsequent litigation.[35]

b. Formal Settlements

In deciding whether to accept a post-hearing formal settlement agreement, the Board in *K & W Electric*,[36] reaffirmed the settlement standards set out *Independent Stave Co.*[37] A settlement agreement bar is an affirmative defense that is waived unless timely asserted.[38]

---

[32]327 NLRB No. 133, 160 LRRM 1178 (1999).

[33]NLRB v. Dynatron/Bondo Corp., 176 F.3d 1310, 161 LRRM 2395 (11th Cir. 1999).

[34]Reno Hilton Resorts v. NLRB, 196 F.3d 1275, 162 LRRM 2961 (D.C. Cir. 1999).

[35]Outdoor Venture Corp., 327 NLRB No. 133, 160 LRRM 1178 (1999).

[36]327 NLRB No. 21, 160 LRRM 1174 (1999).

[37]282 NLRB No. 76, 127 LRRM 1204 (1987).

[38]Richard Mellow Elec. Contractors, 327 NLRB No. 171, 161 LRRM 1018 (1999).

5. The Complaint and the Answer

In determining whether or not the allegations of the complaint are sufficiently related to the underlying charge, the Board, in *Nickles Bakery of Indiana, Inc.*,[39] adopted the three-part test of *Redd-I, Inc.*[40] of whether (1) the allegations involve the same legal theory as the allegations of the charge; (2) the allegations arise from the same factual circumstances or sequence of events; and (3) a respondent would raise similar defenses to both allegations.[41]

In *McKenzie Engineering Co.*[42] the Board found that the general counsel's failure to allege an unlawful withdrawal of recognition is not adequately cured by a motion to amend the complaint, made for the first time in an answering brief to the Board.

While a respondent's answer should comport with the Board's Rules and Regulations, the Board ordered a hearing on an unfair labor practice complaint despite deficiencies in the employer's answer. Specifically, the Board considered the fact that the respondent was pro se, that the answer and amended answer clearly and specifically denied the unfair labor practice allegations, and that the employer tried to cure the deficiencies.[43] The Board also reiterated the policy that its rules permit an answer to be amended any time before trial. In *Eckert Fire Protection*,[44] however, the Board found that an employer's one-page faxed memorandum did not constitute a proper answer to the complaint, even under the more lenient standard applicable to pro se respondents. The memorandum failed to address any of the factual or legal allegations of the complaint, and failed to specifically deny any of the complaint allegations.

6. The Unfair Labor Practice Hearing

The Ninth Circuit, in *NLRB v. Kolkka*,[45] addressed the issue of consolidating unfair labor practice proceedings involving the same respondent. The court held that the Board's refusal to consolidate

---

[39]296 NLRB 927, 132 LRRM 1249 (1989).

[40]290 NLRB No. 140, 129 LRRM 1229 (1988).

[41]*See also* Seven Seventeen HB Denver Corp. dba Adam's Mark Hotel, 325 NLRB No. 91, 160 LRRM 1206 (1999).

[42]326 NLRB No. 50, 161 LRRM 1175 (1998).

[43]A.P.S. Prod., 326 NLRB No. 130, 161 LRRM 1015 (1998).

[44]329 NLRB No. 79, 162 LRRM 1281 (1999).

[45]170 F.3d 937, 160 LRRM 2810 (9th Cir. 1999).

separate proceedings involving distinct legal and factual issues is not an abuse of its discretion.

The Board did not violate Section 10(c) by promulgating Rule 102.45, which altered procedure by giving an ALJ discretion to decide whether written briefs or oral argument would be utilized in a particular case.[46] The ALJ did not abuse this discretion by waiting until the bulk of evidence was presented prior to notifying the parties that, despite the employer's objection, they would present oral arguments, rather than written briefs.

A post-hearing motion to reopen a record to receive certain evidence will be denied absent a showing that the evidence is newly discovered, became available only after the close of the hearing, or otherwise satisfies the requirements of Section 102.48(d)(1) of the Board's Rules and Regulations.[47] In addition, an ALJ does not abuse his discretion by refusing to reopen the administrative record to admit new evidence, where such evidence would not compel or persuade him to contrary results,[48] or where the parties had an opportunity to and did introduce evidence in an objections hearing based on substantially identical conduct and the parties were not prejudiced by the ALJ's rulings.[49]

With regard to the issue of whether a respondent was afforded a full and fair opportunity to defend the charges filed against it, a respondent will be deemed to have been accorded due process if the record shows that it understood the issues and was afforded a full opportunity to meet the charges.[50]

The Board's Rules regarding examination of witnesses in unfair labor practice hearings require that "[w]itnesses shall be examined orally under oath."[51] The Board applied a strict interpretation of this rule in holding that it required the physical presence of the witness in the hearing room and that testimony taken telephonically during a hearing was inadmissible under the Rule.[52] The Board ruled that the *only* exception to the physical presence requirement is the taking of testimony by deposition upon a showing of good cause.[53]

---

[46]NLRB v. Beverly Enters.-Mass., 174 F.3d 13, 160 LRRM 2935 (1st Cir. 1999).

[47]Goski Trucking Corp., 325 NLRB No. 192, 160 LRRM 1078 (1998).

[48]Reno Hilton Resorts v. NLRB, 196 F.3d 1275, 162 LRRM 2961 (D.C. Cir. 1999).

[49]Teamsters Local 299, 328 NLRB No. 178, 162 LRRM 1327 (1999).

[50]McKenzie Eng'g Co. v. NLRB, 182 F.3d 622, 161 LRRM 2641 (8th Cir. 1999).

[51]Rules and Regs. §102.30.

[52]Westside Painting, Inc., 328 NLRB No. 110, 161 LRRM 1177 (1999).

[53]*Id.* slip op. at 1; Rules and Regs. §102.30.

In another decision involving the use of testimony taken outside of a hearing, the Board held that deposition testimony of witnesses obtained during the investigation of an unfair labor practice charge pursuant to an investigatory subpoena and prior to the issuance of a complaint was admissible in the subsequent unfair labor practice hearing.[54] Unlike the aforementioned Rule allowing for deposition testimony in lieu of live testimony during a hearing under limited circumstances, the Board did *not* rule that depositions taken during a pre-complaint investigation may be admitted in lieu of live testimony; rather, it was noted that counsel stipulated that all of the witnesses whose depositions were offered would testify as they had in their depositions, and that all but one did testify during the hearing.[55]

10. Applicability of the Equal Access to Justice Act

Courts of Appeals will determine appropriate fees and costs to the prevailing employer even though the court ordinarily would remand the case to the Board for such determination, because the Board, which had rejected the employer's fee application as untimely, may be placed in an awkward situation.[56]

IV. PROCEDURES APPLICABLE TO ALL CASES

A. In General

The D.C. Circuit held that an ALJ did not engage in an improper ex parte communication under any applicable rules, including the Board's own rules,[57] by consulting with a colleague on the correct manner for handling a procedural issue in the matter before him, noting that the Board's rules prohibit only communications with interested parties *outside* the Agency, and that the consultation was over a procedural, not a factual, issue.[58]

The Board held that the use of a same-day delivery service to file an answering brief with the Board on the date it was due, but which arrived too late to be received that day, did not satisfy the

---

[54]North Bay Plumbing, Inc., 327 NLRB 899, n.1, 161 LRRM 1139 (1999).
[55]*Id.*
[56]E.W. Grobbel Sons, Inc., 176 F.3d 875, 161 LRRM 2229 (6th Cir. 1999).
[57]Rules and Regs. §§102.126–102.134.
[58]Pioneer Hotel, Inc. v. NLRB, 182 F.3d 939, 161 LRRM 2785 (D.C. Cir. 1999).

requirements of the Board's "postmark" or "excusable neglect" rules.[59] The postmark rule provides that for a document which is received by the Board after the due date to be considered as timely filed, the document must be postmarked no later than the day before the due date and that if a delivery service is used, it must be shown that the document was tendered to the delivery service with sufficient time for it to be delivered by the due date, but no later than the day before the due date.[60] Upon good cause shown based on excusable neglect, the filing of a document within a reasonable period of time after the date due may be considered as timely.[61] The Board rejected the argument that the delivery service's failure to deliver as promised satisfied the excusable neglect rule, which applies only to the party filing; it noted further that the filing party did not argue, or present any reason to conclude, that its failure to comply with the Rule by depositing its brief with the delivery service the day before it was due based on any excusable neglect. Therefore, in light of the explicit language of the rule regarding the use of a delivery service, it acted at its own risk by using same-day service.[62]

B. Discovery[63]

In a decision that did not involve the Board policy of not allowing any discovery in its own proceedings, the Board addressed the extent to which a party may use state court discovery procedures to obtain information from the Board which it would be unable to get in a Board proceeding. In *Wright Electric, Inc.*,[64] the Board held that an employer committed an unfair labor practice by seeking, through discovery in a state court lawsuit against a union, to obtain the authorization cards submitted to the union by its employees. Citing *National Telephone Directory*,[65] the Board reinforced its zealous protection of the confidentiality of the identity of employees engaged in organizing activity.

---

[59]Carpenters Metropolitan Regional Counsel of Philadelphia (R.M. Shoemaker), 332 NLRB No. 140, 166 LRRM 1001 (2000).
[60]Rules and Regs. §102.111(b).
[61]Rules and Regs. §102.111(c).
[62]*Supra* note 59.
[63]*See also* discussion in text at notes 51–55.
[64]327 NLRB 1194, 163 LRRM 1077 (1999).
[65]319 NLRB 420, 150 LRRM 1290 (1995).

C. Subpoenas

The Board denied a petition to revoke a Board subpoena to a video production company, which produced an organizational campaign videotape, for documents related to an employer's purchase of the videotape.[66] The Board rejected the argument that the subpoenaed documents were protected from disclosure by Section 8(c) of the Act regarding the right of an employer to freely express its views on unionism during a campaign. The Board held that the subpoena inquiry was narrowly limited to whether the production company and the employer had an agency relationship and did not seek to determine the legality of its content.

The Sixth Circuit held that a federal district court lacked discretion to delegate to the Board's ALJ the function of conducting an *in camera* review of the employer's documents subpoenaed by the Board during unfair labor practice proceedings.[67]

Under Section 102.113(e) of the Board's Rules and Regulations, an attorney's unsworn affirmation of service of a subpoena constitutes sufficient proof of service. As a result the Board directed the regional director to institute proceedings to enforce the subpoena.[68]

The Board reaffirmed the principle that a party is not entitled to a Board subpoena if its broad request for records is a mere "fishing expedition"; there must be some basis in the hearing record that establishes that the records may contain relevant evidence.[69]

In an unfair labor practice hearing the Board affirmed the taking and introduction into the record of pretrial depositions that had been obtained during the investigation of the unfair labor practice charge pursuant to investigatory subpoenas issued by the regional director.[70]

D. Request for Information Under the Freedom of Information Act

The Board added a FOIA web page to its website in February 1999. This page includes a number of features, including a detailed

---

[66]Projections, Inc., 331 NLRB No. 135, 165 LRRM 1135 (2000).

[67]NLRB v. Detroit Newspapers, fka Detroit Newspaper Agency, 185 F.3d 602, 161 LRRM 3051 (6th Cir. 1999).

[68]Best Western City View Motor Inn, 327 NLRB No. 92, 160 LRRM 1221 (1999).

[69]Millsboro Nursing & Rehabilitation Center, 327 NLRB No. 153, 160 LRRM 1209 (1999).

[70]North Bay Plumbing, 327 NLRB 899, 161 LRRM 1639 (1998).

FOIA reference guide that explains the right to obtain records under FOIA and instructions for making a FOIA request, a sample FOIA letter, and guidance on where to file a request. It also provides links to the electronic reading room that provides direct links to NLRB records on the Internet. It is located at www.nlrb.gov, where the FOIA web page may be accessed by clicking on the FOIA "button" appearing on the website home page.

In November 1999, the Board published a comprehensive FOIA Manual for guiding agency employees in making determinations concerning the public release of agency records under FOIA and in litigating FOIA-based lawsuits. The Manual supersedes all previous General Counsel guideline memoranda concerning the processing and litigation of FOIA matters.

Chapter 32

NLRB ORDER AND REMEDIES

I. GENERAL PRINCIPLES

The Board adheres to the view that it does not have the authority to compel a party to make a bargaining concession or agree to a proposal. Thus, good faith bargaining does not require the parties to agree to a proposal.[1] However, the Board held in *TNT Skypak, Inc.*[2] that the employer committed an unfair labor practice when it reneged on tentative agreements with the union after it became apparent that the union was going to accept virtually all of the company's positions, making a contract inevitable.

The Board continues to hold that the Section 10(b) period does not begin running until the aggrieved party receives actual or constructive notice of the conduct that constitutes the alleged unfair labor practice.[3] It is the respondent's burden to establish that the charging party was on notice more than 6 months before the charge was filed. However, the Board has allowed the General Counsel to litigate situations in which the "time barred" allegations were found to be "closely related" to the allegations in the original, timely filed charge.[4]

II. ORDERS IN REPRESENTATION CASES (SECTION 9)

The "certification year" rule is within the Board's administrative authority and is reviewed only for an abuse of discretion.[5]

The Board overruled its prior decision in *Southern Moldings, Inc.*[6] and held that once a successor employer's obligation to recognize an incumbent union attaches, the union is entitled to a rea-

---

[1]Dependable Storage, Inc., 328 NLRB No. 6, 164 LRRM 1268 (1999). *Accord* Naomi Knitting Plant, 328 NLRB No. 180 (1999).

[2]328 NLRB No. 67, 163 LRRM 1299 (1999), *aff'd*, 208 F.3d 362, 163 LRRM 2989 (2d Cir. 2000).

[3]Nieman, 328 NLRB No. 91 (1999).

[4]*See* Ross Stores, Inc., 329 NLRB No. 59, 163 LRRM 1137 (1999) (overruling Nippondenso Mfg. U.S.A., 299 NLRB 545, 135 LRRM 1100 (1990), to the extent it conflicts with Nickles Bakery of Ind., 296 NLRB 927, 132 LRRM 1249 (1989), and other precedent on the ground that *Nippondenso* is an unreasonably restrictive view of the factual-relatedness requirement of the *Nickles Baker/Redd-I* test). *See also* Seton Co., 332 NLRB No. 89 (2000); Bridgestone/Firestone, Inc., 332 NLRB No. 56 (2000); Office Depot, 330 NLRB No. 99 (2000) ("closely related" charges not barred by §10(b)).

[5]NLRB v. Beverly Health & Rehabilitation Servs. Inc., 187 F.3d 769 (8th Cir. 1999).

[6]219 NLRB 119 (1975).

sonable period of bargaining without a challenge to its majority status.[7]

III. Orders and Remedies in Complaint Cases (Section 10)

A. Provisional Remedies

1. *Provisional Remedies—General Principles*

a. Discretionary Injunctions Under Section 10(j)

(3) Judicial Standards

In *Wells ex rel. NLRB v. Brown & Root, Inc.*[8] the court found that in the absence of a clear statement of legislative intent or Eleventh Circuit precedent, the court would use traditional equitable principles in interpreting and applying the "just and proper" standards.

(4) Temporary Restraining Orders

A temporary restraining order was issued, pending a hearing on the preliminary injunction, in *Blyer v. Platt Towers, Inc.*[9]

(5) Delay in Filing Petition

The issue of the effect of the delay continues to be litigated. In *Sharp ex rel. NLRB v. Webco*[10] the court, while recognizing that the reasonableness of the Board's delay is largely determined on a fact-specific basis, found a 7-month delay in the filing of a petition was not unreasonable.

In *Blyer v. Platt Towers, Inc.*[11] the employer questioned whether injunctive relief was just and proper given the regional director's

---

[7]St. Elizabeth Manor, 329 NLRB No. 36, 162 LRRM 1146 (1999); Ferri Supermkts., Inc., 330 NLRB No. 156 (2000) (rejecting employer's defense of good faith doubt in union's majority status based upon information provided by employer's predecessor).

[8]65 F. Supp. 2d 1264 (S.D. Ala. 1999). *Accord* Blyer v. Platt Towers, Inc., 124 F. Supp. 136 (E.D.N.Y. 2000) (applying "reasonable cause" and "just and proper" standards). Silverman v. J.R.L. Food Corp., 196 F.3d 334, 162 LRRM 2771 (2d Cir. 1999) (district court erred in denying NLRB regional director's petition for temporary injunction where court did not accord ALJ's decision appropriate deference and thus district court's finding of no reasonable cause was not supported by record).

[9]124 F. Supp. 136 (E.D.N.Y. 2000).

[10]225 F.3d 1130, 165 LRRM 2353 (10th Cir. 2000).

[11]*Supra* note 9, quoting Dunbar v. Carrier Corp., 66 F. Supp. 2d 346, 161 LRRM 2119 (N.D.N.Y. 1999).

delay in filing the subject petition. The court stated that delay should not be taken into consideration unless, between the alleged unfair labor practices and the filing of the petition, circumstances have changed that affect the appropriateness of such relief. The employer argued that the regional director's delay compromised the necessity for injunctive relief, and that it would be disruptive to its operations if, assuming the Board declined to adopt the ALJ's recommended order with regard to reinstatement, the employer again had to discharge the employees. The regional director presented evidence demonstrating that the case has been prosecuted with reasonable diligence, the Section 10(j) petition was timely, and absent injunctive relief, the employees' ability to organize would be significantly curtailed. This led the court to grant the regional director's request for injunctive relief.

(6) Injunctions Against Employers

In *Dunbar v. Carrier Corp.*[12] the district court found an order for interim bargaining regarding location, pending the outcome of an unfair labor practice proceeding, appropriate. The court refused to lift its order precluding the employer from completing certain construction tasks related to the relocation.[13]

b. Mandatory Injunctions Under Section 10(*l*)

(1) Standards for Issuance

In *Kobell v. African American Workers Union*[14] the court granted injunctive relief in favor of the Board and against a labor organization whose picketing at a job site was directed toward municipal and county authorities, as opposed to the contractors working at the site. The court recited several standards involved in reviewing a petition for Section 10(*l*) relief: (1) "the Board faces a relatively insubstantial burden of proof" in Section 10(*l*) proceedings because they are ancillary to the Board's exclusive jurisdiction over unfair labor practices; (2) "[t]he Director's burden is to demonstrate that reasonable cause exists to believe that the elements of an unfair labor practice are present, and that the Director's theory is substantial and not frivo-

---

[12]66 F. Supp. 2d 346, 161 LRRM 2119 (N.D.N.Y. 1999).
[13]*See also* Moore-Duncan ex rel. NLRB v. Aldworth Comp., Inc., 124 F. Supp. 2d 268, 166 LRRM 2338 (D.N.H. 2000) (interim injunction, including reinstatements and bargaining order, approved in light of array of violations asserted).
[14]162 LRRM 2235 (W.D. Pa. 1999).

lous"; (3) the Board must demonstrate an evidentiary basis for its Section 8(b)(4) violation claim; and (4) the "reasonable cause" standard applies to all legal, factual, and jurisdictional elements as to the violation.

In *Moore-Duncan v. Metropolitan Regional Council of Philadelphia & Vicinity*[15] the court issued a temporary injunction, pursuant to Section 10(*l*), again a labor organization, prohibiting it from broadcasting protest messages over a sound system outside specified time periods and above acceptable noise levels.

B. Final Orders and Remedies

2. *Special Remedial Problems Involving Employers*

a. Flagrant Violations

The Board continues issuing "extraordinary" remedies in cases in which the employer has committed pervasive or outrageous unfair labor practices.

In *Avondale Industries, Inc.*[16] the Board ordered the respondent to comply with the special remedies imposed in *Fieldcrest Cannon, Inc.*[17] The Board concluded that the quantity and severity of the unfair labor practices warranted the imposition of special mailing and published notice remedies, although the ALJ's order was modified to provide that the notice could be read to employees by either a responsible supervisory official of the respondent above the departmental level, or, at the respondent's option, by a Board agent, with the responsible supervisory official present while it was read. The judge had ordered the company president to sign the notice or to be present when it was read.

The Board also concluded that, in light of the Fifth Circuit's direction of a second election among the respondent's employees, special access remedies were necessary to eliminate the effects of the respondent's widespread, serious, and pervasive unfair labor practices and to ensure a fair and free election. These special remedies required the respondent to: (1) supply the union, on request made within 1 year of the date of the decision and order, the full names and addresses of its current employees; (2) on request, grant the union and its representatives reasonable access to the respondent's

---

[15]162 LRRM 2615 (E.D. Pa. 1999).
[16]329 NLRB No. 93 (1999).
[17]318 NLRB 470, 473–74, 152 LRRM 1173 (1995).

bulletin boards and all places where notices to employees were customarily posted; (3) on request, grant the union reasonable access to its facilities in nonwork areas during employees' nonwork time; (4) give notice of, and equal time and facilities for the union to respond to, any address made by the respondent to its employees on the question of union representation; and (5) afford the union the right to deliver a 30-minute speech to employees, on working time, prior to any Board election that may be scheduled in which the union is a participant. These additional access provisions were imposed for a period of 2 years from the date of the posting of the notice, or until the regional director issued an appropriate certification following a fair and free election, whichever came first.

Exceptional notice requirements were also found appropriate in *Audubon Regional Medical Center*[18] based upon the nature and range of the employer's violation of the Act.

In *Overnite Transportation Co.*[19] the Board adopted the ALJ's decision and order issuing *Gissel* bargaining orders, after finding that the respondent engaged in extensive unfair labor practices that involved "hallmark" violations. These included the granting of unprecedented wage increases, threats of job loss and closing of business, assertions that bargaining would be futile, promises of better benefits, overtime policies, and vacation, and threats of stricter discipline and more onerous working conditions.[20]

In *Dorsey Trailers, Inc.*[21] the Board ordered the respondent to reestablish the operations of a closed facility and to bargain with the union. In *Traction Wholesale Center Co.*[22] the Board ordered the issuing of a *Gissel* bargaining order, but Member Brame dissented on the issue of the authenticity of the signed union cards. In *U.S.A. Polymer Corp.*[23] the Board issued a *Gissel* bargaining order, despite the passage of several years, because the respondent committed numerous, egregious violations that constituted Category I conduct within the meaning of *Gissel* (such as laying off nearly one-half of the bargaining unit, coupled with statements that the lay-offs were due to the employees' support of the union). In *State Materials, Inc.*[24] the

---

[18]331 NLRB No. 42 (2000).
[19]329 NLRB No. 91 (1999).
[20]*See also* General Fabrications Corp., 328 NLRB No. 166, 162 LRRM 1100 (1999).
[21]327 NLRB No. 155 (1999).
[22]328 NLRB No. 148 (1999).
[23]328 NLRB No. 177 (1999).
[24]328 NLRB No. 184 (1999).

Board held that a bargaining order was justified, despite the passage of time, because of the employer's *Gissel* Category II violations at the time the unfair labor practices were committed. There was evidence that the respondent remained committed to an antiunion position and that a substantial number of unit employees remained in the respondent's employ. In *Allied General Services, Inc.*[25] the Board ordered reinstatement, reestablishment of closed operations, and a *Gissel* Category I order. In *Climatrol, Inc.*[26] the Board held that the respondent engaged in conduct that justified imposition of a *Gissel* order under Category I.

In *Servco Automatic Machine Products Co. Inc.*[27] the Board ordered the respondent to bargain with the union concerning the effects of closing its facility on its employees, and accompanied the order with a limited backpay requirement. Additionally, the Board required the respondent to mail a copy of the notice to the Union, and to the last known address of its former employees, in order to inform them of the outcome of the proceeding.[28]

In *Traction Wholesale Center Co. v. NLRB*[29] the court upheld a *Gissel* bargaining order imposed on the employer (which had committed unfair labor practices during the union's organizing campaign) because of the magnitude of the respondent's unfair labor practices, the small size of the units, and the involvement of the respondent's owners. The Board found that the unfair labor practices created fear so pervasive that a rerun election would not fairly reflect the views of a majority of the unit. Additionally, the Board determined that the employer's proposed remedy (having the employer's representative read the Board notice to the employees before the new election) would be insufficient to cure the employer's gross interference with free choice in the election.

In a number of cases, however, the Board declined to issue *Gissel* orders when there was a long delay between the alleged unfair labor practices and the Board's decision. In *Comcast Cablevision,*[30] for example, the Board directed a second election rather than imposing the *Gissel* bargaining order due to a 9-year delay from the date of the

---

[25] 329 NLRB No. 58 (1999).

[26] 329 NLRB No. 83 (1999). *See also* Bonham Heating & Air Conditioning Inc., 328 NLRB No. 61, 161 LRRM 1113 (1999); Regional Home Care, Inc., 329 NLRB No. 6 (1999); Wire Prods. Mfg. Corp., 329 NLRB No. 23 (1999).

[27] 332 NLRB No. 119 (2000).

[28] *See also* K & C Supply, Inc., 332 NLRB No. 141 (2000).

[29] 216 F.3d 92, 164 LRRM 2769 (D.C. Cir. 2000).

[30] 328 NLRB No. 74, 161 LRRM 1166 (1999).

election to the Board's decision in processing the case and to avoid further litigation. The Board did, however, order the employer to supply the union with the names and addresses of all current unit employees, if requested to do so within 1 year of the date of the decision and the order.[31]

In several other cases, for a variety of reasons, the Board refused to issue a *Gissel* order. In *Masterform Tool Co.*[32] the Board held that there was an insufficient basis for concluding that a fair election could not be held. In *Eby-Brown Co.*,[33] a *Gissel* order was not warranted because the district court had addressed several remedial issues through a consent decree. In *Naomi Knitting Plant*[34] the Board held that the bargaining order was not appropriate. In *Hospital Shared Services, Inc.*[35] there were no "hallmark violations" and, thus, traditional remedies were sufficient to correct any violations. In *Menlo Food Corp.*[36] the Board held that violations were minor and not a significant impact on the election process.

b. Litigation Costs, Attorneys' Fees, and Union Expenses

In cases involving frivolous charges or defenses, the Board continues ordering the payment of attorneys' fees and other litigation costs. In *Sandusky Mall Co.*[37] the Board determined that the employer unlawfully refused to permit nonemployee union representatives to distribute "area standards" handbills and that it unlawfully called the police to have the representatives arrested. Because of its decision to involve the police, the Board required the employer to reimburse the union and its representatives for "all reasonable legal fees and costs incurred as a result of the arrest."[38]

The Board also addressed a claim for attorneys' fees and costs incurred by the unions in defending themselves against a civil suit

---

[31] *See also* Cooper Indus., 328 NLRB No. 21 (1999) and Wallace Int'l de P.R., Inc., 328 NLRB No. 3, 161 LRRM 1123 (1999), where there were 5-year-delays between the elections and the Board's decisions; Research Fed. Credit Union, 327 NLRB No. 182, 161 LRR 1156 (1999) (almost a 9-year delay between election and Board's decision); and Regal Recycling, Inc., 329 NLRB No. 38 (1999) (7-year delay between date of election and Board's decision).

[32] 327 NLRB No. 185 (1999).

[33] 328 NLRB No. 75 (1999).

[34] 328 NLRB No. 180 (1999).

[35] 330 NLRB No. 40 (1999).

[36] 330 NLRB No. 45 (1999).

[37] 329 NLRB No. 62, 1999 WL 812243, 162 LRRM 1191 (1999).

[38] *Id.*, 1999 WL 812243, at *6.

filed by the respondent in federal district court.[39] The district court previously granted the unions' motions for partial summary judgment and found that the unions' conduct was not unlawful. After concluding that the respondent's suit was filed for retaliatory motives and violated Section 8(a)(1), the Board awarded attorneys' fees to the union.

However, the Board denied fee requests where there was an absence of repeated displays of bad faith or capricious conduct prolonging the litigation.[40]

c. Imposing Remedial Order on Successor to Wrongdoer

Successor employers remain liable, under certain circumstances, for their predecessors' violations of the Act.[41] In *Tellem v. The New Silver Palace Restaurant*[42] the court held that during the pendency of proceedings before the Board, the NLRB regional director was entitled to a remedial order requiring that a successor restaurant that had engaged in discrimination against union employees restore the status quo ante.

3. Final Orders and Remedies for Union Misconduct

a. Sections 8(b)(1)(A) and (B) Violations

In a Section 8(b)(1)(A) case involving a union agent and another person vandalizing an employer's vehicle, the Board adopted the ALJ's order requiring the union to cease and desist from damaging property owned by the employer or any employer.[43] In line with prior Board cases, the Board noted that when misconduct takes place in the presence of a union agent who does nothing to disavow it or to discipline the offenders, the union assumes responsibility for the conduct. The Board did not award damages.

The Board has reaffirmed the holding of *California Saw & Knife Works*[44] that a union violates its duty of fair representation by failing

---

[39]BE&K Constr. Co., 329 NLRB No. 68, 162 LRRM 1217 (1999). *See also* Petrochem Insulation, Inc., 330 NLRB No. 10 (1999).

[40]Halle Enters., Inc., 330 NLRB No. 163 (2000); Sea-Jet Trucking Corp., 327 NLRB No. 107 (1999) (holding that employee's defenses were not frivolous).

[41]Wyandanch Engine Rebuilders, Inc., 328 NLRB No. 119 (1999), relying on Golden State Bottling Co. v. NLRB, 414 U.S. 168 (1973).

[42]164 LRRM 3062 (S.D.N.Y. 2000).

[43]Electrical Workers (IBEW) Local 98, 327 NLRB No. 113 (1999).

[44]320 NLRB 224, 151 LRRM 1121 (1995).

to grant employees who resign their union membership a separate window period following resignation in which to file a *Beck* objection.[45]

The Board found that the union's imposition of a window period limitation on the filing of *Beck* objections on employees who have recently resigned their union memberships violates the union's duty of fair representation.[46] Such a limitation operates as an arbitrary restriction on the right to resign from the union and thus, the union violated Section 8(b)(1)(A) by refusing to accept the *Beck* objection. The Board also ordered the union to accept the employee's objection, provide him with post-objection financial information consisting of (1) the assurance that the union would refrain from charging him for nonrepresentational functions; (2) the percentage by which his dues and fees would be reduced; (3) the basis for the union's calculations, including the percentage of expenditures that were representational and nonrepresentational; and (4) the assurance that he would have the opportunity to challenge the union's determination. The Board required the union to make the employee whole for any excess dues and fees paid to the union for nonchargeable expenditures, through a refund of such excess amounts commencing with the filing of the employee's objection with interest. The Board also ordered the union to amend its policy "concerning the processing of the objections to make clear that they will accept objections from recently resigned perfected *Beck* objectors that are filed within a reasonable time following their resignations."

b. Section 8(b)(2) Violations

In a situation where the union caused the employer to unlawfully discharge an employee, the Board directed the union to notify the employer in writing, copied to the employee, that it not only has no objection to his reinstatement, but affirmatively requests reinstatement.[47] In addition, the Board ordered the union to make the employee whole for lost wages and benefits (less interim earnings) running from termination until such time as the employee is reinstated to the same or a substantially equivalent position with his

---

[45]*See* Polymark Corp., 329 NLRB No. 7 (1999); Steelworkers (George E. Failing Co.), 329 NLRB No. 18, 162 LRRM 1097 (1999); American National Can Co., 329 NLRB No. 41, 162 LRRM 1289 (1999); *In re* Office & Professional Employee Int'l Union, 331 NLRB No. 15 n.105, 164 LRRM 1105 (2000).

[46]Transport Workers, 329 NLRB No. 56 (1999).

[47]Incisa, U.S.A., Inc., 327 NLRB No. 111 (1999).

former employer or finds substantially equivalent employment else-where.[48]

(2) Scope of Order

The Board continues, in accordance with its holding in *Hickmott Foods*,[49] ordering perpetrators of widespread and egregious miscon-duct to cease and desist from violating the Act "in any other manner."[50]

(3) Hiring-Hall Cases

The Board found the production of hiring-hall records, to com-pute backpay, appropriate in *In re Electrical Workers Local 3 (White Plains)*.[51]

In *Steamfitters Local 342 (Contra Costa Electric)*[52] the Board over-ruled *Iron Workers Local 118 (California Erectors)*,[53] and other decisions holding that a union's mere "negligence" in its failure to dispatch an applicant in the proper order from an exclusive hiring hall violates the duty of fair representation. The Board held that mere "negli-gence" in failing to following hiring-hall procedures does not violate Section 8(b)(1)(A) and is independent of the duty of fair represen-tation, because simple mistakes do not carry the coercive message that hiring-hall users "had better stay in the good graces of the union" if they expect to be treated fairly in job referrals.

The Board followed *Contra Costa* when it held a union dis-patcher's failure to refer an applicant did not breach the applicant's duty of fair representation or violate Sections 8(b)(1)(A) and (2).[54]

However, in *Jacoby v. NLRB*[55] the court reversed and remanded *Steamfitters Local 342*[56] on the basis of the Board's reading that *Steel-workers of America v. Rawson*[57] and *Air Line Pilots Ass'n Int'l v. O'Neill*[58]

---

[48]*Accord* Newspaper & Mail Deliverer's Union of New York, 332 NLRB No. 77 (2000); Laborers' Local 1184, 332 NLRB No. 124 (2000).

[49]242 NLRB 1357, 101 LRRM 1342 (1979).

[50]Overnite Transp. Co. Inc., 332 NLRB No. 138 (2000); *In re* Ryan Iron Works, Inc., 332 NLRB 49 (2000); *In re* Bridgestone/Firestone, Inc., 332 NLRB No. 56 (2000); Pacific FM, Inc., 332 NLRB No. 67 (2000); Far West Fibers, Inc. dba E-Z Recycling, 331 NLRB No. 116 (2000).

[51]331 NLRB No. 150 (2000).

[52]329 NLRB No. 65, 162 LRRM 1156 (1999).

[53]309 NLRB 808, 142 LRRM 1168 (1992).

[54]H.C. Price Constr. Co., 330 NLRB No. 55, 163 LRRM 1041 (1999).

[55]233 F.3d 611, 165 LRRM 2993 (D.C. Cir. 2000).

[56]*Supra* note 52.

[57]495 U.S. 362, 134 LRRM 2153 (1990).

[58]499 U.S. 65, 136 LRRM 2721 (1991).

cannot be reconciled with *Plumbers & Pipe Fitters Local 32 v. NLRB* [59] in the context of a union's operation of a hiring hall.

c. Fair Representation Cases

The Board has continued to follow its rule requiring the union to produce information improperly withheld from employees.[60] In a duty of fair representation case where a union unlawfully failed to process a grievance, the Board reaffirmed the position it took in *Iron Workers Local 377*,[61] concerning the allocation of evidentiary burdens.[62]

e. Section 8(b)(4) Violations

In *Electrical Workers (IBEW) Local 3* [63] the Board adopted the judge's recommended broad remedial order, specifically noting that the union had recently consented to entry of an order by the Second Circuit requiring compliance with its obligations under prior outstanding court judgments and that it not further violate Section 8(b)(4) of the Act. The Board noted that the union's violation of Section 8(b)(4)(ii)(B) in the instant case, just a little more than 2 years later, sufficiently demonstrated that the union has a proclivity for violating the Act, and thus warranted a broad order.

Having found that the union violates Sections 8(b)(4)(A), (i), and (ii)(B), by coercing employees in the exercise of their Section 7 rights and by enmeshing neutrals in the primary labor dispute, the Board ordered a broad cease-and-desist order.[64]

---

[59] 50 F.3d 29, 148 LRRM 2833 (D.C. Cir. 1995).

[60] *In re* Laborers Local 294, 331 NLRB No. 28, 164 LRRM 1169 (2000).

[61] 326 NLRB No. 54, 159 LRRM 1097 (1998); *see also* Branch 3126, National Ass'n of Letter Carriers, 330 NLRB No. 85, 163 LRRM 1190 (2000).

[62] Communication Workers Local 3410 (BellSouth Telecommunications, Inc.), 328 NLRB 135 (1999).

[63] 329 NLRB No. 34 (1999).

[64] Service Employees Local 525, 329 NLRB No. 64 (1999).

Chapter 33

JUDICIAL REVIEW AND ENFORCEMENT

II. APPELLATE REVIEW AND ENFORCEMENT

B. Scope of Review

3. Issues That Can Be Raised on Review

A reviewing court may not consider an issue that was not raised before the Board unless there are extraordinary circumstances.[1]

---

[1] *See* Woelke & Romero Framing v. NLRB, 456 U.S. 645, 110 LRRM 2377 (1982); *see also* Joseph T. Ryerson & Son, Inc. v. NLRB, 216 F.3d 1146, 164 LRRM 2856 (D.C. Cir. 2000) (holding that responsibility of Board to uphold "fundamental principles of labor law" does not qualify as extraordinary circumstance). *See, e.g.,* Deferiet Paper Co. v. NLRB, 235 F.3d 581, 166 LRRM 2107 (D.C. Cir. 2000); Beverly Cal. Corp. v. NLRB, 227 F.3d 817, 165 LRRM 2257 (7th Cir. 2000); Vulcan Basement Waterproofing of Ill., Inc. v. NLRB, 219 F.3d 677, 164 LRRM 2961 (7th Cir. 2000); Traction Wholesale Ctr. Co. v. NLRB, 216 F.3d 92, 164 LRRM 2769 (D.C. Cir. 2000); Schnurmacher Nursing Home v. NLRB, 214 F.3d 260, 164 LRRM 2531 (2d Cir. 2000); Elizabethtown Gas Co. v. NLRB, 212 F.3d 257, 164 LRRM 2257 (4th Cir. 2000); Cast North American (Trucking) Ltd. v. NLRB, 207 F.3d 994, 163 LRRM 2995 (7th Cir. 2000).

To preserve an issue for review, a party must make more than just a passing reference to the issue in the litigation phase of the case.[2]

The courts apply this principle not just to bar new issues but new arguments regarding old issues, as well. In *MacMillan Publishing Co. v. NLRB*[3] the D.C. Circuit refused to consider different grounds offered by Board counsel to support an order where those grounds were not adopted by the Board at the administrative level.

In addition, to preserve an issue for judicial review, a party subject to a ruling by an ALJ must respond to any new issues raised by the opposing party on appeal to the Board, despite the fact that they were not raised before the ALJ. In *NLRB v. Monson Trucking*[4] the ALJ ruled for the employer and the general counsel filed exceptions on grounds not raised before the ALJ. The employer filed a response, but did not address the general counsel's new argument. The Board agreed with the general counsel's new argument, and the employer filed an appeal. The Eighth Circuit held that it did not have jurisdiction to consider the employer's appeal because the employer failed to raise its objection in its response to the general counsel's exceptions.

Even the grounds for a subject-matter jurisdiction appeal must be carefully preserved. The Seventh Circuit followed the rule set forth in *NLRB v. Konig*,[5] that although "the Board's statutory jurisdiction may be raised at any time, the facts upon which the Board determines it has jurisdiction may be challenged only upon timely exception."[6] In *Sommerville Construction Co.*[7] the answer to the complaint admitted that the employer performed services valued in excess of $50,000 in states other than its own. The ALJ relied on this admission in determining that the Board had subject-matter jurisdiction. The court held that because the employer did not file an exception

---

[2]*See Elizabethtown, supra* note 1, at 265.

[3]194 F.3d 165, 162 LRRM 2769 (D.C. Cir. 1999) (court refused to entertain new arguments from general counsel in favor of enforcing Board's order for second election).

[4]204 F.3d 822, 824, 163 LRRM 2592 (8th Cir. 2000) (court refused to consider employer's objections to Board's order where employer had not raised them before board).

[5]79 F.3d 354, 151 LRRM 2682 (3d Cir. 1996).

[6]NLRB v. Sommerville Constr. Co., 206 F.3d 752, 756, 163 LRRM 2762 (7th Cir. 2000).

[7]*Id.*

to that determination, the employer was barred from raising that issue for the first time on appeal.

4. Judicial Review of Equal Access to Justice Determinations

In *E.W. Grobbel Sons, Inc. v. NLRB*[8] the Sixth Circuit awarded the employer attorney's fees and costs pursuant to the Equal Access to Justice Act, after the Board had rejected an identical request by the employer as untimely. The Court of Appeals rejected the Board's argument that only the Board had jurisdiction to consider the fee request, holding that the court had retained jurisdiction with regard to the issues on remand and therefore had the authority to consider the fee request arising out of the remand proceedings.

5. Disposition of Cases by Reviewing Court

In *Cooper/T. Smith, Inc. v. NLRB*[9] the Eleventh Circuit refused to review de novo the Board's determination regarding the nonsupervisory status of certain employees included in the bargaining unit, rejecting the employer's argument that de novo review was warranted because of the Board's "demonstrated inconsistency in past supervisory cases."

In *NLRB v. Hilliard Development Corp.*[10] the First Circuit similarly refused to depart from the usual standard of deference regarding the Board's determination about which employees are supervisors, despite the employer's argument that the Board has displayed a policy bias against finding supervisory status with respect to members of the nursing profession.

7. Interlocutory Relief Pending Review [New Topic]

A court of appeals may grant interlocutory relief pending its final determination on appeal. In *Beverly Farm Found., Inc. v. NLRB*[11] the Seventh Circuit granted the Board's injunction pendent lite requiring the employer to recognize and bargain with the union, among other things, pending the Court of Appeals' decision on the Board's petition for civil contempt against the employer.

---

[8]176 F.3d 875, 161 LRRM 2229 (6th Cir. 1999).
[9]177 F.3d 1259, 161 LRRM 2526 (11th Cir. 1999).
[10]187 F.3d 133, 161 LRRM 2966 (1st Cir. 1999).
[11]1999 U.S. App. LEXIS 34979, 162 LRRM 2729 (7th Cir. 1999).

III. DIRECT REVIEW AND ENFORCEMENT

B. Review of Unfair Labor Practice Proceedings

In *Detroit Newspaper Agency v. Schaub*[12] the federal district court applied the *Kyne* exception to grant an employer's application for injunction to bar the Board from prosecuting unfair labor practice charges filed more than 6 months after they accrued. The court rejected the Board's argument that the charges were "closely related" to timely filed charges, and exercised its power to prevent the Board from engaging in activities that are expressly prohibited by statute.

---

[12]108 F. Supp. 2d 729, 165 LRRM 2113 (E.D. Mich. 2000).

TABLE OF CASES

Cases are referenced to chapter and footnote number(s); e.g., *13*: 19, 23 indicates the case is cited in Chapter 13 at footnotes 19 and 23. Union locals and other subdivisions are included with the parent unions. Alphabetization is letter-by-letter (e.g., Farmer precedes Farm Fresh). Numerals are alphabetized as if spelled out *except* for union locals, which are in numerical order.

A

ABF Freight Sys. Inc., 325 NLRB No. 93, 160 LRRM 1027 (1999) *13*: 10

Abrams v. Communications Workers, 59 F.3d 1373, 149 LRRM 2928 (D.C. Cir. 1995) *26*: 55

Addicts Rehabilitation Ctr. Fund, Inc., 330 NLRB No. 113, 2000 WL 248214 (2000) *8*: 3, 7, 11, 26, 28–30, 58

Adel Jewelry Corp., 326 NLRB 53, 159 LRRM 1295 (1998) *9*: 24

Advance Stretchforming Int'l, Inc., 208 F.3d 501, 164 LRRM 2001 (9th Cir. 2000), *enforced in part and remanded in part*, 233 F.3d 1176, 165 LRRM 2890 (9th Cir. 2001) *15*: 35–39

Adventure Resources, Inc. v. Holland, 137 F.3d 786 (4th Cir.), *cert. denied*, 525 U.S. 962 (1998) *29*: 27

Aeronautical Indus. Dist. Lodge 91 v. United Techs. Corp., Pratt & Whitney, 230 F.3d 569, 165 LRRM 2641 (2d Cir. 2000) *17*: 24–26, 31; *28*: 58

Aerospace Corp., The, 331 NLRB No. 74 (2000) *11*: 3

Agosto v. Correctional Officers Benevolent Ass'n, 107 F. Supp. 294, 83 FEP 1042 (S.D.N.Y. 2000) *28*: 71

Aguilera v. Pirelli Armstrong Tire Corp., 223 F.3d 1010, 165 LRRM 2203 (9th Cir. 2000) *28*: 33, 36

Air Line Pilots Ass'n Int'l v. O'Neill, 499 U.S. 65, 136 LRRM 2721 (1991) *7*: 82; *25*: 44, 45; *32*: 58

Alamo Rent-A-Car, 330 NLRB No. 147 (2000) *10*: 2; *11*: 7

Albany Specialties, Inc. v. Board of Educ., 162 LRRM 3071 (N.D.N.Y. 1999) *27*: 5; *29*: 4, 5, 7

Albertson's Inc., 332 NLRB No. 104, 166 LRRM 1003 (2000) *6*: 80; *21*: 4; *22*: 44, 45

Albertson's/Max Food Warehouse, 329 NLRB No. 44, 162 LRRM 1169 (1999) *26*: 21; *2*: 58, 59; *31*: 29

Aldworth Co., Inc., 200 NLRB LEXIS 241 (2000) *6*: 167

Alexander
—v. Laborers Local 496, 177 F.3d 394 (6th Cir. 1999), *cert. denied*, 528 U.S. 1154 (2000) *26*: 36
—v. UDV N. Am., Inc., 78 F. Supp. 2d 614, 163 LRRM 2606 (E.D. Mich. 1999) *28*: 33

Allegheny Ludlum, 320 NLRB 484, 152 LRRM 1142 (1995) *9*: 37

Allen Health Care Servs., 332 NLRB No. 134 (2000) *11*: 1

Allentown Mack Sales & Serv. v. NLRB
—316 NLRB 1199, 149 LRRM 1051 (1995), *enforced*, 83 F.3d 1483, 152 LRRM 2257 (D.C. Cir. 1996), *rev'd and remanded*, 522 U.S. 359 (1998) *10*: 8; *12*: 53
—333 NLRB No. 105 (2001) *12*: 64

Allied Chem. & Alkali Workers Local 1 v. Pittsburgh Plate Glass Co., 404 U.S. 157, 78 LRRM 2974 (1971) *16*: 2

Allied Gen. Servs., Inc., 329 NLRB No. 58 (1999) *32*: 25

Allied Sys. Ltd. v. Teamsters Local 327, 179 F.3d 982, 161 LRRM 2493 (6th Cir.), *cert. denied*, 528 U.S. 965, 162 LRRM 2704 (1999) *17*: 34, 35, *19*: 18; *28*: 55, 56

Allis-Chalmers Corp. v. Lueck, 471 U.S. 202, 118 LRRM 3345 (1985) *28*: 26, 30

Allison Corp., 330 NLRB No. 190 (2000) *13*: 48

Allstate Ins. Co., 332 NLRB No. 66, 165 LRRM 1293 (2000) *6*: 12, 148, 204; *27*: 36, 37, 45

Altorfer Mach. Co., Lift Truck Div., 332 NLRB No. 12 (2000) *13*: 1, 15

Aluminum Casting & Eng'g Co.; NLRB v., 230 F.3d 286, 165 LRRM 2513 (7th Cir. 2000) *6*: 128

H